Migration in the

Routledge Advances in Sociology

For a full list of titles in this series, please visit www.routledge.com.

40 **European Integration as an Elite Process**
The Failure of a Dream?
Max Haller

41 **Queer Political Performance and Protest**
Benjamin Shepard

42 **Cosmopolitan Spaces**
Europe, Globalization, Theory
Chris Rumford

43 **Contexts of Social Capital**
Social Networks in Communities, Markets and Organizations
Edited by Ray-May Hsung, Nan Lin, and Ronald Breiger

44 **Feminism, Domesticity and Popular Culture**
Edited by Stacy Gillis and Joanne Hollows

45 **Changing Relationships**
Edited by Malcolm Brynin and John Ermisch

46 **Formal and Informal Work**
The Hidden Work Regime in Europe
Edited by Birgit Pfau-Effinger, Lluis Flaquer, & Per H. Jensen

47 **Interpreting Human Rights**
Social Science Perspectives
Edited by Rhiannon Morgan and Bryan S. Turner

48 **Club Cultures**
Boundaries, Identities and Otherness
Silvia Rief

49 **Eastern European Immigrant Families**
Mihaela Robila

50 **People and Societies**
Rom Harré and Designing the Social Sciences
Luk van Langenhove

51 **Legislating Creativity**
The Intersections of Art and Politics
Dustin Kidd

52 **Youth in Contemporary Europe**
Edited by Jeremy Leaman and Martha Wörsching

53 **Globalization and Transformations of Social Inequality**
Edited by Ulrike Schuerkens

54 **Twentieth Century Music and the Question of Modernity**
Eduardo De La Fuente

55 **The American Surfer**
Radical Culture and Capitalism
Kristin Lawler

56 **Religion and Social Problems**
Edited by Titus Hjelm

57 **Play, Creativity, and Social Movements**
If I Can't Dance, It's Not My Revolution
Benjamin Shepard

58 **Undocumented Workers' Transitions**
Legal Status, Migration, and Work in Europe
Sonia McKay, Eugenia Markova and Anna Paraskevopoulou

59 **The Marketing of War in the Age of Neo-Militarism**
Edited by Kostas Gouliamos and Christos Kassimeris

60 **Neoliberalism and the Global Restructuring of Knowledge and Education**
Steven C. Ward

61 **Social Theory in Contemporary Asia**
Ann Brooks

62 **Foundations of Critical Media and Information Studies**
Christian Fuchs

63 **A Companion to Life Course Studies**
The social and historical context of the British birth cohort studies
Michael Wadsworth and John Bynner

64 **Understanding Russianness**
Risto Alapuro, Arto Mustajoki and Pekka Pesonen

65 **Understanding Religious Ritual**
Theoretical approaches and innovations
John Hoffmann

66 **Online Gaming in Context**
The social and cultural significance of online games
Garry Crawford, Victoria K. Gosling and Ben Light

67 **Contested Citizenship in East Asia**
Developmental politics, national unity, and globalization
Kyung-Sup Chang and Bryan S. Turner

68 **Agency without Actors?**
New Approaches to Collective Action
Edited by Jan-Hendrik Passoth, Birgit Peuker and Michael Schillmeier

69 **The Neighborhood in the Internet**
Design Research Projects in Community Informatics
John M. Carroll

70 **Managing Overflow in Affluent Societies**
Edited by Barbara Czarniawska and Orvar Löfgren

71 **Refugee Women**
Beyond Gender versus Culture
Leah Bassel

72 **Socioeconomic Outcomes of the Global Financial Crisis**
Theoretical Discussion and Empirical Case Studies
Edited by Ulrike Schuerkens

73 **Migration in the 21st Century**
Political Economy and Ethnography
Edited by Pauline Gardiner Barber and Winnie Lem

Migration in the 21st Century
Political Economy and Ethnography

**Edited by Pauline Gardiner Barber
and Winnie Lem**

NEW YORK LONDON

First published 2012
by Routledge
711 Third Avenue, New York, NY 10017

Simultaneously published in the UK
by Routledge
2 Park Square, Milton Park, Abingdon, Oxfordshire OX14 4RN

First issued in paperback 2014

*Routledge is an imprint of the Taylor & Francis Group,
an informa business*

© 2012 Taylor & Francis

The right of the editors to be identified as the authors of the editorial material, and of the authors for their individual chapters, has been asserted in accordance with sections 77 and 78 of the Copyright, Designs and Patents Act 1988.

All rights reserved. No part of this book may be reprinted or reproduced or utilised in any form or by any electronic, mechanical, or other means, now known or hereafter invented, including photocopying and recording, or in any information storage or retrieval system, without permission in writing from the publishers.

Trademark Notice: Product or corporate names may be trademarks or registered trademarks, and are used only for identification and explanation without intent to infringe.

Library of Congress Cataloging-in-Publication Data
Migration in the 21st century : political economy and ethnography / edited by Pauline Gardiner Barber and Winnie Lem.
    p. cm. — (Routledge advances in sociology ; 73)
Includes bibliographical references and index.
1. Emigration and immigration—Economic aspects—History—21st century. 2. Emigration and immigration—Political aspects—History—21st century. 3. Immigrants—Social conditions—21st century. I. Barber, Pauline Gardiner. II. Lem, Winnie.
    JV6033.M562 2012
    304.8—dc23
    2011049059

ISBN 978-0-415-89222-3 (hbk)
ISBN 978-0-415-71663-5 (pbk)
ISBN 978-0-203-11649-4 (ebk)

Typeset in Sabon
by IBT Global.

Contents

Acknowledgements		ix
1	Migration, Political Economy, and Ethnography PAULINE GARDINER BARBER AND WINNIE LEM	1

PART I
Perspectives

2	Panoptics of Political Economy: Anthropology and Migration WINNIE LEM	17
3	Migration and Development without Methodological Nationalism: Towards Global Perspectives on Migration NINA GLICK SCHILLER	38
4	Theorizing Transnational Movement in the Current Conjuncture: Examples from/of/in the Asia Pacific DONALD M. NONINI	64

PART II
Cases

5	With Crossings in My Mind: Trinidad's Multiple Migration Flows, Policy, and Agency BELINDA LEACH	89

6 Selecting, Competing, and Performing as 'Ideal Migrants':
   Mexican and Jamaican Farmworkers in Canada   109
   JANET MCLAUGHLIN

7 In Search of Hope:
   Mobility and Citizenships on the Canadian Frontier   132
   LINDSAY BELL

8 Constructing a "Perfect" Wall:
   Race, Class, and Citizenship in US-Mexico Border Policing 153
   JOSIAH MCC. HEYMAN

9 The Aftermath of a Rape Case: The Politics of
   Migrants' Unequal Incorporation in Neoliberal Times   175
   BELA FELDMAN-BIANCO

10 Gender, Migration, and Rural-Urban
   Relations in Post-socialist China   196
   YAN HAIRONG

11 "Value Plus Plus": Housewifization and
   History in Philippine Care Migration   215
   PAULINE GARDINER BARBER AND CATHERINE BRYAN

12 Migration, Political Economy, and Beyond   236
   PAULINE GARDINER BARBER AND WINNIE LEM

   Contributors   243
   Index   247

Acknowledgements

This volume is the result of continuing dialogues with colleagues, scholars, and friends in many different contexts. The editors wish to thank the participants of the Anthropology and Political Economy Seminar (APES) for their commitment to critical scholarship which includes conversations about the complexity of the issues we engage in this volume. Many of the chapters in this book are also shaped by conversations with colleagues in the pan-Canadian and international Metropolis project networks, which include the Atlantic Metropolis Centre, supported by the Social Sciences and Humanities Research Council of Canada (SSHRC). In addition to several panels at the national conferences of the Canadian and American Anthropology Associations in 2009, further notable collaborations were hosted by the European Center of Excellence at Dalhousie University in 2009 and 2010. We would particularly like to thank second year summer school students in the 2011 Erasmus Mundus European Master in Global Studies Program at the University of Leipzig, whose comments on the penultimate draft helped us to clarify some of the ideas that appear in the volume. Gavin Smith and Bruce Barber are also to be thanked for their critical commentary and encouragement during various phases in the preparation of this book and others. Natasha Hanson, a PhD student at Dalhousie deserves our gratitude for her indispensable work in preparing this manuscript. We would also like to acknowledge Max Novick at Routledge for his enthusiastic support, kindness, and patience. Also, at the press, we thank Ryan Kenney and Jennifer Morrow for their diligent work in overseeing the production of the publication. A final note of thanks is owed to our anonymous reviewers for their insightful comments and support of the volume.

1 Migration, Political Economy, and Ethnography

Pauline Gardiner Barber and Winnie Lem

As the aftershocks of the financial crisis of 2008 continue to shake our world, the search for paradigms to explain the economic turmoil has been undertaken with some urgency. Increasingly analysts in the academy[1] and elsewhere[2] have turned to political economy perspectives for guidance on how to understand not only the financial upheaval but also the very nature, causes, and effects of such recurring global recessions, downturns, and crises. Political economy, particularly in its Marxian iterations, is explicitly dedicated to deciphering the inner workings of capitalism. Marx's work has inspired many generations of scholars to debate the character of economies and societies. Today, no less than in earlier periods of upheaval and dislocations, his theories, concepts, and methodologies are devoted to analyzing the nexus of forces and social processes that contribute to capitalism's formations, transformations, and crises. For scholarship on migration, this renewed interest in the diagnostics of political economy is propitious, for it has long been established that migration and capitalism are entwined in a relationship of complexity and inextricability.[3] This intricate relationship is evidenced by the fact that the instabilities of capitalism and its cycles of crises are often accompanied by the intensification of the cross-border movements of people. Indeed, the vicissitudes of economic turbulence compel multidirectional human mobility, dislocation, and relocation. The perspective of political economy, therefore, promises significant insights into migration as one process that is deeply implicated in capitalism and its transformations both in the past and in the present.

In history, the movement of populations under the imperatives of colonialism and also imperialism has been allied with the development of capitalism as a global phenomenon,[4] or as some would suggest, as a world system.[5] At least since the last half of the twentieth century, migration has become more salient as a force in contemporary capitalism. Indeed, the restructuring of capitalist economies across the globe in the era of post-fordism and the realization of neoliberal doctrines that increasingly embed societies in market relations have both contributed to the intensification of migration within, as well as between nations. Migration then is as much a sign of ongoing trajectories of growth in the development of capitalism as it is of under- or uneven development. Migrant labor is deployed to the projects of capitalist development in mines, fields, and factories, or in the services that support such schemes. Moreover, both the development and the continuation of capitalism are consequences of migration. As participants in national economies, migrants may also incorporate themselves into societies in which they relocate as members of the entrepreneurial class who sustain capitalist economies by engaging in the pursuit of profits.

Furthermore, remittances provided by migrants of different classes can be seen to foster the redistribution of resources across the globe, albeit sometimes in a multidirectional as well as circular fashion. Often they are directed to societies of migrant provenance for supporting market economies and capitalist development when they are deployed in consumption and sometimes production. But sometimes remittances can also disguise migrant indebtedness, so it is controversial as to whether or not migrant remittances actually foster development in any straightforward manner. Countries of emigration are also sites for capital to draw upon labor reserves where costs of social reproduction are lower than in more established and diverse economies. Moreover, funds garnered through the remittance process are also used by labor-exporting states to service foreign currency loans to transnational banking agencies. The processes of capitalist change and development, therefore, both form and are in turn informed by the movement of people across space and time, while the very character of migration itself is contoured by changing economies and politics under capitalism. Hence the imbrication of capitalism and migration suggests that a diachronic application of a mode of analysis whose purpose is to apply the complexities of capitalism to the study of migration would also serve to disentangle the inner workings of migration itself. We argue, therefore, that a renewed interest in a theoretical orientation that is pre-eminently devoted to the study of the dynamics of capitalist formations and transformations is particularly salutary for scholarship on migration.

In this current period of economic crisis and turmoil, migration scholarship is coming of age. There is now a burgeoning literature that spans a variety of disciplines and constitutes the framework for new interdisciplinary modes of enquiry. The questions are numerous and the analytical perspectives are diverse. Such questions have been surveyed, for example by Brettell and Hollifield (2000), who also offer a comprehensive overview of theoretical, methodological propositions across the many disciplines that address questions of migration. Similarly, Hirschman, Kasinitz, and DeWind (1999), Massey et al. (1998, 1994, 1993), and Portes and DeWind (2007) provide a compendium of different analytical approaches from several disciplines.[6] In reviewing these studies, it is evident that there are few sustained discussions of the relationship between migration and capitalism, and we hazard that a condition of theoretical stasis seems to prevail. Overviews of migration theory tend to be repetitive, continually rehearsing the strengths and weaknesses of a standard and predictable set of theories and ideas. This set includes neoclassical approaches to migration studies, structural approaches, and more recently migration systems theory, as well as transnational analysis.[7] Indeed, in studies of migration the analytical framework of transnational analysis seem to stand alone as a significant innovative advancement in migration theory.[8] Proposed by political economists, transnational analysis as theory and methodology promises insights into the fundamental forces that structure migration in its relationship to capitalism. But here also, as will be made clear by authors in this volume, blind spots prevail. Further, as a mode of analysis transnationalism becomes problematic. To an important extent, it is often rendered troublesome with respect to frameworks that stress "securitization" as both discourse and agenda. Methodological nationalism results from such an emphasis (Glick Schiller, this volume; Wimmer and Glick Schiller 2003).

The issue of the novelty of transnationalism may well belie our claim of a prevailing theoretical stasis. Still we suggest that a tendency toward limited advancements in theory might stem from the fact that much research on migration is state sponsored and therefore driven by policy imperatives. On the one hand, such imperatives reflect the predominant concern to execute forms of neoliberal governance including the project of ensuring that immigrants are, or can be turned into, economically productive citizens. Hence much research is inclined toward a focus on mechanisms of social inclusion and on how immigrants can be incorporated through processes of (neoliberal) assimilation, and integration. On the other hand, such imperatives also reflect the efforts by states to establish secure frontiers in the post-9/11 world. From an alternative viewpoint, responding to perceptions of migrants as threats, the directives of states tend to focus attention upon immigrant exclusion and to be pre-eminently concerned with securing borders against migrant influxes. Because of the complexities of implementing neoliberal policies combined with border securitization strategies, issues of migration and immigration have become matters of urgency on many state agendas. So much of the current research on migration reflects these concerns. Moreover, such directives and agendas for migration studies are often sustained through major international networks where migration research is deliberately targeted to policy-makers and migration agents. Examples of these include the International Metropolis Project (http://www.internationalmetropolis.com/) which hosts major international conferences on migration as well as the ESRC Centre on Migration, Policy and Society (COMPAS) (http://www.compas.ox.ac.uk/) and International Migration, Integration, and Social Cohesion (IMISCOE) (http://www.imiscoe.org). Scholarship on migration then is often curtailed by a clutter of different and often competing agendas, leading toward what we perceive as a limited form of theoretical advancement, if not outright theoretical stasis

Such limitation, at least in the discipline of anthropology, has also resulted in part from the post-structural turn in the social sciences in which deconstruction and the use of literary metaphors has become dominant. In migration studies, this discursive turn is particularly reflected in the idea of 'flows.'[9] Uprooted and oftentimes celebratory discourses about global flows have arguably displaced questions about the structure, power, class, and economy that give capitalism's flows, countercurrents, and blockages their particular character, including those associated with the mobilities of people as economic agents, not just cultural producers.[10] We contend that despite and also because of the complexities of varying applications of neoliberalism as well as border securitization, any appreciation of the social consequences of the contemporary iterations of global capitalism is broadened by a deeper understanding of the relationship between migration and the transformations of capitalism. We further contend that state policies reflect concerns that can be productively examined through the lens of an ethnographically grounded political economy that takes account of both state agendas and migrant responses. In a context in which such directives promote incorporation rather than transformation, radical or critical perspectives are few, as are focused, critical, and sustained meditations on the relationship between migration and capitalism.

This book then brings together the work of anthropologists whose interventions in the field of migration studies are undertaken through an engagement with the analytics of political economy and Marxism. This engagement is undertaken in two ways. First, our work considers migration—or what we call here the "migration question"—in relation to the key concerns in political economy. As the contributors illustrate, we problematize migration, in various global contexts, with respect to the nature of production, the processes of accumulation, the dynamics of social reproduction, hegemony, exploitation, as well as class formation, power, and divisions of labor. Of particular significance to anthropologists is that Marx insisted on the social nature of the economy, that it is composed of social relationships which come to be ordered as classes relative to productive resources and labor. In focusing attention on the key thematic of class, authors illustrate the methodologies for class analysis, while illuminating the varied but comparable articulations of power that inform the lives of migrants and condition different forms of migration relative to questions of political economy. Our volume further illustrates how power infuses the malleable articulations between class, gender, and ethnicity relative to geographic scale. It can be seen that in different settings, varied social aspects of migrants' identities become highlighted in negative ways and thus subjected to power mobilized by discourses of difference which renders migrants even more vulnerable to exploitation.

The second way of undertaking this engagement involves an attempt to move beyond orthodoxies of political economy that many critics, rightly or wrongly, suggest reduce and simplify.[11] Cognizant of such objections, our collaboration must be read as a *critical* engagement with political economy and also Marxism in that we try to shift optics and push analytical boundaries, while remaining faithful to fundamentals. Furthermore our method of engagement with a political economy of migration is one that is dialectical. It is premised on the relationship of reciprocal formation and transformation that prevails between the social conditions of migration and the categories that are employed for its apprehension. It is a critique that emerges through our investigations as ethnographers of migration attuned to the realities of migrants' lives livelihoods and the local logics of their migratory journeys. Hence the book illustrates the productive tension between field-derived observations, with due attention to historical conditions shaping migration trajectories, and the theoretical debates that define anthropological ethnography. Our book therefore is as much an exegesis on a method of inquiry as it is ethnography.

The authors in this volume are committed to asserting the heuristic significance of the theoretical and methodological apparatuses offered in political economy and Marxism, as it has been translated within anthropology to the study of migration. While retaining a commitment to framing the problematics of migration through political economy and Marxism, we attempt to move beyond the limits of orthodox, reductionist, and also static tendencies in materialism to illuminate the increasing complexities of migration and migrants' lives. We argue, therefore, that an understanding of people's spatial mobility is significantly advanced through the analytic lens of an anthropological approach to political economy, particularly in its Marxist variant. Each chapter, through deployment of a comparable conceptual language used with varying emphases and nuance, is an illustration of the key analytics in a reconstituted political economy for problematizing global migration within contemporary capitalism.

Part I, *Perspectives*, is devoted to a delineation of the theoretical and conceptual terrain of a political economy of migration in the discipline of anthropology. The chapters in Part I examine the ways in which migration is refracted through such core concepts as class, divisions of labor, accumulation, structure, agency, social reproduction, surplus population, value, power, and global capitalism. Also pivotal in a framework of political economy are broader questions about processes of class differentiation, dispossession, and exploitation, all of which are of concern to researchers contributing to this book.

Lem, for example, in Chapter 2 attempts to outline the points of departure in navigating through the theoretical and conceptual terrain of a political economy of migration for anthropology. She attempts this task by drawing attention to the foundations of political economy as a form of Marxist analysis and investigation. The chapter begins by outlining some ways in which political economy and Marxism have been understood as method and theory in anthropology. The second part of the chapter is an attempt to think through migration by using concepts in political economy to illuminate the processes of capitalist transformation and class formation in contemporary Chinese transregional and transnational migration.

Her focus is on the ways in which dispossession through capitalist accumulation, particularly primitive accumulation, enables the formation of a class of freed labor which is segmented into a proletariat on the one hand and a relative surplus population on the other. By focusing on the example of Chinese migration she focuses on the processes of differentiation through members of the 'surplus population,' which by its very nature is a highly differentiated population, may follow varied trajectories to become incorporated into different classes over space and time. Class formation as a condition of possibility suggests ways of developing and deepening Marx's ideas of the 'relative surplus population' in relation to the tensions and transformations in the contemporary world. In this way her chapter engages with the dialectics of political economy as a mode of analysis that illuminates the social and economic conditions of migration.

In Chapter 3, Glick Schiller tackles a conundrum in migration theory: how to reconcile contradictory positions in migration policy (and research) whereby migrants are seen as agents of development through the provision of remittances, yet they are also increasingly denied mobility rights. Reconciling these two positions, she proposes that migration studies adopt a critical perspective on global power, one which transcends the distorting effects of persistent methodological nationalism. The author suggests, for example, that various bounded models such as the treatment of immigrants in terms of ethnic categorization have lead to a preoccupation in migration scholarship with immigrant integration. Such work revives historical themes in migration studies, leading Glick Schiller to speak of a 'born-again assimilationism' that can ultimately, if inadvertently, be seen to reflect the neoliberal project of restructuring nation-states. What is absent from contemporary migration studies, she argues, is a critical global power perspective that can link contemporary forces of capitalist restructuring to the specific localities within which migrants live *and* their transnational social fields of uneven power. Her methodological framework addresses countervailing hegemonic processes seen in the disjunction between development rhetoric and migration policies. Of particular significance in the analytics of this volume is her proposition on geographic scale and the mutually constitutive dynamics of local and global processes associated with globe-spanning hierarchies of economic and political power. These processes can be apprehended in a 'locality analysis' which enables ethnographic examination of how migrants are implicated in processes of restructuring and the reproduction and destruction of capital in several locations simultaneously.

The problematics of capital accumulation are also addressed by Nonini (Chapter 4). The author attempts to demonstrate the relationship between the shifting dynamics of capital accumulation in the global system through attention to processes of value creation and the multifaceted nature of social reproduction. Understanding patterns of transnational mobility requires, he suggests, close consideration of the changing dynamics of capitalist markets and accumulation in three major competing regions—Europe, the US, and East Asia. Related to this, he proposes, we should attend to the ways in which citizenship regimes set constraints on the social reproduction of particular groups of migrants. Thus the ethnographic project Nonini models for us concerns how transnational migrants navigate these two sets of contradictory constraints: the articulations of capitalist markets and the particular prescriptions of the relevant multiple citizenship regimes with their attendant bureaucratic complexities. Through ethnographic examples drawn from fieldwork with Chinese groups in Malaysia and Indonesia, with Chinese families who have provisionally relocated from Southeast Asia to Australia, Canada, New Zealand, and elsewhere in the Pacific basin, and lastly with Chinese Malaysian laborers whom he first encountered when they were migrants from Malaysia to Japan in the 1980s, Nonini's chapter acutely demonstrates how migration scholars can combine ethnography and political economy to 'transcend methodological nationalism.' Arguing that value creation and associated processes of social reproduction in capitalism always take place somewhere, Nonini thus situates various distinct groups of transnational labor migrants within a broader comparative class framework. His purpose in so doing is to better illuminate the circumstances of transnational laborers in contrast with other groups of transnationally mobile classes, each confronting different relationships with respect to the mechanisms of social reproduction and facing class-specific dilemmas stemming from their varied forms of mobility. Hence, a primary contribution from Nonini's chapter is to theoretically advance our approach to transnational class formation which remains a central challenge for scholars of the 'migration question.'

The authors in Part II, *Cases*, draw upon ethnographic projects in more detail to illustrate the ways in which conceptual configurations of political economies of migration articulate and inform our understanding of the movement of populations as a process and lived reality. Like Nonini, they do this by ethnographically analyzing distinctive processes of class formation, reformation, and differentiation under historical and contemporary capitalisms. Contributions to this section focus on cases of transregional migration in national and transnational settings.

Also exemplifying Glick Schiller's global power approach, Leach's study in Chapter 5 animates the historical significance of Trinidad's strategic geographic location as a 'crossing point' for various global flows, including labor migration. Part of the theoretical challenge advanced in the chapter, as demonstrated earlier by Nonini, is to situate labor migration in relationship to the circuits of mobility for other commodities, trading relationships, and vice versa. As the demands of global capital change so too do we see changes in the social relations of labor in Trinidad. Working from the history of multiple migrations to and from Trinidad, Leach explores the complexities of migration and class formation through attention to the dialects of migrant agency, political economy, and policy constraint. Ethnographic analysis of contemporary migration to Canada shapes an argument about the co-presence of three particular migration flows from and to the country. These migrant streams are themselves products of various constraints in political economy shaping migrants' decisions about staying and leaving, in turn configured in the light of what is possible given the demands of migration policy regimes. Migration is thus central in constituting gendered and racialized class relations in Trinidad and fundamental to the political struggles of global workers.

A focus on states and their role in the formation of a class of mobile labor is also present in McLaughlin's contribution in Chapter 6. Along with Barber and Bryan (Chapter 11), the author considers how multiple states and capital interests converge to influence the selection of the 'ideal' transnational migrant worker as well as how prospective migrants adapt to these expectations. She also explores the consequences of such enactments, particularly for migrants, but also for the societies in which they live and work. McLaughlin analyzes these questions through an exploration of how relationships of class, race, gender, and nationality interact and inform the participation of migrants in Canada's Seasonal Agricultural Workers Program (SAWP), a managed migration program which employs migrant farmworkers from Mexico and several English-speaking Caribbean countries for up to eight months each year. The author then suggests the ways in which workers who participate in this managed migration program respond to these expectations by conforming to demands that they perform the role of an 'ideal migrant worker.' Migrant workers work hard, obey rules, become flexible, while never aspiring to improve their skills or to develop relationships and settle in Canada. Complementing Lem's discussion of the role of relative surplus population in migration, McLaughlin's intervention illustrates the ways in which states enact 'exception' (Agamben 2005) in conjunctural moments. In so doing they render a particular class of migrant workers as members of that distinct population.

In a different context within Canada, Bell (Chapter 7) explores the complexities of class formation and the contradictions associated with mobility and settlement within the Canadian Northwest Territories. Her chapter is framed by a discussion of how the dynamics of the global 'labor crisis' are insinuated within one pillar of Canadian political economy, primary resource extraction of diamonds and oil, both sectors notorious for instabilities associated with global commodity market fluctuations. Because of market vagaries, mining industries also depend upon both migrant labor and where possible a labor surplus with the capability to sustain themselves in situ in accord with industry demands for labor and in relation to market volatility. Complicating assumptions about labor mobility and fixity, as well as the social characteristics and identities of who is mobile and who is settled, the author maps contradictions associated with a popular narrative opposition of migrant/settlers and fixed, timeless indigenous populations. While local development policy is aimed at directing the 'benefits' of primary extraction work to 'Aboriginals' and 'Northerners,' a severe labor shortage across sectors requires more bodies than this sparsely populated territory can provide. As such, migrant labor figures centrally in local class formation and the ongoing articulation of Northern social inequalities. Focusing on two different work trajectories, one historical and one contemporary, both at once migrant and Aboriginal, the author shows the inscription of surplus populations as central to processes of Northern capital accumulation. With this analysis she highlights the chaotic and destructive nature of legal-political-economic regimes that are reliant upon institutionalized identity categories and differentiated citizenships.

In Chapter 8, Heyman's essay on US-Mexico border enforcement directs attention to class power and the state enforcement regime. Through analysis of various assumptions underlying the tactical procedures of border control, the author demonstrates the logics of how border issues become transformed into security issues, and how these in turn produce intractable inequalities of class and power relentlessly to the disadvantage of migrants. Border agenda-setting prerogatives are seen to be aligned with various groupings of corporate power, whose contradictory interests are served through securitization. Heyman thus links border rhetoric and redesign to the need on the part of elites for a sizeable, relatively inexpensive, and readily disciplined transnational migrant labor force. Here again, debates over border redesign seek optimum efficiency in the smooth flow of labor (preferably authorized yet readily managed) and commodities. Yet constructs of the 'perfect border' are flawed, the rhetoric contradictory, the goals unobtainable. Instead, Heyman argues, American 'addictions' to drugs and cheap labor are displaced onto the symbol of a threatened then defended border. Thus he makes a case for a truly dialectical engagement with class, political economy, and border securitization. Migration and border policies of states are seen as responsive albeit in complex ways to class interests and capital agendas. A political economy analysis of multiple and contradictory aspects of migration and borders should, Heyman demonstrates, be both at once historical and multifaceted.

In Chapter 9, Feldman-Bianco also problematizes the relationship between a shifting global political economy, the intersection between gender, race, and class, and processes of transnational migrants' unequal incorporation in a locality. Avoiding what Glick Schiller calls 'born-again assimilationism' and the de rigueur paradigms of the 'ethnic group' as the unit of analysis, as well as the corollary constructs 'assimilation,' 'integration,' or 'transnational paradigms,' she focuses on the internationally infamous New Bedford 1983 gang rape in which a Luzo-American woman was attacked by a handful of Azorean unemployed immigrant workers in a barroom. Exacerbated by intense media coverage and a televized trial, that dramatic event incited major political confrontations between groups rallying around gender or ethnic issues. These conflicts served to heighten existing xenophobia and discrimination against immigrants of Portuguese origin and ultimately led to the targeting of New Bedford as the "Portuguese rape city of America." The author analyzes the social drama and its aftermath in the context of the social history of a neoliberal transformation. Class and gender conflicts underscore the changing positioning of New Bedford's Portuguese and reveal the unequal processes of incorporation of immigrants relative to local and global restructuring dynamics.

Questions of subjectivity and gendered class identities are also addressed by Yan, and Barber and Bryan in Chapters 10 and 11 respectively. By focusing on Chinese transregional migration, Yan examines experiences in the Mao and post-Mao eras and traces the formation of rural subjectivities in the inter-related fields of state policies, ideology, community, and patriarchal families. By comparing two generations of migrants, she argues that their different experiences, particularly their relationship with rurality, arise from how rural-urban relations had been constituted in the political economies of socialist and post-socialist modernity. The epistemic shift of post-socialist transformation has created in rural youth a crisis of subjectivity that compels and naturalizes their search for modern experiences through migration. By focusing on how their underclass status in the city offers only the lack of fulfillment of their pursuit, Yan emphasizes, in a similar vein to McLaughlin and Bell, how this contributes toward maintaining migrants as flexible and disposable labor. Indeed, she argues their exodus from the countryside and their very survival in the city depends on their being flexible and disposable.

The role of Manila as a long-standing 'hub' for the staging of global migrations and the feminization of Philippine labor export constitutes a powerful case for examining the 'migration question' through a gendered political economy lens, the subject of Barber and Bryan's contribution in Chapter 11. They argue that contemporary care migration can be productively understood as a global reinitiating of a gendered (and increasingly racialized) process of 'housewifization,' as proposed in mid-twentieth-century feminist scholarship (Mies 1986). Through global processes that continually adjust and readjust social reproduction labor—who performs it on behalf of whom and the values assigned to it—class by class, location by location, the fundamental social and economic contributions of such labor remain mystified. Yet, they propose, social reproduction is central to global capitalism. Their Philippine ethnographic examples show how gendered class relations in the provision of care labor, be they defined through kinship and other forms of patronage and/or commoditized, are foundational to national policies of feminized labor export. Because, as Glick Schiller makes clear in her chapter, migration and development narratives are implicated in perpetuating migration, rendering it a normative expectation in the Philippine case; migrants 'invest' more in preparing to migrate. This includes obtaining higher levels of education and risking more indebtedness as migrants target particular labor markets, such as care industries.

Increasingly then, employers in global markets receive measurably higher levels of 'skill' and 'value,' thus playing into processes of accumulation noted by Nonini (Chapter 4). Hence the dialectics of migration in the case of the Philippines, Barber and Bryan argue, reproduces new economic subjectivities that can be linked to neoliberalism's desire for both flexibility and subordination. Migrant labor is cheapened through stratification in the global political economy. The sheer repetition of negative stories shared through migrants' social networks contribute to migrants' low expectations. Here again we are reminded of Glick Schiller's theoretical proposition to juxtapose migration and development scenarios and migration policy dynamics, and furthermore the alignment of these with neoliberal initiatives in political economy.

Migrants in all our cases, whether they are from the Philippines, rural China, the Azores, Mexico, Northern Canada, the Caribbean, or the Asia Pacific, provide powerful examples for what Eric Wolf (1982) termed "new laborers" in the global political economy. Throughout the book, the authors demonstrate how political economy provides migration scholarship with a critical and coherent framework for problematizing the complexity of the migration-capitalism nexus, and most particularly for addressing the question of how migrants as a distinctive population are produced, sustained, and transformed. Our cases also demonstrate how the perspectives we use provide conceptual apparatuses and methodologies for analyzing the everyday domain of migrants' lives by adressing the forces that create differences and inequalities of class, both within and between migrant populations and the constituencies that receive as well as ultimately profit from their movement. Our objective therefore is to assert the primacy and scope of political economy as a paradigm that explicates the nexus of migration and capitalism as forces which shape the contemporary world.

NOTES

1. See for example Ho (2009), Wade (2008), and McNally (2008).
2. See for example Masse (2008), Fox (2008), and Collins (2008) whose articles appear in conservative newspapers.
3. See for example Sassen (1998), Castles and Miller (2009), and also Lem and Barber (2010).
4. See Wolf (1982).
5. See Wallerstein (1980).
6. See also Foner, Rumbaut, and Gold (2000), as well as Castles and Miller (2009) for some useful overviews.
7. See for example Castles and Miller (2009), Chapter 3 this volume, and also Massey et al. (1998).
8. See Basch, Glick Schiller, and Szanton Blanc (1994) and Rouse (2002).
9. Inda and Rosaldo (2002); Appadurai (1996).
10. See Heyman and Campbell (2009) for a critique of the idea of flows. See also Leach (this volume).
11. See Chapter 12 (this volume).

REFERENCES

Agamben, Giorgio. 2005. *State of Exception*. Chicago: University of Chicago Press.
Appadurai, Arjun. 1996. *Modernity at Large: Cultural Dimensions of Globalization*. Minneapolis: University of Minnesota Press.
Basch, Linda, Nina Glick Schiller, and Christine Szanton Blanc. 1994. *Nations Unbound: Transnational Projects, Post-colonial Predicaments and De-territorialized Nation-States*. New York: Gordon Breach.
Brettell, Caroline, and James Hollifield, eds. 2000. *Migration Theory: Talking across Disciplines*. New York: Routledge.
Castles, Stephen, and Mark Miller. 2009. *The Age of Migration: International Popular Movements in the Modern World*. London: Palgrave.
Collins, Philip. 2008. "Karl Marx: Did He Get It Right?" *Time*, October 21.
Foner, Nancy, Ruben Rumbaut, and Steven Gold, eds. 2000. *Immigration Research for a New Century: Multidisciplinary Perspective*. New York: Russell Sage Foundation.
Fox, Claire. 2008. "Not, Please, in Marx's Name." *Independent*, October 27.
Heyman, Josiah McC, and Horward Campbell. 2009. "The Anthropology of Global Flows: A Critical Reading of Appadurai's 'Disjuncture and Difference in the Global Cultural Economy'." *Anthropological Theory* 9(2): 131–148.
Hirschman, Charles, Philip Kasinitz, and Josh DeWind, eds. 1999. *The Handbook of International Migration: The American Experience*. New York. Russell Sage.
Ho, Karen. 2009. *Liquidated: An Ethnography of Wall Street*. Durham and London: Duke University Press.
Inda, Jonathan Xavier, and Renato Rosaldo, eds. 2002. *The Anthropology of Globalization: A Reader*. Malden, MA and Oxford: Blackwell.
Lem, Winnie, and Pauline Gardiner Barber, eds. 2010. *Class, Contention, and a World in Motion*. New York and London: Berghan Books.
Masse, Michael. 2008. "Bailout Marks Karl Marx's Comeback." *Financial Post*, September 29.
Massey, Douglas S., Joaquin Arango, Ali Koucouci, Adela Pellegrino, and J. Edward Taylor. 1993. "Theories of International Migration: A Review and Appraisal." *Population and Development Review* 19(3): 431–446.
———. 1994. "An Evaluation of International Migration Theory: The North American Case." *Population and Development Review* 20: 699–752.
———. 1998. *Worlds in Motion: Understanding International Migration at the End of the Millennium*. Oxford: Clarendon.
McNally, David. 2008. "Global Instability and Challenges to the Dollar: Assessing the Current Financial Crisis." *New Socialist*, June 14.
Mies, Maria. 1986. *Patriarchy and Accumulation on a World Scale: Women in the International Division of Labor*. London: Zed Books.
Portes, Alejandro, and Josh DeWind. 2007. "A Cross-Atlantic Dialogue: The Progress of Research and Theory in the Study of International Migration." In *Rethinking Migration Theory*, edited by Alejandro Portes and Josh DeWind, 3–26. London: Berghahn.
Rouse, Roger. 2002. "Mexican Migration and the Social Space of Postmodernism." In *The Anthropology of Globalization: A Reader*, edited by Jonathan Xavier Inda and Renato Rosaldo, 157–171. Malden, MA and Oxford: Blackwell.
Sassen, Saskia. 1998. *Globalization and Its Discontents: Essays on the New Mobility of People and Money*. New York: The New Press.
Wade, Robert. 2008. "Financial Regime Change." *New Left Review*, September–October.

Wallerstein, Immanuel. 1980. *The Modern World-System*. Vol. 2, *Mercantilism and the Consolidation of the European World-Economy, 1600–1750*. New York: Academic Press.

Wimmer, Andreas, and Nina Glick Schiller. 2003. "Methodological Nationalism, the Social Sciences, and the Study of Migration: An Essay in Historical Epistemology." *The International Migration Review* 37(3): 576–610.

Wolf, Eric. 1982. *Europe and the People without History*. Berkeley and Los Angeles: University of California Press.

Part I
Perspectives

2 Panoptics of Political Economy
Anthropology and Migration

Winnie Lem

It is commonly asserted that migration has been growing in salience since World War II.[1] This salience is often linked to the transformation of 20th century migration from a transatlantic phenomenon to one that is truly global, in manifesting the processes of change generally glossed as globalization. As the mantra insists, in a global age people along with capital, commodities, and ideas all flow through borders made increasingly permeable by strategies of governance that promote economic liberalization. Globalization, of course, has been the focus of much debate as analysts continue to argue over its effects as well as its status as a new player on the stage of world history.[2] In the literature on migration, such arguments have provoked much rethinking about paradigms that prevail in the analysis of the cross-border movement of populations.[3] Such re-evaluations—of current conceptual schemes, extant theoretical frameworks, and established analytical approaches—have revolved around several axes. On the temporal axis, for example, scholars have argued that "traditional approaches" cannot contend with contemporary migration, as they were developed in previous eras to explain earlier forms of migration that were limited in scope and geographic scale (Massey et al. 1998: 8).[4] So, "new" perspectives must be engaged to analyze the intensified cross-border, multination commitments, activities, and orientations of migrants.[5] New approaches include social capital theory, the new economics of labor migration, and the transnational framework of analysis[6] (Portes, Guarzino, and Landolt 1999; Glick Schiller, Basch, and Szanton Blanc 1995, 1992).

Re-evaluations continue on the disciplinary axis and it has been suggested that the theoretical repertoire of any one discipline is not up to the task of contending with the complexities of global migration. Rather, cross-disciplinary collaborations as well as interdisciplinary perspectives are considered more apposite (Brettell and Hollifield 2000; Foner, Rumbaut, and Gold 2000; Hirschman, Kasinitz, and DeWind 1999). Many reassessments have been undertaken on the epistemological axis as well. For example, Massey et al. (1994) have suggested that a comprehensive interdisciplinary theory of international migration must be built and this must be done by integrating the most rigorous components of new theories. Such a unitary theory could avoid the duplications, reinventions and bickering between disciplines and adherents of particular analytical paradigms (Massey et al. 1994). Yet, it is precisely migration's protean character that has led other scholars to proclaim that attempts at producing a comprehensive or grand theory of migration are misguided and bound to fail (Portes and DeWind 2007; Hirschman, Kasinitz and DeWind 1999). For instance, citing the theory of colonial capitalist penetration as a key example of "grand theory", Portes points out that while this approach plays a significant role in explaining the initiation of large scale labor migration from less developed countries it says nothing about who among the population of those countries is more likely to migrate (Portes 1999).[7] Portes continues, "Nor can it be tested at the level of individual decision making" (1999: 27). Given such failings, what is advocated is a retreat from grand theory in favor of the development and application of a set of mid-range concepts and theories to research agendas (Portes and DeWind 2007; Hirschman, Kasinitz, and DeWind 1999).[8]

The caution extended in such critiques about the explanatory limits of any theory, "grand" or otherwise, is judicious. However, predictions of the inevitable failure of unitary paradigms are, as I will suggest, less prudent. For the purposes of this chapter and this volume, the claim of the failure of grand theory and in particular of what is called the "theory of colonial capitalist penetration" is particularly provocative. For this theory is in fact one variant of political economy, a paradigm that is explicitly dedicated to the critical investigation of the inner workings of capitalism. As migration is a process that is intrinsic to and varies with the changing dynamics of capitalism, it seems that political economy and its variants will necessarily aid our understanding population movements both in the past and also in the present. In this chapter then, I will argue that by deploying key precepts and the conceptual apparatus of political economy, not only is our understanding of the movement of populations significantly advanced but many of the concerns that have been raised in rethinking migration theory are addressed.

The first part of this chapter is an attempt to broadly outline the conceptual parameters of political economy as a theoretical and methodological framework in anthropology. I do this by drawing attention to some of the foundational concepts that are used in Marx's analysis and investigation. To begin to set out any of even the most fundamental principles of inquiry is an ambitious undertaking. The scope of political economy is vast and its analytics are used in many disciplines. Thus any endeavor to delineate its parameters will be necessarily telegraphic. My effort here therefore must be read as an attempt simply to set out some of the possibilities of a conceptual approach in one discipline with a view to addressing the problematic of migration. The second part of the chapter consists of an illustration of a way to think through the processes, context, and dynamics of Chinese transregional and transnational migration by using the optics of Marxist analysis. In doing this it is an instantiation of what Barber and Lem (this volume) call a "dialectical method of engagement" for I seek to illuminate the "relationship of reciprocal formation and transformation that prevails between the social conditions of migration and the categories that are employed for its apprehension." In the final section, I return to the concerns raised in critical rethinking of migration theory.

POLITICAL ECONOMY AND ANTHROPOLOGY

In anthropology, many scholars lay claim to using the perspective of political economy to work through the complexities of the processes of transformation under capitalism.[9] These processes include not only the forces of economic change, but also transformations in socio-cultural formations. Yet attempts to define political economy as a theoretical school in the discipline are few. This dearth combined with convolutions in the history of the relationship between anthropology, political economy, and Marxism has resulted in conceptualizations that are variegated, confused. This point was underscored by Roseberry (1988), in one of the few attempts to grapple with definitions published in *Annual Review of Anthropology*.[10]

As a key interpreter of Marxist ideas in the discipline, Roseberry argued against what had become an accepted view in anthropology that political economy and Marxism was bifurcated into gut or visceral Marxism and cerebral Marxism (1988: 161).[11] He notes that this binary was first suggested by Raymond Firth (1972) and it coincided with a transatlantic divide between American and French Marxists. Later, it was rendered into a slightly different form by Ortner (1984) in which political economy became conflated with world systems theory. World systems analysis itself included strands of Marxist and neo-Marxist thinking which produced a further layer of conflation. The assumption that political economy is co-extensive with world systems theory has become accepted by many anthropologists and according to Roseberry, serves as the understanding of political economy that prevails in anthropology. While this conflation pervades the discipline of anthropology, it also permeates the literature on the anthropology of migration as well as migration studies in general (see for example Silverstein 2004: 25; and also, Brettell 2000; Massey 1999; Massey et al. 1994).

World systems analysis, of course, has been subjected to many criticisms. One of the most significant is the failure of its proponents to define the conceptual apparatus that sustains the framework (Pieterse 1988). Moreover, critics have noted the scalar vagueness that besets world systems analysis and neo-Marxist theories. Indeed critiques of world systems theory have also come from Marxists. Critiques from a Marxist perspective have focused on the lack of analytical attention to class and the state as well as the misattribution of trade as key in the formation and transformation of capitalism (Brenner 1977). The neglect of class in neo-Marxist theory, so they argue, has meant that the role played by class and conflict as a force of change in history is not addressed. That Marxists find fault with world systems analyses suggests that assumptions about the co-extensiveness of the two theoretical orientations are indeed problematic. It also highlights the confusion that persists over the scope of political economy.

Confusions in current understandings about the nature and usage of political economy may be traced to its roots as method and theory as well as to events in US history. The roots of political economy are found in the works of A. Smith (1776), Ricardo (1817), Malthus (1798, 1820), as well as Marx (1867). It is often debated whether Marx himself was a political economist, as Marx did actually engage in a radical critique of the political economy of his day. Indeed, the three volumes of *Capital* are subtitled *A Critique of Political Economy* (emphasis mine). In *Capital* and in other writings[12] Marx set himself against the ideas of Smith, Ricardo, and Malthus, the political economists who laid the foundations for the analysis of capitalism. The central project of Marx's critique of political economy was to illuminate the forces and laws of motion of capitalism and capitalist change through history. His central critique was that political economy was only appropriate for the study of the societies of that era and the political economists saw their perspectives as transhistorical. Moreover, the political economists were concerned to understand the genesis and the distribution of wealth under capitalism, while Marx's critique focused on an analysis of the structural contradictions in class society—between labor and capital—which would erupt in class conflict propelling the transformation in time of the fundamental nature and organization of society.[13] As Barber and Lem emphasize in the introductory chapter (this volume), of particular significance to anthropologists is that Marx, unlike his contemporaries, insisted on the social nature of the economy, that it is composed of social relationships which come to be ordered as classes relative to productive resources and labor.

So Roseberry states that many anthropologists—but by no means all—who consider themselves political economists accept the radical critique of political economy. In earlier decades, they did this through a self-consciously limited engagement with the work of Marx. For example, the work of such scholars as Eric Wolf and Sidney Mintz, which appeared in the 1950s and early 1960s, was characterized by a constrained involvement with the work of Marx. Such timidity was a function of the political climate of the Cold War and McCarthyism in the US. So anthropologists who engaged with Marxist ideas called themselves "political economists" and not "Marxists." Wolf and Mintz focused on the analysis of the structure of communities and called their approach "cultural history" as they argued that the *formation* of communities was intimately connected with of colonialism, empire-building, international trade, and state formation. Their work is characteristically "historical" in the sense that it attempted to see local communities as products of centuries of social, political, economic, and cultural processes, and those processes were global. The work of these anthropologists (and their students) can be distinguished from later world systems theories, as the goal of historical investigation was not to subsume local histories within global processes but to understand the formation of anthropological subjects; "real people doing real things" (see Roseberry 1988: 163–164). Anthropologists then sought to address questions of class formation and cultural production with a tentative application of Marx's schemas and produced works that were related but not entirely consistent with the Marxist roots of political economy. Political economy thus became a code for the work done scholars in the US who engaged, though in a constrained fashion, with Marxist enquiry in the 1950s and 1960s. This legacy of ambiguity and tentativeness continues today.

While Wolf and Mintz concentrated on the understanding of the dialectic of local and global histories with the development of capitalism, other political economists, particularly Leacock and Nash, brought the analysis of gender into political economy. They stressed that the labor process and divisions of labor under capitalism are fundamentally gendered.[14] Leacock's work questioned the origins of inequality, especially gender inequality and the effects of colonialism (and, later, of state formation) on class formation.[15] Later such scholars as Roseberry (1996, 1983) and G. Smith (1999, 1989) also produced a systematic and sustained engagement with Marxist epistemologies by offering theoretically robust accounts of class formation, cultural production, capitalist reproduction, and conflict under capitalism.[16] For example, G. Smith's (2007, 1999, 1989) work centers on capitalism's inexorable capacity to reproduce itself through the dialectics of exploitation and inequality, while asserting the human capacity for contestation and mobilization in both predictable and unexpected forms. Furthermore, Smith's idea of *historical realism*, which is premised on Marx's notion of historical materialism, insists on the significance of history in shaping social relations and class processes. This theoretical and methodological intervention is to be deployed in confronting the dynamics of capitalism. In *Coffee and Capitalism in the Venezuelan Andes* (1983) Roseberry offers a detailed historical study of the rise of merchant capitalism and transformation of the social relations of coffee production in a region of the Andes. In this text he also wrote a short manifesto for Marxist scholars: "We should have to look a long time to find a Marxist who did not take class analysis seriously as a point of departure. Our histories, after all are written in terms of class relations and class struggles" (Roseberry 1983: 10).

These attempts at a deep engagement contrast with some recent interventions that tend to both misapply and misrepresent Marxism and political economy. While offering significant insights on forces and effects of capitalist change on institutions and the entanglements of people in global capitalism, many such interventions display a tendency to abstract Marxist concepts from the framework of Marxist analysis. For example, in a study of nongovernmental institutions in Indonesia, T. Li (2007) lays claim to the analytics of political economy to explicate continuities in the relations between state-sponsored development projects and Indonesian communities which become the 'objects of development.'[17] In her analysis, questions of class are addressed as are questions of economy but in a way which is appended to a dominantly Foucauldian analysis. The transformations of capitalism themselves, then, tend to be reduced to an epiphenomenon of governmentality (T. Li 2007) or what might be called a logic (see also Ong 1999). As some authors have noted (see for example G. Smith 2002, 1999; O'Malley, Weir, and Shearing 1997), the tendency to frame discussions with a Marxist lexicon without embedding them in the framework of Marxist analysis inhibits our understanding of the forces and contestations in capitalism which condition the emergence of certain 'logics' of governmental or ruling schemes as prevailing representations.[18]

In other studies, there has been a tendency also to misread political economy and Marxist analysis. In a discussion of flexible specialization and transformations in the social relations of family firms engaged in the Italian silk industry, Yanagisako (2002) for example, criticizes political economy and Marxism for its economic reductionism and determinism. She suggests that the economy is less significant than culture in shaping the organizations and institutions that appear in capitalist societies.[19] Marxist scholars such as Gramsci (1971) and Althusser (1969), as well as anthropologists such as Godelier (1977) and Friedman (2002) noted that the charge of economic determinism results from both a misreading and a selective reading of Marx. Also this very common critique has long ago been dismissed as a conflation of "vulgar" Marxism with Marxism itself. The instrumental use of Marxism to assert the primacy of other analytical paradigms notwithstanding, the positioning of culture as determinant is, of course, equally reductionist. By contrast, many accounts exist in the anthropological literature that address the relationship between culture and capital as one that dialectical.[20] The commitment of scholars to different theoretical schools aside, the conflations and confusions to which I earlier refered have no doubt contributed to misreadings of Marx. My efforts in what follows may not correct these tendencies nor influence scholars with inclinations against Marxism and political economy. Still, my attempt to set out some analytical possibilities of this conceptual orientation, I hope, will be salutary at least for those efforts that are directed at illuminating the dynamics of capitalist transformation and its relationship to migration.

POLITICAL ECONOMY AND MIGRATION

Political economy as a form of Marxist inquiry involves engaging with a distinctive conceptual framework that begins and ends with analyzing the formation of capitalism. Central in this framework is the examination of the processes which labor is transformed into a commodity, for they enable accumulation and therefore the reproduction of capitalism in both time and space. Such processes are social in that they refer to the relationships of class, which are themselves formed through the immanent and intentional forces in market economies, that promote differentiation, dispossession, and proletarianization. According to Marx, the central relationship that enables accumulation under capitalism is the relationship between classes. This is, of course, the relationship between owners of capital and industrial wage labor. Through the appropriation of the value that was created by workers under industrial capitalism, accumulation was assured and the system sustained through cycles of production and reproduction. Contemporary analysts have expanded this conceptualization to consider the ways in which differentiations of gender and the racialization of ethnicity also contribute to the creation of an expression of value in these cycles. The *telos* of this conceptual orientation is a political project that is premised on the principle that conflict between classes can potentially propel societies toward structural transformation and breaking free of these cycles. Anthropologists who have employed this framework have enhanced our understanding of the development and expansion of capitalism in into territories and nations as well as analyzed how different nations have broken away from capitalism (Wolf 1982, 1969). This orientation is also prescient in identifying the modalities of change in the contemporary world which allow capitalism to further expand and re-absorb economies and societies that once broke away.

In this contemporary period, then economic elites and supranational institutions have acted in concert to fashion regimes of deregulation, privatization, and to expand the rule of the market.[21] Originally intended to stem the global economic crises in the 1970s this project continues into the twenty-first century and such governing practices have become regnant in many national economies. Guided by the doctrines and principles of neoliberalism, this project is of course commonly referred to as globalization or the imposition of the capitalist market on a global scale (Kalb 2004; Brown 2003). Anthropologists who have applied the conceptual tools of a political economy both from the Marxist and neo-Marxist school of thought have suggested that the restructuring of places in different nations and states as sites for sustained accumulation has resulted in the intensification of the differentiation of populations into classes. They have also suggested that class differences are amplified (Friedman 2004b, 2002). For a vast number of people then, globalization has implied joining the ranks of the proletariat, which has become increasing mobile in the last quarter of the twentieth century.[22] Indeed in China, the emergence of a huge population of migrants, members of a mobile proletariat, is the result of efforts made by a nation that once made a radical break from capitalism to re-enter the mainstream of the global economy.

CHINA, CAPITALIST TRANSFORMATION, AND MIGRATION

Since the late 1970s, the Chinese state has been engaged in an effort to service the drive toward accumulation. This has been done by refashioning the socialist command and control system into a socialist market system. Originating as the project of officials and cadres, the reform and opening of the economy came to be executed in league with such players as Chinese business, the World Trade Organization (WTO), and international corporate capitalists. As Walker (2008) has observed, the turn away from socialist economics in China coincided with the shift to neoliberalism in the advanced capitalist world and was much aided by international players who were eager to facilitate the re-entry of a nation that would release hitherto unavailable assets into the mainstream of capitalist accumulation (Walker 2008: 463; also see Yan, this volume). China's re-entry into the capitalist mainstream was initiated by legislative reform, which enabled a process that can be likened to what Marx called primitive accumulation. While there are many debates over the nature and dynamics of primitive accumulation, according to Marx, this is a process that ensures the "separation of the direct producers from the means of production though non-economic means" (1867: 874–875).[23]

In the countryside such extra-economic means meant modifications in legislation governing land and property tenure, land-use rights, as well as leasing systems in order to pave the way for private ownership. A program of agrarian reform was therefore initiated in the late 1970s with the dismantling of rural collectives and the development of private forms of cultivation. Reform also included the institution of a "responsibility system" which permitted resources to be contracted to individuals, households, or groups of households and the terms of such contracts came increasingly close to de facto ownership. Communes were replaced with local governments and mixed (private and public) forms of economic organization. The reforms also entailed the revival of a market for labor power, thus labor became recommodified and hiring labor became legal. Private marketing was also revived and agricultural products as well as other factors of production were, along with labor, recommodified. Furthermore, state control over production was reduced, allowing private enterprises to emerge both in the countryside and in the city (Oi 1999). As a result of these reforms, in the years between 1978 and 1984, rural incomes grew but this growth could not be sustained over the longer term.[24] Further reforms combined with the deeper penetration of the market into the countryside undermined rural livelihoods and increased rural-to-urban migration.

Among the forces that contributed to intensifying migration were the policies for industrial development that have been pursued since the late 1950s and the end of the period of rural collectivization. Since that time, economic planning in China, so some observers have noted, has consistently favored the development of an industrial urban economy with its series of Five Year Plans and in particular with the Great Leap Forward of 1958–1961 (see Zhang 2003). This growth based strategy has led to the rapid expansion of industries particularly along the coast in China's eastern-most provinces. What Lipton (1977) described as "urban bias" prevails in Chinese development strategy and this is manifested in the increasing inequality in the terms of trade between agriculture and industry, where agricultural commodities are relatively underpriced and industrial commodities overpriced relative to their respective "labor values."[25] Indeed as Zhang (2003: 47) has noted, in the reform era, while official attention and resources were diverted to the development of the urban industrial economy, remittances obtained through migration came to be regarded as the least expensive and most efficient way of developing the rural regions. Moreover, legislative changes also allowed the appropriation of agricultural land in the process of urbanization, and enabled land transfers for infrastructure, real estate, and industrial development.[26] As Deepak (2011) has observed China's economic growth has been driven by heavy investment in infrastructural and real estate development. Such investments require land and millions of hectares of arable land have been lost as a result of "land enclosure rushes" which took the form of speculation, industrial development, and rehousing.[27] Because of these developments, low living standards in the countryside relative to the city prevail, and rural poverty has increased (Zhang 2003: 30). This has led to a situation in China in which wages rather than assets such as land are the source of higher relative incomes, and work in industry yields higher incomes than incomes gained through farmwork.[28]

As expressions of the processes of primitive accumulation, changes in legislation have paved the way for the entry of capital and capital accumulation in the land market. Moreover, as demands for accumulation become more generalized and insistent, the state's role in governing populations, for example in ensuring that the needs of social reproduction are met, must be weighed against the role it plays in servicing accumulation in its various forms. It is in this sense and under these conditions, that migration can be seen to result from struggles over accumulation and indeed, hyperaccumulation. The case of Chinese migration and the forces of peasant dispossession in the late twentieth and early twenty-first century illustrates this amply.

The practices through which peasants have become deprived of or have lost control of their land are many and varied but the result has been rather uniform—transformation of peasants into a migrant labor—a mobile proletariat that provides the low-skilled laborers for the coastal export-oriented industries (Walker 2008; Solinger 1999).[29] In such industries, migrants from rural areas tend to be preferentially hired over local labor (see Yan, this volume). Lacking formal rights of residence and treated with contempt by the local urban population, employers regard them as highly controllable and easily exploitable. The methods of exploitation and the deplorable conditions of work and insecurity of contracts and tenure in industrial employment have been extensively documented.[30] Such conditions of the precariousness of work are exacerbated by the decline in formal wage employment in cities. Indeed in 2011, roughly 8 percent of the urban population was unemployed and much of this resulted from the restructuring of state owned industries after accession to the WTO in 2001.[31] So phases of unemployment can alternate with phases of employment for many migrant laborers as rural surplus labor can also translate into urban surplus labor for those who flow into China's cities. As the rates of unemployment rise both in the country and in the city and also given the precarious nature of contracts, migrant workers can be transformed into a population of contingent labor—a floating population—that drifts around industrializing cities in search of employment or re-employment.

This "floating population" in official and popular discourse refers to people who have crossed over an administrative boundary but have not altered their permanent registration or *hukou*. *Hukou* refers to a registration system, which restricted the inter-regional migration and the movements of people during the pre-reform period.[32] *Hukou* registration is tied to the household registration system that was first implemented in rural areas in 1955. It became a part of state policy in 1958 to ensure that the peasantry would stay tied to the land in the context of the restructuring agriculture.[33] During the reform era, controls over residence that were in place were relaxed and this facilitated the creation of a population of migrants for China's industrialization drives.

Under the *hukou* system migrant flows in China are grouped into three categories: migration with residency rights (*hukou* migration), migration without *hukou* residency rights, and migrants who are engaged in short-term movements such as visiting, circulating, and commuting. *Hukou* migration, or official migration, is endowed with state resources and is referred to as "planned migration" by the government. Migrants whose movements occur outside state plans and whose movements planners describe as "anarchic" and "chaotic" are called in China the "floating population." They have not migrated officially and thus are not allowed to be permanently settled. According to Solinger (1999: 15), "floaters" are a "self-flowing population" and their chief characteristic then is that they "float and move" (see also Murphy 2002; Chan 1999).[34] This designation of members of the migrant population as "floaters" very powerfully evokes Marx's writing on the "relative surplus population."

SURPLUS POPULATION

According to Marx, the surplus population includes members of society who are unable to work and hence unable to become members of the working class and he often used the term synonymously with the reserve army of labor and the industrial labor reserve (see Marx 1867: 794–795; also Magdoff and Magdoff 2004). The relative surplus population appears in three forms—the floating, the latent, and the stagnant forms. The *floating* segment of the relative surplus population refers to the temporarily unemployed. The *latent* part consists of that segment of the population not yet fully integrated into capitalist production—for example, part of the rural population. Members of the latent surplus population form a pool or reservoir of potential workers for industries. The third is the stagnant segment. This segment is composed of those who have irregular employment, and marginalized people "who dwell in the sphere of pauperism," including first those still able to work, second orphans and pauper children, and third the "demoralized and ragged" or "unable to work" (Marx 1867: 795–796). As the term is used in China, the three forms are conflated. Nonetheless, Marx's writings on surplus populations provoke question both about the genesis, character, and also the fate of the relative surplus population as its members contend with the exigencies of the rule of the market in different nations and states.

Marx argues that through the operation of the laws of capitalist accumulation, part of the working population will tend to become surplus to the requirements of capital accumulation over time (see Marx 1867: 781). In the context of China, Marx's intervention suggests that it is prudent to problematize the processes which contribute toward the creation of a surplus population. This problematization in fact serves to correct a perception that prevails regarding the floating population in China. As Nielson, Smyth, and Zhang (2006) observe, it is commonly assumed by journalists and scholars alike that members of the floating population do not experience unemployment. Yet a good portion of the floating population can be and are often unemployed for periods of up to twelve months. For those earning marginal livelihoods, this is a significant period of time to be wageless. These observations suggest a need to further problematize the relationships that prevail between accumulation, dispossession, pauperization, as well as proletarianization and the forces that which avoid this bifurcation and reductionism by propel people from place to place both within the nation and also beyond it. While members of the surplus population can also float from city to city as transregional migrants in search of but not engaged in wage work, occasionally, perhaps exceptionally, such floaters have become members of a mobile population who have followed capital on a transnational trajectory.[35] The example of Ping below embodies the relationship that can prevail between such forces and a trajectory of transnational migration that extends from China to France.

PING, WENZHOU, AND TRANSNATIONAL MIGRATION

In the early 1990s Ping, a middle-aged woman and mother of three, migrated to Paris from Wenzhou. The prefecture of Wenzhou is located in the coastal province of Zhejiang in eastern China.[36] As one of the first places that was remade into a site of rapid accumulation through the privatization of industry and agriculture, it became an important destination for rural migrants from other parts of the country as well as from its own rural hinterland.[37]

The population living outside the investment zones in villages in the coastal areas often gained little from investment and much like their counterparts in the rural interior, they were underemployed and sought access to employment opportunities not available locally (Pieke et al. 2004: 45). For example, Ping's family were farmers whose land, and located in the prefecture of Wenzhou, was taken over for redevelopment of industry in the late 1980s.

As the oldest daughter of a family that was deprived of its means of livelihood, Ping felt the responsibility of having to support her family and migrated to the city in order to find work in a manufacturing firm. She had difficulty finding her first job because, as she puts it, there was much competition from the growing population of migrants from other areas of China who were arriving in Wenzhou. She eventually found work in a garment factory, where she also met her husband, Tan, a migrant from another part of Wenzhou. After marrying and working for two years, she became pregnant and was forced to give up her job for a period of time, since there was no provision for maternity leave. They managed for a while as Ping took up a job as a part-time nanny for a Hong Kong business family that had relocated temporarily to Wenzhou. After the family left, she was again unemployed for a few months but soon found a job in an electronics factory. However, she quit after a few months as she could not endure the inhumane working conditions in which she was forced to breath in toxic chemicals for seemingly endless hours. She was getting ill but without *hukou* rights, Ping could only get heath care by paying extortionate prices to doctors in clinics that were set up unofficially to cater to the large market of floaters. Meanwhile, her husband had been fired for not meeting his production quotas and had been searching for jobs in nearby cities and thinking of relocating the entire family. Realizing too that her child would not be entitled to an education in Wenzhou or that she would have to pay huge fees to the private schools that catered to non-*hukou* migrants, she decided to quit and her mind turned toward migrating to Europe as a way of making a living. Many villagers from her home had left for Europe, including an aunt and a cousin. Eventually, Ping was able to obtain a loan from a relative in France to pay the travel costs for her, Tan, and their three-year-old daughter. They arrived in France on a tourist visa but they stayed on after their visas expired. Both worked in restaurant kitchens for several years. Eventually, through obtaining small-scale loans and savings, they managed to set up a small restaurant of their own. Ping now operates a family-run restaurant-catering business that serves prepared Chinese meals to a largely non-Asian clientele in the sixteenth district in Paris.

As Ping and Tan's case illustrates, far from continually hovering around the edges of industrial centers in China, some members of a population socially defined and made surplus have become incorporated into the class of a global mobile proletariat and eventually joined the ranks of the petty bourgeoisie. The ability of different members of the floating population to engage in migration across national borders varies considerably among different class segments of the surplus population, as does the means through which this is accomplished. Also, it has long been established that the economically most pauperized are seldom able to mobilize resources needed to migrate. Indeed, during a trip to Wenzhou in 2009, I observed that many in fact were dwelling in the sphere of pauperism, inhabiting shacks and rudimentary houses located near luxury apartments, shops, and hotels. Nonetheless, through the mobilization of resources of families and networks of transnational kin, a search for livelihood overseas is one means by which members of surplus populations become transformed into global mobile proletariat and some into members of the petty capitalist class. This pattern for the formation of classes within and across national boundaries has been common for migrants to France who originate from Wenzhou. Such patterns are further discussed in other chapters in this volume (see Nonini, and Barber and Bryan, in particular).

FROM SURPLUS POPULATION/TRANSNATIONAL MOBILE PROLETARIAT TO PETTY CAPITALISTS

As in the case of Ping and her husband Tan, migrants who have relocated to France often spend a considerable period of time as part of a national and then global mobile proletariat. Many sojourn in different countries before arriving in France, often working as undocumented workers in the informal economy of services and manufacturing.[38] Many like Ping and Tan have also made the transition from transnational mobile proletariat to petty capitalists by establishing themselves as small entrepreneurs and pursue strategies of accumulation by becoming incorporated into the economic mainstream in European cities and towns. This incorporation is facilitated by the hegemony of neoliberal citizenship norms that support the entrepreneurial ethics of a nation's denizens, whose activities are oriented toward accumulation.[39] Such strategies of accumulation and its effects are transnational. The capital generated though work and small entrepreneurship reinforces processes of accumulation and class formation in France. It also does this in China through cross-national flows of resources that are remitted to societies and communities of provenance. Among Chinese migrants, it is common for members of the working class and petty bourgeoisie alike to invest in the economies of their areas of origin. Cash remittances for example are used for investing in businesses and factories in Wenzhou, as well as for buying and refurbishing houses, and also for acquiring production materials such as chemical fertilizers to support the everyday expenses of members of kin and households. Such funds are also used to assist in the enterprises of kin who have settled in other countries. In Wenzhou, the visible evidence of such monetary flows includes spacious homes and large family tombs built with migrant remittances and this materially reinforces the association of accumulation through migration (Li 1999; Massey 1998: 187). Therefore, the relatively better-off households are positioned to engage in strategies of further accumulation supported by interregional and also international migration (see also Nonini, this volume). Migration is not simply a strategy used to improve the standard of living for the family and kin of individual migrants, but the circulation of commodities through the remittance economy contributes towards reinforcing wealth and also class differentials in many localities.

CONCLUSION

In this chapter, I have examined the ways in which some key precepts in the conceptual apparatus of political economy can be deployed to illuminate the complexities of contemporary transregional and transnational migration. As mentioned earlier, political economy is a mode of inquiry that has its origins in the nineteenth century and had much analytic purchase in the social sciences in the 1960s and 1970s. In these respects, it could possibly conform to what has been described as a "traditional" school of thought (Massey et al. 1998). However, as I have attempted to show, it is far from being outmoded. This school not only retains its relevance for understanding the dynamics of contemporary migration but also persists as a potent theoretical and methodological framework that enhances our understanding of the dialectal relationship between migration and contemporary capitalism. Moreover, in a context in which many efforts are directed at constructing new paradigms, much scholarship has tended to advocate a theoretical eclecticism in the study of global migration, particularly in the absence of an acceptable comprehensive theory of migration.[40] While eclecticism allows migration studies to be broad and theoretically flexible, an expanded field of theoretical options can result in research that is inchoate and unsystematic. In the contemporary context when the structures, processes, and formations of capitalism systematically enforce the differentiation of people into groups that are exploitable and marginalized, systematic and perhaps "unitary" or "grand" theories are in indeed order. In this discussion, I have suggested that one such "traditional" or comprehensive intervention—that of political economy—perforce provides a systematic framework, for it addresses itself to problematizing the ways in which distinctive groups of people contend with laws of motion that pervade their lives in contemporary capitalism. Moreover, political economy also fulfills the call for cross-disciplinary collaborations in the study of migration. As a mode of inquiry, it is a paradigm that is inherently multidisciplinary and its reach cuts across disciplinary boundaries by providing a common theoretical foundation as well as a lexicon for interdisciplinary collaboration. In these ways, political economy addresses itself to the concerns raised by scholars who have called for a critical rethinking of migration theory.

I conclude by returning to the field of anthropology and some familiar critiques that are leveled at political economy and Marxism. As I mentioned earlier, some anthropologists have cited the tendency for political economy and Marxism to be overly economistic. They identify a failure to come to terms with the ways in which culture structures capitalism (see for example Yanagisako 2002: 12–15, 174–175). Other critics have cited a tendency toward capital centricity (Ortner 1984) or simply react viscerally to some of the concepts and premises of the paradigm.[41] Yet, as I have mentioned earlier, many recent anthropological works that engage with Marxist analysis consist of a problematization of the relationship between culture, economy, and capitalism. Such relationships are conceived as dialectical rather than deterministic and culture, history, and practice begin and end with an analysis of class and power within capitalism. Moreover, as capitalism prevails as the dominant system which organizes our world, those analyses that are "capital-centric," that is, centered on capitalism, are most appropriate to understanding our world.

NOTES

1. See for example Castles and Miller (2009); Basch, Glick Schiller, and Szanton Blanc (1994); Massey et al. (1998).
2. See for example Ohmae (1991) and the "hyperglobalist" school of thought, which insists that globalization represents a new and logical final phase for human development. Friedman (2004c: 67) by contrast suggests that it is in fact a configuration of a world system, which is a phase in a larger cycle of expansion and contraction.
3. See for example Portes and DeWind (2007); Glick Schiller, Basch, and Szanton Blanc (1995); Massey et al. (1998); Hirschman, Kasinitz, and DeWind (1999). On internal migration, see Skeldon (2006) and King, Skeldon, and Vullnetari (2008).
4. Massey et al. (1998: 8–14) identify "traditional theories" as those that were developed within the framework of micro-economics and its assumptions regarding rationality as well as macro-economics and its push-pull models. Their comments, however, betray a common concern in the social science regarding the applicability of older theoretical paradigms in explaining contemporary phenomenon.
5. The ways in which migration is periodized in the literature varies. Castles and Miller divide migration history into two and the pre-1945 period is characterized largely by transatlantic migration. The post-1945 period is one of global migration (2009: 2). Massey et al. divide the modern history of international migration into four rough periods: the mercantile period from 1500 to 1800; the industrial period from approximately 1800 to 1925; the period of limited migration from 1925 to 1960, and the post-industrial period beginning in 1960 (1998: 1–3).
6. Others include segmented labor market theory, world systems theory, and the theory of cumulative causation (Massey et al. 1998: 16).
7. He also mentions he once used a variant of this theory also used by Sassen (1988).
8. These areas include: transnationalism and transnational communities; the new second generation; households and gender; state and state systems; cross-national comparisons (see Portes and DeWind 2007; Hirschman, Kasinitz, and DeWind 1999).

9. Significant scholars include Wolf (1969), Mintz (1985), and Nash (1979).
10. Other attempts include Ortner's (1984) discussion published in *Comparative Studies in Society and History* as well as O'Laughlin's (1975) discussion. Ortner's contribution is actually embedded in a longer treatise on anthropological theory. See also Bloch (1983) and Godelier (1977).
11. For a further discussion of Marxist anthropology see Roseberry (1997). Also see Smith's (2007) special issue on William Roseberry and anthropology in *Critique of Anthropology* 27, no. 4.
12. See for example Grundisse, preface to *A Critique of Political Economy* (Marx 1857–1858).
13. For a discussion of Marx's critique of the political economists, see De Angelis (1996).
14. See Nash (1979); Nash and Fernandez-Kelly (1984); Nash and Safa (1980).
15. See Etienne and Leacock (1980); Leacock (1981, 1982).
16. Other later scholars include, but are not limited to, Sider (1986) and Donham (1999) and of course my own work (Lem 1997).
17. A review of the literature in which such tendencies appear is clearly beyond the scope of this chapter. Here, I focus very briefly on some anthropological works which explicitly address themselves to issues in the study of capitalism or Marxist analysis.
18. Smith argues that compounded processes of selection from 'history' and prioritizations in the present produce the conditions, for example, the processes of thought, the policies as well as the visions of the future that frame contemporary material reality (2002: 256).
19. Marxist scholars such as Gramsci (1971), Althusser (1969), as well as anthropologists such as Godelier (1977) and Friedman (2002) have long ago suggested that the charge of economic determinism results from a selective reading of Marx.
20. In addition to the chapters in this volume, see Smith (1989), Roseberry (1983), and Sider (1986).
21. See for example Harvey (2005).
22. See Davis (2004) and Kalb (2004).
23. A good summary of the debates on primitive accumulation is provided by Webber (2008). Also see Harvey (2003) who has discussed this process as accumulation by dispossession.
24. Rural incomes fell due to a combination of rising costs, increased taxation, and lowered government price quotas. They also fell as a result of embezzlement by corrupt local cadres and officials and particularly after 1992 when business men and capitalists were first allowed to become party members (Walker 2008).
25. For example, in 1993, 50 kilograms of rice was worth only a bottle of pesticide. Furthermore, while prices for certain agricultural crops were fixed by planning mechanisms, industrial commodities such as chemical pesticide, chemical fertilizers, and other industrial commodities were sold at market prices (Zhang 2003: 32).
26. For example, by 1995, five million hectares of arable land was transferred to infrastructure and real estate in China. In Fujian Province, thirty-five million hectares were transferred to industry (Banerjee-Guha 2011).
27. According to Deepak (2011) three were three such rushes. The first was during the mid-1980s when cities expanded, town and township enterprises mushroomed, and peasants started to build new houses. The second 'land enclosure rush' occurred between 1992 and 1993 in the form of land speculation; huge tracts of arable land were seized for constructing commercial houses. The third land enclosures took place between 2002 and 2004 when

the government invited and sold land to developers at a very low price. There was also a fourth which was to be driven by the government's resolve to convert the rural population into non-rural by building 'mini cities' in the rural areas (see also Guldin 2001).
28. Zhang (2003: 33) lists differences in income between urban and rural areas between 1978 and 2000. With the exception of 1984, urban incomes were at least double that of rural incomes.
29. For a discussion of the mechanisms which enabled such transfers see Webber (2008) and Banerjee-Guha (2011). For details of the effects of the reform program on agrarian livelihoods see Zhang (2003) and Murphy (2002).
30. Both Lee (2007) and Ngai (2005) detail such conditions in their studies of industrial labor in China.
31. See Banerjee-Guha (2011) and Tian (2004).
32. Both interregional migration and international migration were common in pre-communist China. However, in the pre-reform period, international migration was forbidden. For a discussion of pre-reform migration see Lary (1999).
33. Under this registration system, each household was allocated an occupational category, either agricultural or non-agricultural, and a place of residence or *hukou*. Hukou confers rights in residence and eligibility for certain jobs particularly in urban areas as well as subsidized welfare benefits. Changes in *hukou* must be approved by the official authorities who have historically granted them when they were not at odds with the state's developmental objectives and policies (for more details see Zhang 2003; Judd 1994).
34. In 2011, the floating population of China is estimated to exceed 221 million; see www.chinadaily.com.cn/china/2011–02/28/content_12091797.htm (retrieved August 11, 2011).
35. Castles and Kosack (1985) and Sassen (1984) for example have discussed migrants as members of this transnational and global labor reserve.
36. I met Ping (a pseudonym) and her family during fieldwork in Paris in 2006.
37. For discussion of the Wenzhou model of development see Liu (1992), Parris (1993), and Nolan and Dong (1991).
38. See Levy and Lieber's (2008) discussion of women who have migrated from northwestern China, who turn to prostitution as a way of making a living in the underground economy.
39. For case studies of this transition and a more detailed discussion of migrant incorporation, neoliberalism, and citizenship see Lem (2009).
40. See for example Brettell and Hollifield (2000), Massey et al. (1994), and Castles and Miller (2009).
41. As Friedman (2004a: 180) has noted, one anthropologist of globalization has remarked, "When I hear the word *class*, I go for my gun."

REFERENCES

Althusser, L. 1969. *For Marx*. London: Verso.
Banerjee-Guha, Swapna. 2011. "Status of Rural Migrant workers in Chinese Cities." *Economic and Political Weekly* 46(26&27): 33–37.
Basch, Linda, Nina Glick Schiller, and Christine Szanton Blanc. 1994. *Nations Unbound: Transnational Projects, Post-Colonial Predicaments and De-territorialized Nation-States*. New York: Gordon Breach.
Bloch, Maurice. 1983. *Marxism and Anthropology: The History of a Relationship*. Oxford: Clarendon.

Brenner, Robert. 1977. "The Origins of Capitalist Development: A Critique of Neo-Smithian Marxism." *New Left Review* 104: 25–92.
Brettell, Caroline. 2000. "Theorizing Migration in Anthropology." In *Migration Theory: Talking across Disciplines*, edited by Caroline Brettell and James Hollifield, 97–136. New York: Routledge.
Brettell, Caroline, and James Hollifield, eds. 2000. *Migration Theory: Talking across Disciplines*. New York: Routledge.
Brown, Wendy. 2003. "Neoliberalism and the End of Liberal Democracy." *Theory & Event* 7(1).
Castles, Stephen, and Godula Kosack. 1985. *Immigrant Workers and Class Structure in Western Europe*. 2nd ed. Oxford: Oxford University Press.
Castles, Stephen, and Mark Miller. 2009. *The Age of Migration: International Popular Movements in the Modern World*. London: Palgrave.
Chan, Kam Wing. 1999. "Internal Migration in China: A Dualistic Approach." In *Internal and International Migration*, edited by Frank Pieke and Hein Mallee, 49–72. London: Curzon.
Davis, Mike. 2004. "Planet of Slums: Urban Involution and the Informal Working Class." *New Left Review* 26: 5–30.
De Angelis, Massimo. 1996. "Social Relations, Commodity-Fetishism and Marx's Critique of Political Economy." *Review of Radical Political Economics* 28(4): 1–29.
Deepak, B.R. 2011. "China's Rural Land Grabs: Endangering Social Stability." *South Asia Analysis Group*. Paper 4412. http://www.southasiaanalysis.org.
Donham, Donald L. 1999. *Marxist Modern: An Ethnographic History of the Ethiopian Revolution*. Berkeley: University of California Press.
Etienne, Mona, and Eleanor Leacock, eds. 1980. *Women and Colonization: Anthropological Perspectives*. South Hadley, MA: Bergin.
Firth, Raymond. 1972. "The Skeptical Anthropologist? Social Anthropology and Views on Society." *Proceedings of the Historical Academy* 58: 3–39.
Foner, Nancy, Ruben Rumbaut, and Steven Gold, eds. 2000. *Immigration Research for a New Century: Multidisciplinary Perspectives*. New York: Russell Sage Foundation.
Friedman, Jonathan. 2002. "Globalization and Localization." In *The Anthropology of Globalization Reader*, edited by Jonathan Xavier Inda and Renato Rosaldo. Oxford: Blackwell.
———. 2004a. "Globalization." In *A Companion to the Anthropology of Politics*, edited by David Nugent and Joan Vincent, 179–197. London: Blackwell.
———. 2004b. "Anthropology of the Global, Globalizing Anthropology: A Commentary." *Anthropologica* 46(2): 231–240.
———. 2004c. "Globalization, Transnationalization and Migration: Ideologies and Realities of Global Transformation." In *Worlds on the Move: Globalization, Migration and Cultural Security*, edited by Jonathan Friedman and Shalini Randeria, 24–63. London: I.B. Taurus.
Glick Schiller, Nina, Linda Basch, and Cristina Szanton Blanc, eds. 1992. *Toward a Transnational Perspective on Migration: Race, Class, Ethnicity and Nationalism Reconsidered*. New York: New York Academy of Sciences.
———. 1995. "From Immigrant to Transmigrant: Theorizing Transnational Migration." *Anthropological Quarterly* 68: 48–63.
Godelier, Maurice. 1977. *Perspectives in Marxist Anthropology*. Cambridge: Cambridge University Press.
Gramsci, Antonio. 1971. *Selections from the Prison Notebooks*. London: Lawrence and Wishart.
Guldin, Gregory Eliyu. 2001. *What's a Peasant to Do?* Boulder: Westview Press.
Harvey, David. 2003. *The New Imperialism*. London: Oxford University Press.

———. 2005. *A Brief History of Neo-liberalism*. London: Oxford University Press.
Hirschman, Charles, Philip Kasinitz, and Josh DeWind, eds. 1999. *The Handbook of International Migration: The American Experience*. New York: Russell Sage.
Kalb, Don. 2004. "Time and Contention in the 'great globalization debate'." In *Globalization and Development: Themes and concepts in Current Research*, edited by Don Kalb, Wil Pansters, and Hans Siebert, 9–47. Dordecht: Kluwer Academic Publishers.
King, Russell, Ronald Skeldon, and Julie Vullnetari. 2008. "Internal and International Migration: Bridging the Theoretical Divide." Working Paper 52, Sussex Centre for Migration Research, University of Sussex.
Lary, Diane. 1999. "The 'Static' Decades: Inter-provincial Migration in Pre-reform China." In *Internal and International Migration: Chinese Perspectives*, edited by Frank Pieke and Hein Mallee, 29–48. Richmond: Curzon.
Leacock, Eleanor. 1981. *Myths of Male Dominance*. New York: Monthly Review.
———. 1982. "Marxism in Anthropology." In *The Left Academy*, edited by Bertell Ollman and E. Vernoff, 242–276. New York: McGraw Hill.
Lee, Ching Kwan. 2007. *Against the Law: Labor Protests in China's Rustbelt and Sunbelt*, Berkeley: University of California Press.
Lem, Winnie. 1997. *Cultivating Dissent: Work, Identity and Praxis in Rural Languedoc*. Albany: State University of New York Press.
———. 2009. "Mobilization and Disengagement: Chinese Migrant Entrepreneurs in Urban France." *Ethnic & Racial Studies* 33(1): 1–16.
Levy, Florence, and Marylene Lieber. 2008. "Northern Chinese Women in Paris." *Social Science Information* 47(4): 629–642.
Li, Minghuan. 1999. "'To Get Rich Quickly in Europe!' Reflections on Migration and Motivation in Wenzhou." In *Internal and International Migration*, edited by Frank Pieke and Hein Mallee, 181–198. London: Curzon.
Li, Tania. 2007. *The Will to Improve: Governmentality, Development, and the Practice of Politics*. Durham and London: Duke University Press.
Lipton, Michael. 1977. *Why Poor People Stay Poor: Urban Bias and World Development*. Temple Smith and London: Harvard University Press.
Liu, Yia-Ling. 1992. "Reform from Below: The Private Economy and Local Politics in the Rural Industrialization of Wenzhou." *The China Quarterly* 130: 293–316.
Magdoff, Fred, and Harry Magdoff. 2004. "Disposable Workers: Today's Reserve Army of Labor." *Monthly Review* 55: 11. http://monthlyreview.org/0404magdoff.htm
Malthus, Thomas R. 1798. *An Essay on the Principle of Population*. Oxford World's Classics reprint: xxix Chronology.
———. 1820. *Principles of Political Economy*. London: William Pickering.
Marx, Karl. [1867] 1976. *Capital*. Vol. 1. New York: Penguin Books.
———. [1857–1858] 1993. *Grundrisse: Foundations of the Critique of Political Economy*. London: Penguin.
Massey, Douglas S. 1999. "International Migration at the Dawn of the Twenty-First Century: The Role of the State." *Population and Development Review* 25(2): 303–322.
Massey, Douglas, Joaquin Arango, Graeme Hugo, Ali Kouaouci, Adela Pellegrino, and J. Edward Taylor. 1998. *Worlds in Motion: Understanding International Migration at the End of the Millennium*. Oxford: Clarendon.
Massey, Douglas S., Joaquin Arango, Ali Koucouci, Adela Pellegrino, and J. Edward Taylor. 1994. "An Evaluation of International Migration Theory: The North American Case." *Population and Development Review* 20: 699–752.

Mintz, Sidney. 1985. *Sweetness and Power: The Place of Sugar in Modern History*. New York: Viking.

Murphy, Rachel. 2002. *How Migrant Labor is Changing Rural China*. Cambridge: Cambridge University Press.

Nash, June. 1979. *We Eat the Mines and the Mines Eat Us*. New York: Columbia University Press.

Nash, June, and Maria Patricia Fernandez-Kelly, eds. 1984. *Women, Men and the International Division of Labor*. Albany: State University New York Press.

Nash, June, and Helen Safa, eds. 1980. *Sex and Class in Latin America: Women's Perspectives on Politics, Economics and the Family in the Third World*. South Hadley, MA: Bergin.

Ngai, Pun. 2005. *Made in China*. Durham: Duke University Press.

Nielsen, Ingrid, Russell Smyth, and Mingqiong Zhang. 2006. *Unemployment within China's Floating Population: Empirical Evidence from Jiangsu Survey Data*. ABERU Discussion Paper 6.

Nolan, Peter, and Dong Fureng, eds. 1991. *The Wenzhou Debate*. London: Zed Publishers.

Ohmae, Kenichi. 1991. *The End of the Nation State*. London: Harper Collins.

Oi, Jean C. 1999. "Two Decades of Rural Reform in China: An Overview and Assessment." *China Quarterly* 159: 616–628.

O'Laughlin, Bridget. 1975. "Marxist Approaches in Anthropology." *Annual Review of Anthropology* 4(1): 341–370.

O'Malley, Pat, Lorna Weir, and Clifford Shearing. 1997. "Governmentality, Criticism, Politics." *Economy and Society* 26(4): 501–517.

Ong, Aiwa. 1999. *Flexible Citizenship: The Cultural Logics of Transnationality*. Durham and London: Duke University Press.

Ortner, Sherry. 1984. "Theory in Anthropology since the Sixties." *Comparative Studies in Society and History* 26: 126–166.

Parris, Kirsten. 1993. "Local Initiative and National Reform: The Wenzhou Model of Development." *The China Quarterly* 134: 242–263.

Pieke, Frank, Pal Nyiri, Mette Thuno, and Antonella Ceccagno. 2004. *Transnational Chinese: Fujianese Migrants in Europe*. Stanford: Stanford University Press.

Pieterse, Jan Nederveen. 1988. "A Critique of World Systems Theory." *International Sociology* 3(3): 251–266.

Portes, Alejandro. 1999. "Immigration Theory for a New Century: Some Problems and Opportunities." In *The Handbook of International Migration: The American Experience*, edited by Charles Hirschman, Philip Kasinitz, and Josh Dewind, 21–33. New York: Russell Sage.

Portes, Alejandro, and Josh DeWind. 2007. "A Cross-Atlantic Dialogue: The Progress of Research and Theory in the Study of International Migration." In *Rethinking Migration Theory*, edited by Alejandro Portes and Josh De Wind, 3–26. London: Berghahn.

Portes, Alejandro, L.E. Guarzino, and P. Landolt. 1999. "The Study of Transnationalism: Pitfalls and Promise of an Emergent Research Field." *Ethnic and Racial Studies* 22(2): 217–237.

Ricardo, David. 1817. *On the Principles of Political Economy and Taxation*. London: John Murray, Albemarle-Street.

Roseberry, William. 1983. *Coffee and Capitalism in the Venezuelan Andes*. Austin: University of Austin Press.

———. 1988. "Political Economy." *Annual Review of Anthropology* 17: 161–168.

———. 1996. "The Rise of Yuppie Coffees and the Re-imagining of Class in the United States." *American Anthropologist* 98: 762–775.

———. 1997. "Marx and Anthropology." *Annual Review of Anthropology* 26: 25–46.
Sassen, Saskia. 1984. "Notes on the Incorporation of Third World Women into Wage Labor and Off-Shore Production." *International Migration Review* 18(4): 1144–1167.
———. 1988. *The Mobility of Labor and Capital*. London: Cambridge University Press.
Sider, Gerald. 1986. *Culture and Class in Anthropology and History: A Newfoundland Illustration*. Cambridge: Cambridge University Press.
Silverstein, Paul. 2004. *Algeria in France: Transpolitics, Race, Nation*. Bloomington and Indianapolis: Indiana University Press.
Skeldon, Ronald. 2006. "Interlinkages between Internal and International Migration and Development in the Asian Region." *Population, Space and Place* 12: 15–30.
Smith, Adam. [1776] 1976. *An Inquiry into the Nature and Causes of the Wealth of Nations*. New York: Oxford University Press.
Smith, Gavin. 1989. *Livelihood and Resistance: A Study of Peasants and the Politics of Land*. Berkeley: University of California Press.
———. 1999. *Confronting the Present: Towards a Politically Engaged Anthropology*. Oxford: Berg.
———. 2002. "Out of Site: The Horizons of Collective Identity." In *Culture, Economy, Power: Anthropology as Critique, Anthropology as Praxis*, edited by Winnie Lem and Belinda Leach, 250–266. Albany: State University of New York Press.
———, ed. 2007. Special issue, *William Roseberry and Anthropology: Critique of Anthropology* 27(4).
Solinger, Dorothy. 1999. *Contesting Citizenship in Urban China: Peasant Migrants, the State and the Logic of the Market*. Berkeley: University of California.
Tian, Qunjian. 2004. "Agrarian Crisis, WTO Entry, and Institutional Change in Rural China." *Issues & Studies* 40(2): 47–77.
Walker, Kathy le Mons. 2008. "From Covert to Overt: Everyday Peasant Politics in China and the Implications for Transnational Agrarian Movements." *Journal of Agrarian Change* 8(2–3): 462–488.
Webber, Michael. 2008. "Primitive Accumulation in China." *Dialectical Anthropology* 32:299–320
Wolf, Eric. 1969. *Peasant Wars of the Twentieth Century*. New York: Harper and Row.
———. 1982. *Europe and the People without History*. Berkeley and Los Angeles: University of California Press.
Yanagisako, Sylvia. 2002. *Producing Culture and Capital: Family Firms in Italy*. New Jersey: Princeton University Press.
Zhang, Mei. 2003. *China's Poor Regions: Rural Urban Migration, Poverty, Economic Reform and Urbanization*. London: Routledge Curzon.

3 Migration and Development without Methodological Nationalism
Towards Global Perspectives on Migration[1]

Nina Glick Schiller

On a phone booth in Manchester, England—where I now live as a transmigrant—I saw an advertisement that read "Send money home from closer to home." It went on to announce that you can now send funds to locations around the world from any British Post Office. The Post Office, whose sales operations have now been privatized, has joined businesses around the world that seek to profit from migrant remittances. Spanish banks extend mortgages to migrants living in Spain who are building houses 'back home' in Ecuador and elsewhere in Latin America, while appliances stores in Brazil process orders for customers whose source of payment comes from family members living abroad (Lapper 2007a). Migrants' money transfers, purchases of costly commodities, and homeland investments figure large in the recent policies of powerful globe-spanning financial institutions, such as the World Bank, which have proclaimed migrant remitters as the new agents of international development (Fajnzylber and López 2008; de Hass 2007; Lapper 2007b; World Bank 2006). Meanwhile, researchers of development and migration, while noting the possibilities and contradictions of migrant remittances on sending and receiving localities, take for granted that migrants are both local and transnational actors (Faist 2008; Dannecker 2007; Fauser 2007; Guarnizo 2007; Østergaard-Nielsen 2007; Pries 2007; Raghuram 2007).

Yet, at the same time that the transnationality of migrants is being both routinely documented and celebrated, politicians and the mass media in Europe and the United States are focusing their concern primarily on questions of 'integration,' and portrayed migrants' transnational ties as threats to 'national security.' In these discourses, migrants are attacked for their supposed lack of loyalty to their new homeland. Politicians, demagogic leaders, and media personalities blame migrants for national economic problems, including the growing disparity between rich and poor, the shrinking of the middle class, the reduction in the quality and availability of public services and education, and the rising costs of health care and housing. Calls for tightening borders and ending the influx of migrants are widespread and countries around the world are shutting their doors in the faces of people desperate to flee war, rape, and pillage. In the meantime, rates of deportation are rising dramatically.

Within these anti-migration discourses, little is said about migrants' provision of vital labor, services, and skills to their new land or their role in the reproduction of workforces—including their sustenance, housing, education, and training—in countries around the world. It is true that there is some appreciation for one current in the migrant stream. States as diverse as Singapore and Germany welcome 'global talent' in the form of professional and highly skilled immigrants. Yet this differentiation only serves to reinforce the viewpoint that most migrants are undesirable and migration should cease.

What is the response of migration theorists to the current contradictory positions on migration whereby migrant remittances are defined as a vital resource, and yet those who send remittances are castigated and increasingly denied the right to move across borders? To date, I would argue, migration scholars have not established a critical perspective that can adequately make sense of the contradictions. They have not developed a global perspective that can place within the same analytical framework debates about international migration and development, national rhetorics on migration and refugee policies, and migration scholarship. Instead, migration scholars have adopted the perspective of their respective nation-states.

Much of the European and US scholarship on migration is confined to questions such as 'how well do they fit into our society,' 'what are the barriers that keep them from fully joining us,' or 'which cultures or religions do not fit in?' In the United States, migration scholars who see themselves as pro-immigration increasingly embrace what I call 'born-again assimilationism' to show that migrants do indeed become part of the national fabric and contribute to it (Smith 2006; Waldinger and Fitzgerald 2004). New assimilationists and integrationists distinguish themselves from the old by updating what they mean by immigrants becoming an integral part of their new society (Alba and Nee 2003; Heckmann 2003; Sackmann, Peters, and Faist 2003; Morawska 2003; Joppke and Morawska 2002). Although these scholars accept the persistence of ethnic identities, home ties, and transnational networks as in some cases compatible with integration, they continue to see migration as a potential threat to the nation-state. They belive that international migration warrants investigation because it is fundamentally problematic for the cohesion of the 'host society.'

For example, Michael Bommes and Andres Geddes (2000: 6) are concerned that "migration can be taken as part of a process that erodes the classical arrangement by which welfare states provide an ordered life course for the members of the national community, i.e. for their citizens in exchange for political loyalty." As Bommes (2005) has noted, "assimilationists conceptualise . . . society as a big national collective.". In Europe, the term used is 'integration,' which is often differentiated from assimilation (Esser

2006, 2003). However, whether the concept being deployed is integration or assimilation, most scholars of migration reflect and contribute to an approach to the nation-state that depicts a nation and its migrants as fundamentally and essentially distinct—both socially and culturally.[2]

It is likely that future scholars will demonstrate that the revival of assimilationist theory and the 'new' integrationism at the beginning of the twenty-first century, rather than representing an advance in social science, reflected the neoliberal project of the restructuring of nation-states. Rescaled but not replaced in relationship to regional and global reorganizations of economic and political power, nation-states began, as they did at the turn of the twentieth century, and with the assistance of migration scholars, to build national identities at the expense of immigrants. Even the scholars of transnational migration, including those who highlight the role of migrants in transnational development projects, are now concluding their articles with reassurances that migrants' transnational activities are relatively minimal or contribute to their integration into the nation-state in which they have settled (Smith 2006; Guarnizo, Portes, and Haller 2003). They have not provided a perspective on migration that explains why major global financial institutions, which portray migrants as agents of development through remittances that sustain impoverished communities, seem unconcerned that these very same people are increasingly disdained and excluded in their countries of settlement.

In this chapter I build on scholars who advocate an institutional analysis of contemporary migration policies and discourses, but I continue the argument further by proposing a 'global power perspective' that can link contemporary forces of capitalist restructuring to the specific localities within which migrants live and struggle. After a post-modern period in which any attempt to use or develop globe-spanning perspectives was dismissed as a 'grand narrative,' scholars in an array of disciplines, and with very different politics, have once again tried to connect the local and particular with an analysis of broader forces. Contemporary globe-spanning trends have been approached as globalization (Mittleman 1996), network society (Castells 1996), and empire (Hardt and Negri 2000). Yet ironically, many migration scholars who study cross-border population movements remain inured to concepts of society and culture that reflect historic nation-state building projects. These projects obscure the past and contemporary transnational fields of power that shape political and economic development.

A global power perspective on migration could facilitate the description of social processes by introducing units of analysis and research paradigms that are not built on the methodological nationalism of much migration discourse. It would allow researchers to make sense of local variation and history in relation to transnational processes and connections. Such a framework would allow us to identify contradictions and disjunctures in contemporary scholarship, as well as forms, spaces, ideologies, and identities of resistance to oppressive and global relations of unequal power.

One chapter cannot, of course, do more than outline such an alternative analytic framework. In sketching a different approach to migration and development that builds on a global power perspective, this chapter briefly (1) critiques methodological nationalism; (2) addresses neoliberal restructuring of localities of migrant settlement and ongoing connection; (3) situates the topic of remittances within transnational social fields of uneven power; and (4) analyzes the countervailing hegemonic processes that are encapsulated in state migration policies and development discourses.

I want to be clear from the very beginning that by eschewing methodological nationalism and establishing a global framework for the study of migrant settlement and transnational connection, I am not saying—and never argued—that the nation-state is withering away.[3] I am asserting that to understand the restructuring of globe-spanning institutional arrangements, including the changing role and continuing significance of states, we need a perspective that is not constrained by the borders of the nation-state. This is because nation-states are positioned and transformed within global fields of power, and consequently these fields affect the migration process, including movement, settlement, and transnational connection. At the same time, through their connections between places and their actions that affect places, migrants are active agents of the contemporary transformations on local, national, and global scales. My particular interest is the way in which migrants' settlement and transnational connections both shape and are shaped by the contemporary restructuring of capital and the scalar repositioning of specific localities (Glick Schiller and Çaglar 2011, 2009; Glick Schiller, Çaglar, and Guldbrandsen 2006).

TRACING THE LINEAGES OF METHODOLOGICAL NATIONALISM IN MIGRATION SCHOLARSHIP

A growing number of social theorists have argued that methodological nationalism has been central to much of Western social science (Wimmer and Glick Schiller 2002a, 2002b; Beck 2000; Smith 1983; Martins 1974). Methodological nationalism is an ideological orientation that approaches the study of social and historical processes as if they were contained within the borders of individual nation-states. Nation-states are conflated with societies, and the members of those states are assumed to share a common history and set of values, norms, social customs, and institutions. Some writers label this orientation the 'container' theory of society to highlight that most social theorists, including Emile Durkheim, Max Weber, and Talcott Parsons, have contained their concept of society within the territorial and institutional boundaries of the nation-state (Urry 2000; Basch, Glick Schiller, and Szanton Blanc 1994; Wolf 1982). A methodological nationalist perspective in migration scholarship led to the separation of development studies from the study of immigrant incorporation into a new country. To reject methodological nationalism requires migration scholars to recover an approach to migration that does not use nation-states as units of analysis but rather studies the movement of people across space in relationship to forces that structure political economy. These forces include states but are not confined to states and their policies. Furthermore, national and international policies are considered within the same analytical lens (Nye 1976).

I am calling for scholars to recover rather than develop a global perspective on migration, since aspects of this approach were widespread during the period of globalization that took place from the 1880s to 1920s. At that time, there was broad interest in the diffusion of ideas and material culture through the migration of people. Scholars such as Fredrick Ratzel (1882) treated all movements of people over the terrain as a single phenomenon linked to the distribution of resources across space. Ratzel's writing reflected the assumptions of his times, namely, that the movements of people were normal and natural. The fact that migrants came and went, and maintained their ties to home by sending back money to buy land, initiate businesses, and support families and village projects—all this was understood as a typical aspect of migration. Workers migrated into regions in which there was industrial development and returned home or went elsewhere when times were bad. England, Germany, Switzerland, France, the United States, Brazil, and Argentina built industrialized economies with the help of millions of labor migrants, who worked in factories, fields, mills, and mines. In general, during that era of globalization and imperial penetration, most European countries abolished the passport and visa system they had installed in the first half of the nineteenth century (Torpey 2000). The United States did not restrict migration from Europe and required neither passports nor visas.[4]

This period of unequal globalization was shaped by the fierce competition among many states for control of far-reaching transnational commercial networks. The wealth and workforce of many nations were produced elsewhere, and colonial projects were the basis of the accumulation of nationally based capital. Governmental regimes increasingly deployed the concepts of nation, national unity, and national economy in ways that obscured the transnational basis of their nation-state building projects. The people who lived in these states faced increasing pressure to use a single national language, to identify with a national history, to understand their practices and beliefs to be part of a national culture, to equate concepts of blood and nation, and to be willing to sacrifice their lives for the nation's honor.

Both international migrants and citizens of migrant-receiving states sought explanations for the rapid changes they were experiencing. Political theories and social movements that could speak to global transformations flourished, including international socialism, anarchism, pan-Africanism, feminism, nationalism, scientific racism, and anti-imperialism (Gabaccia and Ottanelli 2001; Gilroy 1992; Potts 1990; van Holthoon and van der Linden 1988; Bodnar 1985). However, state officials, politicians, and intellectuals supported nationalist ideologies that portrayed individuals as having only one country and one identity. In so doing, they contributed to the view that immigrants embodied cultural, physical, and moral characteristics that differentiated them from their host society and therefore merited study. It was at the moment—and in conjunction with the mounting pressure to delineate national borders more firmly by closing them—that a scholarship of immigrant settlement became delineated. The transnational social fields of migrants and their engagement in internationalism and other forms of non-state-based social movements increasingly were seen as problematic, and finally disappeared from view. The study of migration was divided between demographers and geographers, who studied movement between nation-states, and sociologists, who studied settlement and assimilation.

As a result of that moment, several complementary but differentiated logics were deployed: (1) the sociology of migration was situated exclusively within national territories; (2) the notion of national origin was racialized through the popularization of the concept of national stocks; (3) assimilationist theory was developed within the hegemonic narrative of race and nation; and (4) national stocks came to be seen as differentiated by culture and designated either as 'nationalities' or as 'national minorities' who resided within a state of settlement. Current scholarship on migrant incorporation and transnational connection continues to be shaped not only by these past approaches but also by the current historical conjuncture in which the leaders of migrant-receiving states are emotively legitimating national discourses and narratives.

Today, the 'ethnic group' continues to serve as the primary unit of analysis with which to study and interpret migration settlement, transnational migration, and diaspora. Often termed 'communities,' the ethnic group has become the bedrock of studies of migrant settlement. This remains true despite a voluminous historical and ethnographic literature that (1) identifies the constructed nature of ethnic identities and ethnic group boundaries, (2) includes detailed ethnographies of institutional processes through which ethnic categories and identities are constructed and naturalized by local and transnational actors, and (3) provides copious accounts of divisions based on class, religion, region of origin, and politics among the members of the supposedly 'same' group (Brubaker 2004; Kastoryano 2002; Glick Schiller 1999, 1977; Çaglar 1997, 1990; Sollors 1989; Gonzalez 1988; Glick Schiller et al. 1987; Barth 1969). The use of ethnic groups as units of analysis is a logical but unacceptable consequence of the methodological nationalism of mainstream migration studies.

The problematic framing of migration research in terms of ethnic groups within nation-states obscures the effects of the global restructuring of capital on the population, both migrant and non-migrant, in a specific locality. Even studies of migrants' transnational connections that seemed to offer an analytical perspective beyond the nation-state have tended to examine specific ethnic trajectories and have said little about the ways in which the restructuring of economic, political, and social capital affects specific forms of migrant settlement and transnational connections. Few researchers noted the significance of locality in shaping migrants' transnational social and economic fields.[5]

In short, the methodological nationalism of many migration scholars, reflecting the entanglements of disciplinary histories with nation-state building projects, precludes them from accurately describing the transnational social fields of unequal power that are integral to the migrant experience. Because their scholarship is built on units of analysis that developed within nation-state building projects, few migration scholars situate national terrains and discourses within an analysis of the restructuring of the global economy, the rescaling of cities, and the rationalization of a resurgent imperialist agenda.[6]

ADDRESSING THE NEOLIBERAL RESTRUCTURING OF LOCALITIES OF MIGRANT SETTLEMENT AND ONGOING CONNECTION

Working with a Marxist framework, David Harvey (2005, 2003) and a number of geographers have emphasized that while one can talk about the intensification of global processes of capital flow and flexible accumulation, capital reproduction always comes to ground somewhere. Since capital is ultimately a social relationship, when it is reconstituted in a specific place, the process destroys previously emplaced social relationships and the infrastructures and environments in which they were situated and constructs others. Although differentiated in terms of the path-dependent trajectories of a specific place, the effects of the restructuring of capital are not confined to only one place; rather, the transformation of one place affects many others. The reconstitution of capital disrupts previous arrangements of power and structures new relationships of production, reproduction of labor, distribution, and consumption that extend into other localities.

The processes of the creation and destruction of capital—as it represents the concentration of relationships of production within time and space—is an ongoing feature of capitalism. However, beginning in the 1970s, this general process was reconfigured on a global scale through the uneven and disparate implementation of a series of initiatives widely known as the 'neoliberal agenda.' Neoliberalism can be defined as a series of projects of capital accumulation that have reconstituted social relations of production in ways that dramatically curtail state investment in public activities, resulting in the reduction of state services and benefits and the diversion of public monies and resources to develop private service-oriented industries from health care to housing (sometimes in arrangements termede 'public-private partnerships'). At the same time, the neoliberal project also relentlessly pushes towards global production through the elimination of state intervention in a host of economic issues—from tariffs to workers' rights—including the organization of labor, space, state institutions, military power, governance, membership, and sovereignty (Harvey 2005; Jessop 2003). Neoliberalism has allowed for the creation of wealth by destroying and replacing previous relations of production, consumption, and distribution and by generating new forms of desire. These transformations have affected the quality of life of migrants and natives alike.

Neoliberal projects take the form of specific sets of ideas and policies that may or may not be successfully implemented. These ideas are held, shaped, defended, and contested by a range of actors, including social scientists, whether or not they are directly linked to policy. The broader projects involve not just the domain of economics but also politics, cultural practices, ideas about self and society, and the production and dissemination of images and narratives. Neoliberal plans are implemented on the ground and differentially, depending not just on different national policies but also on specific local histories, including that of migration.

The work of geographers on the neoliberal restructuring of capital and space highlights the various mechanisms that require all places to compete for investments in new economies (Brenner 2004; Smith 1995). All of the resources that cities have, including their human resources, which encompass the migrants and their skills and qualities, acquire a new value and become assets in this competition. Migrants are not only part of the new, just-in-time sweatshop industries that accompany the restructuring of some cities. They provide highly skilled labor that also contributes to the human capital profile of various cities. The 'cultural diversity' of migrants is an important factor in the competitive struggle between the cities. Beyond the marketing of ethnic culture, migrants contribute to the cultural industries of the cities in which they are settling, from media to cuisine, fashion, and graphic design (Çaglar 2007, 2005; Scott 2004; Zukin 1995). The place and role of migrants in this competition might differ, depending on the scalar positioning of these cities.

The implementation of neoliberal agendas had disrupted fixed notions of nested, territorially bounded units of city, region, state, and globe. The scholarship on neoliberalism documents the ways in which all localities have become global in that none are delimited only by the regulatory regime and economic processes of the state in which they are territorially based. The state itself is rescaled to play new roles by channelling flows of relatively unregulated capital and participating in the constitution of global regulatory regimes enforced by the World Trade Organization (WTO) and international financial institutions. To emphasize the processual, competitive, and political aspects of the spatial restructuring of capital, some geographers speak of 'rescaling.' They note that when localities change the parameters of their global, national, and/or regional connectedness and lines of power that serve to govern territory, they in effect 'jump scale' (Swyngedouw 1997). Rather than understanding the local and global scale as either discrete levels of social activities or hierarchical analytical abstractions, as in previous geographies of space, "the global and the local (as well as the national) are [understood to be] mutually constitutive" (Brenner 2001: 134–135). Localities do, however, differ in their positioning in terms of globe-spanning hierarchies of economic and political power.

The scalar positioning of a locality—its success in competing for investments, a range of industries, and businesses services and in attracting highly skilled new economy workers—shapes the incorporation, if differentially, of all residents of that locality. Hence, the research framework I am suggesting—what I call a 'locality analysis' of a global power paradigm—places migrants and natives in the same conceptual framework. Locality analysis turns our attention to the relationships that develop between the residents of a place and institutions situated locally, regionally, nationally, and globally, without making prior assumptions about how these relationships are shaped by ethnicity, nationality, or national territory. All these factors and others that affect opportunity structures remain a matter of investigation.

Although scale theorists have said almost nothing about migrant incorporation, it is evident that a locality analysis built on that scholarship provides important theoretical openings with which to approach the significance of locality in migrant incorporation. The relative positioning of a place within hierarchical fields of power may well lay the ground for the life chances and incorporation opportunities of migrants and those who are native to the place. In order to understand the different modes and dynamics of migrant and transnational incorporation, we need to address the broader rescaling processes affecting the cities in which migrants are settling. A scalar perspective can bring into this discussion the missing spatial aspects of socio-economic power, which is exercised differently in various localities. The concept of scalar positioning also introduces socio-spatial parameters to the analysis of locality in migration scholarship (Glick Schiller and Çaglar 2011, 2009).

For students of migration, this perspective reminds us that migrants, as part of the processes of capital reproduction, are agents of the reshaping of localities. Migrants become part of the restructuring of the social fabric of the several localities to which they may be connected through their transnational networks and become actors within new forms of governing territory. Of course migrants' roles in each place are themselves shaped in the context of rescaling processes themselves. At the same time, pathways of migrant settlement are shaped by the opportunity structures and restrictions of particular places, including the type of labor needed and the way that labor is recruited and organized within those places.

It is through making this type of locality analysis that we can assess the variety of ways that migrants contribute to the opportunity structures of various locations and the degree to which they become one of several factors in the restructuring of a place. This places the migrants as actors within larger global forces and moves our discussion beyond the limitations of a model of migration, development, and remittances. Some of the roles that migrants play as agents of global restructuring are described in the transnational migration literature but are not sufficiently analyzed within broader processes of capital development and destruction. Other migrant contributions are rarely acknowledged because they are not clearly visible through an ethnic lens. My list of forms in which migrants serve as agents of restructuring and rescaling includes their role in contributing to the rise of property values, gentrifying neighborhoods, creating new industries or businesses, developing new trade connections and patterns of marketing and distribution, and changing patterns of consumption.

Contingent on the positioning of a place globally, migrants make different kinds of contributions, which, depending on the stance of the observer, may be judged good or bad. Take, for example, the role of migrants as gentrifiers both in their place of settlement and in localities to which they are transnationally connected. In cities of settlement, which are in the process of successful restructuring, migrants may contribute to the reinvention of urban neighborhoods previously considered undesirable by buying property in particular localities where property values have been low (Goode 2011; Salzbrunn 2011). Migrants may be well placed to buy property because they are able to draw on family credit or pooled resources to invest in and improve the housing stock or local neighborhood businesses (Glick Schiller, Çaglar, and Guldbrandsen 2006). Thus, migrants may stabilize, restore, or gentrify neighborhoods, and may even contribute to the global marketing of a city. Migrant investments in housing and property may transform neighborhoods within their transnational social field in ways that increase economic opportunities or economic disparities between localities.

As I have argued elsewhere (Glick Schiller and Çaglar 2011, 2009), migration scholarship's binary division of foreigner and natives, which is legitimated through the adoption of the nation-state as the unit of both study and analysis, leaves no conceptual space to address questions of the global restructuring of region and locality that serves as the nexus of migrant incorporation and transnational connection and to which migrants contribute in ways that may rescale cities. Except for global cities theory, the insightful and powerful social theorizing of locality and scale produced by urban geographers has not entered into either migration theory or discussions about migration and development. To note that migrant departure, settlement, and transnational connections are shaped by the positioning of localities and regions within globally structured hierarchies of economic and political power would disrupt the homogenization of the national terrain that is imposed by migration theory and echoed in development discourses.

PLACING REMITTANCE FLOWS WITHIN TRANSNATIONAL SOCIAL FIELDS OF UNEVEN POWER

A transnational social field is a complex of networks that connects people across the borders of nation-states and to specific localities (Glick Schiller

2006, 2003). Here I use the term 'social field' to refer not to a metaphoric space but to a set of social relations, unequal in terms of the power of the various actors, through which people live their lives. Migrants who send remittances may reconfigure social relations as part and parcel of the transnational processes that reconstitute localities. These localities may be hometowns, but migrants may also choose to invest in property and businesses in capital or key cities that were not their places of origin. Migrants' labor, cultural and social capital, and agency contribute to the positioning of localities within unequal transnational relationships of power.

Migration processes cannot be seen as a *sui generis* activity with an internal dynamic that can be studied in its own right, without reference to the global-local interface of the reconstitution of capital. This is not to deny that one can track the development of an internal logic within a migration stream as Douglas Massey (Massey et al. 1998) has done so well in his research on Mexican migration. As migration takes on its own logic with transnational networks, a specific migration trajectory and the networks that connect places become part and parcel of the restructuring of those places (Smith 1998). And each place has its own particular history as Jennifer Robinson (2006) has argued in calling for an appreciation of each city as 'ordinary.' However, in order to make sense of migration processes and their variations, we need to theorize not only the agency of migrants, whose networks restructure a specific locality, but also the global flows of capital of various kinds, which contribute to stark differences between the competitive positioning of different localities with consequence for all the inhabitants of each city and town.

A global power perspective that addresses migration and its relationship to the neoliberal restructuring of locality leads us to a more nuanced view of the impact of remittances than is currently available in the migration and development field. This global perspective highlights the dual role played by migrant remittances in relation to the impact of neoliberal restructuring. On the one hand, the impact of privatization of public service is somewhat deflected as migrant remittances pay for vital needs, such as health care, education, and infrastructure. On the other hand, remittance flows within a neoliberal context highlight locational disparities that are no longer addressed by state policies that would aim to even out regional disparities. On the contrary, as the flow of wealth becomes concentrated in specific localities, and these towns and cities reposition themselves within local and even global economies through this restructuring, states may further these disparities (de Haas 2010). For instance, they may facilitate air travel and other infrastructural developments and industries such as tourism in areas developed through migrant remittances, while other places become backwaters, whose residents are severely disadvantaged. Yet studies of development and migration tend to ignore both the specificities of localities that migrants connect through their networks of social relations, and the insertion of these locations within broader structural disparities of wealth and power. It is important to assess how we frame our questions and analyses and to identify which migrants and which localities are winners or losers because of the role played by migrants in restructuring processes.

The implications of this perspective are many for the study of processes termed 'development' in sending countries and 'urban restructuring' in settlement countries. Migrants are seen as remittance senders without sufficient discussion of how migrants are positioned in a new locality in terms of class and occupation, why migrants should want to send remittances, and to whom and where their transnational relations extend. Migrants' cultural values offer an insufficient explanation as to why migrants send large amounts of remittances and frequently support family members living elsewhere. Such explanations cannot address the fact that migrants from around the world—with different concepts of family and moral obligation—engage in very similar behavior when confronted by similar migration contexts.

The contexts that facilitate migrants sending remittances and investing in localities within their transnational field seem to be related to the conditions faced by migrants in their place and country of settlement, as well as those that confront relatives and other members of their social network who have been 'left behind' or who are living elsewhere. Because discussions of migration and development have increasingly taken the sending of remittances for granted, we have too little research on this subject. However, existing ethnographies and surveys about the remittance-sending contexts have indicated that remittances are sent under one or more of the following conditions: (1) when children, spouses, or parents are left behind; (2) when migrants face insecure conditions in a place of settlement because of racism, anti-immigrant sentiment, or other forms of political, social, or economic discrimination; (3) when migrants secure a steady income in their place of settlement, whatever its size or source; (4) when migrants suffer great status loss through the migration process and a remittance-receiving economy provides them with opportunities to maintain or improve their status and class position; and (5) when a possible remittance-receiving locality—whether a hometown or elsewhere—provides alternative economic possibilities, allowing the migrants to 'hedge their bets.' These factors together help explain whether or not a migrant establishes and maintains a transnational social field.

By linking migrants' remittance-sending patterns and motivations to the conditions that they experience in specific localities, we can better account for why some people remain committed to sending remittances or making investments transnationally, while others disengage. The restructuring of localities through neoliberal processes described above may facilitate or diminish the ability of migrants to send remittances. For example, neoliberal policies may lead to increased hiring of part-time workers and the inability of migrants to find steady employment. Or the privatization of public services may mean there is more demand for low-wage migrant labor and more possibilities for migrants to send money regularly to their hometown or homeland. And in the home locality, structural adjustment policies may lead to the reduction of transportation services and increased public insecurity, which would curb investments in businesses or new housing.

THE COUNTERVAILING HEGEMONIC PROCESSES ENCAPSULATED IN STATE MIGRATION POLICIES AND DEVELOPMENT DISCOURSES

Culture remains an important variable in a global power analysis of migration, but cultural differences between natives and migrants within a nation-state are not assumed to be the central topic of concern. Instead, a global power analysis queries not only points of contention in which migrants are constructed as culturally different but also the domains of commonality, social relations, openness, and conviviality between migrants and natives. Migration scholars often fail to address daily social activities that unite migrants and natives within workplaces, neighborhoods, and leisure activities. They also disregard the forces that construct differences, such as the intersections of the global political economy and local forms of differentiating power, including those that racialize, feminize, and subordinate regions, populations, and localities. As a means of addressing these concerns, Ramon Grosfoguel (2006) argues for an analytical framework that he calls the 'colonial power matrix.' He is developing a scholarship that analyzes the role of repressive force and discursive power with regard to the North/South divide. Building on the work of Anibel Quijano (2000), Grosfoguel (2006 : 12) speaks of the coloniality of power as

> an 'entanglement' or 'intersectionality' . . . of multiple and heterogeneous global hierarchies ('heterarchies') of sexual, political, epistemic, economic, spiritual, linguistic and racial forms of domination and exploitation where the racial/ethnic hierarchy of the European/non-European divide transversally reconfigures all of the other global power structures.

Grosfoguel (2006) emphasizes that the concepts of racial and gender differences and the hierarchies that they substantiate are central to the legitimization of the dominance of the location and dominance of finance capital in Northern states and institutions. The 'coloniality of power' framework addresses the disparities of wealth and power that link together the lack of development in the global South, the root causes of migration flows, and the interests of migrants and financial institutions in investments in remittance flows. This framework brings together in a single analytical structure the processes of capital accumulation, nation-state building, the restructuring of place, and the categorization of labor by race and gender.

When applied to migration scholarship, the coloniality of power approach allows us to understand better the current contradictory forces that denigrate migrants and celebrating migrant remittances. We can assess how constructions of migrants are used to dehumanize certain sectors of the workforce in order to legitimate more readily their insertion in neoliberal labor demands. The national discourses of exclusion—which portray migrants as unskilled, threatening, and disruptive invaders and which seem rampant in states around the world, from Singapore to Italy—contribute to the current neoliberal labor regime. Dehumanized through rhetorics of national difference, migrant labor, which is increasingly contractual, meets the needs of localized neoliberal restructuring more efficiently than the previous, and still current, situation of family reunion, asylum, and the use of the undocumented workers as a form of flexible and politically silenced labor.

Over the last few decades, growing international competition led to the development of global assembly lines. Production moved from former centers of capital accumulation in North America and Europe to factories in far-flung regions, where labor is cheap and unregulated. Tariff barriers were demolished, and untaxed export processing zones were established throughout the world. Today, agricultural and industrial corporations based in Europe and North America increasingly face a contradiction in their production processes—the balance between near and far production. This contradiction is heightened by the huge rise in the price of oil and hence transport, which means it is more profitable to locate production processes closer to the areas of high consumer demand. One increasingly popular solution is to use a workforce that is cheap and controllable. As many observers in Europe have pointed out, these contradictions will be heightened by the low birth rate and aging composition of European and North American populations (Castles 2006).[7]

For several decades, undocumented migrants—first in the United States and increasingly in Europe—made up the quiescent, hyper-exploited, and flexible workforces needed within urban restructuring processes. They furnished labor not only for agriculture but also for 'just-in-time' production close to centers of capital and for the various domestic and service industries needed in restructured cities geared toward consumer industries and tourism. In some countries in Europe, such as the United Kingdom, asylum seekers and refugees have provided this form of labor, both legally and illegally. The denigration and criminalization of asylum seekers and the growing capacity of bio-surveillance measures that limit mobility are essential features of a transition to a form of labor more fitted to the production needs of neoliberal economies.

It seems likely that we are witnessing a movement toward an EU labor regime made up of circulating labor from within the European Union and new and very controlled forms of contract labor from elsewhere. As Steve Vertovec (2007: 2) has pointed out, "Circular migration is . . . being advocated as a potential solution (at least in part) to a number of challenges surrounding contemporary migration." The expansion of the EU labor market by the inclusion of the accession states with labor policies that emphasize the merits of circulation are part of this larger policy shift. Contract workers and labor circulation are now hailed as arrangements that benefit all parties, and short-term labor contracts are increasingly part of the production process for agricultural and factory work in places as disparate as Canada and Albania.

Migration researchers are contributing to the legitimization of new forms of exploitation by emphasizing the benefits of transnational remittances while neglecting to address the severe and permanent restriction of rights that accompanies short-term contract work and the decreasing access of migrants to naturalization. Some migration scholars such as Alejandro Portes (2007: 272) have continued to sing the praises of circular short-term migration for development:

> Cyclical migrations work best for both sending and receiving societies. Returnees are much more likely to save and make productive investments at home; they leave families behind to which sizeable remittances are sent. More important, temporary migrants do not compromise the future of the next generation by placing their children in danger of downward assimilation abroad.

This kind of rosy picture reinforces the desirability of the new migration regime of contract labor, which makes migrant settlement increasingly difficult. New migration laws leave migrants with short-term options. Absent from this scenario of the benefits of circular migration are the increasing difficulties of sustaining any form of viable existence in many sending areas. Also absent are the dehumanizing aspects of short-term labor contracts with their dramatic restrictions on, or denial of, rights and privileges to the individuals who are producing wealth, paying taxes, and sustaining infrastructures and services to which they have no entitlement. The mantras about migrants as major agents of development are also part of this new global labor regime. International financial institutions have made migrant remittances a growing industry just at the moment when migrants may be both less interested in transnational strategies and yet less able to choose to settle permanently in a new land.

Transnational migration has in part reflected a strategy on the part of migrants to avoid committing themselves since they were unsure of the long-term welcome they might receive in the states in which they were settling, even if citizenship rights were available and utilized. However, migrants sending remittances make certain assumptions about the viability of local economies in sending states. They assumed that there would be enough security of persons and enough of an opportunity structure for those with capital to support their own investment in a home and family. Increasingly, these assumptions no longer hold in many regions of the world due to environmental degradation, destabilization because of structural adjustment policies, and the hollowing out of national economies through trade agreements such as NAFTA (North American Free Trade Agreement) and WTO (World Trade Organization) restrictions. The result is continuing waves of migration as well as a possible growing disinterest among migrants to invest in their homelands. This may be linked to an increased desire to reunite families in the country of settlement and to unilateral rather than simultaneous incorporation. Transnational migration and connection are not inherent features of migration but rather reflect conditions in both localities.

By examining the relationships between the neoliberal restructuring of capital and the need for ever more controllable and flexible labor, the connection between the various seemingly disparate trends in migration policy and discourse begin to emerge. Nationalist rhetoric and exclusionary policies pave the way for production regimes that rely on the capacity to control labor. The faceless migrating workforce is portrayed as potentially lawless border invaders who require restriction, regulation, and contractual constraints that limit their rights to change employers or challenge working conditions. The depersonalizaton of labor as contractual services allows for labor policy statements in which the separation of workers from home and family, without rights of settlement and family reunion, becomes good economic policy. The depersonalization of the process allows such workers to be categorized as unskilled, despite the fact that many of them have relatively high degrees of education and may be nurses, doctors, teachers, or even university professors. Their willingness to migrate is integrally related to the structural adjustment and privatization policies in their home localities that reduced wages and ended state-funded public services that had provided employment for professionals.

At first glance, the 'global war for talent,' in which multinational corporations compete for highly educated workers, would seem to stand outside the emerging labor regime that I am describing. However, short-term contracts with restructured rights of settlement are increasingly part of this labor market as well, although in many countries highly skilled professionals are still being allowed to settle. Such short-term contracts often regulate high-tech workers to ensure that the currect workforce gives way to the next wave of newly educated and eager bodies and brains. Moreover, the very prominence and desirability of the sought-after few highlight the disposability of the faceless many, despite the fact that both labor streams are needed to sustain many contemporary cities.

The dehumanization of migrants allows for them to be manipulated and controlled as various forms of unfree contracted labor. Meanwhile, migrant professionals can be welcomed in specific places as contributors to the neoliberal restructuring and rescaling of various cities. Also, migrant remittances can be relied on to transmit foreign currency to families, localities, and regimes left behind, enabling their inclusion, however unequally, in global patterns of consumption and desire. In short, the seemingly discrepant narratives are part of the globally structured and locally situated mutual reconstitution of social relationships and values that a global power perspective allows us to analyze. Such a perspective facilitates advocacy of alternative policies and agendas.

It is insufficient, however, to reduce the flood of anti-immigrant sentiments to a justification for exploitative labor. Returning to the 'coloniality of power' framework and using it as part of our global perspective on migration can yield further insights into the current moment of anti-immigrant attacks and contradictory discourses. At the same time, this perspective highlights how US and European imperialist projects are simultaneously justified and obscured through a politics of fear that portrays migrants as the chief threat to national security.

I have noted that states are still important within the globe-spanning economic processes that mark our contemporary world, but of course not all states are equal. Unequal globalization rests on a framework of imperial states that serve as base areas for institutions that control capital, the productions of arms, and military power. These powerful states claim and obtain rights and privileges in states around the world and define the institutional limits of less powerful states. The core imperial states also are the key players in institutions that claim to be global, including the World Bank, the World Trade Organization, and the United Nations Security Council. Increasingly, theorists on the right and the left have recently returned to the concept of imperialism. They stress the significance of warfare, but often ignore the relationship between neoliberal restructuring, migration, and the construction of images of the foreigner as enemy and terrorist (Reyna 2005; Cooper 2003; Harvey 2003; Mann 2003; Ikenberry 2002)

In the face of intense global economic, political, social, and cultural interconnections, and of growing inequality due to racialized and gendered hierarchies, the popularization of the notion of the migrant as the outsider rehabilitates earlier myths that nation-states contain homogenous cultures shared by native populations. Once again, the migrant is constructed to reinforce and validate the nationalism that continues to socialize individuals to identify with their nation-state. Once again, a portrayal of the world as divided into autonomous nation-states is becoming hegemonic.

Increasingly, as states are hollowed out in terms of infrastructure and discrete realms of economic production and are ever more integrally linked to production and consumption processes elsewhere, state narratives stress national identities and cultural difference. In short, nation-states are increasingly identity containers that maintain and disseminate images of the nation as a society that have little to do with the contemporary, transnational institutional structures within which social life and relations of power are produced. The less services and rights that states provide for their citizens and the more that they produce citizens who have been educated to identify as customers enmeshed in cultures of consumption rather than forms of civic and social engagement, the more these states promote discourses of social cohesion and national community. The inside is increasingly constructed in relation to framing foreigners as the source of disruption,—as being responsible for the decline of social services, and of community. The more ordinary citizens in states around the world find their futures circumscribed by poverty or lack of social mobility, the more that they are told by political leaders that the problems are caused by persons from elsewhere. Anti-immigrant discourse remains a nation-state building process, a ritual of renewal that engages its participants in defining their loyalty to a country by differentiating them from stigmatized racialized others.

CONCLUSIONS

Migration studies too rarely address the global system that is reducing the opportunity for social and economic equality and justice around the world and the human costs of new short-term labor contracts. While potent critiques have been made about each strand of the contemporary and apparently contradictory narratives that address migration and development, the critiques remain encapsulated within different literatures. This has made it too easy to keep debates about migration separate from discussions of neoliberal restructuring and the human toll this agenda exacts around the world. Short-term labor contracts resurrect older forms of indenture, with limited rights and mobility. Families separated by migration regulations that allow no family reunion means the reproduction of social life at great personal sacrifice, with parents separated from children, and spouses from each other, and elderly parents left to survive without the assistance of children. Developing a global power perspective on migration that directs attention to the contemporary neoliberal moment allows us both to establish a research agenda that calls attention to human costs of neoliberal restructuring and to trace its various trajectories and the resistances it engenders.

A global perspective on migration can provide an analytical lens that would allow scholars of migration and development to think beyond the reimposition of nationalist interests. Migration studies are at a crucial juncture. We can follow the pattern of the past, let our research be shaped by the public mood and the political moment, and revive old binaries, fears, and categories. Or we can engage in research that clarifies this moment by developing new frameworks for analysis. In short, we need a new scholarship that can build on our understanding of global processes, and highlight them, so that we can actually document how migrants live their lives as constitutive actors in multiple social settings. This scholarship will reconstitute migration theory so that it explains current observations and facilitates new ones. To do this we need to discard methodological nationalism so that our units of analysis do not obscure the presence of imperial globe-spanning power and its internal contradictions, its inability to provide consistent development, and its dependence on migrant labor.

The new scholarship should popularize the concept that migration as well as development processes are part of global forces experienced by people who move and those who do not move. This means migration scholars must enter into the public debate about social cohesion by identifying the forces of globalization that are restructuring the lives of migrants and non-migrants alike and by speaking to the common struggle of most of the people of the world for social and economic justice and equality. When delimited by their methodological nationalism, migration theorists confine their units of analysis to the nation-state and the migrant. They are thus unable to track structures and processes of unequal capital flow that influence the experience of people who reside in particular localities. Migration scholars often fail to look at relationships between migrants and natives that are not framed by concepts of cultural or ancestral difference. Furthermore, they ignore the way in which local institutions that incorporate residents of states in a variety of ways are configured by power hierarchies that interpenetrate into states and regions.

Development discussions that laud migrant remittances yet do not address transnational fields of unequal power serve to obfuscate rather than promote analysis. Many states dominated by imperial power and its new regulatory architecture are struggling because a sizeable proportion of their gross national product is channeled into debt service, leaving migrants to sustain the national economy through their contributions. Meanwhile, remittances and the flow of migrant capital across borders contribute to the profitability of banks and other financial institutions (Guarnizo 2003).

A global perspective on imperial power can also facilitate our ability as socially engaged scholars to theorize the contradictions of imperial dilemmas and find ways in which they can contribute to progressive social transformation. But we can do this only do if we set aside born-again assimilationism and other forms of integrationist theory that posit migrants as disruptors of national communities. It is necessary for migrants and natives of countries around the world who find their lives diminished by unequal globalization to understand what the problem is and what it is not. It is not putative hordes of illegal aliens or migrants' transnational connections that are threatening the majority of people in the imperial core countries. Rather, we need to draw attention to the ways in which anti-immigrant rage and subjective feelings of despair, the precariousness of life, and life's unmet aspirations reflect and speak to the global fragility and exploitive character of contemporary capitalism, its restructuring of economies, labor regimes, and states, and its dependence on war and plunder.

NOTES

1. Acknowledgments: This chapter originally appeared in *Social Analysis, Volume 53, Issue 3, Winter 2009, 14–37* . Portions of this chapter are built on a co-authored paper with Ayse Çaglar entitled "Migrant Incorporation and

City Scale: Theory in the Balance" delivered at the conference MPI Workshop: Migration and City Scale, Halle/Salle, Germany, May 2005. Earlier versions of this chapter were delivered at the Second International Colloquium on Migration and Development: Migration, Transnationalism and Social Transformation, Cocoyoc, Mexico, October 26–28, 2006; the Volkswagen Foundation Conference on Migration and Education, Hamburg, Germany, February 22–23, 2007; the RDI Conference on New Essentialisms, Paris, France, May 22–25, 2007; and the ZIF Conference on Transnational Migration and Development, Bielefeld, Germany, May 30–June 1, 2007. My thanks to the conference organizers and participants who are not responsible for the perspective of this chapter. Special thanks to the James H. Hayes and Claire Short Hayes Professorship of the Humanities that I held and to Burt Feintuch, Center for the Humanities, University of New Hampshire, for summer support, to Günther Schlee, Max Planck Institute for Social Anthropology, for broader conceptualizations of integration and conflict, to Hartwig Schuck for formatting and website posting, and Darien Rozentals for editorial assistance.

2. As Peter Kivisto (2005) has pointed out, the 'new assimilationists' actually are not that different from the old. The classic asssimilationists such as Robert Park and Milton Gordon (1964) did not predict an inevitable melting away of cultural difference within the American crucible. In arguing their case for the new integration or attacking immigrants for their supposed failure to integrate, these scholars generally compare statistics on level of education, workforce integration, and criminality that continue the divide between native and foreigner and sometimes compares different 'ethnic groups' without regard to questions of class background and national or local opportunity structures (Huntington 2000). The defining and essential act for these integrationists continues to be the crossing of the border.

3. I have consistently been quoted as arguing that nation-states are declining in significance and for calling for a post-national world. I have never taken this position. Together with most scholars of transnational migration, I see nation-states, their legal system, migration policies, and institutional structures as significant in the establishment and persistence of transnational social fields (Glick Schiller 2003, 1999; Levitt and Glick Schiller 2004; Levitt 2001; Faist 2000; Smith and Guarnizo 1998; Basch, Glick Schiller, and Szanton Blanc 1994; Glick Schiller et al. 1992). Despite this now-extensive literature, some analysts persist in accusing these scholars of ignoring the persisting importance of nation-states. See for example Bommes (2005) and Waldinger and Fitzgerald (2004).

4. The restrictions on entry of persons from China beginning in 1882 were the precursors of efforts at broader restrictive legislation but the gate was not shut against most migration until the 1920s. The 1917 law not only continued the Chinese exclusion but kept most people from Asia from entering. The bulk of the restrictive legislation that followed was based on nationality until 1965. Migrants were categorized by country of origin; tens of thousands of some nationalities were admitted while no more than one hundred of other 'national origins' including Greek, Bulgarian, Palestinian, and Australian. Most public discussions of migrants from the 1920s identified migrants by their 'nationality,' popularizing the dividing line between American and those identified by other national origins.

5. In contrast to this general failure of transnational migration scholars to theorize locality, Michael Peters Smith (2001) has developed a concept of transnational urbanism. Smith's concern is to generate a new category of urbanism. The weakness of the concept is that the category of transnational urbanism readily becomes an ideal type, rather than an analytical tool through

which to study specific localities and their various positionings as a result of regional history and global restructuring.
6. For important exceptions see Dannecker (2007), Delgado Wise (2007), de Haas (2010), Faist (2008), and Guarnizo (2007).
7. The US birth rates have been higher than Western Europe until recently and have exceeded the rate of replacement, in part because of the higher birth rate of people of "Asian" migrant backgrounds and "Hispanic" backgrounds. However the Population Reference Bureau (Kent 2011) reported that the birth rate began to fall in 2009 among almost all sectors of the population and that the "total fertility rate, or average number of lifetime births per woman, for 2009 was 2.01, the lowest level since 1998." The recent drop in births puts the US total fertility rate below the replacement level of about 2.1 births per woman (preliminary figures for the first half of 2010 show births down about 4 percent compared with the same period in 2009; Kent 2011). "While this was the highest total fertility rate since 1992, it remained well below replacement level of 2.1 children per woman. This is the fertility rate that must be maintained to replace the population in the absence of migration" (Kent 2011).

REFERENCES

Alba, Richard, and Victor Nee. 2003. *Remaking the American Mainstream: Assimilation and Contemporary Immigration.* Cambridge, MA: Harvard University Press.
Barth, Fredrick. 1969. *Ethnic Groups and Boundaries: The Social Organization of Cultural Difference.* Boston: Little Brown.
Basch, Linda, Nina Glick Schiller, and Cristina Szanton Blanc. 1994. *Nations Unbound: Transnational Projects. Postcolonial Predicaments, and Deterritorialized Nation-States.* New York: Gordon and Breach.
Beck, Ulrich. 2000. "The Cosmopolitan Perspective: Sociology of the Second Age of Modernity." *British Journal of Sociology* 51(1): 79–105.
Bodnar, John. 1985. *The Transplanted: A History of Immigrants in Urban America.* Bloomington: Indiana University Press.
Bommes, Michael. 2005. "Transnationalism or Assimilation?" sowi-online e.V., Bielefeld. Accessed December 30, 2008 http://www.sowi-onlinejournal.de/20051/transnationalism_assimilation_bommes.htm.
Bommes, Michael and Andrew Geddes 2000. "Introduction: Immigration and the Welfare State." In *Immigration and Welfare: Challenging the Borders of the Welfare State*, edited by Andrew Geddes and Michael Bommes, 89–107. London: Routledge.
Brenner, Neil. 2001. "World City Theory, Globalization and the Comparative-Historical Method: Reflections on Janet Abu-Lughod's Interpretation of Contemporary Urban Restructuring." *Urban Affairs Review* 36(6): 124–147.
———. 2004. *New State Spaces: Urban Governance and the Rescaling of Statehood.* New York: Oxford University Press.
Brubaker, Rogers. 2004. *Ethnicity without Groups.* Cambridge, MA: Harvard University Press.
Çaglar, Ayse. 1990. "Das Kultur-Konzept als Zwangsjacke: Studien zur Arbeitsmigration." *Zeitschrift für Türkei-Studien* 1: 93–105.
———. 1997. "Hyphenated Identities and the Limits of 'Culture.'" Pp. 169–185 in *The Politics of Multiculturalism in the New Europe: Racism, Identity and Community*, ed. Tariq Modood and Pnina Werbner. London: Zed.

———. 2005. "Mediascapes, Advertisement Industries: Turkish Immigrants in Europe and the European Union." *New German Critique* 92: 39–62.
———. 2007. "Rescaling Cities, Cultural Diversity and Transnationalism: Migrants of Mardin and Essen." *Ethnic and Racial Studies* 30(6): 1070–1095.
Castells, Manuel. 1996. *The Rise of Network Society.* Cambridge, MA: Blackwell.
Castles, Stephen. 2006. "Back to the Future? Can Europe Meet Its Labour Needs through Temporary Migration?" Working Paper 1, International Migration Institute, Oxford University. http://prospero.qeh.ox.ac.uk:8080/imi/pdfs/wp1-backtothefuture.pdf.
Cooper, Frederick. 2003. "Modernizing Colonialism and the Limits of Empire." *Items and Issues* 4(4): 1–9.
Dannecker, Petra. 2007. "The Re-ordering of Political, Cultural and Social Spaces through Transnational Labour Migration." Paper delivered at Transnationalisation and Development(s): Towards a North-South Perspective. Zentrum für Interdisziplinäre Forschung, Bielefeld University, May 31 and June 1.
de Haas, Hein. 2010 "Migration and Development: A Theoretical Perspective." *International Migration Review* 40(4): 227–264.
Delgado Wise, Raúl. 2007. "The Migration and Development Mantra in Mexico: Toward a New Analytical Approach." Paper delivered at Transnationalisation and Development(s): Towards a North-South Perspective Zentrum für Interdisziplinäre Forschung, Bielefeld University, May 31 and June 1.
Escalante, Ana. 2007. "Building Futures." *Financial Times*, August 29. Accessed September 27, 2007. http://www.ft.com/cms/s/0/1bf0b258-55d3-11dc-b971-0000779fd2ac.html.
Esser, Hartmut. 2003. "Ist das Konzept der Assimilation überholt?" *Geographische Revue* 5(Summer): 5–22.
———. 2006. "Migration, Language and Integration." AKI Research Review 4. Arbeitsstelle Interkulturelle Konflikteund gesellschaftliche Integration (AKI) Wissenschaftszentrum Berlin für Sozialforschung (WZB).
Faist, Thomas. 2000. *The Volume and Dynamics of International Migration and Transnational Social Spaces.* Oxford: Oxford University Press.
———. 2008. "Migrants as Transnational Development Agents: An Inquiry into the Newest Round of the Migration-Development Nexus." *Population, Space and Place* 14(1): 21–42.
Fajnzylber, Pablo, and J. Humberto López. 2008. *Remittances and Development: Lessons from Latin America.* Washington, DC: The World Bank. Accessed July 2009. http://siteresources.worldbank.org/EXTLACOFFICEOFCE/Resources/RemittancesandDevelopment.pdf.
Fauser, Margit. 2007. "The Local Politics of Transnational Development Cooperation: On the Interaction between Migrant Organizations and Local Authorities in Spanish Cities." Paper delivered at Transnationalisation and Development(s): Towards a North-South Perspective Zentrum für Interdisziplinäre Forschung, Bielefeld University, May 31 and June 1.
Gabaccia, Donna, and Fraser M. Ottanelli. 2001. *Italian Workers of the World: Labor Migration and the Formation of Multiethnic States.* Urbana: University of Illinois Press.
Gilroy, Paul. 1992. *The Black Atlantic: Modernity and Double Consciousness.* Cambridge, MA: Harvard University Press.
Glick Schiller, Nina. 1977. "Ethnic Groups Are Made Not Born." In *Ethnic Encounters: Identities and Contexts*, edited by George Hicks and Philip Leis, 23–35. North Scituate, MA: Duxbury Press.
———. 1999. "Transmigrants and Nation-States: Something Old and Something New in the U.S. Immigrant Experience." In *The Handbook of International*

Migration: The American Experience, edited by Charles Hirshman, Philip Kasinitz, and Josh DeWind, 94–119. New York: Russell Sage Foundation.
———. 2003. "The Centrality of Ethnography in the Study of Transnational Migration: Seeing the Wetland instead of the Swamp." In *American Arrivals: Anthropology Engages the New Immigration*, edited by Nancy Foner, 99–128. Santa Fe: School of American Research Press.
———. 2006. "Introduction: What Does Transnational Studies Have to Offer to the Study of Localized Conflict and Protest?" *Focal—European Journal of Anthropology* 47: 3–17.
Glick Schiller, Nina, and Ayse Çaglar. 2009. "Towards a Comparative Theory of Locality in Migration Studies: Migrant Incorporation and City Scale." *Journal of Ethnic and Migration Studies* 35(2): 177–202.
———. 2011. Locality and Globality: Building a Comparative Analytical Framework in Migration and Urban Studies. In *Locating Migration: Rescaling Cities and Migrants*. Ithaca: Cornell.
Glick Schiller, Nina, Linda Basch, and Cristina Blanc-Szanton, eds. 1992. *Towards a Transnational Perspective on Migration: Race, Class, Ethnicity, and Nationalism Reconsidered*. New York: New York Academy of Sciences.
Glick Schiller, Nina, Ayse Caglar, and Thaddeus Guldbrandsen. 2006. "Beyond the Ethnic Lens: Locality, Globality, and Born-Again Incorporation." *American Ethnologist* 33(4): 612–633.
Glick Schiller, Nina, Josh DeWind, Mare Lucie Brutus, Carolle Charles, Georges Fouron, and Luis Thomas. 1987. "All in the Same Boat? Unity and Diversity among Haitian Immigrants." In *Caribbean Life in New York City*, edited by Constance R. Sutton and Elsa M. Chaney, 167–184. Staten Island, NY: Center for Migration Studies.
Gonzalez, Nancie L. 1988. *Sojourners of the Caribbean: Ethnogenesis and Ethnohistory of the Garifuna*. Urbana: University of Illinois Press.
Goode, Judith. 2012. "The Campaign for New Immigrants in Philadelphia: Imagining Possibilities and Confronting Realities." In *Locating Migration: Rescaling Cities and Migrants*, edited by Nina Glick Schiller and Ayse Çaglar, 143–165. Ithaca: Cornell.
Gordon, Milton. 1964. *Assimilation in American Life: The Role of Race, Religion and National Origins*. New York: Oxford University Press.
Grosfoguel, Ramón. 2006. "Decolonizing Political-Economy and Post-colonial Studies: Transmodernity, Border Thinking, and Global Coloniality." Accessed March 2009. http://www.afyl.org/descolonizingeconomy.pdf.
Guarnizo, Luis. 2003. "The Economics of Transnational Living." *International Migration Review* 37(3): 666–699.
———. 2007. "The Migration-Development Nexus and the Post-Cold War World Order." Paper delivered at Transnationalisation and Development(s): Towards a North-South Perspective Zentrum für Interdisziplinäre Forschung, Bielefeld University, May 31 and June 1.
Guarnizo, Luis, Alejandro Portes, and William Haller. 2003. "Assimilation and Transnationalism: Determinants of Transnational Political Action among Contemporary Migrants." *American Journal of Sociology* 108: 1211–1248.
Hardt, Michael, and Antonio Negri. 2000. *Empire*. Cambridge, MA: Harvard University Press.
Harvey, David. 2003. *The New Imperialism*. Oxford: Oxford University Press.
———. 2005. *A Brief History of Neoliberalism*. New York: Oxford University Press.
Heckmann, Frederik. 2003. "From Ethnic Nation to Universalistic Immigrant Integration: Germany." In *The Integration of Immigrants in European Societies, National Differences and Trends of Convergence*, edited by

Frederik Heckmann and Dominique Schnapper, 45–78. Stuttgart: Lucius und Lucius.
Huntington, Samuel. 2000. *Reconsidering Immigration: Is Mexico a Special Case?* San Diego: Center for Immigration Studies. http://www.cis.org/articles/2000/back1100.html.
Ikenberry, John. 2002. "America's Imperial Ambition." *Foreign Affairs* 81(3): 44–62.
Jessop, Bob. 2003. "The Crisis of the National Spatio-Temporal Fix and the Ecological Dominance of Globalizing Capitalism." Lancaster: Department of Sociology, Lancaster University. http//www.comp.lancs.ac.uk/sociology/papers/Jessop-Crisis-of-the-National-Spatio-Temporal-Fix.pdf.
Joppke, Christian, and Ewa Morawska. 2002. *Toward Assimilation and Citizenship: Immigrants in Liberal Nations*. Basingstoke, UK: Palgrave.
Kastoryano, Riva. 2002. *Negotiating Identities: States and Immigrants in France and Germany*. Princeton: Princeton University Press.
Kent, Mary. 2011. "US Population Fertility in Decline." Population Reference Bureau. Accessed October 5, 2011. http://www.prb.org/Articles/2011/us-fertility-decline.aspx?p=1.
Kivisto, Peter. 2005. *Incorporating Diversity: Rethinking Assimilation in a Multicultural Age*. Boulder, CO: Paradigm Publishers.
Lapper, Richard. 2007a. "Building Futures." *Financial Times*, August 29. Accessed September 27, 2007 http://www.ft.com/cms/s/0/1bf0b258-55d3-11-dc-b971-0000779fd2ac.html
———. 2007b. "The Tale of Globalisation's Exiles." *Financial Times*, August 27. Accessed September 15, 2007. http://www.ft.com/cms/s/0/11c878de-54bf-11dc-890c-0000779fd2ac.html.
Levitt, Peggy. 2001. *The Transnational Villagers*. Berkeley: University of California Press.
———. 2001b. "Transnational Migration: Taking Stock and Future Directions." *Global Networks* 1(3): 195–216.
Levitt, Peggy, and Nina Glick Schiller. 2004. "Transnational Perspectives on Migration: Conceptualizing Simultaneity." *International Migration Review* 38(145): 595–629.
Mann, Michael. 2003. *Incoherent Empire*. London: Verso.
Martins, Herminio. 1974. "Time and Theory in Sociology." In *Approaches to Sociology: An Introduction to Major Trends in British Sociology*, edited by John Rex, 248–294. London: Routledge and Kegan Paul.
Massey, Douglas, Joaquín Arango, Graeme Hugo, Ali Kouaouci, Adela Pellegrino, and J. Edward Taylor. 1998. *Worlds in Motion: Understanding International Migration at the End of the Millenium*. Oxford: Clarendon Press.
Mittleman, James, ed. 1996. *Globalization: Critical Reflections*. London: Lynne Reinner.
Morawska Eva. 2003. "Immigrant Transnationalism and Assimilation: A Variety of Combinations and the Analytical Strategies It Suggests." In *Towards Assimilation and Citizenship: Immigrants in Liberal Nation-States*, edited by Chistian Joppke and Eva Morawska, 133–176. London: Palgrave-McMillan.
Nye, Joseph, Jr. 1976. "Independence and Interdependence." *Foreign Policy* 22(Spring): 130– 161.
Østergaard-Nielsen, Eva. 2007. "Perceptions and Practices of Codevelopment in Catalunya." Paper delivered at Transnationalisation and Development(s): Towards a North-South Perspective Zentrum für Interdisziplinäre Forschung, Bielefeld University, May 31 and June 1.
Portes, Alejandro. 2007. "Migration, Development, and Segmented Assimilation: A Conceptual Review of the Evidence." *The Annals of the American Academy*

of Political and Social Sciences Quick Read Synoposis 610: 270–272. http://ann.sagepub.com/cgi/reprint/610/1/266.pdf.

Potts, Lydia. 1990. *The World Labour Market: A History of Migration.* London: Zed Books.

Pries, Ludger. 2001. "Transnationalism: Trendy Catch-All or Specific Research Programme." Paper delivered at Transnationalisation and Development(s): Towards a North-South Perspective Zentrum für Interdisziplinäre Forschung, Bielefeld University, May 31 and June 1.

Quijano, Anibal. 2000. "Coloniality of Power and Eurocentrism, and Latin America." *International Sociology* 15(2): 215–232.

Raghuram, Parvati. 2007. "Which Migration, What Development: Unsettling the Edifice of Migration and Development." Paper delivered at Transnationalisation and Development(s): Towards a North-South Perspective Zentrum für Interdisziplinäre Forschung, Bielefeld University, May 31 and June 1.

Ratzel, Friedrich. 1882. *Anthropogeographie.* Stuttgart: J. Engelhorn.

Reyna, Stephen. 2005. "American Imperialism? The Current Runs Swiftly." *Focaal* 45(Summer): 129–151.

Sackmann, Rosemarie, Bernhard Peters, and Thomas Faist, eds. 2003. *Identity and Integration: Migrants in Western Europe.* Aldershot, UK: Ashgate.

Salzbrunn, Monika. 2012. "Rescaling Processes in Two Cities: How Migrants Are Incorporated in Urban Settings through Political and Cultural Events." In *Locating Migration: Rescaling Cities and Migrants,* edited by Nina Glick Schiller and Ayse Çaglar, 166–189. Ithaca: Cornell.

Scott, Allen. 2004. "Cultural-Products Industries and Urban Economic Development." *Urban Affairs Review* 39(4): 460–490.

Smith, Anthony. 1983. "Nationalism and Social Theory." *British Journal of Sociology* 34: 19–38.

Smith, Michael Peter. 2001. *Transnational Urbanism: Locating Globalization.* Malden, MA andOxford: Blackwell.

Smith, Michael Peter, and Luis Guarnizo, eds. 1998. *Transnationalism from Below.* New Brunswick: Transaction Publishers.

Smith, Neil. 1995. "Remaking Scale: Competition and Cooperation in Pre-national and Post-national Europe." In *Competitive European Peripheries,* edited by Heikki Eskelinen and Folke Snickars, 59–74. Berlin: Springer Verlag.

Smith, Robert. 1998. "Transnational Localities: Community, Technology and the Politics of Membership within the Context of Mexico and US Migration." In *Transnationalism from Below,* edited by M.P. Smith and L.E. Guarnizo, 196–238. New Brunswick, NJ: Transaction Publishers.

———. 2006. "Black Mexicans, Nerds and Cosmopolitans: Key Cases for Assimilation Theory." Paper delivered at Segundo Coloquio Internacional Sobre Migración Y Desarrollo: Migración, transnacionalismo y transformación social, Cocoyoc, Morelos, Mexico, October 26–28.

Sollors,Werner, ed. 1989. *The Invention of Ethnicity.* New York: Oxford University Press.

Statistics Canada. 2009. "Births." Accessed October 5, 2011. http://www.statcan.gc.ca/daily-quotidien/090922/dq090922b-eng.htm.

Swyngedouw, Erik. 1997. "Neither Global nor Local: 'Glocalization' and the Politics of Scale." In *Spaces of Globalization,* edited by Kevin R. Cox, 137–166. New York: Guilford Press.

Torpey, John. 2000. *The Invention of the Passport: Surveillance, Citizenship and the State.* Cambridge: Cambridge University Press.

Urry, John. 2000. *The Global Media and Cosmopolitanism.* Paper presented at Transnational America Conference, Bavarian American Academy, Munich,

June 2000. Electronic document. Accessed September 20, 2003. http://www.comp.lancs.ac.uk/sociology/soc056ju.html.

van Holthoon, Frits, and Marcel van der Linden. 1988. *Internationalism in the Labour Movement, 1830–1940*. Leiden: E.J. Brill.

Vertovec, Steven. 2007. "Circular Migration: The Way Forward in Global Policy?" Working papers 4, International Migration Institute Oxford University. http://www.imi.ox.ac.uk/pdfs/wp4-circular-migration-policy.pdf.

Waldinger, Roger, and David Fitzgerald. 2004. "Transnationalism in Question." *American Journal of Sociology* 109: 1177–1195.

Wimmer, Andreas, and Nina Glick Schiller. 2002a. "Methodological Nationalism and Beyond Nation-State Building, Migration and the Social Sciences." *Global Networks* 2(4): 301–334.

———. 2002b. "Methodological Nationalism and the Study of Migration." *Archives of European Sociology* 43(2): 217–240.

Wolf, Eric. 1982. *Europe and the People without History*. Berkeley: University of California Press.

World Bank. 2006. "Global Economic Prospects: Economic Implications of Remittances and Migration." Washington, DC. Accessed July 2009. http://www-wds.worldbank.org/servlet/WDSContentServer/WDSP/IB/2005/11/14/000112742_20051114174928/Rendered/PDF/343200GEP02006.pdf.

Zukin, Sharon. 1995. *The Cultures of Cities*. Oxford: Blackwell.

4 Theorizing Transnational Movement in the Current Conjuncture
Examples from/of/in the Asia Pacific

Donald M. Nonini

INTRODUCTION

In this chapter I seek to place the situation of transnational labor migrants within a broader comparative class framework than they are often viewed by examining not only the conditions they face, but also the situations confronting migrants belonging to classes different from the working class—whether owners of petty productive property, professionals, or managers and owners of capitalist firms.[1] My approach is to examine how persons moving transnationally mediate the relationship between two aspects of life in contemporary capitalist societies—capitalist processes of value production, including the operation of circuits of finance and rentier capital, and the processes of social reproduction which make possible the reproduction of the labor process of capitalist production, the continuity of the capital/labor relation, and beyond these processes as such, the reproduction of the conditions of everyday life in capitalist societies. Let us take these two aspects in turn.

The work of value creation in capitalism, in its multivariate forms, is always local, always has to take place *somewhere*. Members of different classes participate not only in territorially specific labor markets, but also in territorially specific commodity markets, and in the case of a relatively small number of financial capitalists—despite the Internet—in territorially specific capital markets. Some markets, including labor markets, operate within the nation-states in which the people who participate in them are born and reside, while others operate outside the countries of birth and residence ("abode") of those who participate in large numbers in them.

Like the creation of value, social reproduction in the extended sense has to occur *somewhere*, i.e., be undertaken by someone as specific forms of labor performed in *various social spaces*, whether these are state law courts, the household, schools, universities, or elsewhere. I take "social reproduction" to encompass a large number of processes that ensure the viability of capitalism and of the class relationships and positions central to it. In addition to the operation of the legal and political apparatuses of states that fundamentally protect capitalist property relations, these processes include the forms of non-commodified (and commodified) labor that *care for* the laborer and must take place if the laborer is to "appear at the factory gates" when she or he is needed by capital. However, I am also interested in what kinds of caring labor are needed, who performs it, and under what conditions not only for the working class, but also for other classes, such as owners of petty productive property,[2] professionals, farmers, and capitalists, because the question of caring labor within the social reproduction of the members of a class is an essential one to ask when it comes to the reproduction of capitalism as a system. Large numbers of people are induced and at times coerced in everyday life by their place in capitalist relations of production, exchange, and consumption to seek to reproduce or improve their own class positions within the system. Without engaging in functionalist circularity, therefore, one can say that these everyday forms of caring labor may be more or less sufficient for the adequate performance of labor by members of specific classes, although in specific spaces in times of economic and ecological crisis they may fail entirely, and thus represent a contingently necessary but not sufficient condition for the reproduction of capitalism as a spatially and temporally bounded system.

Transnational labor migration is not the only form of transnational movement, for one can also refer to transnational processes of commuting, temporary residence for business (e.g., for expatriate managers), educational sojourning, tourism, and family relocation not directly related to participating in labor markets, as among the forms of transnational travel undertaken by different classes and class fractions of contemporary capitalist societies. In this chapter, I am particularly concerned with such forms of transnational mobility that people engage in that mediate the contradictions between their participating in labor markets and other markets (e.g., real estate, capital), and their access to the labors which others perform to ensure their (the former's) social reproduction. Specifically in this chapter I seek to describe and analyze relationships between the shifting dynamics of value creation and capital accumulation in the global system and certain distinctive practices of transnational movement that are part of strategies of social reproduction, with special respect to Chinese populations in/from Southeast Asia and their involvement in the capitalist economies of the Asia Pacific region.

My interest in comparing transnational labor migrants with those who belong to other classes when it comes to transnational movements as a means of mediating the contradictions between capitalist production and social reproduction has at least three rationales. First, the specificity of the class conditions facing transnational laborers can best be understood by illuminating not only their own situation, but also the situations of other classes in capitalist societies—since, for the latter, the necessity of mediating this contradiction is by no means absent, although the mediation takes different manifestations from that of the working class.

Another justification for my topic is that we need to reconceptualize what transnational movement means in a world where many of those who move live within and are abused by regimes of social inequalities grounded not only in class exploitation, but also in asymmetries of power between groups based on national, racial, cultural, and gender differences institutionalized within the citizenship regimes of nation-states. These differences are important when it comes to social reproduction. To understand the conditions laboring people face when they migrate transnationally, we need to have a more complex sense not only of their positions as owners of labor power but also as persons in need of the caring labor that makes it possible for them to participate in the capitalist economy–labor whose performance is dependent on the national, racial, and gender identities imposed on them by nation-states. This investigation can best be undertaken by way of contrast to the members of other classes—capitalists, owners of petty productive property, or professionals—who are not only in quite different relationships to the means of production from the working class, but also in different relationships with respect to the mechanisms of social reproduction.

The third rationale for treating not only transnational labor migrants but also those belonging to other classes who are mobile transnationally is not just that the situations of the latter are worth studying in their own right, but also that in terms of class position transnational labor migrants are often not only laborers, but also aspire to become small-scale merchants or professionals, or to move their children into these classes. Workers and others living in capitalist societies are affected by dominant hegemonic discourses and ideologies about the opportunities for upward mobility. I am referring to the empirical messiness and ambiguity of class positions among the culturally constrained actors who form our ethnographic subjects in migration studies.

My main theoretical contention is that members of different classes engaged in transnational movement face class-specific dilemmas in how they seek to position themselves and are positioned with respect to two kinds of constraints—one associated with the nation-states where the labor markets and other markets which they participate in are located, and the other associated with the nation-states where their conditions of class and social reproduction are most ensured. The transnational strategies and subjectivities of people confronting the prospects and risks of transnational movement are not only intimately connected to their class situations, but also to their positions within state citizenship regimes that stratify the populations they rule, including those who migrate into their national territories, along lines of ethnoracial and gender differences, where such "bureaucratic logics" (Handelman 2004) have major implications for their social reproduction. On one hand, it is impossible to understand patterns of transnational mobility and why people move where they do without paying close attention to the historically shifting dynamics of capitalist markets and of capital accumulation within the global capitalist economy. On the other, we (like they) must also take into account the ways in which specific citizenship regimes throughout the global economy set constraints on their social reproduction. To study how persons in motion transnationally mediate these contradictory two sets of constraints has everything to do with the investigation of their strategies of self-fashioning and attempts to fashion others like them.

In what follows, I first discuss the processes of social reproduction relevant to the Chinese groups in Malaysia and Indonesia whom I have studied ethnographically in order to argue for the importance for anthropologists of paying greater attention to social reproduction processes when they investigate transnational labor migration and other forms of transnational travel. Second, I then set out very briefly the processes of capital accumulation over the last thirty to forty years, as these have implicated in particular a shift in the centers of accumulation from North America and Europe to East Asia and Southeast Asia with which my informants' lives have been implicated. I then discuss two examples of transnational movement by aspiring "large-scale" Chinese capitalists in order to compare the quite disparate connections they have to the older centers of accumulation—the United States, Europe, and their Anglophone outliers—and to China, the center of the ascendant region in the world economy. In this discussion, I consider the case of "middling transnationalists," Chinese families (and their enterprises) who have provisionally relocated from Southeast Asia to Australia, Canada, New Zealand, and to other Pacific-basin outliers of the US center of accumulation, in a traversal from one region to another (Nonini 1997). Finally, I examine the condition of Chinese Malaysian laborers who were labor migrants from Malaysia to Japan in the 1980s, and what has happened to them since then, and how very different their situations have been from those of other ethnic Chinese from Southeast Asia belonging to more dominant groups engaged in transnational movement.

SOCIAL REPRODUCTION IN TRANSNATIONAL PERSPECTIVE

Marx wrote little in detail about the processes of social reproduction as such. In "Simple Reproduction," Chapter 23 of *Capital*, Vol. 1, he writes, "The capitalist process of production, therefore, seen as a total, connected process, i.e. a process of reproduction, produces not only commodities, not only surplus-value, but it also produces and reproduces the capital-relation itself; on the one hand the capitalist, on the other the wage-laborer" (Marx 1976: 724). He did however write about the value of the labor power offered by the worker for the sale to the capitalist whose value has to be determined within his overall argument about the production not only of this "necessary" value but also of the "surplus value" that is the secret source of capitalist wealth (Marx 1976: 270–280). In determining the value of the labor power the worker sells and capitalist buys, Marx specifies this as the "labor time necessary for the production, and consequently also the reproduction" (1976: 274) of human labor power and of the human who sells it as a commodity. But that then led Marx into a list of the kinds of commodities the laborer requires to produce and reproduce his labor power, whose value in terms of the labor power required for their production must be calculated: the "means of subsistence" necessary for his "maintenance . . . in his normal state as a working individual. His natural needs, such as food, clothing, fuel and housing" (which are historically specific and culturally specified) (Marx 1976: 274–275).

But not only these commodities—because the worker is mortal and must be replaced, the list goes on: "Hence the sum of means of subsistence necessary for the production of labor-power must include the means necessary for the worker's replacement, i.e., his children" (Marx 1976: 275). But there is more, given the quality, as distinct from the quantity, of the labor power sold by the worker, which must be replaced by that of his children: "In order to modify the general nature of the human organism in such a way that it acquires skill and dexterity in a given branch of industry, and becomes labor power of a developed and specific kind, a special education or training is needed, and this in turn costs an equivalent in commodities of a greater or lesser amount" (Marx 1976: 275–276). Not only the kinds but also the quantity of such commodities in this list can be summed up, their exchange value determined by calculating the value of labor power that went into their production, and a total amount of value arrived at for the reproduction of the laborer.

Socialist and progressive feminists (Folbre 2001; Gibson-Graham 1996) have critiqued the logical shortcoming arising from the patriarchal bias in Marx's argument: that "food, clothing, fuel and housing" needed for the laborer himself, the multiple of such items needed not only for the laborer per se but also for "his" spouse and children, and the "special education" the latter require, all demand and receive the everyday expenditure of large and indefinite amounts of *non-commodified caring labor* which these items require to be put to use, most of it expended by women—in preparing food, gathering fuel, making and mending clothes as well as buying them, maintaining the housing the worker rents, and tending, feeding, socializing, and educating "his" labor-power replacements so that grown children come to possess "labor-power of a developed and specific kind." But of course that is not all, for women expend other kinds of non-commoditized caring labor for the laborer himself, to defer that time when "the labor-power [is] withdrawn from the market by wear and tear, and by death" (Marx 1976: 275)—by not only ensuring the day-to-day nurturing of men who are workers, but also looking after them when that time arrives when they are injured or made ill by the labor process, or simply too old to work. Working-class women of Marx's time, moreover, were themselves working as "the laborers" whose self-care they also were called on to perform in the ways listed. This, if you will, is the hidden abode (in plain sight) of unremunerated reproductive labor which underwrites capitalism's "hidden abode of production" (Marx 1976: 279–280).

It is an irony that it is only when such kinds of caring labor have become commodified as waged domestic labor that they are then included within Marx's inventory of "commodities" whose value in terms of labor power must be determined in order to ascertain the necessary value of the labor power expended by the worker. While the value of the caring labor expended on those belonging to the working classes remains non-commoditized when applied to the reproduction of their own families and households, in some settings (e.g., Hong Kong, Singapore, the Gulf States, and North America), caring household labor has become increasingly commoditized as waged domestic labor power where women who are capitalists, professionals, and owners of petty property purchase it to substitute for their own caring labor in their households. But women employed as domestic workers, whether within their countries of birth and permanent residence (abode) or in other countries, thereby withdraw their caring labors from their own children, and from their own households of birth or marriage (see Barber and Bryan, this volume).[3] Remittances from overseas, when they are possible, are only partial compensation for this loss: no direct equivalence can be made between the value of caring labor lost within domestic units and that gained by remittances these households receive. One could therefore plot, in a world-systems way, complementary surpluses and deficits of caring labor in the world economy: e.g., so much caring labor added to the United States, so much subtracted from Mexico or the Philippines.

It is crucial to include as forms of caring labor devoted to social reproduction the labor expended on the education and training of those who labor, as well as of those who participate in the capitalist economy as members of other classes. Such caring labor represents the work that animates what Althusser (1971) called the "ideological state apparatuses," but his conception of such labor as no more (and no less) than that which reproduces capitalism as a system was simplistic. Some educational and training labor may be commoditized in the form of salaries and wages to caregivers, teachers, trainers, and university faculty members, among others, but the rest of it which is not commoditized cannot be so simply calculated, but arises from "family" and "society." This could take the form of a peer showing a youth how to "have a laff" to make the working (or school) day pass more quickly (Willis 1981) or hands-on instruction by a friend or relative in a mechanical craft that has market value (Crawford 2009), or in some other form.

This brings up a broader issue. The foregoing analysis of caring could and should also be applied to those who belong to other classes: caring labor as well as the commodities it deploys are necessary to the social reproduction of not only laborers, but also to that of owners of petty productive property, professionals, and capitalists themselves, among other classes in contemporary capitalism. Marx points out that the "necessary requirements" for the reproduction of the worker are historically (and therefore culturally) specific, being dependent on "the level of civilization attained by a country" and thus "the conditions in which, and consequently on the habits and expectations with which, the class of free workers has been formed" (Marx 1976: 275). A similar consideration should be applied to the members of other classes, both dominated like laborers (e.g., farmer smallholders, lumpenproletarians) and dominating (e.g., professionals, owners of petty productive property, capitalist managers, and owners of productive property).

There appear to be several reasons why Marx paid this issue so little attention. Marx assumed that the wealth expended on consumption was always sufficient "on average" for the social reproduction needs of the working class, in short that its wages received were sufficient in quantity to pay the costs of their social reproduction. He noted that other classes than capitalists and laborers existed but, because of increasing class polarization and the falling of the great majority of humanity into the proletariat, failed to analyze either the fundamental roles of these classes in the capitalist economy or in meeting social reproductive needs (see Nicolaus 1967); and as mentioned above, Marx neglected the role of caring labor in social reproduction.

Nonetheless, Marx pointed to the existence of certain transhistorical human needs that had to be satisfied by use-values in any class formation (Marx 1976), and it is certainly the case that the social reproductive needs of all classes of capitalist society require both the provision of certain use-values and the expenditure of caring non-commoditized labor. Are we simply to assume that this issue is irrelevant to all other classes except the working class either because they, e.g., capitalists, live under the sign of material plenty where *anything* can be bought—and what measure of reproductive sufficiency is that?[4]—or because neither they, e.g., owners of petty productive property, professionals, lumpenproletarians, and farmers, nor their social reproduction, are on the Marxian view ultimately relevant to the history of capitalism and its supersession?

As noted above, various forms of caring labor associated with social reproduction—child care, domestic labor, socialization, schooling, training, care of the elderly, etc.—are tied to nation-state citizenship regimes, because who has access to government-provided care services and civil society resources in a specific country is a matter of stratified eligibility along the lines of nationality, ethnoracial, and gender identities. When it comes to decisions about where people can best—or even at all—obtain such caring labor to meet their social reproduction needs, not all nation-states are the same for all people.

Therefore, as the case studies that follow demonstrate, transnational movements by capitalists, owners of petty productive property, and professionals, as well as by labor migrants among Chinese in Southeast Asia, were part of strategies that were based on decisions about transnational moves that not only considered opportunities in the labor and other markets across the Asia Pacific region in which informants sought to participate, but also took into account their social reproductive needs and the caring labor, in the most expanded sense, that met such needs.

If the examples that follow illustrate a more general situation, it is that transnational subjects have had to reconcile or mediate the contradictions/tensions between where they might seek to participate in labor or other markets in specific Asia Pacific spaces, and where in these spaces they believe their reproductive needs could best be met. In the case of the Chinese of Malaysia and Indonesia who have been my informants, much of this reconciliation/mediation has to do with family and household. Among my urban male Chinese Malaysian informants regardless of their class status, discourses of familism, of effort, and sacrifice expended "for my family" or "for my children" predominated in discussing decisions about transnational moves. As Cohen (1970) long ago pointed out, the "Chinese family," *jia*, has historically taken a variety of forms across space and time, and the deployment of these different kinds of family organization (e.g., concentrated or dispersed), I would argue, is crucial to the various strategies through which those of different classes primarily seek to reconcile this contradiction.

CHANGING CORES OF CAPITAL ACCUMULATION IN THE GLOBAL SYSTEM 1970–2010

The current financial catastrophe in the US and Europe has come about due to the end of a three-decades-long period of hypertrophy of financial capital and of proliferation of speculation centered in these two regions of the world capitalist system. There is wide agreement that such a pattern of financialization and speculation came out of the crisis of falling industrial capitalist profitability in the early 1970s, although the causes of this crisis and its effects are in dispute (Arrighi 2007; Brenner 2006).

As a result, the profitability crisis of the early 1970s led to the emergence of a new regime of "flexible accumulation" involving new forms of hyper-exploitation of labor forces in the US, Europe, and Japan (Harvey 1989). There has also been the creation of new circuits of movement of financial capital into speculative and rentier ventures in the older centers of accumulation, North America and Europe and Japan—a process of intensification in the appropriation of surplus value through financial means, especially debt creation leveraged by asset inflation (Foster and Magdoff 2009; Itoh 2005). Through electronic global capital flows, speculation and financialization has extended from the US to Europe, and—most relevant to this chapter—to Australia and New Zealand (but not, notably, Canada), as has the subsequent "contagion" from panic over asset devaluation since 2007.

In global terms, the shrunken standing of the US as a leader of the coalition of Western and Asian capitalist states, its disastrous record of military adventures, its failing domestic finances, its massive debt held by foreign governments, and its declining seigniorage through the US dollar as a reserve currency have begun to converge in a global withdrawal of "confidence" from the US state as the hegemon of the world capitalist order (Arrighi 2007: 149–172). In a complementary move, during the same period from the 1980s to 2000s, capitalist accumulation due to industrialization and the realization of surplus value in the labor process has expanded rapidly in the regional centers of accumulation in East Asia, notably China, beginning with its liberalization after the death of Mao in 1978, and in Southeast Asia and South Asia. As will be illustrated below by my first case study, overseas Chinese in Southeast Asia have come to play major roles as capitalist brokers and innovators in the coordination of subcontracting in the production supply chains active in a currently flourishing *intraregional* trade between China and Southeast Asia (Arrighi 2007: 348–350).

While the foregoing summary of shifts within the global political economy is familiar to many readers, what may be less well known are the ways in which ethnic Chinese Southeast capitalists, professionals, laborers, students, et al. have played a role in these shifts by connecting different regions of the world economy through circuits of production, exchange, and consumption; by shifting capital from productive to financial–speculative forms across regions; and by migrating transnationally to sell their labor power under what prove to be hyperexploitative conditions. What will be even less known are the tensions and difficulties Chinese Southeast Asians face in reconciling their strategies of accumulation with the culturally defined imperatives for their social and class reproduction.

TRANSNATIONAL MOVEMENT OF CAPITALISTS AND OF CAPITAL ACROSS THE EMERGENT REGIONS OF CAPITAL ACCUMULATION IN ASIA: FROM MALAYSIA TO CHINA AND BACK, AND ON TO AUSTRALIA?

Capitalists in Southeast Asia over the last decade have invested in industrial operations in China, which is followed on previous instances of capital investment from Hong Kong and Taiwan in China that began in the 1980s (Smart and Smart 1999; Hsing 1997). What I wish to do here is to connect this process to the actual movement of capitalists from Southeast Asia to and from China. In this connection, has anyone noticed that one doesn't call such routine commuting "migration"? This suggests strongly that the very idea of migration is already a classed concept, although, as I suggest below, it is raced as well. So let me briefly discuss one example of a capitalist in motion from my fieldwork of 2007 in Bukit Mertajam, in the state of Penang, Malaysia.

Jason Tan was one of the most wealthy young business men among the Chinese in Bukit Mertajam; he was then only in his early thirties, and the son of a prominent local merchant. Jason was the proprietor of a clothing

Theorizing Transnational Movement in the Current Conjuncture   73

wholesale enterprise that sold apparel manufactured in China to supermarket chains throughout Malaysia. He was thus an importer, but beyond being in commerce had moved into the production side of the inter-Asian supply chain that designs, commissions, and manufactures apparel. Jason solicited orders for specific lines of apparel from supermarket managers in Malaysia, and then commissioned the orders based on these designs with factories in China. These factories manufactured these garments to-order on a just-in-time basis. He then imported these garments, brought them through Bukit Mertajam, and distributed them to supermarkets throughout Malaysia. He said the total time elapsed between the placement of an order by supermarket manager and its delivery is about one month.

Jason often commuted to China, at least once per month, where he visited the factories with whose managements he had a relationship, in order to oversee the quality of their production. Currently (2007), however, he said he was dissatisfied because the cost of production was still too high in the areas of China he had access to. One day, I asked him about his travels to China. He began by saying:

JT: It is really difficult to make money in Malaysia as a Chinese businessman. What I really hope to do is to invest in a factory in China.

DMN: Where would you invest—would it be around Guangzhou for example?

JT: No, I am planning on investing in a factory in Anhui province . . . in the city of Hefei.

DMN: Why are you going to invest in such an out-of-the-way place?

JT: The labor costs are so much lower in an internal province like Anhui compared to Guangzhou or nearby, as in Shenzhen. In Shenzhen, the wages for factory labor could be as high as 200 Malaysian ringgit per month [about US$100], whereas in Hefei wages were as low as 50 to 70 ringgit per month. Besides, in Anhui they are eager for investors to come in.

Jason's residence where he, his wife and their two young children lived, and the headquarters of his enterprise were in Malaysia. But note that he identifies himself as a "Chinese businessman." His fluency in Mandarin Chinese, and competence in deploying a discourse of *guanxi* personalism and other ascribed items of "Chinese culture" (cuisine, Buddhist/Daoist beliefs, etc.) are elements in a shared habitus he mastered with his counterparts in China, which smoothed the way for his capital accumulation strategy. For example, he shared with his China partners in China an interest in drinking the famous Pu-er brand of tea from Yunnan, and in collecting and speculating in "disks," *pian*, of the tea on the international market.[5] The preparation, brewing, and drinking of Pu-er revolves around a distinctive aesthetic shared transnationally between Southeast Asian Chinese merchants and their counterparts in China which Jason put on display for me when I interviewed him in his business office.

Despite his aspiration to open a factory to manufacture apparel in inland China, his long-term plans were quite different. Stating that Malaysian government officials and agencies mistreat Chinese, and that the government is "incompetent," he told me he sought to make his fortune in manufacturing in China, but then to retire to Australia, and once he has moved there to engage in day-trading in stocks as a way of making his income. "First my children will go to Australia for education, and later I will join them." Jason's envisioned geographic, economic, and social mobility—from Malaysia where he was born, raised, and schooled, to China, first to visit and later to open a factory there, and then, fortune made, to go to Australia and not to return to Malaysia—recapitulates a common strategy among Malaysian Chinese business families, who have sent their grown children overseas for university schooling over the last thirty years.

From the inception of the New Economic Policy in the early 1970s onward, the discrimination against ethnic Chinese students by entry quotas into the government universities set by the Malaysian government has been a universally acknowledged "social fact" among Chinese in Malaysia. These quotas have been set for each of the major recognized ethnic groups in Malaysia by a government that systematically favors the entry by Malays into universities over members of other ethnic groups, as a consequence of the control of the government by the United Malays National Organization (UMNO) since Independence in 1957. UMNO leaders have regarded such discrimination as one foundation for the uplift of Malays out of poverty, and as justified by "Malay supremacy," *ketuanan Melayu*, established in the Malaysian Constitution. In a strong and hostile reaction, over the last three decades, thousands of Chinese Malaysian families have sent their grown children to universities in Australia, New Zealand, Canada, the US, the UK, and other countries for formal degrees and certification (Munro-Kua 1996). Like most other Chinese business men, Jason plans to do the same, and has constructed a mobility strategy around this decision which has fundamentally to do with reproduction, for his children, of his privileged class position. The caring labor of education in the class reproductive process shapes his strategies for his family and children. Let me now turn to the history of this pattern of transnational social reproduction, within which Jason Tan's movement—actual and envisioned—can be situated.

TRANSNATIONAL MOVEMENT OF SMALL-SCALE CAPITALISTS: AVOIDING THE PETTY ACCUMULATION TRAP

Despite both the contrasted affirmative romance of an adoring Western business press about the "empires" of "Chinese tycoons" which have entered the lists of the "World's Billionaires" (Kroll and Fass 2009), the actual transnational movement by most Chinese who engage in it is far more mundane and contingent. The vast majority of Chinese Malaysians who move transnationally are small-scale capitalists, professionals, students, and their family members. Transnational movement for them is by no means easy or straightforward, nor is it undertaken lightly; it has a high co-efficient of friction. For instance, petty capitalist families have fixed investments in their business inventories, facilities, real estate, customers, suppliers, and credit, the latter often acquired over long periods of steady repayment of funds or goods lent. Liquidating these assets so that capital can be relocated elsewhere is by no means an easy matter, yet once underway is not easily reversible.

Small-scale capital-owning Chinese families in Malaysia with fortunes accumulated through self-exploitation and the exploitation of unpaid family members and of a few non-familial employees, face a petty accumulation trap (Nonini 2003) which bears directly on their capacity to reproduce their own class positions, but which, paradoxically, also impels them to overcome the frictions just mentioned that impede their moving transnationally. Small-business family fortunes would be quickly dissipated through the *practice* of equipartible inheritance of business assets, yet equipartible inheritance is strongly *normative* among Chinese Malaysians. It is unlikely that the owner of a small-business enterprise will be able to pass down a viable share of it to more than one child, if by "viable" is meant capital sufficient to reproduce the entry or continuity requirements for a petty capitalist enterprise. The dominant norm is that in such a situation, the eldest son will inherit all or most of the family enterprise, with minority shares being passed to other children. But this leaves the latter little. What then to do about—and for—a couple's other children? The proprietor—almost always a man, except in the case of an exceptional, still vigorous widow—has obligations to seek the social or class reproduction of his sons and daughters.

As part of being "modern," Chinese Malaysian parents who own and operate a small business interpret such an obligation toward their children in terms of two requirements—first, to either provide a son with a viable share in the family business, or to provide him with a university education which is a pre-requisite to becoming a professional, hirable by a corporation—e.g., computer engineer, accountant, or physician; and second, to follow the norm of "not favoring the male over the female" (*buzhong nan qingnu*), by providing their daughters with similar university educations but not (be it noted, despite the invocation of the "modern") providing the latter with a viable share of the family enterprise, unless there are no sons. Subsidizing the university educations of grown daughters and sons, that is, converting some of the economic capital of the owning parents into the educational or cultural capital of grown children (Bourdieu 1986), is the means by which this petty accumulation trap is avoided.

However, facing this petty accumulation trap, Chinese business couples have found their children being discriminated against by state policies that limit the entry of their children into Malaysian universities on ethnic grounds. Moreover, their post-colonial sense of being "modern" has led them to identify sources of modern professionalization with the English language, the supposed global language, and with international norms of professionalization associated with the West. This has encouraged them to send their grown children overseas to Australia, Canada, the US, New Zealand, Great Britain, and even India, for university education. (One variant is to send grown children who have been primarily Mandarin-educated to Taiwan for university study, degrees, and certification.)

As I have pointed out elsewhere (Nonini 1997), petty capital-owning families engaged in a process of traversal in which their grown children established residency as qualified professionals in these Anglophone settings. This often was the prelude to the liquidation after the retirement of the older male owner of the couple's fixed capital in Malaysia and its export to the Anglophone country, accompanied by the movement of the older couple to live with their grown children overseas. This is precisely what, for example, Jason Tan anticipated doing many years hence, and I interviewed informants who had done precisely this, when they were visiting Malaysia. However, it is also possible that the older couple—particularly if the older man is still surviving and is vigorous—will remain after his retirement in Malaysia, living with the eldest son who has inherited the family business. In neither case was a successful traversal assured, of course: a grown child might fail at university in New Zealand, might find herself without the requisite cultural skills in the country's labor market, or suffer from low job demand during a recession there; it might prove difficult for an elder couple to liquidate all their assets in Malaysia to shift them overseas in liquid form.

For instance, in 2007, when I visited him in Bukit Mertajam, Mr. Toh was in his seventies, and said he had retired from his truck transport business, which I had interviewed him about in the early 1980s. He said he had given over the operation of the business to his eldest son. This man had gone to Taiwan for his university education, married a Taiwanese woman, and had come back to Malaysia to take over operations from his father some ten years previously. Mr. Toh, however, had three other sons. All three he had sent, he said, to Australia for university degrees—one in Sydney and two in Melbourne—at a cost of $500,000 Malaysian ringgit (US$100,000–$200,000) because "this was fundamental." He told me that two adult middle sons, having graduated from Australian universities, now live in Australia, where one is a computer engineer, and the other in some other profession, and are employed by corporations there. The youngest son, just graduated in information science from the Royal Melbourne Institute of Technology, had been called back by his father to assist the eldest son in the transport business. I met the youngest son, who said to me that he was unhappy to be back in Malaysia, and wanted to return to Australia to enroll in post-graduate study. Mr. Toh said that he has visited his sons in Australia several times: "Australia is a nice place to live. The streets are very clean and broad, and this is really desirable." Still, he found some of the customs there strange ("People are allowed to sleep in doorways there"), and he noted that his youngest son had suffered a racially motivated assault by white Australians which he had fought off.

TRANSNATIONAL MOVEMENT AS SPECULATIVE PRACTICE AND THE EXIGENCIES OF SOCIAL REPRODUCTION: CHINESE INDONESIANS, 2000–2003

I indicated above that migration is a classed concept. But also, at times, transnational movement by elites is far from routine—as when they exit from or flee conditions of political repression, economic instability, and social persecution—which suggests that migration is also a raced concept as well (see Ley 2010; Mitchell 1997). Such migration in the case I now discuss is organically and simultaneously connected to the challenges of social reproduction and to the new speculative economies of the Asia Pacific region.

The new inter-Asian ties of capital investment in industrial production, and the appropriation of inter-Asian surplus value, allow for a form of transnational movement that connects wealthy property owners, technocrats, factory managers, and other business professionals who are employed in the new centers of accumulation in East and Southeast Asia to the older centers of accumulation, particularly those in the Asia Pacific—Australia, New Zealand, the western United States, and Western Canada. This was the situation for the extremely wealthy Chinese Indonesian business families I studied in Australia in 2000 and again in 2003.

In their situation, what connected the new centers of accumulation to the older ones were flows of capital from sources in Asia generating the accumulation of surplus value—the new industrial centers like those of China noted above—into speculative ventures in the older centers of accumulation. That is, despite neoliberal immigration incentives that call on foreign investors to do so, why would any Asian entrepreneur seek to invest capital in *factories* in Canada, Australia, the western United States, or New Zealand, where the costs of labor were so much higher than in China; where environmental regulations against industrial pollution were not only present but enforced; and labor activism not completely quelled by state power? As a global process, the accumulation of capital through the appropriation of surplus value now occurs predominately in the rising East Asian centers of accumulation. Nonetheless, if one engaged in short-term speculation in real estate, there was still much money to be made—or at least there was until the collapse of the real estate bubble in late 2007. Similar speculative potential for repeating profits through the deployment of financial capital has existed in Australia and New Zealand on the western and southern edges of the Pacific Rim.

Why, however, did Chinese Indonesian business men speculate in *these specific* economies? Why not speculate in real estate in Korea, Japan, or for that matter, in Russia? One cannot understand transnational movement unless one takes into account the exigencies and demands of the social reproduction of class. How, that is, do the members of this class reproduce not only their capacities for capital accumulation, but also their lifestyles, their civil privileges, and prospects for further upward mobility?

The Chinese Indonesian entrepreneurs I interviewed in Sydney, Melbourne, and Perth, Australia had left Indonesia with part of their fortunes in the wake of the anti-Chinese riots in Jakarta that accompanied the fall of the Suharto New Order regime in mid-1998, and were much wealthier than my Chinese Malaysian informants. Yet these men soon sought to restart their own capital accumulation by maintaining their capital investments and resuming their executive and managerial positions in Indonesian industrial enterprises. At the same time, they sought to take advantage of the new speculative opportunities of the late 1990s–early 2000s to invest their capital in real estate "development" and speculation in the Anglophone edge nation-states of the Pacific Rim, i.e., in the older, declining centers of capitalist accumulation (Nonini 2004).

These Chinese Indonesian executives and technocrats were wealthy jet-setting commuters who positioned their wives and children in Australia, where the latter lived out their lives as Australian permanent residents and citizens, as housewives, school pupils, university students, and real estate brokers. They were thus similar to the so-called Cantonese "astronauts" whose industrial operations were in southern China, while their family members lived in, say, Vancouver (Ong 1993). The latter rode the "transpacific shuttle" that took them on a weekly basis back and forth between the western North America and China—often allowing them also to take mistresses and establish second families in China, while their wives and children from the first marriage remained in Canada, Australia, or wherever. Similarly, Chinese Indonesian business men commuted on the "Jakarta Express" between the residences of their family members in the affluent suburbs of Sydney, Melbourne, and Perth and their factories in Indonesia where they stayed for several weeks before returning for quick visits to families in Australia for a week or two (Nonini 2004). They did not face the poignant petty capital accumulation trap of less well-off Malaysian petty capitalists, but instead saw Australia, or Canada, as refuges from political instability, or from anti-Chinese violence in Southeast Asia, as countries to raise and school their children.

Their lives and careers were predicated on habitual absenteeism from their families in Australia. Their younger children they left primarily in the care of their wives for years, as these children sought to adjust to the vagaries of Australian public school and university education. Men whose first priorities were their duties and perquisites as high-level executives in firms in Jakarta provided little caring labor to their children or their wives in the suburbs of Sydney, Melbourne, or Perth. But at least some showed a keen awareness of the problem of who cared for whom, although their solution was specifically upper-class Indonesian. This came out in a focus interview I conducted in 2000 with three wealthy older men in Perth, when one major complaint they had about the Australian immigration regime was that it did not allow their family servants to accompany their wives from Jakarta! As one of them put it, "Why is Australia so different from Hong Kong or Singapore, where can bring in the servants from Indonesia to help the wives? Why not in Australia? If the wives and children are taken care of in this way, the husbands will feel much better. So the wife won't have to suffer so much." And the wives did have much suffering to undergo, as did their children. It is perhaps unsurprising that other Indonesian expatriates in Australia spoke of the wives of these men as "bored housewives," and as their grown children in Australian universities as "spoiled" and frequently suffering from compulsive gambling, sexual predation, alcoholism, and depression.

For both transnational Malaysian and Indonesian business families, despite the class differences between the two populations, the social reproduction of class represented a central challenge posed by the conditions of state formation and citizenship which have arisen in the course of the rise and consolidation of the new Asian centers of capital accumulation, and of the decline of older centers characterized by the dominance of speculative over productive capital within systems of neoliberal governance. Neoliberal citizenship policies in the declining centers of the West allowed these groups to engage in a national repositioning—as "new citizens" in the former case, as those who have the privilege to engage in citizenship arbitrage in the latter case (see Ong 1999).

LABOR MIGRATION TO THE OLDER CENTERS OF ACCUMULATION: MALAYSIA 1997–2007

As has been noted, declining rates of accumulation in the older centers of capital accumulation have led to new forms of hyperexploitation involving increased extraction of both absolute and relative surplus value in these older centers. Central to such a process of exploitation in the older centers has been the creation of new immigrant proletariats whose precarious legal and economic positions allow them to be kept in a vulnerable position within the labor process, and to supplant the previous domestic proletariat as the labor force of choice for exploitation. Nonetheless, this process since the 1970s has itself been progressively destabilizing, as a new proletarian immigrant labor force, with lower labor costs, greater pliability, and more culturally suited than the current one, displaces the latter, only itself over time to be displaced in turn. Here we come into "labor migration" in its true form.

Malaysian men and women migrated in large numbers from the 1980s through the early 1990s to work as transnational laborers in what were then the rapidly maturing industrial economies of Japan and Taiwan. In 1992, Malaysians (the vast majority of whom were ethnic Chinese) formed the largest contingent of illegal foreign workers in Japan—an estimated fourteen thousand in 1993 (Shimada 1994), although the estimate of forty-two thousand in 1992 was given by a Malaysian government official I spoke with. There were an estimated four to six thousand Malaysians working illegally in Taiwan, the number varying from year to year (Choi 1992; Li and Wang 1992). From the early 1990s onward, as Japan fell into its long (and still ongoing) "lost decade" due to the deflation of real estate and other assets and economic stagnation arising from deindustrialization, it became progressively more difficult for working-class Chinese Malaysians to attain the visitor's visas that allowed them to "overstay" and work illegally in Japan; during the same period, Malaysian workers became excluded from Taiwan's markets for foreign labor after the Taiwanese government legalized temporary employment of foreign workers and the Taiwanese labor brokers came to prefer cheaper Indonesian, Thai, Philippine, and Vietnamese laborers over Malaysians (Tierney 2008). Although informants have reported that Chinese Malaysians have migrated transnationally to work in Europe, the UK, and Gulf states, they appear to be few in number. If Malaysia's post-colonial export of Chinese labor is now largely over, it is worth an assessment of this episode in terms of the themes of this chapter.

From the 1980s through the early 1990s, Chinese Malaysians workers traveled to Japan as presumptive tourists on visitors' visas, then "overstayed" their visas to remain illegally in Japan and labor for wages on informal urban and rural markets there. The trade in labor power was organized transnationally through Chinese Malaysian brokers working on behalf of specific Japanese employers or crew bosses. Overstayers found work either through the brokers (either long-term work or more commonly "day labor"), through relatives (e.g., a brother or father) already in Japan, or through employers directly if they had previously worked for them in Japan. Some, especially women, worked in restaurants in Tokyo and other cities; other women worked in factories, while a very few were prostitutes. Most men were employed in construction, especially in "3-D" (Dirty, Dangerous, and Difficult) labor at the bottom of the segmented labor market in urban construction. This work was indeed dangerous, and informants told me they personally experienced or witnessed falls from high places, the collapse on workers of concrete structures, and other serious accidents.

My interviews in Malaysia with "airplane jumpers," *tiaofeijiren*—Chinese Malaysian men who had migrated to Japan to work as overstayers in the 1980s to early 1990s—point to a gendered imaginary which my informants shared (Nonini 1997). Most airplane jumpers were single, and in their twenties and thirties. They told me that they hoped to work in Japan for two to four years, earn high wages based on Japanese living standards, remit part of their earnings back to their families in Malaysia while they worked in Japan, and finally return to Malaysia with a small fortune in earnings saved, sufficient to buy a house and start a small business. Airplane jumpers also confided, however, that they had been interested in the adventure of going to visit Japan, to "look around" on their own, to "have a good time" and make friends with other airplane jumpers. There was thus an adventurous, even picaresque air to their ambitions.

So, at least, this was the ideal. However, my informants mentioned many ways in which their experiences fell short of the ideal. In addition to construction accidents, Malaysian workers suffered from poor nutrition; this took the form where many men tried to save on food costs by purchasing "instant mee" noodles that, they claimed, were laced with preservatives which, consumed in quantity as many did, were toxic to the liver. I was later told by one airplane jumper in 1997 that another man whom I interviewed in 1991 about his experience in Japan had subsequently returned to Japan, fell ill there with liver disease, and returned to Malaysia only to die there a few months later. A risk of a different kind for an airplane jumper was to fall into compulsive gambling, particularly in pachinko parlors that catered to poor working-class men, where most of a man's earnings could easily be lost, and he would be unable to remit money to his family or save it for his return. And every airplane jumper, I was told, might face extended periods of unemployment, with attendant misery; one who could not find work for three months spent all day sleeping or watching videos in his dormitory, and became severely depressed. What was not a risk, in contrast, were airplane jumpers' contacts with Japanese government officials; several said while in Japan they found local police to be friendly and courteous, even though it would have been obvious to the latter that they were foreigners; and they rarely, if ever, came into contact with officials from the Immigration Department, and raids were uncommon.

Central to the gendered imaginary of airplane jumpers was their dependence on the caring labor of the women they were related to in Malaysia: their mothers, sisters, and—for the married minority of men—their wives. These women looked after the children of the married men, and kept up with the news of family and relatives to be relayed during the telephone calls home that men made every week or every other. Mothers received the money remitted home by unmarried sons, who in this way showed their filial compliance, *xiao*, toward their parents; wives collected the money of married men for their and their children's support—so at least was the ideal, when airplane jumpers did send money.

It is now possible to ask: what did social reproduction mean for a Chinese Malaysian man who had left Malaysia to work as an airplane jumper in Japan in the 1980s to 1990s and indeed, why would he do so, to begin with, when Malaysia during this period had one of the most rapidly industrializing economies in the world? Like other Chinese Malaysians, workers experienced discrimination imposed by a national government that implemented long-term indigenist policies systematically disadvantaging Chinese not only in applying for university entry, but also in seeking government civil service, armed forces and police employment, and for jobs with large private corporations, which were either government owned or controlled, and were required to implement employment quotas that favored Malays over non-Malays. Chinese laborers, school leavers by Standard 3, were educationally unqualified for many of these jobs in any case; but even if they had not been, there were the ethnic quotas that severely restricted Chinese entry. Formal policies were reinforced on the interpersonal level by imperious or hostile officials and managers who referred to Chinese laborers as *kasar,* "unrefined," as "people of no position," *orang yang tiada pangkat,* or, more vulgarly but not uncommonly, by the epithet, *babi,* "pig." The message of these large-scale administrative and corporate employers to Chinese laborers was *Sulit!*—"we're closed," or more colloquially, "get lost." Laboring men could apply to work in the industrial estates and export processing zones as factory operatives at poor pay and under onerous industrial discipline, and a few did so and were hired.

Most Chinese laboring men turned to the local Chinese-owned petty capitalist sector. Here some sought out skilled work for small employers as truck and bus drivers, stone masons, mechanics, machinists, and similar trades. A few moved into illicit activities like becoming a lottery number runner or working for a "boss" in some illegal hustle or smuggling operation. These occupational possibilities required personal intercession by a kinsman or relative, neighbor or friend who would put in a good word with a potential employer, and offer help in learning the actual skill or trade required by the work: how to drive a truck between Bukit Mertajam and Kuala Lumpur, craft a cemetery stone, machine an auto part, learn the skills required to work for the illegal lottery boss, etc.

But a large number of men—even many of those who found skilled work—aspired to upward class mobility by engaging in what was called in its most abstract and ambiguous form *zuo shengyi,* or "doing business." Covering a vast array of petty commercial possibilities depending on where one already was positioned in the class system, for most laborers this meant something quite specific—opening a small hawker's or vendor's stall to sell quick snack food, small lots of produce, apparel, etc. Here, the imaginary went, one might really come to prosper, pick up a business secret, accumulate a small fortune, and with extraordinary hard work and the help of the Buddhist/Daoist gods, move one's family and oneself up into the class of petty property owners. One might become a person of "position," or *pangkat;* give one's children the opportunity to get extra tutoring to pass the "school leavers" exam at Standard 6; thus go on to secondary school, and attempt high marks on the national examinations; and perhaps move on to a glorious future.

What was needed to start doing business, however, was a stake of capital. The personal accumulation of such capital, given the racial barriers to entry set by the state, was almost completely impossible on the Malaysian national labor market. Going out made sense; for many young men with no other option, it became imperative. It was here that the gendered imaginary of the male airplane jumper idealized the rapid accumulation of a small fortune by working in Japan for high wages in 3-D work or similar work that one might save and bring back to Malaysia to start "doing business," and by so doing, improve one's class position. As in the case of Chinese Malaysians with wealth, the concept of "social reproduction" for laboring men needs to be reconceived as a historical construct that does a specific kind of conceptual work to reflect the messy realities of class-based claims, identities, and ambiguities about how people situate themselves within, and are situated by, the capitalist order. As Chinese laboring men have sought out their options domestically and internationally, the sources of the reproductive and caring labor that makes their productive labors possible and that connects them to the general process of the reproduction of capitalism remain fixedly rooted in their relationships of family, neighborhood, and workplace within Malaysian space, and I thus conclude with a short discussion of their "being stuck" (Gooding-Williams 1993).

1997–2007 Epilogue

Since the early 1990s, as noted above, Chinese transnational labor migration to Japan and Taiwan has ceased due to political and administrative restrictions in these countries. Moreover, these restrictions were themselves signs of a process of ongoing displacement of one nationalized migrant proletariat by another within the hyperexploitative sectors of the capitalist economies of the Asia Pacific.

Of greatest relevance to Chinese laborers in Malaysia, from the early 1990s onward, a tiered division of labor of racialized (and nationalized) migrant proletariats has emerged within the Asia Pacific. In Malaysia, since the late 1980s, Indonesian migrant workers, which even earlier played a major role in Malaysia's rural plantation sector, have moved in even greater numbers into urban housing construction, and, more recently, into full-time factory work in the country's industrial estates and export processing zones, thus displacing the more costly and rights-bearing Malay industrial proletariat; over the same period, Indonesian and more recently Philippine women have moved into domestic work and into general laboring jobs in the Chinese petty capitalist sector. Indonesian migrants, in turn, have been pressed by Pakistani and Afghani migrant laborers, who have moved into the onerous labor of road and public-works construction.

The result, of course, has been to put further downward pressure on the wages and on the working conditions of Malaysian workers of all ethnic groups, thereby disciplining all Malaysian working-class citizens, including Chinese. How have Chinese workers responded? The successful export-oriented industrialization of the last thirty years has increased the wealth of the property-owning bourgeoisie, both Chinese and non-Chinese, many times over from the 1970s, and rising living and consumption standards have been in evidence over the last two decades. Yet the political denial of rights of access to employment and education by Chinese Malaysians and most of the discriminatory policies against Chinese of Malaysia's New Economic Policy from the early 1980s on behalf of Malays remain in place.

The social reproduction of the Chinese workers I knew two decades previously therefore places them between a multitude of rocks and hard places. Men I knew then who labored long hours under trying physical conditions are now in their fifties, sixties, and even seventies but continue to work if they are physically able, because they have no choice. Pensions and Employee Provident Fund retirement payments from the government are exiguous. Some of my informants who were vigorous and active men as airplane jumpers, and truck drivers and stone masons in the 1980s and early 1990s when I first interviewed them are now ill or dying from diseases and injuries caused by their working conditions. The caring labors of kin women for Chinese laborers have become no easier over the last two decades. An occasional worker with kidney or heart disease becomes featured in the local media as the publicized poster-person to promote a charity drive to build a kidney dialysis center or new wing of a hospital for heart patients organized by the richest merchants in Bukit Mertajam in acts of kindly condescension. If the grown sons and daughters of these men can now "get by" economically as small vendors or hawkers, or as skilled laborers employed by local Chinese petty capitalists, these men count their children fortunate. An occasional Chinese laborer gets caught trafficking in narcotics, and is hung by the government. Life goes on.

Working Chinese Malaysians are in the condition of "being stuck": where one finds oneself in the shadow of ordinary, everyday, and largely inescapable structural violence perpetrated by state and capitalist class forces, and saturating one's life. As Gooding-Williams (1993: 3) puts it, "Being stuck ... is a matter of being inexorably caught up in a network of political, economic, and cultural legacies that escape the aura of the extraordinary."

NOTES

1. A preliminary version of this chapter was prepared for the panel, "Political Economy and Migration II," organized by Winnie Lem and Pauline Gardiner Barber, CASCA/AES Joint Annual Meeting, May 13–16, 2009, Vancouver, Canada. The research for this chapter was funded by the National Science Foundation, and the Carolina Asia Center of the University of North Carolina, Chapel Hill. I want to thank Winnie Lem, Pauline Gardner Barber, and two anonymous reviewers for their comments and suggestions on this chapter.
2. Owners of petty productive property can be distinguished from capitalists, in that the former, like the latter, own the means of production, but unlike capitalists, employ primarily their own labor and that of family members in the labor process. Unlike the situation of capitalists the enterprises of owners

of petty productive property involve both a substantial degree of self-exploitation and the unremunerated exploitation of family members, and the small scale of the labor process, with a resultant small volume of surplus (profits) that can be generated by the production process.
3. In this situation, the provision of caring labor by women as mothers, aunts, etc. must not be naturalized, but understood within the patriarchal domestic division of labor within which it is situated, in which men in the countries from which domestic workers migrate maintain gendered privileges of not providing caring labor to children and elders—irrespective of whether women are "withdrawing" their labor or not.
4. Of course, not everything *can* be bought. In response to readers who may see this as an argument to "pity the poor capitalist!"—my contention would be that it might be best to understand more completely the resources that allow one's class antagonists to thrive, which might also be a source of their weakness as well. The requirement that capitalists beyond a certain point must meet their own needs of social reproduction—and may experience the alienated conditions of commoditized caring labor which their class has imposed on others—may represent one such vulnerability of capitalist domination, leading to the cultivation of class traitors, etc.
5. The "disks" of Pu-er tea are strands of tea leaves twisted together in a bolus or doughnut shape, weighing several ounces, and are the basic unit in which it is produced and sold.

REFERENCES

Althusser, Louis. 1971. "Ideology and Ideological State Apparatuses: Notes Towards an Investigation." In *Lenin and Philosophy and Other Essays by Louis Althusser*, edited by Louis Althusser, 127–188. New York: Monthly Review Press.

Arrighi, Giovanni. 2007. *Adam Smith in Beijing: Lineages of the Twenty-First Century*. London and New York: Verso.

Bourdieu, Pierre. 1986. "The Forms of Capital." In *Handbook of Theory and Research for the Sociology of Education*, edited by J.G. Richardson, 241–258. New York: Greenwood.

Brenner, Robert. 2006. *The Economics of Global Turbulence: The Advanced Capitalist Economies from Long Boom to Long Downturn, 1945–2005*. London: Verso.

Choi, Tuck Wo. 1992. "Rise in Illegal M'sian Workers in Taiwan." *Star*. Penang, Malaysia.

Cohen, Myron L. 1970. "Developmental Process in the Chinese Domestic Group." In *Family and Kinship in Chinese Society*, edited by M. Freedman, 21–36. Stanford: Stanford University Press.

Crawford, Matthew B. 2009. *Shop Class as Soul Craft: An Inquiry into the Value of Work*. New York: Penguin Press.

Folbre, Nancy. 2001. *The Invisible Heart: Economics and Family Values*. New York: New Press.

Foster, John Bellamy, and Fred Magdoff. 2009. *The Great Financial Crisis: Causes and Consequences*. New York: Monthly Review Press.

Gibson-Graham, J.K. 1996. *The End of Capitalism (As We Knew It)*. Oxford: Blackwell Publishers.

Gooding-Williams, Robert. 1993. "Introduction: On Being Stuck." In *Reading Rodney King / Reading Urban Uprising*, edited by R. Gooding-Williams, 1–12. New York: Routledge.

Handelman, Don. 2004. *Nationalism and the Israeli State: Bureaucratic Logic in Public Events.* Oxford and New York: Berg.

Harvey, David. 1989. *The Condition of Postmodernity.* Oxford: Basil Blackwell.

Hsing, You-tien. 1997. "Building Guanxi across the Straits: Taiwanese Capital and Local Chinese Bureaucrats." In *Ungrounded Empires: The Cultural Politics of Modern Chinese Transnationalism,* edited by A. Ong and D.M. Nonini, 143–166. New York: Routledge.

Itoh, Makoto. 2005. "Assessing Neoliberalism in Japan." In *Neoliberalism: A Critical Reader,* edited by A. Saad-Filho and D. Johnston, 244–250. London and Ann Arbor, MI: Pluto Press.

Kroll, Luisa, and Allison Fass. 2009. "The World's Billionaires." *Forbes Magazine.* http://www.forbes.com.

Ley, David. 2010. *Millionaire Migrants: Trans-Pacific Life Lines.* Chichester, West Sussex: Wiley Blackwell.

Li, Qingyuan, and Xun Wang. 1992. "Tong shi tianya tiaofeijiren [All are faraway airplane jumpers]." In *Xingzhou Ribao* 22–23. Kuala Lumpur.

Marx, Karl. 1976. *Capital.* Vol. 1, *A Critique of Political Economy.* Translated by B. Fowkes. London and New York: Penguin Books.

Mitchell, Katharyne. 1997. "Transnational Subjects: Constituting the Cultural Citizen in the Era of Pacific Rim Capital." In *Ungrounded Empires: The Cultural Politics of Modern Chinese Transnationalism,* edited by A. Ong and D.M. Nonini, 228–258. New York: Routledge.

Munro-Kua, Anne. 1996. *Authoritarian Populism in Malaysia.* New York: St. Martin's Press.

Nicolaus, Martin. 1967. "Proletariat and Middle Class in Marx: Hegelian Choreography and the Capitalist Dialectic." *Studies on the Left* 7(1): 22–49.

Nonini, Donald M. 1997. "Shifting Identities, Positioned Imaginaries: Transnational Traversals and Reversals by Malaysian Chinese." In *Ungrounded Empires: The Cultural Politics of Modern Chinese Transnationalism,* edited by A. Ong and D. Nonini, 204–228. New York and London: Routledge.

———. 2003. "All Are Flexible, But Some Are More Flexible than Others: Small-Scale Chinese Businesses in Malaysia." In *Ethnic Business: Chinese Capitalism in Southeast Asia,* edited by K.S. Jomo and B.C. Folke, 73–91. Studies in the Growth Economies of Asia, 50. London and New York: Routledge Curzon.

———. 2004. "Spheres of Speculation and Middling Transnational Migrants: Chinese Indonesians in the Asia Pacific." In *State/Nation/Transnation: Perspectives on Transnationalism in the Asia-Pacific,* edited by B.S.A.Y. Yeoh and K. Willis, 37–66. London: Routledge.

Ong, Aihwa. 1993. "On the Edge of Empires: Flexible Citizenship among Chinese in Diaspora." *Positions* 1(3): 745–778.

———. 1999. *Flexible Citizenship: The Cultural Logics of Transnationality.* Durham: Duke University Press.

Shimada, Haruo. 1994. *Japan's Guest Workers: Issues and Public Policies.* New York: Columbia University Press (Imprint for University of Tokyo Press).

Smart, Josephine, and Alan Smart. 1999. "Personal Relations and Divergent Economies: A Case Study of Hong Kong Investment in South China." In *Theorizing the City: The New Urban Anthropology Reader,* edited by S.M. Low, 169–200. New Brunswick, NJ: Rutgers University Press.

Tierney, Robert. 2008. "Inter-ethnic and Labour-Community Coalitions in Class Struggle in Taiwan since the Advent of Temporary Immigration." *Journal of Organizational Change Management* 21(4): 482–496.

Willis, Paul. 1981. *Learning to Labor: How Working Class Kids Get Working Class Jobs.* New York: Columbia University Press.

Part II
Cases

5 With Crossings in My Mind[1]
Trinidad's Multiple Migration Flows, Policy, and Agency

Belinda Leach

> "Then every day in Trinidad will be Departure Day. And not just for Indians—our African brothers and sisters are leaving also. But it is Arrival Day for Chinese labourers."[2]

In the closing pages of *Europe and the People without History*, Eric Wolf writes:

> Capitalist accumulation thus continues to engender new working classes in widely dispersed areas of the world. It recruits these working classes from a wide variety of social and cultural backgrounds, and inserts them into variable political and economic hierarchies. The new working classes change these hierarchies by their presence, and are themselves changed by the forces to which they are exposed. On one level, therefore, the diffusion of the capitalist mode creates everywhere a wider unity through the constant reconstitution of its characteristic capital-labor relationship. On another level, it also creates diversity, accentuating social opposition and segmentation even as it unifies. Within an ever more integrated world, we witness the growth of ever more diverse proletarian diasporas. (Wolf 1982: 383)

In the same chapter Wolf writes of the "flow" of labor from "regions where people were unemployed, or displaced ... toward regions of heightened industrial or agricultural activity." (Wolf 1982: 362). He cautions us not to distinguish too sharply between "'intracontinental' and 'intercontinental' flows of population" since historically barriers "between town and country, between classes, and between regions were not different in kind from those that faced the migrant in external or intercontinental movement" (361). In characteristic fashion, he presages more recent anthropological concerns with migration flows, but migration scholars have not often followed his guidance, tending largely to pay insufficient attention to his insistence on attention to history and power. As Nina Glick Schiller notes in this volume, migration theorists have not yet developed a global perspective that permits debates about migration, development, national policies and discourses, and global capital restructuring to co-exist within a single analytical framework.

Not long after Wolf was writing, an idiom of flows issued rather freely from the pens of anthropologists. Referring variously to people, ideas, commodities, finance, media, the notion of flow came to characterize an era in the study of globalization. For Inda and Rosaldo (2002), for example, globalization speaks to a "world of complex mobilities and (uneven) interconnections" (4). Empirically there is a certain undeniability to the idea of flows. As I try to focus my research on the migration of Trinidadians to Canada, I begin to understand that this particular flow of people is but one of a number of migration flows—intraregional and intercontinental, historical and contemporary—which implicate Trinidad. Each is configured differently in terms of class, gender, and racialization. All are constrained by state and suprastate agendas and the demands of restructuring international capital within global fields of power (Glick Schiller 2009). They flourish through people's agency and ingenuity, and sometimes their corruption, and each flow affects the others.

Anna Tsing critiques the imagery of flow used by many anthropologists to conjure late-twentieth-century global processes, arguing that "flow is valorized but not the carving of the channel. . . . We lose touch with the material and institutional components through which powerful and central sites are constructed" (2000: 330). The notion of flow provided a convenient—and fashionably literary—metaphor to capture the causes and consequences of global cultural change. It allowed for the possibility of shifts in routes, direction, and strength. But to push Tsing's imagery further, it relied more on connotations of the gentle meandering of streams, or of rivers in spate cutting powerfully through new terrain, than of managed and manipulated water-courses, where flows are actively channeled, dammed, and sluiced, through the combined actions of those in power and of the relatively powerless.

The history of multiple migrations to and from Trinidad makes it a good place from which to address questions of migrant flows. Trinidad's contemporary demography emerged from earlier histories of African, Indian, European, Chinese and Middle Eastern migration flows, which has made Trinidad and some other Caribbean nations of special interest to analysts concerned with how plural societies negotiate racial, religious, and cultural dynamics in order to function (Smith 1965). Aisha Khan argues that Trinidad's colonial past created a race-class-color hierarchy that provided the foundations for a post-colonial society based in "ethnic group competition, fostered by class inequalities and state control of certain resources and couched in terms of racial antipathies between Indo- and Afro-Trinidadians" (2004: 9). But empirically there is also much evidence of what Khan describes as "mixing." Despite a discourse of difference and ethnic distinction especially at the political level, intermarriage and co-residency within neighborhoods are and in the past have been common. Furthermore, Trinidad has a history of solidarity among migrants and longstanding residents. Santiago-Valles (2006) documents a period of widespread working-class protest, education, and organization in the 1930s and 1940s. This activism managed to cut across the division between Indo- and Afro-Trinidadians that had emerged out of slavery and it incorporated returning migrants from Europe and North America. It also extended the conversation to unionized workers on other islands, bringing about a form of transnational resistance to globalization.[3]

Yet despite these historical dynamics, a recent newspaper headline reads, "Chinese Go Home." These are the words of a local contractor who demands, "Stop giving the Chinese contracts. Time to send them home. . . . thousands of whom are in our country when our people cannot find work" (Tait 2009: 1). The global recession is hurting locally, whereas most of the new offices, major hotels, and industrial parks are being built by Chinese laborers contracted by Chinese construction companies. For several years a building boom has brought construction workers to Trinidad. Smaller construction projects use the labor of Filipinos and Grenadians, Guyanese and South Americans. But other opportunities bring migrants to Trinidad and lead them elsewhere. South Americans enter illegally to work in low-skill jobs and the sex trade, whereas middle-class Trinidadians take their skills and professional qualifications to Britain, the US, and Canada, leaving behind gaps in health care and other professions that are filled by Nigerians, Indians, and Cubans.

The demands of restructuring global capital are changing the social relations of labor in Trinidad[4] and at the same time changing Trinidadians' role in global labor markets. My starting place—Trinidadian migration to Canada—touches only one tiny aspect of the migration flows to and from Trinidad. Most people in Trinidad, and those who have left, have past, present, and future crossings in their minds. In this chapter[5] I demonstrate that an understanding of contemporary migration from Trinidad to Canada cannot be dissociated from an exploration of other migration flows in which Trinidad is implicated. The factors that influence people's decisions to move to Canada are closely tied, sometimes in not so obvious ways, to other people's decisions to move to and from Trinidad. They are also tied to the shifting political agendas of states and global institutions that ground individual migration decisions in policy processes, including the shape that labor markets take in a range of locales.

In recent years Trinidad's new inflows and longstanding outflows of migrants have been reshaped by changing international migration regimes combined with and closely linked to the shifting demands of globalized capital. A political-economy approach to Trinidadian migration then invites attention to migrant flows, but in a more theoretically productive fashion than that to which the notion of flow has usually been subjected. My aim here is to consider the conjunction and layering of historical and geographical flows, shaped by global and local political and economic exigencies. Nina Glick Schiller (2009: 22) calls for migration scholars to conduct "locality analysis" that considers the relative positioning of a place within global hierarchical fields of power. Doreen Massey argues that "localities are *constructions* out of the intersections and interactions of concrete social relations and social processes in a situation of co-presence" (1994: 138). I argue that the co-presence of migrant flows and the political and economic constraints that shape them[6] result in contestations over meaning, including the meaning of place, and are constitutive of gendered and racialized class relations in Trinidad.

In what follows I first describe the political-economic positioning of Trinidad and Tobago, demonstrating the importance of locality analysis in challenging some of the assumptions about countries whose main function is seen to be migrant-sending. My research with actual and potential Trinidadian migrants to Canada then operates as a starting place for describing the regional and intercontinental migration flows that imbricate in Trinidad. I address how issues of agency and policy operate to shape those flows, and conclude by briefly considering the implications of shifting migration flows for global working-class mobilization.

A POINT OF CROSSINGS

Trinidad and Tobago sit geographically where the Caribbean region meets Latin America and global flows of people, commodities, languages, and ideas have historically crossed paths. Colonized first by the Spanish, who wiped out the indigenous population and held it until the late eighteenth century when it was lost to the British, Trinidad was also fought over by the Dutch and French. All these colonial influences remain in one form or another. Commonwealth links to Britain, fuelled by historical preferential trading status now denied by the World Trade Organization, have been more or less superseded by economic relations with hemispheric partners facilitated by actual and anticipated regional trade agreements. But Commonwealth relationships remain politically important, such that Trinidad hosted the Commonwealth Heads of Government Meeting in 2009. In recent years Trinidad has tried to use its geographical location to position itself as the center of the Western hemisphere: politically by hosting the Summit of the Americas (also in 2009) and economically by developing itself as a center for business and commerce. Heavily dependent on oil revenues for much of the past several decades, the economy is now somewhat more diversified with the investment of US $1 billion in the Atlantic liquefied natural gas industry, reported to be the largest-ever single industrial investment in the Caribbean. Trinidad is an active member of the CARICOM community of Caribbean states, but the US is its major trading partner, for whom it provides two-thirds of all imported natural gas. Brazil, Venezuela, and Jamaica are its next most important trading partners.

Although by no means immune to global economic ups and downs, the relatively strong economy underwritten by oil and gas has maintained relatively low levels of unemployment and a fairly stable welfare state. These have allowed Trinidad to follow a rather different path to neoliberalism than that of other countries usually associated as migrant-sending. One major consequence is that remittances from overseas migrants represent only a small contribution to the national economy (0.5 percent of GDP—gross domestic product) in officially recorded remittances, although the actual amount is likely to be far higher (World Bank 2009). This figure should not diminish the importance of those remittances to particular families living in poverty.

Trinidad's position along the transit route from South to North America has made it a key hub for two major illegal global trades, drugs and women. Reportedly controlled by international and local crime gangs, these have contributed to a murder rate that is among the highest in the world,[7] fuelled by the availability of handguns. Also contributing to crime rates is the quite widely held opinion that the benefits of Trinidad's oil and gas wealth are not being distributed among the population, but rather are concentrated in the hands of a few.

As Rowbotham (1998) has argued, the Caribbean region has been formed over the past five hundred years, all of that time within the framework of global capitalism. In this way it is unlike some other world regions where the task of global capitalism has been as Rowbotham puts it, "radical rupture" with a non-capitalist past. Slavery and indentureship in the Caribbean context are some of the earliest and most brutal examples of the ways capitalists actively moved labor to the locations where they wanted to use it. For Slocum and Thomas the Caribbean can be "understood as a site composed of and charted through global connections" (2003: 554), rooted in continual movement, both forced and voluntary. These global connections comprise deeply historical transnational linkages that are South-South as well as North-South (Rowbotham 1998: 310), including well-established flows of migrants such as those taking place *within* the Caribbean region, which have been subjected to little attention by mainstream migration scholars.[8]

THEORIZING LABOR FLOWS WITHIN AND AGAINST GLOBALIZATION

A shift in anthropological approaches to global migration taking place in the late 1980s and 1990s led to a greater focus on human agency in migration, grounding migration flows in the rather more precise concept of transnationalism. Scholarly attention to Caribbean migration has focused mainly on the large-scale movement of people to higher-wage countries (see for example Foner 2001). But the particular character of this Caribbean flow made a strong contribution to the development of the idea of transnationalism. Writing about Caribbean migrants to the US, Constance Sutton argued that unlike earlier European immigrants, these people were not fully incorporated into American society (not least because they faced racism), and given the close proximity of where they had come from they cultivated a bidirectional flow of people, ideas, practices, and goods between the Caribbean region and the US (Sutton 1987).

Roger Rouse coined the term "transnational migrant circuit" to argue against the more conventional notion of migration as a unidirectional process. More firmly anchored in material processes, Rouse's term refers to the ways in which workers themselves have responded to the transnationalization of capital by developing "continuous circulation of people, money, goods and information" (Rouse 2002: 162) and creating new socio-spatial arrangements that stretch across national borders. Adopting the concept of transnationalism produced methodological challenges for anthropologists. Rouse argues that for migrant Aguilillans "the various settlements [in Mexico and the US] have become so closely woven together that, in an important sense, they have come to constitute a single community spread across a variety of sites" (2002: 162). Eriksen suggests that employing the term "transnational flows" instead of globalization allows anthropologists to follow "informants and cultural production wherever they go" (2003: 5) rather than taking global processes as given.

In the past twenty years the attention of most analysts has been on those migrant flows, or circuits, that incorporate workers whose origins are in parts of the world where there is a surfeit of labor but little economic opportunity (usually in the capitalist periphery), who move to regions of the world where labor, or more precisely certain kinds of labor, is in short supply and there are expanded opportunities for work and far higher wages (usually in the rich countries of the North, Australia, and New Zealand). This transnational migration flow from south to north remains at the center of the multidisciplinary field of migration studies. This orientation has been shown by Wimmer and Glick Schiller (2002) to be closely connected to metropolitan notions of nation-state building and the role that immigration has played in state development. Glick Schiller (2009) argues that migration scholarship requires a perspective not constrained by the borders of the nation-state. A new broader analytical framework would pay far greater attention to how "the reconstitution of capital disrupts previous arrangements of power" (2009: 20) and restructures them into new ones that, with little respect for national borders, extend into other localities.

As the Trinidad example shows, to meet the shifting international labor demands of capital, the south-to-north flow of migrants may be only one of several migrant flows that exist in a particular place. Focusing attention on this one in isolation impoverishes our understanding of how multiple migration flows intersect, interact, and are mutually constitutive, reshaping social relations in these places of crossings. Furthermore, attention to the multiple strands of what is going on in situ can tell us much about transnational ambitions, possibilities, and outcomes. In this chapter I try to show the value of examining the complexity of social relations in places where migrant flows intersect, where outward flows demand new flows inward. In a sense, as a corollary to the strategy of those promoting multisited ethnography where several sites become one (Hannerz 2003), I suggest that one site contains several layers that need to be kept within the analytical frame, as I have suggested for a different context in which migrants encounter nonmigrants, shaping the sense of belonging and capacity for agency of both (Leach 2008).

TRINIDAD'S REGIONAL AND INTERCONTINENTAL MIGRATIONS

Contemporary Trinidad is shaped by the convergence of historical and present-day migration flows, financial and commodity flows, and the policies of government that constrain or enable all of these. For the purpose of my analysis I identify three region-based, post-emancipation migration flows in which Trinidad is enmeshed, and I consider each of these in terms of its history and its contemporary character. Each flow emerges from specific histories of uneven development in the places where labor originates and the places to which it goes. The one that has been most often and for the longest time considered in academic and policy analyses of Caribbean migration is the flow *from Trinidad* to the high-wage countries, especially Britain, the US, and Canada. This is where my investigations began, as I interviewed actual and potential migrants to Canada from Trinidad in the context of shifting Canadian immigration agendas. It was through conversations with these people, as well as observations on the ground in Trinidad, that I began to expand my understandings of Trinidad's multiple migration flows. The second flow I identify is that of migrants *to Trinidad* from other Caribbean states, notably those poorer than Trinidad, mainly in the English-speaking Caribbean islands, especially Guyana and the nearby islands but also Jamaica. The third is the flow *to Trinidad* from locations outside the English-speaking Caribbean. This is the flow that has changed most noticeably over time in terms of source countries and skill. Some of the first migrants to Trinidad after emancipation were white-collar managers, experts, and professionals from Europe and North America. In recent years, professionals are as likely to be from Nigeria and Cuba. In addition to these new source regions for highly skilled migrants, there is a new flow of low-skill workers from Africa and China, and other parts of the Asia Pacific region.

I distinguish these flows in terms of their regional origin or destination because analytically one can rather crudely map onto these regional flows particular kinds of national and supra-national policies that work to shape them at one or both ends and one can also map on particular kinds of labor needs being addressed. But such mapping does not work perfectly, largely because of the migration desires and ingenuities of the actual people who constitute migration flows. In the following sections I attempt to characterize these flows in more detail, to show the ways in which they form layers that interconnect through social relations, politics and policy, and economics.

Trinidad to High-Wage Countries—and Sometimes Back Again

Large-scale migrations out of the Caribbean region can be traced to receiving-country legislation in the 1950s and early 1960s that allowed women to travel to Canada, Britain, and the US to work as domestic care workers for prescribed periods. As a result of these policies, it was often women who were the first in their family to migrate overseas. Before that, young people (most of them men) had been encouraged from at least the 1930s to leave the Caribbean, as they were in other parts of the world, to study at the well-established universities overseas, with the hope, often unfulfilled, that they would bring their knowledge back to help build their country's economy and its emerging governmental system. After the Second World War, Trinidadians were among those who having served in the British army were encouraged to move to Britain[9] to assist with the post-war reconstruction, the beginning of a major migration flow between Trinidad and Britain.

The long-standing south-to-north migration ties between Trinidad and Northern countries from the early twentieth century have resulted in dense transnational networks of family and friends that encompass different continents, such that almost everyone in Trinidad, and in every class, has a relative overseas. This flow has changed its character over time with evolving policies in the receiving countries. Mass migration to Britain, for example, was curbed in the late 1960s when the earlier more generous provisions for Commonwealth immigrants were rescinded. At exactly this time opportunities in Canada were expanding and the demand for skilled workers allowed a relatively large number of skilled Trinidadians to move. Trinidad has continued to provide the highest number of skilled workers entering Canada from the Caribbean region, a phenomenon that Plaza (2001: 59) attributes to the higher levels of schooling that Trinidadians have available to them. Nevertheless, since the 1970s most Trinidadians entering Canada have done so as sponsored relatives, and over the years the numbers have dropped quite dramatically.[10]

Potential migrants thinking of coming to Canada these days are either quite highly qualified in terms of formal education, or they already have relatives who live there, and most likely both. Relatives overseas provide fairly accurate knowledge of what they can expect and a potential foothold once they arrive. My field research indicates that those most keenly seeking to leave Trinidad in the early years of the twenty-first century largely fall into two groups. One is middle-class, female, and often Indo-Trinidadian.[11] The other group comprises young university or college graduates.

To an extent, this apparent self-selection is driven by Canadian immigration policies that increasingly privilege highly skilled migrants while limiting the stay of low-skilled workers through temporary worker programs. As I have argued (Leach 2009), the long history of links between Canada and Trinidad associated with permanent migration and eventual Canadian citizenship leads Trinidadians to shun the idea of temporary work in Canada, despite the fact that this is now the fastest way into Canada. The exceptions are around a thousand men, and very few women, who travel each year to engage in seasonal agricultural work. There are also a dwindling number of temporary domestic workers, all women, who under quite stringent conditions may be allowed to remain in Canada when their temporary work permits expire. But the numbers of Trinidadians in both of these categories are dropping every year, as the agriculture program is extended to Mexican and Central American workers, and Filipino domestic workers, available in large numbers and now perceived as the preferred caregiver, replace those from the Caribbean. In this way Canadian immigration policy—itself responding to both domestic labor needs and domestic political exigencies—shapes the flow of migrants out of Trinidad, as does the migration regime in other countries like the Philippines (see Barber and Bryan's chapter in this volume).

The out-migration of Indo-Trinidadians comes up quickly in conversations about migration. This is also a popular topic in the media and as the opening quote shows, more broadly. Immigration consultants (most whom I know are themselves Indo-Trinidadian, perhaps to address the perceived demand) point first to this flow and to the perception that Indo-Trinidadians are subject to specific, targeted injustices, that "they are not going to get their fair share," as one consultant put it. Much of the commentary by Indo-Trinidadians on Trinidadian politics constructs the party in power (the People's National Movement (PNM), associated with Afro-Trinidadians and in power for all but six of the past fifty-three years) as promoting the interests of Afro-Trinidadians at the expense of Indo-Trinidadians, consistent with the discourse of separate spheres that Khan (2004) notes. Discussion over the recent resignations of several Indo-Trinidadian medical staff at a major medical center included allegations of racial discrimination. There is evidence that Indo-Trinidadians, often thought to be better off financially than others because of their apparent success in business, have been the targets of kidnappings and ransom demands. Thus several factors make the local climate inhospitable for Indo-Trinidadians, and underpin their desire to leave.

Most migrants I have interviewed have been women, and they are also vastly overrepresented on Internet social networking sites that offer peer support to potential migrants from Trinidad to Canada. Although impossible to verify because the government department does not release a gender breakdown, my sense is that this flow is not predominantly of women.[12] Rather, it is women who are pushing the process on behalf of their families.

It is they who are taking the time to investigate what needs to be done and to seek out assistance through their relatives and others who are already abroad. This makes sense in terms of the historical role of women as lead migrants from the Caribbean region (as noted above for domestic service), and because of the ways in which women have historically been economically active and self-supporting in the region. One woman noted wryly that the online application "is not very user friendly." Thus the visibility of women in this process likely also relates to the high levels of education that women achieve in Trinidad, facilitating their navigation of the bureaucratic maze of immigration policy.

Acquiring Canadian citizenship is widely noted as a major benefit of immigration. Dual citizenship is very common and provides people with particular rights and privileges, such as ease of travel between the two countries. Furthermore, a sizeable number of those now living in Trinidad are in fact return migrants holding Canadian (or other) citizenship (recent estimates put the figure at over four thousand [Mahoney 2009]). These have achieved what is often a goal for migration of intending to save enough money to be able to retire comfortably back in Trinidad (see De Sousa 2006). Dual citizenship and the return migrant flow both facilitate the continuing conversation among those who have left and those who would like to leave. The often-ignored back-again flow of those with Canadian and other citizenships is another strand in the multiple migration flows that converge in Trinidad. All of these factors combine with the policies of the other major receiving countries, the US, Britain and Australia, to contribute to the class and gender configuration of the flow of migrants from Trinidad.

Caribbean Region to Trinidad—and Sometimes Beyond

Intra-regional migration is a historical phenomenon in the Caribbean. For centuries people have moved from places with limited economic opportunity to those nearby where they hope to find work. The location of that opportunity has shifted over time. In the 1880s tens of thousands of Caribbean nationals, most from Jamaica and Trinidad, worked on the construction of the Panama Canal where they were segregated in camps, lived in abject poverty, and were subjected to racism. In recent decades economic opportunity in the Caribbean region has been in Trinidad, because of industrial and commercial activities, and in Barbados, with its strong tourism base. Valtonen (1996) notes that "ethnocultural affinity" combines with established chain migration to promote a sense of belonging and ease of integration for low-income intra-regional migrants. The International Organization for Migration (2009) reports that with its "significant oil and natural gas resources, high levels of direct foreign investment and an expanding tourism industry," Trinidad has a strong pull for migrants, such that one-third of intra-Caribbean migrants live there. The higher standards of living in both Trinidad and Barbados compared to other parts of the Caribbean have triggered a regional flow of migrants that until recently was largely undocumented. Policies that permit skilled workers to move exist among thirteen of the CARICOM countries, provisions that have gradually expanded in the last few years as a preliminary step in the Caribbean Single Market and Economy (CSME) initiative.

Whereas some claim that Trinidadians move to places like Barbados because "they are afraid to live in Trinidad at this time" (*Trinidad Express* September 26, 2008), predictably, mobile Caribbean workers, especially those without the skills that might carry them to North America or Britain, still tend to favor Trinidad and Barbados as destinations. This situation led to heated debate at the CARICOM summit in Georgetown, Guyana in 2009, as the Barbados Prime Minister declared that he was determined to manage immigration "in the interest of the local labor force and the foreign workers who may otherwise be subjected to exploitation" (Johnson 2009). This debate over intra-regional migration has become racialized. Trinidadians I talked to, as well as commentators in the press, identify the position of the Barbados government to be an attempt to "keep Barbados black and white" by not admitting Indo-Guyanese migrants even when they comply with the CARICOM policy on free movement for certain kinds of workers. In Trinidad these actions were immediately labeled racist, and despite the racial tensions that exist in Trinidad, Trinidadians have quickly assumed the moral high ground.

The migration of women for the sex trade, sometimes under coerced conditions, is another form of (mainly) intra-regional mobility that engages Trinidad and is currently under scrutiny internally and by the international community. Women have entered Trinidad illegally from the Dominican Republic, Colombia, and Brazil to work in the local sex trade and some will eventually move or be moved to other Caribbean locations, or to North America. The persistence of this flow is attributed to corrupt border officials, but also to the fact that at its southern tip Trinidad is only about six miles from Venezuela. Whereas for several years the press has reported on women caught in police immigration raids and then deported, there are newer reports that residents in some southern villages refuse to report such activities they witness because the industry is controlled by heavily armed crime gangs. Other factors that are likely to contribute to villagers' complicity with these activities include the decline in the local coconut and fishing activities in the area, and the government's general neglect of the southern region's economic well being.

All forms of intra-regional migration are under policy review in the region. Governments are considering amnesties for illegal workers and have been advised by local analysts (e.g., Girvan 2009) to develop a common policy that would grant temporary work permits in sectors not currently covered by CARICOM, such as construction, agriculture, and tourism. Intra-regional migration is often the first step for individuals on a longer journey to the labor markets of North America and Europe. Many migrants to Canada moved first from a poorer island to Trinidad, from where, after gaining work skills and experience and exposure to Trinidad's particular migration nexus, they may make the more demanding move to higher-wage countries. Despite widespread agreement that intra-island migrants fill positions that many Trinidadians refuse, they are also blamed for putting pressure on the local economy, often identified by Trinidadians to be a factor in their own decision to leave.

Outside the CARICOM Caribbean to Trinidad

Labor migration to Trinidad from outside the Caribbean region is traced from the sixteenth century, the beginning of the human trade that brought slaves from Africa to work on the sugar plantations. For a century after the end of slavery in the 1830s workers were brought from India and to a lesser extent China under indentureship programs where they replaced and competed for work with the newly freed slaves (Brereton 2007). In the early twentieth century Syrian Lebanese Christians fled religious persecution and economic hardship at home and established themselves as traders in Trinidad. Another wave of Chinese migrants in the 1920s to 1940s are said to have fled the Chinese Revolution.

Until only a couple of years ago, very few non-CARICOM nationals were granted work permits for Trinidad each year. Most of those were highly qualified personnel required by multinational companies for their operations. Trinidad's major economic sectors have traditionally looked elsewhere for skilled workers, and high skill and racialization as white are the factors that have characterized that flow until fairly recently. Most workers for these jobs were sourced from the predominantly white, educated populations of North America and Europe, especially before the University of the West Indies became established. The oil and gas sector has needed specially qualified workers for about forty years, but for the finance sector this need dates back to the mid-nineteenth century. Other sectors like transportation have also looked overseas to staff certain positions. The high-speed ferry that operates between Trinidad and Tobago, for example, is owned by a European company and staffed by skilled operators and technicians from Europe and North America, as well as Trinidadians. Whereas some overseas staff have relocated their families to Trinidad, others I have talked to live a cyclical work schedule, working one month in Trinidad followed by a month off back in their home countries.

In the contemporary moment Trinidad's need for highly qualified workers has expanded far beyond the small number of Euro-Americans invited to fill positions in the past. The health sector in particular is suffering a massive shortage of professionals, attributed by government officials and others, including the IOM (International Organization for Migration), to the migration of locally trained doctors and nurses to more lucrative positions in richer countries, where they are also in short supply. In August 2009 the government announced that 119 foreign doctors and 450 foreign nurses had been recruited. Many of the doctors would be coming from Cuba, but from Africa as well, and nurses are being hired from the Philippines among other places. The search for highly skilled workers to fill positions in Trinidad has thus shifted in recent years, away from Europe and North America and towards countries further away geographically (or for Cuba, politically).

In 2007 the government announced that it was easing the rules for foreign worker permits in light of the national labor shortage associated with the development boom. In 2009 the government reported that it had granted some twelve thousand work permits to non-CARICOM nationals in 2007 and 2008 combined. Of these 2,800 permits were granted to Chinese nationals, about 80 percent to work in construction in 2008, the remainder in food service occupations. This particular flow of migrant Chinese workers has generated ongoing hot debate within Trinidad. In the last two years conversations about the construction boom, the sound of which is almost always in the background, frequently turned to what people had heard were terrible working and living conditions for Chinese laborers.

Concerns about these workers' conditions had been raised in early 2007 by David Abdulah, President of the Federation of Independent Trade Unions and NGOs (FITUN), who wrote to the Minister of Labor calling on him to investigate. Abdulah noted that minimum wage laws and occupational health and safety laws were being violated. He argued as well that because the work could have been done by Trinidadian nationals, work permits should not have been granted. The government's position has been that no violations are taking place, and that in any case terms and conditions of work are a matter between the employer and the workers. The government has also claimed that the Chinese firms holding the construction contracts are more efficient and their workers far more productive (Abdulah 2009) than their Trinidadian counterparts.

Although these workers became the focus of attention, China is not the only country supplying workers for unskilled positions. The massive and numerous construction projects, as well as perceptions of rising crime levels, have created hundreds of positions for security guards. These are very low-paid positions, taken by workers from all parts of the Caribbean as well as from further away. Economic opportunity has also encouraged undocumented migration from outside the Caribbean region. In October 2008 twenty-three Filipino construction workers were deported for working in Tobago without permits, deemed by government officials to be "victims of unscrupulous employment recruiters in the Philippines" (Homer 2008).

SHAPING MIGRATION FLOWS: LOUD AND QUIET PROTESTS, CAPITAL, AND STATE RESPONSES

In May 2009 people living close to the construction site for a new aluminium smelter in the southern coastal town of La Brea protested an agreement between the government of Trinidad and Tobago and a Chinese bank that required that most of the jobs created both in construction and to operate the smelter would go to Chinese workers, leaving local people unemployed. These protests halted construction for a couple of weeks, as trucks attempting to enter the site were blocked. After assurances that local people would in fact be hired, the community's attention turned to the environmental impact of the smelter. A few months later, several hundred workers at the site, as far as I can tell almost all Trinidadians, walked off the job complaining of health and safety violations in the construction process. They were summarily fired by the company for staging an illegal strike. After a few days of negotiations between the company and the workers' leaders they were reinstated.

The debate over the plight of Chinese laborers has been sharpened as the global economic crisis continues to bite into the local economy. Trinidadian workers' protests at the practice of importing labor when local workers are unemployed raise the stakes in the common government practice of signing contracts that include provisions to bring in foreign workers. It was only after multiple assurances from government officials that local workers would be hired that the protests stopped and construction could resume. But it is not only Trinidadians exercising agency around migrant flows.

In October 2009 about one hundred Chinese laborers involved in the construction of two secondary schools staged a protest on the main north-south highway to draw public attention to not having been paid for two months and to their terrible living conditions. Journalists who returned with them to their living quarters were appalled at "the pungent urine smell. . . . a communal concrete sink . . . a garbage bin was overflowing" (Neaves 2009). The workers described a regular fourteen-hour work day, with overtime required to have the construction site ready for the Commonwealth Heads of Government Meeting in November (Neaves 2009). The press reported that when journalists and opposition politicians arrived later at the Chinese workers' camp, they were met by "Nigerian security guards . . . placed on the compound of the living quarters of Chinese construction workers . . . instructed to keep the steel doors of the camp locked" (Dowlat 2009). About seventy Chinese workers were arrested after they protested their work conditions outside the Chinese Embassy (Pickford-Gordon and Dhalai 2009). The company employing them responded by applying to the Ministry to have their work permits revoked, and they were flown back to China within days. A few days later newspapers reported that the company already had plans to request work permits for new workers to replace them (Honore-Gopie 2009).

People protest, but corporations respond quickly and firmly. Smelter construction workers were given gentle assurances the first time they protested, but the second time they were shown the extent of corporate power. The response to the Chinese migrant first workers' protest was direct, immediate, and enforced by low-paid—but most likely armed—migrant workers from another part of the world. As they persisted in protesting, they were sent home. Attempts at solidarity, albeit of very different kinds, were met with actions underpinned, I would argue, by a reliance on the dominant discourse of difference that operates at the political level. Corporations employ this discourse, consistent with and bolstered by their political allies, rather than the alternative available one of 'mixing' that operates at a more local level.

Individuals also exercise agency in a variety of ways through attempts to circumvent the policies and practices that constrain migrant flows. In the late 1980s a number of Indo-Trinidadians attempted to claim refugee status on arrival in Canada on the basis of racial discrimination at home, where their claims were met with incredulity. These events remain in the memories of those who now seek to leave and often came up in conversations with me. More recently both the US and Britain have identified Trinidadians as among the top 15 percent of "overstayers," those who remain after their tourist visas have expired. In response, the US recently joined Canada and imposed a visa requirement on all Trinidadian nationals (Britain continues not to demand visitor visas for Trinidadians). This move, together with the fact well covered in the press that many if not most such visa requests are denied, has infuriated Trinidadians. They value but have largely taken for granted prior easy access to the US and Canada to visit friends and family, and in the process to consider a more permanent move. This makes the Canadian and US citizenship that people already have more valuable than ever as global routes—even for more casual travel—become increasingly difficult to access for some.

Ironically, consular officials assessing visa requests look for firm ties to Trinidad (such as owning property and other assets in Trinidad, and having close family members still living there) in order to predict the likelihood that the applicant will want to return. It seems quite likely that the very ties that people have carefully nurtured with friends and family abroad will in fact operate against them in attempts to acquire visitor visas.

The ever-changing visa requirements for those trying to move between countries is the most direct method states have to shape migration flows. But an alternative is to encourage and assist development in situ, that is, to encourage economic opportunities that will discourage emigration. In the past couple of years the Canadian government has refocused some of the resources of the Canadian International Development Agency (CIDA) towards the Caribbean. This follows years of virtual neglect of the region in terms of development assistance, in favor of Africa and poorer parts of Latin America. Similar motives are being attributed to CARICOM development initiatives for poorer parts of the Caribbean region, recently promoted by Trinidad's Prime Minister. As commentators have pointed out, the Trinidad government has a vested interest in encouraging Caribbean nationals to stay in their own countries and out of Trinidad.

The imperatives of states and capital to restrict and expand migration flows have shaped them historically in particular ways with regard to gender, race, and class. Plaza (2001) shows that in the 1960s Canadian financial institutions put pressure on the Canadian government to liberalize immigration regulations for the previously excluded non-white immigrants, so that they could send their most promising management staff from the Caribbean to Canada. This opened up a migration stream of non-white skilled workers to Canada and simultaneously removed those people from the Trinidadian labor market. Recent shifts in Canadian immigration policy are more clearly than ever before bifurcating that flow, as Canada chooses only highly skilled migrants for permanent residency, and restricts low-skill workers to temporary migrant programs.

CARICOM migration policy also shapes migrant flows with regard to class. Skilled and semi-skilled workers are permitted to move, whereas unskilled workers attempting to improve their economic status must move to Trinidad either illegally, or as kinship networks show, by manipulating relations through marriage.

The intersection of class and racialization leads to different forms of experience in different places. Even highly skilled Afro-Trinidadians moving to Canada or the US find themselves received there as lower class because of the racialization of class in those places (Rowbotham 1998). Despite a longstanding ethnic Chinese community in Trinidad, the migrant Chinese laborers are racialized in particular class terms. The fact that this migration flow is primarily of men then produces gendered and racialized class effects. Workers from Guyana, with a similar ethnic profile to Trinidad, once in Trinidad are also considered lower class, whereas Valtonen (1996) notes significantly that intranational class cleavage and socio-economic distance in Trinidad are probably more important than the distinction between locals and newcomers. As several hundred nurses are 'imported' from places like the Philippines, this particular flow is also configured in gendered, racialized, and class terms. In these and other ways multiple migration flows are constitutive of gendered and racialized class experience in Trinidad that I argue have the potential to challenge existing stratifications in new and profound ways.

CONCLUSION

Dabydeen's 'crossings' are intended to evoke the Middle Passage that brought slaves to Trinidad and Tobago from Africa and the voyage across the Kala Pani, the dangerous "black water," that brought indentured workers from India. For Trinidadians, thoughts of migration are always underpinned by memories of these migration flows, the power dynamics that accompanied them and that shaped colonial Trinidad, in other words the continuing intersections of political economy and racism. But these references also underpin the sense that migration is always a possibility for Caribbean peoples. Not just a memory in their pasts, it is part of the present, and is likely in their futures too.

Don Rowbotham argues that in the Caribbean globalization has introduced "no radical alteration of the relations of social classes and identities" (1998: 308). Whereas it is possible to view historical migration flows of unskilled and skilled workers to the north and skilled workers to the Caribbean as an extension of established relations, I suggest that contemporary migration flows in and out of Trinidad indicate that this may be changing. Recognizing all of these multiple flows, the policies that constrain them, and the ways that migrants and others attempt to remake them allows us to understand better their consequences for the capacity of global working classes to mount any kind of challenge to the actions of global capital and their state facilitators.

The global economic crisis has put pressure on Caribbean economies in ways that have implications for migration flows. As migrants lose jobs or clients for their businesses elsewhere, remittances to those in need and other benefits to those at home decline. If migrants return they will find that the crisis is already affecting employment and commerce there, and if unemployment rises, protests against the use of foreign workers may well intensify. What emerges as most important is how transnational communities of all kinds are inserted into the current economic system, and how those communities begin to challenge the material conditions of their new lives (Santiago-Valles 2006: 64). Migration flows are shaped by global economics and migrants are not all equally able to exercise agency and to manipulate or lobby for policies to their benefit.

For Slocum and Thomas (2003) studying the Caribbean permits writing against easy analytical binaries. As both sender and receiver of migrants, Trinidad demonstrates the dangers of looking simplistically through a migration-studies lens at localities in the South as only places that people leave. Yet it is equally important to avoid characterizing Trinidad, or other places of crossings, simply as a 'translocality' (Appadurai 1996), a place where because people are often in motion they simply move through. Whereas migrant Chinese laborers, and other transmigrants, may maintain their political affiliation to home and derive important aspects of their identity from that, the protests in 2009 suggest awareness that they can also exercise political agency—that they have a political identity—in the place where they are temporarily living and working. In November 2009 the leaders of the major national unions in Trinidad organized five days of protest actions leading up to and during the Commonwealth Heads of Government Meeting to draw attention to the government's shortcomings with regard to issues of food security and governance. Coalescing into a broad-based action group called People's Democracy and holding public protests around issues of taxation, corruption, and crime, the conditions of migrant workers are identified as one of their concerns, within a framework of broader labor rights. In May 2010 a new government was elected, a coalition that has adopted an anti-neoliberal, pro-people manifesto that closely resembles that of People's Democracy.

It becomes clear that even in the midst of movement, meanings and understandings of place, identity, and belonging are being shaped, and contemporary struggles involving migrants as well as permanent residents in particular places are reframing hegemonic understandings of globalization. Political agendas and individual and collective actions will determine whether there will be a major shift in historically entrenched gendered and racialized class relations.

NOTES

1. "I Come to You with Crossings in My Mind" is the title of a poem by Guyanese-Canadian poet Cyril Dabydeen. Dabydeen was born in Canje, Guyana where he worked as a teacher. He came to Canada in 1970 to pursue postsecondary studies and teaches creative writing at the University of Ottawa.
2. Comment by a reader on an article in the Trinidad and Tobago Guardian, September 17, 2009. Indian Arrivals Day is the Trinidadian national holiday that commemorates the arrival of people from the Indian subcontinent to work as indentured laborers.
3. This was organized by the Negro Welfare Cultural and Social Association. Santiago-Valles (2006: 67) argues that this struggle was clearly very effective. At the trial of the movement's leaders, the colonial administration and the companies affected combined a long list of demands: banning public conversations about world events, the distribution of pamphlets about union organization, and the calypso music shows used as a forum for disseminating information about global and national events.
4. The politics of naming is of course an issue for a twin island nation like Trinidad and Tobago. I follow other authors who use the terms Trinidad and Trinidadian, rather than the full name. In policy and political terms the processes discussed here apply in both islands, although the construction boom, for example, is less evident in Tobago, despite its more advanced tourism development.
5. This chapter is based on research undertaken as part of a comparative research project with Pauline Gardiner Barber, supported by the Social Sciences and Humanities Research Council of Canada.
6. The full analysis, taking account of Glick Schiller's locality analysis, would include the co-presence of flows of commodities, ideas, media, etc., and their attendant social, political, and economic processes.
7. The murder rate in Trinidad is forty-two per one hundred thousand, making it rank seventh in the world according to the UN. Canada's rate is about two per one hundred thousand, the US's about six.
8. Some anthropologists have been exceptions to this trend, such as Karen Fog Olwig, whose research into Caribbean family networks incorporates attention to inter-island migration (Olwig 2007).
9. Andrea Levy's novel *Small Island* deals with the reception Caribbean nationals received when they returned to Britain to live after serving in the British Army during the War.
10. Citizenship and Immigration Canada reported in 2007 that of the sixty-seven thousand people born in Trinidad who are now in Canada, forty-three thousand arrived before 1991. The numbers admitted have dwindled from 11,400 in the period between 1991 and 1995 to 4,500 between 2001 and 2006.

11. I am guided by Khan (2004), one of the few recent ethnographers of Trinidad, in using the terms Indo- and Afro-Trinidadian. However, these terms are not used locally. More likely, as in my opening quote, people refer to each other as "Indian," "African," "Syrian," etc.
12. Gender disaggregated figures are not publicly available after 1996. It is not possible to determine the relative numbers of Indo- and Afro-Trinidadians who emigrate to Canada, because CIC does not keep records of ethnic background for immigrants.

REFERENCES

Abdulah, David. 2009. "FITUN Told You So." *Trinidad and Tobago's Newsday*, October 18.
Appadurai, Arjun. 1996. *Modernity at Large: Cultural Dimensions of Globalization*. Minneapolis: University of Minnesota Press.
Brereton, Bridget. 2007. "Emancipation in Trinidad." http://sta.uwi.edu.resources/speeches/2009/EMANC_LECT.pdf
Citizenship and Immigration Canada. 2007. *Facts and Figures 2006*. Ottawa: Citizenship and Immigration Canada
De Sousa, R.M. 2006. "Trini to the Bone: Return, Reintegration and Resolution among Trinidadian Migrants." In *Returning to the Source: The Final Stage of the Caribbean Migration Circuit*, edited by Dwaine E. Plaza and Frances Henry. Kingston: University of the West Indies Press.
Dowlat, Rhondor. 2009. "Manohar: It's a Humanitarian Crisis." *Trinidad and Tobago's Newsday*, October 18.
Eriksen, Thomas Hylland, ed. 2003. *Globalisation: Studies in Anthropology*. London: Pluto Press.
Foner, Nancy, ed. 2001. *Islands in the City: West Indian Migration to New York*. Berkeley and Los Angeles: University of California Press.
Girvan, Norman. 2009. "Caribbean Xenophobia: Where Will It End." http://www.normangirvan.info/caribbean-xenophobia-where-will-it-end-norman-girvan/.
Glick Schiller, Nina. 2009. "A Global Perspective on Migration and Development." *Social Analysis* 53(3): 14–37.
Hannerz, Ulf. 2003. "Several Sites in One." In *Globalisation: Studies in Anthropology*, edited by Thomas Hylland Eriksen, 18–38. London: Pluto Press.
Homer, Louis B. 2008. "Philippines Government to Foot Bill for Deportees' Plane Tickets." *Trinidad Express*, October 17.
Honore-Gopie, Venus. 2009. "70 Chinese Worker Permits Revoked." *Trinidad and Tobago's Newsday*, October 20.
Inda, Jonathan Xavier, and Renato Rosaldo, eds. 2002. *The Anthropology of Globalization: A Reader*. Malden, MA and Oxford: Blackwell.
International Organization for Migration. 2009. "Trinidad and Tobago: Facts and Figures." http://www.iom.int/Jahia/Jahia/trinidad-and-tobago.
Johnson, Randy. 2009. "Regional Migration Debate Dominates Caricom Summit." *Trinidad and Tobago Express*, July 12.
Khan, Aisha. 2004. *Callaloo Nation: Metaphors of Race and Religious Identity among South Asians in Trinidad*. Durham: Duke University Press.
Leach, Belinda. 2008. "A Clash of Histories." *Focaal* 51: 43–56.
———. 2009. "Shunning Canada's Neoliberal Immigration Project: Trinidadian Transnationalism, Citizenship and History." Paper presented at CASCA annual meeting.

Mahoney, Jill. 2009. "Canada's 'Missing Province' Grows as Ex-pats Opt Out." *Globe and Mail*, October 29.
Massey, Doreen. 1994. *Space, Place and Gender*. London: Polity Press.
Neaves, Julien. 2009. "Chinese Workers' Quarters Not up to Mark." *Trinidad Express*, October 18.
Olwig, Karen Fog. 2007. *Caribbean Journeys: An Ethnography of Migration and Home in Three Family Networks*. Durham and London: Duke University Press.
Pickford-Gordon, Lara, and Richardson Dhalai. 2009. "'Return Blood Money'." *Trinidad and Tobago's Newsday*, October 14.
Plaza, Dwaine. 2001. "A Socio-historic Examination of Caribbean Migration to Canada: Moving to the Beat of Changes in Immigration Policy." *Wadabagei: A Journal of the Caribbean and Its Diaspora* 4(1).
Rouse, Roger. 2002. "Mexican Migration and the Social Space of Postmodernism." In *The Anthropology of Globalization: A Reader*, edited by Jonathan Xavier Inda and Renato Rosaldo. Malden, MA and Oxford: Blackwell.
Rowbotham, Don. 1998. "Transnationalism in the Caribbean: Formal and Informal." *American Ethnologist* 25(2): 307–321.
Santiago-Valles, William F. 2006. "Resistance among Those Displaced to the Caribbean: Suggestions for Future Research." In *Caribbean Transnationalism: Migration, Pluralization and Social Cohesion*, edited by R. Gowricharn, 59–75. Lanham, MD: Lexington Books.
Slocum, Karla, and Deborah Thomas. 2003. "Rethinking Global and Area Studies: Insights from Caribbeanist Anthropology." *American Anthropologist* 105(3): 553–565.
Smith, Michael G. 1965. *The Plural Society in the British West Indies*. Berkeley: University of California Press.
Sutton, Constance. 1987. "The Caribbeanization of New York City and the Emergence of a Transnational Sociocultural System." In *Caribbean Life in New York City*, edited by Constance Sutton and Elsa Chaney, 15–20. Staten Island: Center for Migration Studies.
Tait, Ria. 2009. "Chinese Go Home." *Trinidad Express*, August 27: 1.
Tsing, Anna. 2000. "The Global Situation." *Cultural Anthropology* 15(3): 327–360.
Valtonen, Kathleen. 1996. "Bread and Tea: A Study of the Integration of Low-Income Immigrants from Other Caribbean Territories into Trinidad." *International Migration Review* 30(4): 995–1019. Academic OneFile. Web. Accessed June 10, 2010.
Wimmer, Andreas, and Nina Glick Schiller. 2002. "Methodological Nationalism and Beyond: Nation-State Building, Migration and the Social Sciences." *Global Networks* 2(4): 301–334.
Wolf, Eric. 1982. *Europe and the People without History*. Berkeley and Los Angeles: University of California Press.
World Bank. 2009. "Migration and Remittances Factbook." Accessed May 25, 2010. http://econ.worldbank.org/WBSITE/EXTERNAL/EXTDEC/EXTDECPROSPECTS/0,,contentMDK:21352016~pagePK:64165401~piPK:64165026~theSitePK:476883,00.html.

6 Selecting, Competing, and Performing as 'Ideal Migrants'
Mexican and Jamaican Farmworkers in Canada

Janet McLaughlin

"The globe shrinks for those who own it; for the displaced or the dispossessed, the migrant or refugee, no distance is more awesome than the few feet across borders or frontiers."

Homi Bhabha (2003: 449)

"Human beings make their own history . . . but not in circumstances of their own choosing."

Karl Marx (1963: 15)

GATED MOVEMENTS IN A GATED GLOBE

Until recently, so Douglas Massey observed, theories of international migration had "paid short shrift to the nation-state as an agent influencing the volume and composition of international migration" (1999: 303). Yet—as much recent scholarship has shown (e.g., Heyman, this volume; Griffith 2006; Portes and Rumbaut 2006; Luibhéid and Cantú 2005)—this influence is very present in the current era of expanding international human and labor rights and managing migration within what Hilary Cunningham (2004) calls an increasingly "gated globe." In this era states use such instruments as guestworker programs to access migrants' productive power while abdicating responsibility for the rights of temporary laborers that would normally be expected for citizens or landed immigrants, divesting the costs of reproduction to migrants' "sending" states. In so doing, such "receiving" states construct zones, or what I call "systems of exception," in which partial or differential rights for certain (non-citizen) groups become normalized.[1]

In Canada, as elsewhere, employing migrant labor is not just convenient to capitalism, but has become a central component of the political economy, allowing a captive, disposable/replaceable, "just-in-time" labor force to do the most difficult work with wages, conditions, and benefits deemed unacceptable to most domestic workers. To facilitate this process, the neoliberal state, following the welfare state, has generated a society of multi-unit competition,[2] in which performance or adaptation of a neoliberal subjectivity is a defining element. In this increasingly precarious competition, race, gender, class and "ideas of nation" are endemic to the process of determining who is a worthy *immigrant*, versus who is merely a worthy *migrant* (see Barber and Bryan, this volume; Feldman-Bianco, this volume; Leach, this volume; Sharma 2006). Although the influence of migrant-receiving states on determining migration patterns and parameters has received much more attention in the literature, the role of migrant-sending states is also paramount (Fitzgerald 2009). Indeed, local, national, and global processes surrounding transnational migration are deeply interconnected and mutually constitutive (see Glick Schiller, this volume).

This chapter then is an exploration of how state and capitalist interests influence the selection of "ideal" migrant workers in Canada's Seasonal Agricultural Workers Program (SAWP) in a system of exception spanning Canada, Mexico, and Jamaica, the primary participating countries in the program. The SAWP is a managed migration scheme that legally employs migrant farmworkers from Mexico and several English-speaking Caribbean countries in Canadian agriculture on a temporary—or more accurately, circular—basis. It is among the oldest components of Canada's Temporary Foreign Worker Program, which has expanded rapidly over the past decade to involve migrant workers across numerous sectors.

Migrants' involvement in the SAWP and other temporary foreign worker programs is highly mediated by participating states, who define the parameters of the "types of migrants" they are willing to accept based, primarily, on their presumed ability to be the most efficient workers to support the interests of capital. The primacy of such interests becomes apparent through probing how these "ideal temporary migrants" are selected in each country—a complex process that has distinct differences from the procedures and requirements for permanent immigrants, and one that had been largely overlooked[3] (though see Barber and Bryan, this volume; Barber 2008b; Sharma 2006). In what follows, I also stress that while state and capitalist interests across several countries converge to influence this selection, Mexican and Jamaican workers participating in this managed migration program respond to these expectations, conforming as much as they can to become the ideal. In the face of recruiters and employers, many workers enact what Pauline Gardiner Barber and Belinda Leach have labeled "performances of subordination," to conform to the model image expected of them (Barber and Bryan, this volume; Barber 2008a, 2008b).[4] Ideal workers in the SAWP are those who will work hard, obey rules, and be completely flexible, while never aspiring to advance their position, develop personal or romantic relationships, or settle in Canada. Such conformity has consequences in their lives, and not all are willing to accept them. Yet most feel that the SAWP is the best option for them in a set of increasingly limited alternatives.[5]

My purpose here is to probe how multiple players collude and compete to produce the ideal flexible, subaltern migrant worker within a system of exception, thereby reproducing specific constructions of gender and class, as well as relations of race and citizenship. These players are: first, the employers; second, the states and their bureaucracies, on the one hand of Canada, and on the other hand of Mexico and Jamaica; and third, the migrants themselves. The discourse that organizes and makes possible this collusion is one of perceived competition between players at the same level in each case (though interestingly this sense of competition from perceived peers is perhaps most poignant among state actors and employers). Canadian employers, for example, argue for the use of migrant workers and justify their treatment of workers by reference to the absent presence of other, competing farms.[6] Bureaucracies, especially Mexican and Jamaican, invoke a world in which other nations could reap the benefits currently flowing to them. Canada meanwhile appears to be acting somewhat along the lines of the "Guantanamo legal loophole"—that they cannot be held responsible for practices taking place abroad that would be illegal at home, or for the treatment of non-citizen migrant workers—thereby enhancing Canadian productive society despite Canadian law. And in turn, migrants are then brought into this thus-constituted social arena under terms that shape their necessary collusion.

The Mexican and Caribbean farmworkers hoping to come to Canada learn to enact performances of subordination in order to appear ideal, both during the application process to migrate as well as during their time in Canada as they attempt to secure future employment. I suggest these performances create a dehumanizing context in which migrants can succeed only through appearing docile and underemphasizing their experiences, intelligence, independence, and talents. The continuation of these performances in a program that allows for no job mobility inhibits migrants' class mobility (at least while in Canada). The alternative, however, is a loss of employment and of the means to support their families (and the preclusion of what many aspire toward—the facilitation of their families' advancement through supporting their education, etc.). Potential consequences of performances of subordination are thus complex and often contradictory. For migrants, such enactments may result in both limitations and experiences of dehumanization as well as the potential for (relative) empowerment and improvement of life circumstances. For Canada, the normalization of these performances creates a two-tiered society, in which some residents and citizens may develop their human potential and integrate under conditions of relative freedom, while certain categories of migrant workers are systematically excluded from national membership. Such migrants are only permitted temporarily, so long as they perform a certain script, and accept living and working under conditions of relative unfreedom. Yet the perceived need and demand for such "temporary" migrants has become permanent.

To conceptualize how this system unfolds, the metaphor of a "gated globe" (Cunningham 2004) can be expanded from the notion of borders denoting "lines" over which migrants must pass to physically leave or enter a country, to also include "gates" of screening within their countries of origin as well as their "exceptional" forms of treatment within Canada. Thus, the idea of the border can be extended to include the lines that delineate movement and membership both between and within nations (see Sharma 2006). Núñez and Heyman (2007) note, however, that ethnographic attempts to understand barriers to movement and operationalize the concepts of "mobility and enclosure" must also consider the agency of migrants and their attempts to overcome these barriers for reasons they deem important. As Barber argues in her analysis of the "Janus (double-faced) effect," structural disempowerment does not preclude "individual agency and its empowering possibilities" (2002: 56; see also Leach, this volume). With these considerations in mind, I demonstrate ways in which migrants use networks, creativity, and in some cases false identities, strategies mediated by a "morality of risk" (Núñez and Heyman 2007), in order to circumvent the limitations imposed by these rigid state selection processes to promote their own interests. Findings are based on over three years of ethnographic research in Mexico, Canada, and Jamaica.[7]

THE CANADIAN SAWP: A MODEL FOR TEMPORARY LABOR MIGRATION?

The SAWP began in 1966 as a pilot program between Canada and Jamaica, based on similar guestworker initiatives in the United States and Europe, at a time when these programs were coming under severe criticism and in some cases were even being terminated (see Castles 2006; Griffith 2006; Smith-Nonini 2005; Rothenberg 2000). As seen in the United Kingdom and elsewhere, such guestworker programs institute a bifurcated labor market, in which a near-endless supply of foreign workers provides a highly exploitable reserve army of labor, often working under conditions of structural violence (McLaughlin 2009; Ivancheva 2007).

Initially concerns among Canadian government officials about the effects of the program on domestic employment and the possibility of undesired migrants' permanent settlement led to considerable debate (Satzewich 1991). Canadian growers lobbied extensively for the program, however, arguing that they could no longer secure reliable domestic sources of labor under competitive conditions. From the pilot year, detailed processes were put into place between the participating governments to screen and select ideal migrants for the program, and to ensure that they would return to their countries of origin at the end of each contract (McLaughlin 2009).

Soon after its inception, in the face of diplomatic pressures, the SAWP expanded to include other Commonwealth Caribbean countries. Mexico joined in 1974, a move that provided a near limitless supply of migrant farmworkers to Canada with differently perceived racialized traits (see Preibisch and Binford 2007; Satzewich 1991). The SAWP has continually expanded, now issuing over twenty-five thousand annual visas. In 2002 the federal government announced an expanded temporary foreign worker program (TFWP), which allows the employment of temporary workers in numerous sectors, including agriculture, from any country. This broader program provides employers with even more choice over the national origin of their prospective labor force, and its use has expanded rapidly. In fact, across all industries, there were over 360,000 foreign workers in Canada in 2008, about double the number present five years earlier.[8] Although some agricultural employers have hired workers through this expanded program from countries such as Guatemala, the Philippines, and Thailand, the majority continue to utilize Mexican and Caribbean workers through the SAWP, a program with which they have more experience and familiarity, and which has the advantage of rigid, standardized selection procedures.

Now in its forty-sixth year, the SAWP is often hailed as a model migration program on which others should be based, widely praised for its ability to meet the flexible needs of Canadian employers in an orderly fashion. Although it is a federal government authorized and managed program, the SAWP's day-to-day operations are conducted through privately run user-fee agencies, run "by and for" employers (Verma 2003). SAWP participants are guaranteed many of the same rights and benefits as Canadian workers; they pay taxes, employment insurance, and pension premiums, and are granted such rights as minimum or prevailing wage and (temporary) access to Canadian medical care and workers' compensation. Moreover, the program provides immense economic benefits not only for Canadian employers, but also for many other sectors of the Canadian economy on which agriculture depends. For migrant-sending countries and communities, remittances are ever more important, particularly as relative economic conditions worsen for many countries within the global South (see Kapur 2004). The SAWP thereby generates economic benefits for employers, participating states, and for individual migrants, their families, and communities. But at what cost?

WORTHY MIGRANTS, UNWORTHY IMMIGRANTS

Although the income and protections afforded in the SAWP are undoubtedly appreciated by migrants, the managed, limited nature of the program also has major shortcomings. SAWP participants benefit from the mandatory accommodation provided on their employers' property, for example, but this also subjects them to regulation, monitoring, and control both on and off the job. Moreover, much work has drawn attention to the fact that migrants' rights, though guaranteed on paper, are restricted in practice, while agriculture—long seen as an "exceptional" industry requiring exceptional measures to remain globally competitive—has been exempt from basic labor protections considered standard in other industries in Canada (McLaughlin 2009; Verma 2003; Basok 2002). Farmworkers in Ontario, for example, are denied the right to bargain collectively as part of a union.

The labor performed by migrants is part of a continuum of labor practices, which have become increasingly precarious for both domestic and (im)migrant workers in Canada (see Sider 2003; Winson and Leach 2002), as elsewhere. As part of the hegemony of neoliberalism, states have increasingly taken on the role of "handmaidens" to global capitalism (Winson and Leach 2002: 23). Amid the wider global retreat from the role of states as providers of welfare to those that uphold a neoliberal hegemony, rather than placing workers' interests at the fore with increased wages, protections, and welfare, the state devises arrangements to deliver an unfree labor force to industries, which argue that they could not survive, or thrive, otherwise. Differential citizenship status thus replaces earlier forms of discrimination as a form of "harnessable vulnerability" (Sider 2003) for the lowest paying, most precarious jobs. As Sider argues: "The apparent transition from race to citizenship as the primary way of producing usable difference and inequality is actually a result of the state increasingly and directly assuming almost full control over the production of useful vulnerabilities and delivering these vulnerabilities as a subsidy to capital" (2003: 317). Capitalism, immigration/citizenship regimes, and migrant vulnerability are thereby inextricably linked.

A principal advantage of the SAWP as a *temporary* migration program is that the majority of participants return home and the program generally does not lead to permanent immigration (Basok 2000). Migrants' labor is desired, but they are deemed unworthy of permanent settlement, not only because of long-standing racialized biases against the suitability of uneducated people of color to settle in Canada (Trumper and Wong 2007; Sharma 2006; Satzewich 1991), but also because once immigrants—or even *free* laborers—they could no longer be compelled to work in agriculture, let alone be bound to a single employer. Tanya Basok (2002) thus argues that migrant workers' unfree labor is a "structural necessity" to some sectors of Canadian agriculture. Immigration would undermine the very purpose of the SAWP—to ensure a ready, reliable, and flexible supply of agricultural labor exactly when and where it is needed.

Temporary migrants' strategic advantage to capital is precisely that they are a form of unfree labor in industries that offer conditions so distasteful (e.g., long, inconsistent hours, difficult work, low pay, fewer workplace rights and protections) that free laborers do not normally remain (Basok 2002; Satzewich 1991). Migrant workers are inhibited from labor market mobility because of legal and political restrictions, which effectively bind them to one employer in Canada. Workers are unable to refuse employers' demands and requests for labor, even if conditions are difficult, dangerous, or otherwise undesirable. Even though migrant workers are legally free to leave their job and return home, their often dire economic circumstances and other considerations create a situation in which they feel that they cannot afford to risk losing their employment (Basok 2002). Employers' treatment of workers is extremely variable, along a spectrum of those who claim their workers are like "family," (and who may even visit them in the winters), to those who generally respect and treat workers with dignity, to those who may either neglect workers' needs or actively abuse their rights. The structural dimensions of the program, however, render all workers vulnerable regardless of their individual employers. Migrants' jobs are extremely precarious: they can be fired at the discretion of their employers. A loss of contract means the loss of the right to remain in Canada, and deportation normally follows. Readmission to the program is not secured by seniority or experience, and rather depends largely on employers' evaluation of or request for them (see Binford 2009; Basok 2002). Thus there is a constant pressure for workers to conform to their employers' expectations. Workers, in fact, may feel even more pressure to perform well for employers considered to be friendly, to maintain these more favorable employment relations for years to come.

SHIFTING PREFERENCES AND COMPETITION FOR IDEAL MIGRANTS

Employers assert that amid intense globalized competition, productive, disciplined workers are essential; this rationale not only sustains the SAWP,[9] but also justifies shifting the national and gender composition of workers to create the ideal labor force.[10] Under the SAWP, employers specify the number of workers from each gender and nationality that they desire. These requests are often based on gendered and racialized assumptions of different groups' attributes and abilities, which shift over time. In interviews, many employers commented on migrants' "inherent" qualities, such as the Caribbean men's "hearty make-up" and "tolerance of intense heat," making them ideal fieldworkers, or Mexican women's delicate and obedient "nature," which make them superior workers for specific tasks such as packing soft fruit or picking flowers. Such preferences create a pervasive sense of competition within and between specific gendered, national, and racialized groups. In some cases, cross-mixing by nationality and gender across various parts of the farm is also done in an attempt to circumvent romantic relationships forming between workers, which can, as one employer asserted, "affect productivity."[11]

Meanwhile, workers explain that their high productivity levels are primarily achieved because of their sense of intense competition and desire to please employers for coveted positions in the program. Women, who comprise only 2 to 3 percent of the program's participants, are under particular pressure to perform (see Preibisch and Encalada Grez 2010). As 'Maria,'[12] a worker from Mexico explains:

> We have to work much harder because others around us set the pace very high because they want to show off to the boss. We're not machines, but some try to work like machines—they want to impress the boss and keep up the reputation that one Mexican worker is worth the productivity of three to four Canadians—not just three, but four! (Interview, April 2007)

The reflections of many workers interviewed suggest that the pervasive competition between workers of various ethnic and gender backgrounds, combined with limited labor mobility rights, pushes them to be more productive than Canadian citizens, who have the freedom to seek alternative employment. Employers often argue that hiring workers through the SAWP increases their production costs due to expenses associated with the program, such as transportation and housing costs, that are incurred on top of minimum wages. Most employers, however, also acknowledge that the higher productivity and reliability of migrant laborers more than make up for these added expenses. Thus the SAWP may contribute both to the higher profits for employers—or at least sustainability of agricultural production that could not operate profitably with domestic labor alone—as well as lower food prices and the sustainability of "local food" systems for Canadian consumers, representing an additional subsidy to capital.

This sense of competition between workers has also been reinforced by government officials, who continually assert that workers must work hard and refrain from "causing problems," in order to retain their country's positions in the program. Such messages have been especially pronounced from the Caribbean governments, whose economies are smaller and more dependent on migration programs, and who have been concerned about losing ground in the SAWP to Mexico—which has overtaken all of the Caribbean countries combined as the SAWP's leading participant country. Workers are regularly reminded by their government officials to "give their best," that they are "ambassadors" who must uphold the country's reputation to ensure future positions. These messages often play out in the local media where the success of the program and performance of workers within it earn political bragging rights. For example, a 2005 article quoting Jamaica's Senior Liaison Officer in Leamington, an area of concentrated greenhouse production close to Windsor, Ontario, reports: "While acknowledging that the competition for jobs in the area was stiff, especially from the Mexicans, Mr. Day said, 'What we find is that our workers are much more hardy and they do work much better. They are more apt to go the extra mile sometimes'" (Rose 2005). An earlier article describing Jamaican officials' visits to Canada similarly reports that "Jamaican farmworkers are highly rated for their ability to work harder than their counterparts from Mexico or the Eastern Caribbean" and quotes a Canadian farmer saying: "I couldn't survive without these guys . . . they work much harder than the Mexicans and Eastern Caribbean workers" (*Gleaner* 1995).

Ultimately, however, employers make their own judgments and have decidedly shifted toward Mexican workforces in recent years. There are many possible reasons for this shift.[13] Corroborating recent findings by Preibisch and Binford (2007), in my interviews, employers indicated their conceptions that Mexican workers are superior at certain sectors of agriculture that have expanded, while noting that the cultural and linguistic differences of Mexicans may be seen to limit their politicization and social relationships with Canadians. As one employer explained:

> There were problems on some of the farms with some of the [Caribbean] fellows who were here long enough . . . they sort of start to get a little bit slack and they start to think about some of the good times they can have here and when work isn't the important part anymore, and the Mexican men are more family oriented. I don't think they have two wives or that sort of thing. [One grower switched to Mexicans] . . . because the Caribbean guys could speak English and the Mexicans would come and maybe one in ten can speak English and they don't make a point of trying to learn English and I think that's okay because they don't make a point in trying to carouse for women like the Caribbean workers. (Interview, January 2007)

Both individuals and groups can be punished for such perceived indiscretions. In multiple instances throughout my fieldwork, migrants were fired or removed from the program for developing personal relationships in Canada. One was even let go for making a long-distance phone call to his wife while she was in labor in Jamaica, even though he admitted and apologized for his action. Through such instances, migrants learn that developing romantic or even platonic relationships while in Canada, or prioritizing family contact at inopportune times, can have a negative impact on their employment. The "machines" who must demonstrate the productivity of three to four Canadians to be competitive must also restrain from engaging in any humanizing relationships—thus necessitating yet another layer of performing subordination.

SELECTING MIGRANTS IN MEXICO AND JAMAICA

Amid this atmosphere of intense competition and control, once employers have selected the national and gender compositions of their workforce, migrant-sending countries are charged with selecting appropriate workers based on criteria they further establish. The criteria and mechanisms to select workers stand in stark contradiction to Canada's Employment Equity

Act, which states that "no person shall be denied employment opportunities or benefits for reasons unrelated to ability" (Department of Justice Canada 1995) as well as the Human Rights Act, which features similar clauses against discriminatory hiring practices. But there seems to be little concern with such discrepancies, in part because the hiring processes are divested off-shore and conducted by the sending states. Instead, the sending governments who are charged with worker selection demonstrate a sense of pride and take seriously their job of finding ideal workers for Canadian employers. For example, when I asked an official at the Mexican Ministry of Labor (MOL) how Mexico could improve the program, his response was:

> The Mexican government could improve the quality of the workers who go to Canada, improving the selection of workers, workers who apply themselves in Canada, who will work 10 hours a day from Monday to Saturday, who don't leave the farm, who make their life in the farm nothing else, that go to work only as agricultural workers with experience. They have to be accustomed to a certain way of living, because in Canada, you cannot leave the farms without warning the employer. (Interview, November 2006)

The MOL has determined the kind of laborer most likely to fit this profile—workers with dependents, limited education, and few job prospects are the most likely to work hard, not jeopardize employment, and to return home at the end of the contract, and the MOL has honed a selection apparatus emphasizing these traits. According to 2006 MOL statistics, 94 percent of workers selected were in a marriage or common-law partnership (an additional 3 percent were single, widowed, or divorced women); 96 percent had children (others may have other kinds of dependents, such as elderly or sick parents); 81 percent had two children or more. Workers' average age in 2006 was 37.4, and 78 percent of workers (both new and returning) were between the ages of twenty-five and forty-four. Most had some primary or junior high-school education (approx 96.5 percent), but very few (about 3 percent) had high school or above.

Nicolas is a prototypical ideal migrant in Mexico. He is a young man, married, with five children and a sick parent to support. He has years of agricultural experience, but little land, a sixth-grade education, and his job prospects are scarce. He wants to work in Canada to support his family in Mexico, especially as US-border security has tightened, making the prospects of undocumented migration there increasingly precarious. If he makes it into the Canadian program, he insists that he will not cause any problems to jeopardize his coveted position, and will return home to his family in the winter. By all accounts, he represents the model candidate sought for the SAWP in Mexico.

There are many other prospective migrants, however, who fall outside of the parameters established by the MOL, but still desperately need income

Selecting, Competing, and Performing as 'Ideal Migrants'

to support their families, and cannot find adequate employment in Mexico, or who may want to migrate for other reasons. Through their kin networks of successful migrants, applicants have a good idea of what the MOL seeks, and some deliberately manipulate their profiles to conform. Some workers speak of dipping their hands in *cal* (used to make tamales) to look more as though they are agricultural laborers. Others go to more elaborate means. Forged documents in Mexico, and among Mexican (im)migrants in the United States, are commonplace,[14] and many workers speak of altering theirs to comply with MOL preferences. As Pedro, another migrant, explains:

> The program here is very important and very hard to get into. . . . I live in D.F. (Mexico City), where we had the welding business. I'm 27 and my wife is 20. We don't have any kids. She's trying to learn English and wants to study international business. She's very smart but it's expensive, so I have to send money home to support her. I can't make enough in Mexico. . . . I had to fake papers from my brother's wife, saying that we have children together and that I'm a *campesino* [peasant]. (Interview, July 2006)

Female applicants, who face even stiffer competition for only 3 percent of the program's spots, have also learned to manipulate their circumstances. Although the MOL typically only allows single mothers (the assumption ingrained in this deeply patriarchal society is that married women should stay home while their husbands migrate), some married women have managed to break the mold when their husbands are unable to go to Canada. As Cecilia, a worker in her thirties, explains:

> I applied for the program after my son got cancer. He was very sick and we spent our life savings, including selling our house, on his treatments. I entered the program to pay off these debts and continue to support him. I entered as a 'single mother.' My husband could not go because he was 46 and there is an age limit to enter. (Interview, November 2006)

Although some applicants are successful, with stiff competition, many others are still turned down. It is somewhat ironic that some of these unsuccessful applicants may fit the criteria of what the MOL is seeking more than those who know the rules and have the resources to bend them. In such cases, a lack of education, resources, and literacy may actually pose a barrier to the admittance of those most in economic need, as they may not be able to as easily manipulate their applications to conform to the MOL preferences.

In Jamaica, the applicants' relationship to those in positions of power in their communities is a primary determinant of their consideration for the program. Applicants with the right "connections" are in the best position to make it past the first gatekeeper—their members of parliament (MP), who hand out cards to workers which enable them to attend an "interview" for the program. Although these leaders are supposed to consider applicants with the best likelihood of success in Canada, inevitably in small communities where "everybody knows everybody," cards end up going to applicants with the best relationships to these leaders—family members, friends, and supporters who have demonstrated political loyalty. As one worker explains, "I know I got my job much faster because I know a lot of people in the Ministry . . . It's good if your MP knows you, if you're well known in your community, and if you support your MP. Then he will work for you" (Fieldnotes, January 2007).

MPs play an important function by pre-selecting candidates who suit Canada's needs. A Jamaican MOL official defends the use of political leaders as gatekeepers into the program because:

> They know the type of people we are looking to recruit—people who will come and work and complete their contract and return to Jamaica. That is important to the growth of the program where the Canadian government is concerned—that people come to work and return to their country of origin. You don't want a lot of people running off the program and becoming illegal immigrants; that would be of some concern to the Canadian authorities that we're recruiting workers who aren't coming home. (Interview, July 2007)

That MPs play a critical role and wield a great deal of influence in the selection process is no secret, but it is the program screeners who have the final say in the selection. The pre-selected workers are given cards by their MP or community leader and told to show up on a designated interview day, where they wait around until their names are called. One past recruiter emphasized that their main goal at this point is "getting men who are able to do the work—based on their physical look, farm experience. They should have no criminal record. It's good if they are able to read" (Interview, February 2007). For Jamaica's selection it matters little if applicants are married, how many dependents they have, or whether or not they are unemployed. Instead, selectors seem to be primarily concerned with ensuring that applicants are physically and mentally able to handle agricultural labor; willing to accept an environment where they have little control over their living and working conditions and fully obey their employers; and unlikely to commit a crime, stay in Canada, or cause any trouble.

Like their counterparts in Mexico, Jamaican applicants also learn what qualities are sought, and how to appear to be the ideal candidate. In their case, performances of subordination may involve demonstrating complete flexibility and submissiveness. A key determinant in workers' ability to pass the selectors' test is the attitude they display—basically, if they are willing to do exactly as they are told and appear to be obedient and disciplined. "Selectors might say no to a worker if he has a bad attitude" (Interview, February 2007), explained one past official who performed this role. What

Selecting, Competing, and Performing as 'Ideal Migrants' 121

determines if a worker has a bad attitude and agricultural experience is subject to a peculiar examination. Anthony, a Jamaican applicant, described his experience with the selection process as follows:

> I know someone, one of the councilors who gives out the cards. . . . So after I get that card I go to the place where the Ministry select the guys . . . and they ask me some stupid questions like if you eat pork, because most Jamaicans don't eat pork, but they say when you go on the program you have to eat anything because you don't want to give the employer any problem. They would look at your hand and if it was too soft they wouldn't let you. And they ask you if you ever traveled before. If you go to get a visa before and you didn't get it then they wouldn't use you. They think you going to use the program to run away so they look at your book stamped up they wouldn't use you. But normally they would ask—you want somebody who is a farmer—so they ask you what you farm and if you can't answer they wouldn't bother to use you. They asked me if I want to work seven days a week and I said 'yes if possible' and they looked at my hand and ask if I'm prepared to wash and cook for myself and I said 'yes I will' and then he just let me through. (Interview, February 2007)

Seemingly arbitrary physical "tests" are also used to examine applicants who line up for hours in a field, waiting for their turn to come. Jamaican applicants, like their Mexican counterparts, speak of "roughing up their hands" to look more like hard laborers before the selection. Anthony continues:

> So they just look at you and judge you by how your hands are. . . . And they ask you to touch your toe; you just have to go down very quick—they want to know if you have a back problem so you have to touch your toe and don't bend your knees. And then they ask you to stretch out your hand and you have to do it quick . . . and if not they turn you down. . . . If you're smart you can go and watch the guys before, you see . . . [and can] have a pretty good idea. (Interview, February 2007)

Those who make it past the first stage are then sent to the Ministry of Labor in Kingston, Jamaica's capital, to perform detailed medical exams to ensure their health and fitness before they can be approved. Here, the emphasis on appearance continues: applicants are told to remove any piercings and that men must have short hair.

Many aspects of Jamaica's selection process parallel those of Mexico. The age of recruits, for example, with a bias against younger or older candidates, and the preference for rural candidates with agricultural experience, are similar in the two countries. Also both countries recruit predominantly men, although the gender ratios are entirely employer driven. The low education level of workers in both countries is also somewhat similar. Both countries have also been subject to some accusations of bribery, of intermediaries who charge money to facilitate entry (Hennebry 2008), and workers gaining an upper hand due to personal or family connections with administration officials. Despite the regulations offered by heavy state involvement, Hennebry (2008) argues that there is evidence of a "migration industry" forming around SAWP recruitment. In the end, each country appears to predominantly base its decisions for admittances on what officials deem to be the best method of recruiting a docile labor force for Canadian employers, and one that will return at the end of the season. Officials are clear that if their workers do not comply with the rules, they can easily be replaced not only by other co-patriots, but more important, by workers from other nations. In this arena of intense competition, both countries—within their unique contexts—have created what they view as the most effective schemes for ensuring their workers' compliance to these standards.

In Mexico, a largely Catholic country where deeply ingrained religious norms support the ideal of family unity, the most likely candidates to return are seen to be men who have wives, children, and/or other dependents to support, or single mothers. There is a long history of cyclical migration across the US-Mexico border, and the majority of migrants send remittances and return to their families. *Campesinos* are viewed as "simple people" who want to work to maintain their families, and have no ambitions which may detract from this. Therefore higher education or urban work experience are actually barriers to admittance. Uneducated peasants with families to support are widely seen as the most likely to fit the profile.

Jamaica, by contrast, presents its own unique social features that affect the perceived qualities of desired recruits. For example, having multiple flexible relationships is a widespread form of social behavior. Making marriage or common-law relationships a criterion in a country with low rates of formal unions would be excessively prohibitive. Furthermore, deep historical injustices and political and structural violence—stemming from slavery to the profound effects of global economic restructuring and liberalization—have contributed to current levels of violence and drug use emerging as notorious problems, particularly in urban areas of the country. Finally, as part of the former British Commonwealth, people in Jamaica speak English and many have relatives in Canada, making absconding from the program an easier and more appealing option (see Preibisch and Binford 2007).

Even if these issues are exaggerated in the minds of employers to the point of racialized stereotyping, Jamaican officials are well aware of them and are concerned with recruiting participants who will not worsen Jamaica's image. Perhaps for these and other reasons, good standing and reputation within the community, rural residence, law-abiding behavior, clean-cut appearances, and good attitudes are seen to be particularly important criteria for predicting who will do their jobs, obey the rules, stay out of trouble, and, perhaps most importantly, return home. Such rationalities may help to explain the seemingly much greater emphasis in the Jamaican system on these factors, ensured by the MP vetting process and attitude-based assessment, while in Mexico the emphasis remains on other traits, such as marital status, number of dependents, and lack of higher education and other job prospects.

PERFORMANCES OF SUBORDINATION IN CANADA

Once workers arrive in Canada, their performances of subordination must continue. Those who cannot comply to these standards often face harsh consequences. Workers are well aware that they are easily replaceable and can be dismissed at any time. As Mark, a Jamaican worker, explained, "We couldn't utter a word because if we said something you're on the way home. You go back to Jamaica, your brother's on the way up . . . if you don't behave, your brother's on his way up." Without even a basic level of education, Steve, a second Jamaican worker, came to understand the lived effects of being made a "reserve army": "[Canada is] like a prison and a high school—you go to prison and you learn something. I figured out that we are reserve workers—they have 1,000 extra guys they call on if there are any problems. Any time you stick up for your rights they don't like you." Steve further explained that "well educated" or "intelligent" workers are not liked by employers, and they must pretend not to know anything about their rights in order to maintain favor and, of course, employment (Fieldnotes, February 2007).

Although all employers may share a preference for disciplined and obedient workers, the experience of performing subordination is by no means universal or homogenous, and varies based on the attitudes of workers as well as their employers. Some employers, for example, emphasized that they appreciated those workers who demonstrated intelligence and skills—such as a Mexican who could speak some English and therefore could help translate; a Jamaican who had advanced literacy and could understand written instructions; or workers who could be trusted to competently drive vehicles or operate farm machinery. In fact, in some cases such workers would receive favors, such as supervisorial duties, use of an employer vehicle, or superior accommodations.

Some workers, moreover, determine that the experience of performing subordination is not worth the effort. Lorenzo is an apt example of a migrant who did not fit neatly into the profile of selectors, but was nonetheless accepted into the program by de-emphasizing his education, experience, and fluency in English. Lorenzo, who was working as a greenhouse manager in Mexico, had previously lived for many years in the United States, where he became fluent in English, ran his own businesses, and pursued post-secondary education. He wanted to come to Canada to learn more about greenhouses and thought his experiences managing a greenhouse, combined with his fluency in English, would make him an asset to any farm. When applying for the job, he did not mention his education, experience, or employment. Instead, he posed as a poor *campesino* with no job prospects.

Using these measures, Lorenzo was pleased to be admitted to the program, hoping to contribute something meaningful to his Canadian employer and to gain international experience and skills that could contribute to his greenhouse business in Mexico. Yet shortly after he arrived he became frustrated over several aspects of the job in Canada. Irritated with the lack of transportation options, he purchased a used car, which completely shocked his boss, who forbade him from parking it on the farm property (where Lorenzo lived and worked), forcing him to keep his car at a nearby store parking lot. When he drove the car to Leamington, an area of concentrated greenhouse production about four hours away from his place of employment, to see about transferring to a farm where his skills could be better applied, he was bluntly told by the employers there that the program was not meant to recruit skilled workers. As he summarizes:

> I can see the way they look at Mexican workers. Maybe they think we're not capable to do something like that. They look at Mexicans just as job power, not as people with brains. I've been pretty disappointed, but to me it's just another obstacle. . . . I want to find something else where they can appreciate what I can do . . . They don't allow you to improve . . . and even if you come with an idea, it's not valued. (Interview, June 2006)

Simply requesting access to his own health card (used to attain free medical services) from the employer—who routinely (and illegally) withheld the cards from all workers—caused a problem, even though Lorenzo only wanted to use the card as identification to take out books and access the Internet at the local library. The employer apparently could not understand why a migrant would want to access the community services meant for Canadians. In the end, Lorenzo was fired after only two months in Canada for, he believes, asking too many questions, which, incidentally, he was able to do in English.

After being fired, Lorenzo was partly relieved to be going back to Mexico, a country he said exhibited "much greater freedom" than Canada. He even determined that despite the precarity described by Heyman (this volume), the United States is a better country to work in because at least there you have "freedom of movement and association" (unless you get caught). He had given Canada a try only because of the increased security barriers along the US border, which had got him kicked out of the country after years of living there (and working as a construction manager) without legal status. He vowed upon leaving Canada that if he ever came back as a worker, it would have to be "undocumented" so that he could actually be free to "move around" and "get ahead."

Ultimately, Lorenzo's experience, ability, willingness to communicate, and motivation to apply and advance his skills resulted in his being kicked out of Canada's "model migration program." He could afford to break from the mold of performed subordination as he has a reasonable job prospect in Mexico. Nicolas, a genuine "poor *campesino*" with six dependents, continues on in the program. Like the vast majority of migrants in the SAWP, Nicolas deems the trade-offs of working under poor conditions without complaint as worth the sacrifice. In his mind, the Canadian program is the best available alternative to him.

CONSEQUENCES OF PERFORMING SUBORDINATION

The ideal temporary migrant sought by Canada is someone who will work without complaint and will return home at the end of the contract. The SAWP is considered a success because, for the most part, it complies with these criteria. The ministries of labor in sending countries do their best to conform to these requirements, as they compete against other participating countries to produce the optimal labor force to ensure their continued participation in the program and the related remittances and political acclaim to the government for securing lucrative positions abroad. Workers who are unable or unwilling to successfully perform their subordination are quickly removed from the program.

Although some Canadian union and activist groups have begun to advocate for the rights of migrant workers, labor uprisings and protests over poor conditions among workers are infrequent and when they do occur often lead to the dismissal, deportation, and future exclusion of participants. Most migrants are well aware of this reality, and their structural vulnerability vis-à-vis this restrictive system acts as a significant deterrent. Many workers nonetheless exercise subtle forms of resistance to this domination, utilizing "weapons of the weak" (Scott 1985), such as sneaking out of their employer-provided housing after curfew, filing for benefits against their employer's wishes, or taking farm produce, in some cases expensive items such as ice wine, to consume and give to each other (and sometimes fortunate anthropologists). As Ivancheva (2007) found among farmworkers in the UK, migrants in Canada revealed their "hidden transcripts of resistance" in "safe spaces," among trusted allies and friends. There, they continually articulate their frustrations with a system that does not permit overt public challenge. Outside of such limited spaces, however, most—out of necessity—play the hegemonic script of obedience. As Gabriela, a Mexican worker, explained:

> You have to be there to do what the *patron* tells you . . . if you start to disobey him, you will no longer return. For that reason one has to accept everything. Although you know that it is not the correct thing

or that they are committing injustices against you, you have to allow it. (Interview, November 2006)

There are sometimes severe consequences to continually performing subordination. The emphasis on refraining from engaging in humanizing or romantic relationships can have a particularly profound cost, generating a context of isolation and stress for many workers. Indeed, my health-focused research found that many migrants suffer from depression, anxiety, *nervios*, and other health concerns brought on by the dehumanization of living and working in conditions of high stress and low control without adequate social support (McLaughlin 2009). Some analysts suggest that high education levels among migrant farmworkers may be a predictor for depressive symptomatology, because they may be more sensitive to discrepancies between their treatment and that of other residents, and their jobs as farmworkers may not be allowing them to reach their life's goals (Hovey and Magaña 2000: 129). Lorenzo's experience supports this hypothesis.

Selecting the ideal migrant, then, is a process of ensuring little to no job mobility or integration for migrants in Canadian communities. They are permanently temporary. Thus, Canada successfully separates the laborer from the human, seeking only to extract a specific service and not to develop a well-rounded citizen with various skills to contribute to the country. Ideal migrant workers will never seek to be immigrants. Canadian society thus creates a two-tiered system, in which one group of residents, those deemed worthy of permanent membership, has the chance to develop skills, be mobile, unite with their families, and ultimately, belong; while the other is wanted only to work temporarily—only so long as needed—and is ultimately disposable. People of color from the global South with lower levels of formal education fall into the latter category, even though their labor is just as needed and fundamental to the Canadian economy (if not more so) as more highly educated white-collar (and often white-colored) workers who are afforded the opportunity to immigrate.[15]

Through managed migration programs such as the SAWP, receiving states can control the composition of their imagined communities, while ensuring a ready supply of exploitable labor to support the capitalist interests which are becoming increasingly hegemonic in neoliberal regimes of production and appropriation. Sending states also have a stake in coordinating these flows, even if the primary terms are dictated by receiving states, in order to ensure a steady flow of remittances and to maintain some control over their citizenry abroad. In an ever polarizing world, in which stable job prospects and alternatives are diminishing, increasing numbers of people are willing to enter precarious migratory labor flows that are continuously temporary. Migrants who participate in such systems perform their subordination to survive in a world in which their interchangeable labor is valued, but their human potential is not.

ACKNOWLEDGMENTS

This chapter is a modified version of "Classifying 'Ideal Migrant Workers': Mexican and Jamaican Transnational Farmworkers in Canada," in *Focaal-Journal of Global and Historical Anthropology*, no. 57 (Summer 2010): 79–94. Copyright 2010 Stichting Focaal and Berghahn Books. All rights reserved. Used by permission of the publisher. This research was funded by the Social Sciences and Humanities Research Council of Canada, the International Development Research Centre, the Institute for Work and Health, and the University of Toronto. My doctoral examining committee and advisors, Hilary Cunningham, Gavin Smith, Richard Lee, Valentina Napolitano, Donald Cole, and Linda Green, helped to shape the ideas here within. Gavin Smith, Shaylih Muehlmann, Winnie Lem, Pauline Gardiner Barber, and anonymous reviewers offered insightful comments on various parts of the manuscript. I owe my deepest gratitude to the migrant workers and other research participants whose insights and experiences formed the basis of this analysis.

NOTES

1. Agamben's theorization of the state of exception (2005) is useful in analyzing how such spaces can be rationalized and maintained in a liberal democracy espousing principles of human rights and equality. Agamben postulates that a state of exception arises in the juridical context during which emergency or exceptional measures, which include suspending normal constitutional order and human rights, are deemed necessary and become the norm. Although many authors have written of zones or spaces of exception, in discussing the Seasonal Agricultural Workers Program, I prefer to use the term "system of exception," which recognizes that the program operates as a system, involving multiple zones and actors, across time and space. A system of exception may be understood as a specific way in which a state of exception is realized.
2. I use the term 'multi-unit competition' to imply that there are multiple layers of 'actors' competing among each other simultaneously. In this case, agricultural employers, state officials, and workers of various backgrounds all define the parameters of their participation in a labor migration program vis-à-vis the competition they face from other members of each category.
3. Notably more attention has been paid to the desirable traits of *immigrants* than those admitted as temporary migrant workers. In contrast to the attributes considered valuable among temporary migrants, the Canadian government's construction of ideal "immigrants"—as instituted in the immigration point system—rests on such factors as ability to speak English and/or French, higher levels of post-secondary education, employment experience, and "adaptability" to living in Canada. See Simmons (2010) for further analysis.
4. Performing subordination, according to Pauline Gardiner Barber and Belinda Leach, involves migrants presenting themselves with particular desired identities and downplaying less desired traits, including, in some cases, education and professional experience. Barber (2008b: 1268), for example, discusses how both the Philippine state and Filipino migrants have adapted to suit

the changing immigration demands of Canada. She provides the prototypical example of doctors attempting to fill overseas positions as nurses or nurses aspiring to enter as domestic live-in caregivers. For further discussion, see articles in the *Focaal* 51 (2008) theme section on migration and mobilization.

5. As has been documented, pressures on small producers in countries like Mexico and Jamaica amid expanding neoliberal trade regimes, and an increasingly securitized (and precarious) US border, have influenced many people's desire to migrate, and safer alternatives afforded by legal migration are welcome (e.g., Núñez and Heyman 2007; Smith-Nonini 2005; Cunningham 2004; Basok 2002; Rothenberg 2000). Other factors, such as natural disasters and changing environments, political pressures, family and community networks, and "cultures of migration," also influence these decisions and alternatives (Kandel and Massey 2002).
6. Interestingly their argument works against the principles of comparative advantage, which is the cornerstone of free-trade neoliberalism, because they would lose such advantage should the extra-economic facility of flexible migrant labor be removed.
7. This research explored health and human rights issues among farmworkers and involved multisited fieldwork, which began in the Niagara region of Ontario in 2005, and continued as I followed workers to their homes in central Mexico and southeastern Jamaica and back to Canada again over the course of several annual migration cycles. Primary methods involved participant observation and qualitative interviews with workers, their families and communities, as well as interviews with employers, government officials, labor and community groups, and health-care providers.
8. This number included entries and re-entries for the year, as well as those workers who may have entered previously and were still in Canada in 2008 (CIC 2009).
9. Although the SAWP has undoubtedly helped to maintain labor-intensive agriculture in Canada, this has not necessarily been to the benefit of preserving small, or family-run, farms. Large commercial establishments, sometimes with hundreds of SAWP employees and lucrative corporate chain contracts, benefit from the same access to the dependable ideal migrant worker labor force as do the smaller operations. The SAWP thus does not lessen, and may even facilitate, the replacement of small farms by large corporate operations (see Binford 2010).
10. Although the role of employers is key, I emphasize it less in this chapter because other recent work has provided insightful analyses of employers' racialized (Preibisch and Binford 2007) and gendered (Preibisch and Encalada Grez 2010) preferences for migrant farmworkers in Canada. Griffith (2006) likewise offers a rich exploration of Mexican and Jamaican guestworker composition in the United States.
11. Preibisch and Encalada Grez (2010) report similar findings.
12. All names used are pseudonyms.
13. See Basok (2002), Binford (2002), Preibisch and Binford (2007), and Satzewich (2007) for further analyses of why Mexican labor has grown in the SAWP.
14. Núñez and Heyman (2007) discuss various strategies employed by migrants in the United States to learn and conform "to specific 'legal' social appearances and identities," including the use of documents to stave off arrest.
15. As Canada's temporary foreign worker programs continue to expand, some classes of workers—particularly those from higher skilled categories or professional occupations—have been given the opportunity to apply and even

fast-track applications for permanent residency. This has led critics to contend that temporary labor systems, which depend on employers' preferences, are replacing elements of Canada's traditional system of immigration. This same opportunity has not been equally provided to their "low-skilled" counterparts in industries such as agriculture; SAWP participants are almost never able to immigrate (with very few exceptions, for example if a worker marries a Canadian citizen). Trumper and Wong (2007) argue that race and gender remain central attributes in the organizing of migrant labor in Canada. They note: "By 2005, the number of unfree temporary worker entries (245,426) was almost double the number of free immigrant workers (128,727) who entered Canada" (2007: 155). Unfree workers, they note, are more often from racialized groups. See also Sharma (2006) for extended discussion.

REFERENCES

Agamben, Giorgio. 2005. *State of Exception*. Chicago: University of Chicago Press.
Barber, Pauline Gardiner. 2002. "Envisaging Power in Philippine Migration: The Janus Effect." In *Rethinking Em(power)ment, Gender and Development*, edited by Jane Parpart, Shirin Rai, and Kathleen Staudt, 41–60. London: Routledge.
———. 2008a. "Cell Phones, Complicity, and Class Politics in the Philippine Labor Diaspora." *Focaal—European Journal of Anthropology* 51: 28–42.
———. 2008b. "The Ideal Immigrant? Gendered Class Subjects in Philippine-Canada Migration." *Third World Quarterly* 29(7): 1265–1285.
Basok, Tanya. 2000. "He came, He saw, He . . . Stayed. Guest Worker Programmes and the Issue of Non-return." *International Migration* 38(2): 215–238.
———. 2002. *Tortillas and Tomatoes: Transmigrant Mexican Harvesters in Canada*. Montreal: McGill-Queen's University Press.
Bhabha, Homi K. 2003. "Postmodernism/Postcolonialism." In *Critical Terms for Art History*, edited by R.S. Nelson and R. Shiff, 435–451. Chicago: University of Chicago Press.
Binford, Leigh. 2002. "Social and Economic Contradictions of Rural Migrant Contract Labor between Tlaxcala, Mexico and Canada." *Culture & Agriculture* 24(2): 1–19.
———. 2009. "From Fields of Power to Fields of Sweat: The Dual Process of Constructing Temporary Migrant Labour in Mexico and Canada." *Third World Quarterly* 30(3): 503–517.
———. 2010. *Bound for Canada: Mexican Contract Labor in the Era of National Security*. Unpublished book manuscript.
Castles, Stephen. 2006. "Guestworkers in Europe: A Resurrection?" *The International Migration Review* 40(4): 741–767.
CIC (Citizenship and Immigration Canada). 2009. *Facts and Figures 2008: Immigration Overview: Permanent and Temporary Residents*. Ottawa, ON: CIC.
Cunningham, Hilary. 2004. "Nations Rebound? Crossing Borders in a Gated Globe." *Identities: Global Studies in Culture and Power* 11(3): 329–350.
Department of Justice Canada. 1995. "Employment Equity Act." Accessed February 9, 2012. Retrieved from: http://laws-lois.justice.gc.ca/eng/acts/E-5.401/page-1.html
Fitzgerald, David. 2009. *A Nation of Emigrants: How Mexico Manages Its Migration*. Berkeley and Los Angeles: University of California Press.
Gleaner. 1995. "Farmworkers in Canada Learning French." *Jamaica Gleaner*, August 31. Kingston.

Griffith, David Craig. 2006. *American Guestworkers: Jamaicans and Mexicans in the U.S. Labor Market*. University Park: Pennsylvania State University Press.

Hennebry, Jenna L. 2008. "Bienvenidos a Canada? Globalization and the Migration Industry Surrounding Temporary Agricultural Migration in Canada." *Canadian Studies in Population* 35(2): 339–356.

Hovey, Joseph D., and Cristina Magaña. 2000. "Acculturative Stress, Anxiety, and Depression among Mexican Immigrant Farmworkers in the Midwest United States." *Journal of Immigrant Health* 2(3): 119–131.

Ivancheva, Mariya. 2007. "Strawberry Fields Forever? Bulgarian and Romanian Student Workers in the UK." *Focaal—European Journal of Anthropology* 49: 110–117.

Kandel, William, and Douglas S. Massey. 2002. "The Culture of Mexican Migration: A Theoretical and Empirical Analysis." *Social Forces* 80(3): 981–1004.

Kapur, Devesh. 2004. *Remittances: The New Development Mantra?* G-24 Discussion Paper Series. New York and Geneva: United Nations.

Luibhéid, Eithne, and Lionel Cantú Jr., eds. 2005. *Queer Migrations: Sexuality, U.S. Citizenship, and Border Crossings*. Minneapolis: University of Minnesota Press.

Marx, Karl. 1963. *The Eighteenth Brumaire of Louis Bonaparte*. New York: International Publishers.

Massey, Douglas S. 1999. "International Migration at the Dawn of the Twenty-First Century: The Role of the State." *Population and Development Review* 25(2): 303–322.

McLaughlin, Janet. 2009. "Trouble in Our Fields: Health and Human Rights among Mexican and Caribbean Migrant Farm Workers in Canada," Doctoral thesis, Department of Anthropology, University of Toronto.

Núñez, Guillermina Gina, and Josiah McC Heyman. 2007. "Entrapment Processes and Immigrant Communities in a Time of Heightened Border Vigilance." *Human Organization* 66(4): 354–366.

Portes, Alejandro, and Rubén G. Rumbaut. 2006. *Immigrant America: A Portrait*. Berkeley and Los Angeles: University of California Press.

Preibisch, Kerry, and Leigh Binford. 2007. "Interrogating Racialized Global Labour Supply: An Exploration of the Racial/National Replacement of Foreign Agricultural Workers in Canada." *Canadian Review of Sociology and Anthropology* 44(1): 5–36.

Preibisch, Kerry L., and Evelyn Encalada Grez. 2010. "The Other Side of el Otro Lado: Mexican Migrant Women and Labor Flexibility in Canadian Agriculture." *Signs: Journal of Women in Culture and Society* 35(2): 289–316.

Rose, Dionne. 2005. "J'can Liaison Office in Canada Brings Job Boom." *Jamaica Gleaner*, September 22. Kingston.

Rothenberg, Daniel. 2000. *With These Hands: The Hidden World of Migrant Farmworkers Today*. New York: Harcourt Brace and Co.

Satzewich, Vic. 1991. *Racism and the Incorporation of Foreign Labour: Farm Labour Migration to Canada since 1945*. New York: Routledge.

———. 2007. "Business or Bureaucratic Dominance in Immigration Policymaking in Canada: Why Was Mexico Included in the Caribbean Seasonal Agricultural Workers Program in 1974?" *Journal of International Migration and Integration / Revue de l'integration et de la Migration Internationale* 8(3): 255–275.

Scott, James C. 1985. *Weapons of the Weak: Everyday Forms of Peasant Resistance*. New Haven and London: Yale University Press.

Sharma, Nandita Rani. 2006. *Home Economics: Nationalism and the Making of 'Migrant Workers' in Canada*. Toronto: University of Toronto Press.

Sider, Gerald M. 2003. *Between History and Tomorrow: Making and Breaking Everyday Life in Rural Newfoundland*. Peterborough, ON: Broadview Press.

Simmons, Alan B. 2010. *Immigration and Canada: Global and Transnational Perspectives*. Toronto: Canadian Scholars' Press Inc.

Smith-Nonini, Sandy. 2005. "Federally Sponsored Mexican Migrants in the Transnational South." In *The American South in a Global World*, edited by J.L. Peacock, H.L. Watson, and C.R. Matthews, 59–82. Chapel Hill: University of North Carolina Press.

Trumper, Ricardo, and Lloyd L. Wong. 2007. "Canada's Guest Workers: Racialized, Gendered, and Flexible." In *Race and Racism in 21st-century Canada: Continuity, Complexity, and Change*, edited by B.S. Bolaria and S.P. Hier, 151–170. Peterborough, ON: Broadview Press.

Verma, Veena. 2003. *The Mexican and Caribbean Seasonal Agricultural Workers Program: Regulatory and Policy Framework, Farm Industry Level Employment Practices, and the Future of the Program under Unionization*. Ottawa: North-South Institute.

Winson, Anthony, and Belinda Leach. 2002. *Contingent Work, Disrupted Lives: Labour and Community in the New Rural Economy*. Toronto: University of Toronto Press.

7 In Search of Hope
Mobility and Citizenships on the Canadian Frontier

Lindsay Bell

Canada is often referred to as a "country of immigrants." Its current and historic role as a receiving country has made it a rich site for migration studies (Abu-Laban and Gabriel 2002). Nevertheless, there are facets of migration which have been left unexplored, and which are related to the ways in which Canada's political economy relies on primary resources and their transformation. This political economy depends on the continual production of surplus labor populations within and without the country's borders. These populations are involved in complex and sometimes contradictory processes of mobility and fixity which complicate the narrative of Canada as a receiving country and subsequently home to fixed populations. It also complicates the narrative opposition of migrant/settlers and fixed, timeless indigenous populations (Abele and Stasiulus 1989). Indeed, migration and indigenous studies are usually held as distinct concerns. In this chapter, however, I show how the social categories of 'migrant,' 'Aboriginal,' and other configurations of locality are in fact dimensions of the same processes of social reproduction that have characterized the uneven course of state and capital in Canada.

The primary sector, a foundation of Canada's political economy, produces several scales of labor mobility which structure local and larger forms of social difference and inequality. The rise and fall of commodity prices and changing market conditions translate into the boom and bust of Canadian materials and markets. These highs and lows alongside changes in productive technologies move labor into, out of, and around the country. At the same time, resource extraction, via the state, has attempted to 'fix' populations in place. The bulk of Canadian resource projects today take place on lands marked as 'indigenous' (Gordon 2010). In order to secure access to land for development, the state has needed to arrange rights and property ownerships in a way that gives institutional meaning to Aboriginal collectivities, or put differently, it has reconfigured Aboriginal collectivities in ways that are institutionally recognizable. The contradiction, however, is that large-scale resource development and its accordant forms of (im)migration undermine the political-economic basis on which that Aboriginality was based. In addition, non-indigenous migrant workers frequently lay claim to local authenticity and priority as a way to stake a claim to privileged access to work. They do so by drawing on discourses of liberal citizenship as attached to occupation of the wider territory. Indeed "rights of citizenship" is the dominant trope through which mobility/fixity tensions and contradictions are debated pitting different groups against each other in rival claims to locality.

In this chapter I offer a case study of the mobility/fixity contradiction and the way it produces differentiated citizenships in Canada today. To tell the story of how mobility and fixity work (or not) in resource-rich regions of Canada, I elaborate the work trajectories of two individuals, one historic and one contemporary, who migrated to Hay River, Northwest Territories (NWT). Today, Hay River is a community of four thousand. Just north of the sixtieth parallel and located along its namesake Hay River and the southern shore of the Great Slave Lake, the area has been the 'gateway to the North' for some time. Its location is central to moving goods and labor into, around, and out of the region. John Hope arrived to the area at the end of the British Imperial era and at the dawn of Canadian nationhood and was interpreter at the Hay River Post belonging to the Hudson's Bay Company (HBC) in 1870. Ruth was one of the ten adult mining students I followed through the course of the field research, which was conducted between 2007 and 2009, the years that saw the peak of the Canadian diamond boom and the global financial crisis. Their movements form a chronological account of changing political-economic imperatives and the ways in which they shape mobility and forms of citizenship in the Canadian North, in particular the production and erasure of "Aboriginality." The individuals at the center of the account are both at once migrant and Aboriginal. Both show up to the NWT at times of significant political and economic change as part of the inscription of surplus populations in the continuous processes of primary resource extraction in the NWT from the fur trade to today's diamond industry. Indeed, diamond and oil developments in Canadian Northwest Territories (NWT) account for a substantial portion of the nation's gross domestic product.

The discussion here is based on eighteen months of ethnographic fieldwork in the two urban centers of Canada's diamond basin, Yellowknife and Hay River. At the outset of the research, the area, and the mining sector more generally, were described as experiencing a labor crisis (MITAC 2005). Labor shortages, or the construction thereof, provide an entry point into social dimensions of (im)migration. As capital searches for labor, and vice versa, social categories and positionings are reconfigured, reproduced, and resisted.

The NWT provides a particularly revealing space to explore the relationships between migration, (racialized) locality, and Canadian social reproduction for a variety of reasons. First, in symbolic and economic terms, the North has a history of being perceived as a frontier in the Canadian imagination (Furniss 1999, 1997). Frontiers are spaces where migrants turn up, and equally where territories are struggled over. Second, the NWT, like its neighbors the Yukon and Nunavut, are of peculiar political status. Sometimes referred to as Canada's "internal colonies" (Hodgkins 2009; Coates 1985), the territories are largely managed by the federal government. For example, resource royalties are collected by the federal government and are returned to Territorial governments in the form of per capita transfer payments. Finally, just under 50 percent of the NWT's population is indigenous.

My work and approach to the study of labor, migration, and citizenship stands in stark contrast to the majority of the research on Northern migration, which treats indigenous and non-indigenous migration as separate issues. It has even been argued that these two disparate phenomena require different methodological approaches (Petrov 2007; Cooke and Belanger 2006). Northern migration research generally has one of two emphases: either a focus on the migration of Aboriginal bodies out of the North to urban centers in the South (Peters and Newhouse 2003), or on non-Aboriginal labor in-migration (Heleniak 1999; Zarchikoff 1975). All deploy the same oppositional understanding (see Nugent 1994) of Aboriginal and non-Aboriginal and all posit migration as a threat to the nation-state. Urbanization of Aboriginal populations is described in relation to its burden on social welfare and housing programs (Kuhn and Sweetman 2002) and non-indigenous migration is described as an issue of an "unstable labour force" (Heleniak 1999). In most instances, the primary unit of analysis is the 'ethnic group,' often termed 'community.' As noted by Glick Schiller (this volume), "The problematic framing of migration research in terms of ethnic groups within nation-states obscures the effects of the global restructuring of capital on the population, both migrant and non-migrant, in a specific locality" (64). What a political-economic perspective reveals is, in the case of the Northwest Territories, the institutionalization of ethnic groups—that is, the production of differentiated citizenships;[1] first "Treaty indians" and Métis, now smaller Aboriginal communities, have been essential to changing co-constructions of state and capital and the kinds of migration tendencies it depends on and produces.

At the time when the diamond basin was being described as in crisis, the developments were said to be providing local populations with ample work and training opportunities. To explore how the employment opportunities of resource extraction were being distributed, I organized an ethnographic study of labor recruitment and job training practices in the NWT. Aboriginal job training programs, although seemingly local, are a testament to tensions between labor and global capital, and between citizens and the state.

The first section builds on the story of John Hope to show how the social and economic relations which sustained the long period dominated by merchant capital (fur trade) were undermined by the arrival of industrial capital. As a result, new configurations of Aboriginality were articulated. The second part of the chapter is built around Ruth who, like Hope, is both migrant and Aboriginal. Originally from Eastern Canada, Ruth moved north in search of livelihood after hearing there were abundant opportunities for work in the diamond mines. The constant renegotiation of her mobility/locality in light of economic shifts (notably the financial crisis which occurred as she was halfway through the training program) makes clear the untidiness of migration, ethnicity, and social reproduction. Her story recapitulates that of Hope in many ways, picking up on similar themes: resource exploitation, identity politics, citizenship, mobility, and the shifting character of locality at the frontier, then and now. In the final section, the stories of Ruth and Hope are analytically assembled to show how migration in Canada is linked to labor mobility in ways which make some bodies visible as migrants while pushing others into, or just outside of, a range of differentiated citizenship categories (Aboriginal, Northerner, among others).

IN SEARCH OF HOPE: MIGRATION, RACE, AND THE ADVENT OF A NATION

Around the time of Hope's arrival in the late 1800s, the primary economic activity in the arctic basin drainage at that time was fur trading (Kretch 1984). Labor consisted of mobile "indians" as trappers and a small pool of temporary labor to manage trade and the posts. The inclusion of the Northern regions into the new Canadian state and the onset of mineral prospecting and subsequent industrial extraction (1900–1930) would substantially change the amount of labor coming and staying north. The shift from metropole colonialism to settler-style colonialism undermined local indigenous livelihoods which depended on fur and fish (as subsistence food and as exchange goods) as in-migrants were in search of the same materials. This was resolved through a Treaty-making process which guaranteed fishing and hunting rights for subsistence purposes. When the population grew with the second fur boom and a mineral boom, terms of the Treaty would bar "Treaty indians" from commercial licenses and loans at a time when competition over resources (fish and game) was high. These kinds of conflicts and state-sanctioned resolutions that emerged then, and continue to the present, namely shifting forms of citizenships, are the foundation for the current emphasis on Aboriginal employment and training in resource policy and practice. As other forms of livelihood have been eroded, inclusion in the wage economy has come to be the dominant paradigm for imagining futures.

Hope's name appears in an 1870 account book of the Hudson's Bay Company (HBC). He was one of eight waged employees. The second list of names was of "indians" who received trade goods either for furs or for labor rendered (navigational assistance, providing meat and fish). Hope's occupation was listed as interpreter. Bilingualism among HBC employees was out of the ordinary as translation was usually left to men of the church or to indigenous traders. The number of indigenous languages in the region is a debate which is better left to other authors (Rice 1990), however, in general Cree and English were the two dominant languages of trade, and Slavey (an Athabaskan language) was the local language. I pieced together Hope's path to and from Hay River, and found his movements revealing of the complicated ways in which race and political economy articulate across time and space.

John Hope was baptized an "indian boy" by Reverend J. West at the Red River settlement (now Manitoba) in 1825 (HBC 2002). As a child, Hope showed great promise in his ability to read and write in English. Reverend West selected Hope and three other boys to become missionaries to their own people. Young Hope eventually joined the Hudson's Bay Company, as mission wages were comparatively low. Hope was hired in 1863 to help paddle large canoes northwest into the Mackenzie District. By 1868, Hope had arrived on the south shore of the Great Slave Lake. He helped to establish the Hay River Fort (roughly the same place where later Ruth and I will turn up 140 years later). While the HBC had been in pursuit of fur since 1670, by the time Hope was born their monopoly on the trade was in jeopardy, and fur sources were depleting in and around Hudson's Bay. The company's desire to move inland in search of more furs and to cut off rival traders placed new demands on the company's labor. The HBC had difficulty in convincing their existing labor to move away from the single-season work around the bay which had characterized the industry up until that point, to the lengthier, more dangerous contracts which involved travel to the Northwest (Burley 1997). The response around the 1820s was to hire "Canadian" labor, which, given that the Canadian state did not yet exist, largely meant the descendants of French settlers or Métis trappers who had worked for the rival Northwest Company, and which had now merged with the HBC.

While Hope was busy helping to navigate and change the local landscape, important political-economic changes were underway, both near and far.[2] First, the HBC was sold by the Crown to a group of British financiers whose priorities would shift and split from furs to industrial development. Canadian federation occurred in 1867, but the nascent nation-state would not acquire the land where Hope was (the Northwestern Territory) until the Hudson's Bay Company sold it to Canada in 1870. Envious and fearful of the US's rising industrial production, the new Dominion and British finance capital worked together to expand Canada, drawing western resources eastwards for the expansion of industrial centers in Ontario and Quebec.

With declining interest in furs, the Hay River Fort closed in 1873 and Hope was promoted to postmaster at nearby Fort Simpson. That same year marked the beginning of "the long depression," an international financial crisis, which ended Britain's exclusive claims to industrial dominance. In efforts to recapture some of their losses, expedited plans for development in new and former colonies began. In Canada, this meant primarily rail development through the borrowing of British capital. Across midwestern Canada there was the outstanding issue of unconverted indigenous populations who were without the economic basis which had sustained them (fur and game), and who were increasingly either dying or causing civil 'unrest'— both of which challenged the legitimacy of the new state (Kulchyski 2007, 2006; Kalant 2004).

The state used a series of, now contested, numbered treaties to serially extinguish significant (though not all) Aboriginal claims to land title in exchange for economic and social support from the federal government (Fumoleau 2004; Coates and Morrison 1986). The treaties were pursued from east to northwest between 1871 and 1921[3] turning former fur labor into "Treaty indians."

As he was non-Treaty, Hope was not allowed to settle locally upon his retirement. He went south to the newly formed province of Saskatchewan with his wife and son. He returned to the Church of England which had schooled him long ago. In his final years he served as a Sunday school teacher at the newly instituted vocational residential school for "indians." His knowledge of Cree and his allegiance to the Church made him an asset to the newest venture in indian education. Two years before his arrival to Battleford, Saskatchewan, the small town was the site of the largest mass hanging in Canadian history. Eight "indians" were brought to death over their resistance to unfair terms of their Treaty. The children at the indian vocational school were brought out to watch the deaths. The project of assimilationist Canada was underway in regions where fur sources had been depleted.

Racialized categories used to organize labor and property, like "indian," and "Treaty indian," have uneven applications and effects. Hope's ways of speaking and moral values evaded the term "indian" in reports written about his service. In the notebooks of his superiors and colleagues he was never racialized. My discovery of his shifting status came with the location of his birth record and later from census data of 1881 which all labeled him "indian," the former by birth, the latter as 'nationality.' Like many mission workers in the mid-nineteenth century, converted "indians" (sometimes) lost the distinction of the racialized category in daily practice, however, changing state apparatuses (like the advent of the census) would renew the racialization of some populations.

Hope never became a "Treaty indian" and moved on to a comfortable home with his wife and son in Battleford, Saskatchewan. "Treaty indians" were intended to remain as labor for merchant capital through the fur trade. However, as a form of enclosure, Treaty-making took land that had been commonly used and made it property available for two partially incommensurable uses: subsistence/furs for "Treaty indians" and mineral extraction/exploitation for state and capital. The former depended on limited amounts of in-migration, whereas the latter spurred a surge in the population. In this way, fixing populations within a system which depends on, and produces, mobility is not without consequence. While the Treaty system fixed communities in the hopes of their erasure, resource extraction and labor mobility set up the conditions for the broader resistance to state and capital I outline in the next section.

FROM HOPE TO OPPORTUNITY: MIGRATION AND LOCALITY BETWEEN 1900 AND 1970

This section explores two crucial shifts which happen between the story of Hope and the story of Ruth. First, the numbered Treaty system, which can be shorthanded as 'accumulation by dispossession' (Harvey 2005), is replaced with the comprehensive and specific land-claims processes[4] or 'dispossession by slow bureaucratic grind' (Gordon 2010). This move took civil unrest from the 1970s and brought it safely into the realm of the Canadian legal system where, as we see in the next section, the issues remain largely unresolved although the resources continue to flow out. The second shift is from directly assimilationist policy and colonial domination to liberal multicultural forms of domination. As Povinelli explains (2002), in contrast to colonial forms of domination, multicultural domination works by inspiring subaltern and minority subjects to identify with the impossible object of an authentic self-identity (a domesticated, non-conflicted 'traditional' form of sociality). Further, this requires the transportation of ancient pre-national meanings and practices to the present in whatever language and moral framework prevails at the time of enunciation.

The point of an inquiry into the politics of history in the area in question is not to identify what indigeneity is or should be, rather it is to show how regimes of recognition in and against labor migrations and resource extraction have made specific transformations sensible and acceptable to large segments of the Aboriginal/non-Aboriginal population, and how and when alternative configurations of history and future development are lost in the process (Li 2000). The transformations I focus on here are shifting categories of citizenship, possibilities for livelihoods, and the transformation of ethnic groups into quasi-corporations.

In the early 1900s, seasonal life at posts and missions had become standard for many groups in the region. As a means of drawing labor into submission, posts and missions had conventionally assisted with reproduction of groups during times of difficulty (fauna depletion, epidemics, etc.). As these increased around the turn of the century, the HBC wanted the new state to take over the off-season reproduction of their labor force. The time spent at posts came to increase with the growing number of epidemics that came in with outside goods (Kretch 1980). With a free staking system for mineral prospecting, the gold rush of the late 1800s flooded the area with in-migrants. The HBC slowly turned its attention from trading furs to outfitting prospectors with goods. Competing trade companies arrived, some of whom brought their own labor force to acquire furs. Some local groups had also participated in fish harvesting to supply posts, missions, and new mine projects with food sources. When in-migrants arrived with technology to harvest lake fish faster, many found themselves out of work (Piper 2009).

Between the 1930s and the 1970s the non-enforcement of the area Treaty (Treaty 8), and specifically the state's inability to guarantee rights (to fishing and trapping) while subsidizing state-capital's interests, meant an increasing indigenous solidarity throughout the region. While the state ignored early protests, the political movement of the Indian Brotherhood of the 1970s (based on the civil-rights-style movements in the United States), coupled with the possibility of a Northern oil pipeline running through the Territory, meant that the state, at a discursive impasse, would have to reconstruct itself if it wanted to make new development possible. The ethnic division between "indian" groups and Métis were now points for political mobilization in the interest of reclaiming land rights. The Brotherhood (later renamed the Dene Nation) rejected the categories of Métis, non-status, and "Treaty indian"—which were argued to be imposed categories meant to impede solidarity.[5] The group was able to have pipeline development placed on hold for ten years to allow for new land-claim agreements to be settled.

The Dene Nation was successful at bringing indigenous social and economic equalities to the forefront of the Canadian imagination largely through environmental discourses. Through the 1960s and 1970s, national cohesion had been achieved, in large part, through a liberal multicultural paradigm made popular through Prime Minister Trudeau. Much like other liberal diasporas, Australia in particular (Povinelli 2002), there is a common sentiment among Canadian citizens that decreased harm comes through increased understanding of difference. On all sides of the debate, support was high for the inclusion of 'citizens' on the basis of difference and previous exclusion. But the question remained, on the basis of which differences?

After the Dene Nation rejected the state's initial proposals, the federal government proclaimed that they would no longer negotiate with the allied group—only regionally with smaller groups. Internal divisions within the Dene Nation, which dated back to the fur trade, grew increasingly acute. Their neighbors to the north, the Inuvialuit (who had never been included in the numbered Treaty system), had reached a settlement in 1984. The newly formed Inuvialuit Regional Corporation and its "shareholders" began to receive dividend payments from oil and gas explorations.

By 1993 the fragments began to break away with the groups whose unsettled claim areas stretched along the Mackenzie Valley Gas corridor withdrawing from the Dene Nation. The shift to regional representation unsettled the politics of "indianness" and regional solidarities—at once according more autonomy to Aboriginal groups while at the same time politicizing their respective differences with one another (Kulchyski 2006). These processes made land claims dependent on and exacerbated differences between groups, many of whom had to that point identified more closely with a local community that with a linguistic or cultural entity/nation. Likewise, the economic stakes of large-scale resource allocations drove wedges within groups according to the sorts of internal inequalities that had long beset Aboriginal peoples (see also Dombrowski 2008). The transformation was pronounced: some of the same leaders who had been members of the Indian Brotherhood in the 1970s had, by the 1990s, reinvented themselves as industry consultants, and many have been instrumental in pushing through development projects similar to those they once adamantly opposed. Such turns of events do not seek to place blame on Aboriginal leadership, however, it is to illuminate the ways in which groups' political and economic "room to maneuver" (Li 2003, 2000; Hall 1990) is channeled into particular and narrow pathways by local and larger forces.

To summarize, changing demands and types of capital engenders different forms of migration which existing populations deal with in a number of ways ranging from indifference to resistance. A key strategy for securing livelihood by indigenous populations was to forge a regional identity based on securing access to the means of production. The terms of that access, however, placed them in a different relationship to rights than other citizens (e.g., prohibited them from commercial practices), which, with increased in-migration, would prove to undermine their ability to reproduce themselves in the same way. To overcome this, they sought a second form of formal identification as fixed populations vis-à-vis the state. At the same time, many individuals and families sought other means of reproduction (mobility towards resource projects, participation in the Canadian army during the two World Wars, or mobility to schools and cities where the Canadian project of assimilation would continue). Others stayed and invested in local differences as a means to seek equality in a state which had now spread liberal values of democracy to its frontiers.

In the next section, I move ahead to a portrait of current events in the NWT, specifically the discovery and development of diamonds. Ruth, a student involved in an Aboriginal mine training program, will serve as the center of a discussion of how tensions between mobility and fixity left over from Hope's era, escalating in the 1970s, have come to shape the present state of affairs. Upon arrival, Ruth learned that her citizenship as a "status indian" give her privileged access to subsidized training programs. When the economy declined and industry-state funds for education held back, Ruth found out that her Aboriginality is not always Aboriginal enough, and she was left to take a loan for the rest of her education. Later that year, she debated if she could or should be included in the newer institutionalized form of local citizenship, "Northerner," which normally is reserved for the non-indigenous settler population. All of this happens vis-à-vis narrowing chances for fair waged work.

MOBILITY AND OPPORTUNITY: FROM LIVELIHOOD TO EMPLOYMENT IN THE ERA OF 'COMPREHENSIVE' LAND CLAIMS

In 1991, prospectors Charles Fipke and Stewart Blusson confirmed the presence of chrome diopside, pyrope, garnet, and ilmenite on a parcel of land in Canada's Northwest Territories (NWT). These seemingly insignificant minerals are the geological bread crumbs used to guide explorers to the more eminent gemstone: the diamond. By 2007, the NWT treasure trail was well worn. BHP Billiton's Diavik mine was in operation as of 1998, Rio Tinto's Ekati mine came online in 2003, and DeBeer's Snap Lake project was scheduled to start production within the year. Canada had become the third largest producer of diamonds in the world and the Territorial per capita gross domestic product had increased by 79 percent, making it second only to Luxembourg. Yet, these facts say more about the sparse population (forty thousand) than they do about how wealth is distributed.[6]

Despite ongoing inequalities, the dominant expectation persists that free-market growth in the primary sector will bring socio-economic equality to Canada's North by providing jobs for the local population and drawing new labor north who will use Northern businesses and services. At the same time, the prospect of the project brought concerns. Would the urban centers be able to handle an influx of (im)migrants? Would this project ignore ongoing indigenous land struggles? Would history repeat itself and most benefits flow out of the area? Would it cause environmental harm?

Both the hopes and fears that diamond discovery brought to the North were addressed through two separate but related institutional apparatuses: the Impact Benefit Agreement (IBA) and the Socio-Economic Agreement (SEA).[7] These agreements show us how the tension between mobility and fixity in resource economies unfolds in the present. At the time of their discovery, the NWT diamond deposits were located on contested lands (Bielawski 2003). Since the late 1980s, a growing number of Aboriginal groups in other parts of the Territories had the numbered treaties repealed and settled modern land-claim agreements.[8] To circumvent the formal land-claims process and take the federal government out of the sticky business of dealing with Aboriginal politics, at least temporarily, the state left industry to seek support for resource development directly from groups whose relationship to land and livelihood was uneven and tenuous. They did this through the impact benefit process.

Linked to the Corporate Social Responsibility movement, impact benefit agreements are steeped in the language of the local yet are global industry standards for dealing with indigenous populations (see Sosa and Keenan 2001 for overview).[9] In the NWT, IBAs are confidential documents signed by the developer and the Aboriginal authority and usually specify private arbitration as the means for settling disputes. Given that their terms are secret, they are best described as the exchange development rights of lands for things such as royalty payments, lump sums, infrastructure investments, and educational funding. IBAs were quickly reached with the communities immediately surrounding the deposits and mine construction began. While IBAs acknowledged and gave meaning to varying degrees and forms of property ownership and determined which groups (communities) would be measured and assessed for impacts and benefits of mining, this placed strict temporal and spatial constraints on how the state and industry would be willing to make sense of the economic and social transformations unfolding.

While the IBAs intended to fix populations for the sake of accessing resources, they undermined the ability of the state to reproduce existing mobile labor, or "Northerners" (non-Aboriginal residents, making up over half the population) even as it renewed the conditions that will, once again, draw more labor north to communities like Hay River and Yellowknife. Mining resources in the NWT are managed federally, with royalty payments going to the federal government and then back to the Territorial government through transfer payments based on population. The modest royalty structure in the NWT is often used by both levels of government to attract industry and investors, the anticipated level of direct transfers was low, and the fears of large open-pit mining and the influx of migration it would encourage were common public topics. Such fears were well founded. The current royalty regime in the NWT is among the lowest in the world: low enough, in fact, that BHP's Ekati and Rio Tinto's Diavik mines were able to repay their capital construction costs (prices in the several billion dollar range) in the first three years of production. This type of timeline is almost unheard of in the mining industry. While industry profits climbed, so too did the housing crisis in the capital city of Yellowknife (GNWT 2009). The rising cost of social reproduction put pressure on regional and Territorial governments whose ability to provide for its citizens is stifled by low royalty regimes and further exacerbated by increased temporary labor who are not accounted for in the transfer payment scheme. The only thing the local governments can do is encourage new labor to stay.

In the service of existing local elites and in the interests of encouraging labor to stay north, Socio-Economic Agreements (SEAs) were introduced to guarantee priority employment and business opportunities (tenders and sub-contracts) to residents of the North. SEAs helped pave the road to diamond development by raising public support among non-Aboriginals. Citing employment and training as the key "benefits" of contemporary resource projects, the SEAs were attractive to (those in the process of formally becoming) "Northerners" as most are displaced working-class Canadians who came north for work opportunities. Many of these workers are, like Ruth, from the Eastern Provinces (Newfoundland, New Brunswick) where primary and secondary industry has been in sharp decline since the 1980s and human labor has become the main export (Sider 2003b, 1988).

PUTTING THE LOCAL TO WORK

The emphasis on jobs and training as key benefits of contemporary resource projects is evident in policy and public space. At the Territorial Heritage Center in Yellowknife the renovated ground floor tells the story of Canadian diamonds and the opportunities they afford Northern populations. Photographs of residents from the region capture the ethnic diversity of the industrialized North. Portraits include Aboriginals, Northerners (non-Aboriginal Canadians living in the area for an extended period), and a few recent immigrants to Canada. The wall-length photo collage reads: "A New Economy, A New Lifestyle" and captures the aura of opportunity:

> There are over 3000 direct jobs in diamond mining and polishing as of 2007. There are also hundreds of related jobs that are created in areas such as housing, schools and the service industry ... NWT mine workers are paid competitive wages- average salary $63,700 in 2006- and the benefits of this employment are primarily reaped by northern residents. Hiring preference is given to Aboriginal northerners and other NWT residents with targets that are typically 60% northerners of which half are northern Aboriginals reflecting the NWT's population mix.[10]

The message is rather simple. Diamond mining is good because it makes jobs for the people of the place. Yet, contrary to the idea of a "New Economy," resource extraction, as we have seen, is hardly new. In fact, the Northwest Territories is the site of the densest commercial exploitation of mineral resources in North America. And, true to the logic, mining has brought jobs—usually too many jobs for the sparsely populated area (Morrison and Coates 1994). To harvest resources requires productive labor and reproductive labor (see Nonini, this volume). This amount often exceeds local sources, especially when the demand for a particular commodity is high or large-scale infrastructure projects are required. This rolling demand for labor has laid the groundwork for (im)migrations of various scales and durations (e.g., American military labor for road and airfield construction during World War II, see Morrison and Coates 1994; Japanese workers brought in for fish-processing plants during the 1940s and 1950s, see Piper 2009).

This raises three questions. First, why is there an emphasis on the local when there is a known dependence on migrant labor to make these projects profitable? Next, how did it come to pass that the exclusive benefit of resource extraction for local people is participation in industry's development as individual wage workers? Finally, who counts as "local"? In the short passage on the heritage center's wall, multiple, ambiguous forms of the local emerge: Northern residents, Aboriginal Northerner, NWT residents, Northerners, Northern Aboriginals. As this second ethnographic vignette will show, the ambiguity is not inconsequential.

In December 2008, posters went up all over the Northwest Territories calling for local residents to "BECOME A CERTIFIED ROCKER!" The advertisements were part of an Aboriginal employment initiative and announced a six-week pre-requisite course for a certificate in underground mining. The initiative was developed and funded by a newly formed state-industry partnership, the Mine Training Society. The poster's reference to rocks signaled the intended shift in Northern diamond-mining industry operations from large open pits to underground methods of extraction. Local media and industry enthusiasts had proclaimed the urgent need for labor with new sets of technical skills suitable for the underground work to come. The planned shift in operations from open pit to underground mining was promoted as an opportunity for 'local' labor to benefit from the booming industry.

CONTEMPORARY HOPE: RUTH'S TRAJECTORY

Ruth was one of ten students who signed up for the course at the local community college in Hay River. Ruth moved from New Brunswick to Hay River in 2003. Her brother had moved north for love, then called Ruth to tell her about the money. "They're desperate for people everywhere!" he said, "I hear some people are making $50 an hour in the mines." Ruth has been part of the migrant Aboriginal working class since birth. Her father was born on a reserve in New Brunswick, her mother on a reserve in Quebec. She spent most of her childhood and young adulthood in Boston, where her father worked as a boat mechanic. She was forty-eight at the time of her brother's phone call and exhausted from running a small catering company that always left her just above the breakeven point. She came north, and was immediately hired by the sub-contracted firm responsible for mine catering. She worked in the mine's kitchen for a year, but the pay was a fraction of the imagined rate her brother had reported. The twelve-hour shifts and the two weeks in/two weeks out cycle of remote mining wore on her. For her "out" shifts, she flew back to New Brunswick to be with her husband.

Over the past ten years there has been an influx of in-migration to the North from Canada's eastern Maritime Provinces. With the collapse of primary and secondary processing industries in the region, workers have been taking their skills on the road, many sending remittances back East. Locally, this causes tension, as they are believed not to be 'contributing' to the Northern economy. For those from the East, the high wages of the North are attractive. High rents, however, drain most of the wage and therefore many commute by season, or by two-week cycle. Ruth's husband had worked as a certified carpenter for seven years in New Brunswick. His wage was not enough to have him ever feel secure, despite holding the highest qualification for his trade. Eventually he moved north. Reluctant to leave his grandchildren, the opportunity of tripling his salary seemed worth the risk. He encouraged his wife to do some upgrading to try for a higher-paying job in the mines. When Ruth saw the Rocker poster she too decided to take a risk for opportunity's sake.

Although programs like the Rocker course are designed for 'local' labor, observing their delivery on the ground reveals that 'localness' is a constant negotiation based on shifting political and economic conditions. The term 'migrant labor' is seldom associated with Aboriginal populations, particularly not with those in the Canadian North. In attempts to navigate the uneven employment opportunities in Canada and in the Territory itself, many people, Aboriginal and not, arrive in the NWT's larger centers of Yellowknife and Hay River in search of work. Ruth is but one example. In her class of ten students, only half were from the immediate region.

Ruth arrived north with the intention of taking advantage of the spaces of hope and advertised 'labor shortage' supplies to the Canadian working class. She was one of the top students in the class, however, when she completed the first phase of the program, the political-economic contingencies of the category 'Aboriginal' were revealed. In simple terms, a dramatic downturn in international diamond markets (as part of the broad economic downturn) caused considerable slowdown in all three operations.[11] Between October 2008 and February 2009, BHP laid off one hundred to one hundred fifty workers. During roughly the same period, DeBeers closed its Snap Lake mine for ten weeks leaving four hundred workers to take unpaid leave (or use paid vacation), and Rio Tinto's Diavik mine announced 140 layoffs plus eight weeks of mine closure. Ruth's training course had been offered through a state-industry partnership and industry's contributions and interest in producing underground miners declined. Planned underground expansions for each mine were put on hold. Two of the three operational mines had been functioning at peak production and were about to exhaust open pit operations. Plans to move into underground methods of diamond harvesting was now seen as a risk for capital, as transition costs would be high, and profitability questionable. Despite these facts, the course went ahead with a few adjustments to the funding formula.

Ruth and three other successful Hay River candidates packed their bags and flew to Yellowknife for the final twelve weeks of the program which would be held in a simulated mine camp. Once in camp, the group was told that there had been changes to funding structure. Each individual would have to pay for their flights over and be reimbursed by their band council later. Not being from the Territories, Ruth did not qualify for such funding opportunities. She was never made aware of this until she arrived on the spot. She spoke with her husband on the telephone that night. Together they decided it would be worthwhile to take out a loan so Ruth could continue.[12]

Ruth and her classmates heard a lot of stories about mine employers being present at their graduation. When the day came only one representative from a mine was present. He congratulated the group and talked of the 'downturn' and how they would need to exercise patience. His estimate was that hiring would begin again in six months. A month after the course ended, Ruth called and asked if I could help her apply online for a job. She heard one of the mines was hiring. She also wanted to send out resumes and cover letters to a few other leads in transportation. We sat in front of the computer and worked together at 'selling' Ruth's new skills. As we reread our draft, it occurred to me that something may be missing. The following conversation ensued:

L: Do you want to say you are an Aboriginal woman?
R: Why would I do that? Do you think I should?
L: Hmmm. Well, technically they are supposed to give priority hires to Aboriginals and Northerners.
R: Yeah, but I am not from here.
L: Right, but you have lived here for three years so that makes you a Northerner.
R: Ok, so I should say I am a Northerner. But, I mean, I AM Aboriginal. Is that better?
L: I don't know. I have been trying to figure out how these categories work for the past year.
R: I just don't want to make some big deal out of it. It might look like I am trouble, you know, demanding. What do you think?
L: It's up to you. We could say that a copy of your license and indian Status Card are available upon request. That way they would know, but you wouldn't be making it, like, a big deal. I know that contractors get more "points" if they have Northern and Aboriginal employees. More points means they have a better chance of winning bids. I wouldn't want you to miss out if it really is an advantage. But, like I said I don't know.
R: Let's put it as the 'upon request', then it's there without really being there.[13]

The ambiguity of how the categories will work in the world was apparent to both Ruth and I. The socio-economic assessment process, much like Northern migration research, takes the categories Aboriginal and Northerner as axiomatic objects. Our conversation reveals how these are always negotiations, heavily traversed by relations of power (me being the 'expert' on categories), and related to the struggle over limited resources (in this case jobs). After a little more editing, we sent off Ruth's packages. I checked in with her a month later. She had had no responses. Two years later, she is now working for herself cleaning private homes in town. "I haven't given up on the mines," she tells me over the phone. "Cleaning is really good money, you know. My husband and I are going to go to Boston on holidays. I haven't been back in ages, but my sister still lives there. Not to mention the Boston Bruins will be playing." I ask her if she or her husband plan on moving back to New Brunswick. "It would be hard. There is good-paying, steady work for my husband here. Back home you never know, and wages are less than half what they are here. Plus there is all the overtime. It adds up. It also means he doesn't have much time left to work on fixing up our place, but that's ok. It will come."[14]

CONCLUSION

On several scales, mining depends on the movement of labor into and out of development regions to ensure forms of social regulation and economic productivity commensurate with global industry's imperatives. Ruth and Hope show us that while capital is adept at harnessing expended populations to these ends, it cannot single-handedly produce or reproduce them. In addition to demand for unequally divided labor, capitalist expansion depends on establishing and maintaining sovereignty over areas to access raw resources. Establishing sovereignty and dividing labor pose a dialectical challenge to state and capital. The social process of differentiation aims to meet this dual challenge. The history between Hope and Ruth is meant to elaborate how citizenships and locality, as means of differentiation, are used by state, capital, and social actors in different, and partially incompatible, ways. As a result, forms of social reproduction are destabilized and draw attention to a core contradiction of liberal citizenship, namely unequal inclusion.

John Hope's baptized name is dialectical in the sense that it signals the system is driven by law (in conjunction with the contingencies of capitalist political economy) on the one side, and his own hope and mobility on the other. The changes which situate Ruth and Hope within and against categories of indigeneity reveal how, in the first instance, states reproduce locality to maintain sovereignty and make resources available to capital. At the same time, however, to harvest those same resources and reproduce property relations and labor at a cost attractive to state and capital, populations are circulated to and from frontier zones of extraction. The effects are that these populations increase local competition over resources which drive wages down and cost of living up. The contradiction is that existing (definitively) local populations need to increasingly rely on the state for social reproduction. At moments of economic decline, the state becomes invested in very strict versions of the local.

The appearance of 'Northerner' needs to be understood as a mediation of an internal contradiction of citizenship, the geographically uneven distribution of citizenship rights within nation-states. Mobilizing shifting scales of locality then ("indian," "Treaty indian," Aboriginal, Northerner, and in between) leaves wiggle room for who will and will not be reproduced in moments of economic crisis. Ruth and Hope's stories reveal the constant negotiation of citizenship and its tight links to political economy. While it may be tempting to conclude that citizenship is merely in need of further refinement, or better clarity of conditions of use, Saskia Sassen (2009) makes the following argument:

> [First], citizenship is an incompletely theorized contract between the state and the citizen. This incompleteness makes it possible for a highly formalized institution to accommodate change—more precisely, to accommodate the possibility of responding to change without sacrificing its formal status. Second, . . . the longevity of the institution suggests that it is *meant* to be incomplete, that is to say, capable of responding to the historically conditioned meaning of citizenship. Incompleteness brings to the fore the work of making, whether it is making in response to changed conditions, new subjectivities, or new instrumentalities. (228)

Differentiated citizenships, produced in part out of patterns of migration as a social relation, are thus a cornerstone of a system that necessarily produces the individual chaos of these sorts of (typical) lives (Ruth, Hope) in order to try to tame the vagaries and inevitable self-destructiveness of capitalist forms of development. The state has to keep making profitable opportunities if it expects capital to work as colonizer—this means giving it cheap labor and resources on the one hand, and then dealing with the mess left behind when capital produces its inevitable contradictions and makes it impossible to make a profit even with cheap labor and resources (times of recession and depression). Missionaries/education are usually the clean-up crew, hence Hope's path back and forth from industry to education, and Ruth's as well. In the end, maybe John Hope figured it out by getting a job in education, and melding the two worlds, but only individually (and then his difference disappears—he went unmarked on the 1891 census). What sustains the working side of the equation is not status or cultural difference, as Ruth's story points out—they are far too ambivalent and tainted of concepts. However, hope is sustaining, the idea that they might find a point of steadiness amid the wild ride of capitalism, which even the state cannot tame. But as Gramsci makes clear, this is an individual hope, one for Hope and his wife, or Ruth and her husband, but not for indians in general.

NOTES

1. In the preface to *Living Indian Histories: Lumbee and Tuscorora People in North Carolina*, Gerald Sider (2003a) explains how forms of differential citizenships (that is, differential positionings in relation to rights, benefits, protections) are a crucial feature of modern states (for legitimizing unequal divisions of labour/resources) but cannot be fully managed or produced by

the state itself. These differential citizenships and inequalities that come to be named race, gender (for example), become harnassable vulnerabilities that simultaneously "produce, or deeply participate in the production of enduring inequalities" while allowing the state to claim that it has one set of rules that apply to all (Sider 2003a: xv).
2. The trade of furs did occur before European occupation. The scope of the trade and its economic functions are beyond the scope of this paper. Arguments range from formalist neoclassical interpretations by Innis (1962) to more substantivist interpretations by Rich (1967). Later, White (1984) tried to bridge the divide between market-trade and gift-trade debates by providing a nuanced picture of the complex ways in which native populations fit new economic relationships into existing cultural patterns.
3. A numbered Treaty was not offered to the people of the Great Slave Lake area until 1899, when prospecting had begun in earnest in the area. Up until that point the view of the state was that local people were "best left as indians" (Coates 1993).
4. Although land claims are generally understood as the means through which the past wrongs of colonial exploitation are undone (Hamilton 1994), Aboriginal claims are a key meeting point for state/industry conjunction and negotiation (Dombrowski 2001). Modern land claims are the second phase of state centralization in the Canadian North. Treaty-making was the first. The details of each phase are not explored here; however, it is important to observe that both phases have consistently arranged claims to land and rights in ways that allow for the transfer of significant resources from state control to industrial extraction.
5. In July 1975, the Dene Nation passed the Dene Declaration, which at once affirmed their solidarity across these groups and their right to self-determination (Watkins 1977). Throughout the 1970s and early 1980s Dene Nation Leader George Erasmus adopted a nationalist framework for political mobilization and continued to underscore the danger of fragmentizing policies and continued to lobby the state on behalf of the larger region.
6. Twenty percent of all households in the NWT have incomes below $30,000 and costs of living are substantially higher than other parts of Canada. Outside the few "urban" centers of the Territories, in the smaller communities, 50 percent of households have a total income below $30,000 (Wilson 2009). Rates of cancer and heart disease are higher and life expectancies lower for the population here as compared to southern Canada. Much like Povinelli's (2008) observation of indigenous Australia, Northern health statistics reveal "the unequal distribution of life and death in democratic orders" (513).
7. From social science to media accounts, IBAs and SEAs, and their assessment tools, are usually portrayed as "viable approaches" in assuring Aboriginal people will reap economic benefits of resource extraction (Gibson and Klinck 2005). While criticisms are emerging (Caine and Krogman 2010), rarely is it noted that these same processes have transformed much of the discussion around development from questions of indigenous land and livelihood to questions of labor. Over the course of eighteen months of fieldwork in Canada's diamond basin, it was clear that the majority of Aboriginal residents in the larger region have a distant relationship to the supposed direct economic benefits of diamond development, even when projects happen on what are at various stages of becoming Aboriginal title lands (Bielawski 2003). For this reason, many Aboriginal residents see development projects in terms very similar to non-Aboriginal residents, as a potential source for labor/employment. State and industry have encouraged this process via IBA/SEA agreements which, to an extent, privilege Aboriginal/Northern hiring.

8. The 1986 Comprehensive Land Claims Policy, passed under the Conservative government of Brian Mulroney, redefined land claims such that land and self-government claims would be settled simultaneously. Aimed "to promote Aboriginal groups' economic growth and self-sufficiency," the comprehensive policy held that "resolving land claims will benefit all northerners by creating a stable and predictable environment that will, in turn, encourage economic development in the north" (DIAND 2002: 1).
9. The bottom line of the intent of these programs was made clear at a mining industry conference I attended in 2007. As part of their "sustainable human development panel," an industry-anthropologist declared, "Beyond the feel good, effective CSR maximizes benefit by minimizing slow down . . . Social unrest results in high costs . . . even small groups can cause problems later; women, youth, indigenous people . . . You have to know. Who are the opposition?"
10. Photograph, Author, June 6, 2007.
11. Other economic impacts were also observed in adjacent industries. Smaller industries whose primary clients are the mines cut labor costs, and subcontractors found their services no longer needed. The secondary diamond industry set up to 'diversify' the local economy almost completely shut down: Laurelton Diamonds (a subsidiary of Tiffany & Co) closed its operations in Yellowknife entirely in 2009, and tried to relocate its forty employees to one of its other facilities. This was the fourth plant to close on Yellowknife's unsuccessful "Diamond Row."
12. It is important to underscore that Ruth and the other candidates who moved on to the final phase all had partners (or in one case parents) who had steady incomes. While students did receive a stipend of $50 a day in the first six weeks, it was difficult for many to meet financial obligations on this amount. The program drained surplus capital from those households that had it available. This sits in stark contrast to local/national ideas like "Aboriginals get free education" and "they just don't take advantage of opportunities."
13. Field notes, Author, June 9, 2009.
14. Field Notes, Author, June 12, 2010.

REFERENCES

Abele, Frances, and Daiva Stasiulus. 1989. "Canada as a 'White Settler Colony.' What about Natives and Immigrants?" In *The New Canadian Political Economy*, edited by Wallace Clement and Glen Williams, 240–277. Montreal: McGill Queens University Press.

Abu-Laban, Yasmeen, and Christina Gabriel. 2002. *Selling Diversity: Immigration, Multiculturalism, Employment Equity and Globalization*. Toronto: University of Toronto Press.

Bielawski, Ellen. 2003. *Rogue Diamonds: Northern Riches on Dene Land*. Seattle: University of Washington Press.

Burley, Edith I. 1997. *Servants of the Honourable Company: Work, Discipline, and Conflict in the Hudson's Bay Company, 1770–1879*. Toronto: Oxford University Press.

Caine, Ken J., and Naomi Krogman. 2010. "Powerful or Just Plain Power-Full? A Power Analysis of Impact Benefit Agreements in Canada's North." *Organization & Environment* 23(1): 76–98.

Coates, Kenneth. 1985. *Canada's Colonies: A History of the Yukon and Northwest Territories*. Toronto: James Lorimer & Company.

In Search of Hope 151

———. 1993. *Best Left as Indians: Native-White Relations in the Yukon Territory, 1840–1973.* McGill-Queen's Studies in Ethnic History. Montreal: McGill-Queen's University Press.

Coates, Kenneth, and William Morrison. 1986. *Treaty Research Report—Treaty No. 11 (1921).* Ottawa: Treaties and Historical Research Centre, Indian and Northern Affairs Canada.

Cooke, Martin, and Daniele Belanger. 2006. "Migration Theories and First Nations Mobility: Towards a Systems Perspective." *Canadian Review of Sociology and Anthropology* 43(2): 141–164.

DIAND (Department of Indian Affairs and Northern Development). 2002. *NWT Plain Facts on Land and Self-Government.* Northwest Territories: DIAND NWT Region. http://dsppsd.pwgsc.gc/Collection/R34-9-5-2000E.pdf.

Dombrowski, Kirk. 2001. *Against Culture: Development, Politics, and Religion in Indian Alaska (Fourth World Rising).* Lincoln and London: University of Nebraska Press.

———. 2008. "Subsistence Livelihood, Native Identity and Internal Differentiation in Southeast Alaska." *Anthropologica* 49(2): 211–229.

Fumoleau, Rene. 2004. *As Long as This Land Shall Last: A History of Treaty 8 and Treaty 11, 1870–1939.* Calgary: University of Calgary Press.

Furniss, Elizabeth. 1997. "Pioneers, Progress, and the Myth of the Frontier: The Landscape of Public History in Rural British Columbia." *BC Studies* 1(155/166): 7–44.

———. 1999. *The Burden of History: Colonialism and the Frontier Myth in a Rural Canadian Community.* Vancouver: University of British Colombia Press.

Gibson, Ginger, and J. Klinck. 2005. "Canada's Resilient North: The Impact of Mining on Aboriginal Communities." *Pimatisiwin: A Journal of Aboriginal and Indigenous Community Health* 3(1): 115–139.

GNWT (Government of Northwest Territories). 2009. "Communities and Diamonds: Socio-economic Impacts in the Communities of Bechokö, Gamèti, Whatì, Detah, N'dilo, Åutselk'e, and Yellowknife." In *2008 Report of the Government of the Northwest Territories Under the BhP Billiton, Diavik and De Beers Socioeconomic Agreements.* Northwest Territories: GNWT.

Gordon, Todd. 2010. *Imperialist Canada.* Winnipeg: Arbeiter Ring Publishing.

Hall, Stuart. 1990. "Cultural Identity and Diaspora." In *Identity: Community, Culture, Difference,* edited by Jonathan Rutherford, 222–237. London: Lawrence and Wishart.

Hamilton, John David. 1994. *Arctic Revolution: Social Change in the Northwest Territories 1935–1994.* Toronto: Dundurn Press.

Harvey, David. 2005. *The New Imperialism (Clarendon Lectures in Geography and Environmental Studies).* New York: Oxford University Press.

HBC (Hudson's Bay Company). 2002. Filename: Hope, John (1) (fl. 1843–1854).

Heleniak, Thomas. 1999. "Out-Migration and Depopulation of the Russian North during the 1990s." *Post-Soviet Geography and Economics* 40(3): 155–205.

Hodgkins, Andrew. 2009. "Re-appraising Canada's Northern Internal Colonies." *Northern Review* 30: 179–206.

Innis, Harold. 1962. *The Fur Trade in Canada.* Toronto: Toronto University Press.

Kalant, Amelia. 2004. *National Identity and the Conflict at Oka: Native Belonging and Myths of Postcolonial Nationhood in Canada.* London: Routledge.

Kretch, Sheppard, III, ed. 1980. "Reconsiderations of Aboriginal Social Organization in the North American Subarctic." *Arctic Anthropology* 17(2): 1–63.

———, ed. 1984. *The Subarctic Fur Trade: Native Social and Economic Adaptations.* Vancouver: University of British Columbia Press.

Kuhn, Peter, and Arthur Sweetman. 2002. "Aboriginals as Unwilling Immigrants: Contact, Assimilation and Labor Market Outcomes." *Journal of Population Economics* 15: 331–355.

Kulchyski, Peter. 2006. *Like the Sound of a Drum: Aboriginal Cultural Politics in Denendeh and Nunavut.* Winnipeg: University of Manitoba Press.

———. 2007. *The Red Indians: An Episodic, Informal Collection of Tales from the History of Aboriginal People's Struggles in Canada.* Winnipeg: Arbeiter Ring Press.

Li, Tania. 2000. "Articulating Indigenous Identity in Indonesia: Resource Politics and the Tribal Slot." *Comparative Studies in Society and History* 42: 149–179.

———. 2003. "Resource Struggles: Concepts for Empirical Analysis." *Economic and Political Weekly* 28(48): 5120–5128.

MITAC (Mining Industry Training and Adjustment Council). 2005. *Prospecting the Future: Meeting Human Resources Challenges in Canada's Minerals and Metals Sector.* Ottawa: Government of Canada Sector Council Program.

Morrison, William, and Kenneth Coates. 1994. *Working in the North: Labor and the Northwest Defense Projects 1942–1946.* Fairbanks: University Of Alaska Press.

Nugent, David. 1994. "Building the State, Making the Nation: The Bases and Limits of State Centralization in "Modern" Peru." *American Anthropologist* 96(2): 333–369.

Peters, David, and Evelyn Newhouse, eds. 2003. *Not Strangers in These Parts: Urban Aboriginal Peoples.* Geneva: Policy Research Initiative.

Petrov, Andrey N. 2007. "Revising the Harris-Todaro Framework to Model Labor Migration from the Canadian Northern Frontier." *Journal of Population Research* 24(2): 185–206.

Piper, Liza. 2009. *The Industrial Transformation of Subarctic Canada.* Nature, History, Society Series. Vancouver: University Of British Columbia Press.

Povinelli, Elizabeth. 2002. *The Cunning of Recognition: Indigenous Alterities and the Making of Australian Multiculturalism.* Durham: Duke University Press.

———. 2008. "The Child in the Broom Closet: States of Killing and Letting Die." *South Atlantic Quarterly* 107(3): 509–530.

Rice, Karen. 1990. *A Grammar of Slave.* Boston: Walter de Gruyter.

Rich, Edwin. 1967. *The fur trade and the Northwest to 1857.* Toronto: McClelland and Stewart.

Sassen, Saskia. 2009. "Incompleteness and the Possibility of Making: Towards Denationalized Citizenship?" *Cultural Dynamics* 21(3): 227–254.

Sider, Gerald. 1988. *Culture and Class in Anthropology and History: A Newfoundland Illustration.* Cambridge Studies in Social and Cultural Anthropology. New York: Cambridge University Press.

———. 2003a. *Living Indian Histories: The Lumbee and Tuscarora People in North Carolina.* Chapel Hill: The University of North Carolina Press.

———. 2003b. *Between History and Tomorrow: Making and Breaking Everyday Life in Rural Newfoundland.* Peterborough: Broadview Press.

Sosa, Irene, and Karyn Keenan. 2001. *Impact Benefit Agreements between Aboriginal Communities and Mining Companies: Their Use in Canada.* Calgary, Alberta: Canadian Environmental Law Association.

Watkins, Mel. 1977. *Dene Nation, the Colony Within.* Toronto: University of Toronto Press.

White, Bruce. 1984. "'Give Us a Little Milk': The Social and Cultural Meanings of Gift Giving in the Lake Superior Fur Trade." In *Rendezvous: Selected Papers of the Fourth North American Fur Trade Conference*, edited by Thomas C. Buckley. St Paul: North American Fur Trade Conference.

Wilson, Jeffrey. 2009. *Poverty Reduction Policies and Programs in the Northwest Territories.* Social Development Report Series. Canadian Council on Social Development. http://www.alternativesnorth.ca/pdf/NWTPovertyReductionReport.pdf.

Zarchikoff, William. 1975. "The Development and Settlement Patterns of Hay River Northwest Territories." Unpublished master's thesis, Simon Fraser University, British Colombia.

8 Constructing a "Perfect" Wall
Race, Class, and Citizenship in US-Mexico Border Policing[1]

Josiah McC. Heyman

US policy toward immigrants, and in particular ones from Mexico, revolves around key symbolic formations about the US-Mexico border, as materialized in massive policing of and wall-building at that border. Kitty Calavita (1990) importantly first suggested the symbolic politics analysis of immigration policy, and I extended it to border policing in my work of the 1990s (Heyman 1999a, 1998, 1995). Disturbingly, these ideas have only become more relevant and extreme over time; as I write in 2010, over twelve hundred US troops are being sent to this peaceful border (that is, peaceful on the US side, where the military units are being deployed) (Mendoza 2010). Why and how does this occur? This chapter examines the core idea that the US-Mexico border can be perfectly controlled and sealed off from all harm. It locates this idea in the historical and contemporary dynamics of race and citizenship, attending to those phenomena in the context of ideologies, politics, and economics of the United States in its relationship to Mexican working people. Taking a political-economy perspective, but not one a reductive one, I explore how transnational migration through the US-Mexico border manifests profound contradictions emerging from capitalism seen as a fully socio-cultural phenomenon, including but also extending beyond obvious economic interests.

I begin this essay by delineating how border enforcement operates at the tactical level, and following that I explore the fundamental assumptions behind those tactics. Doing so helps take these technologies and tactics out of the realm of the normal and natural, to examine them as an overall system. I then state what these operations ideally should accomplish, from their immediate law-enforcement goals to the wider social goals that they are supposed to address. In turn, I consider the evidence on whether border enforcement has been effective or not. If it has been ineffective, why is the border wall, literal and metaphorical, being raised higher and higher? To answer this question, I consider how issues such as migration are turned into matters of national security, akin to military imperatives of defense against fundamental threats.

Moves to transform border issues into security issues are, we find, highly contested and contradictory. To tease out these complicated drivers of border policy, I explore some circumstances of the United States at the present moment, and some of the history through which we arrived at this point. This includes insecure prosperity and clinging to order in a world of vast inequalities of lifestyle, class, and power, and how such concerns are expressed in two ways: citizenship differences between deserving insiders and serving (but not deserving) outsiders, and racism against Latinas/os, especially Mexicans and Central Americans. Although having some capitalist-functional effects on labor exploitability, border policy is not calibrated to its economic consequences, and is beginning to threaten the transnational flow of labor so valued by capitalists. Yet it has taken on an extremist political life of its own, the dangerous spawn of right-wing populism usually at the service of capitalist and neo-imperialist elites. The contending coalitions and positions in the current conjuncture are sketched, and some possible paths forward are delineated. Citizenship, openness, security, and prosperity are important values, but I argue that we err in displacing the challenges involved in obtaining them onto a single, illusory answer: border policy that has little effectiveness and causes much suffering.

ATTEMPTS AT A PERFECT BORDER WALL

Enforcement occurs in three broad places along the Mexican border: at the ports of entry from Mexico into the United States; at or near the boundary between the ports; and in the buildings, streets, and roads of the borderlands extending north from the boundary. At ports, literally millions of commercial vehicles, non-commercial vehicles, and pedestrians seek to enter the country. The bulk of this flow is legitimate, including international commerce and manufacturing, cross-border shopping and tourism, legal commuting across the boundary to work, and visits to friends and family living in the adjacent nation. Various laws and regulations are applied by Customs and Border Protection to this flow, such as declarations of imported goods.

Amid this vast array of legitimate entries, the US government attempts to detect law violations. These include the smuggling of a number of restricted or prohibited goods, including drugs. They also include people entering the United States by hiding in vehicles, by falsely claiming US citizenship, by presenting counterfeit documents, or by presenting real documents that have been altered to falsify identity. Likewise, they include detecting people who enter with legitimate documents, such as Border Crossing Cards and non-immigrant visas, but who violate the terms by working or residing in the United States.[2]

The ports of entry face an inherent contradiction, in that they cannot function purely as a wall (for more on ports, see Heyman 2009a, 2004). They must serve as a filter that differentiates among entrants. Legitimate traffic must be cleared through the port for economic and social ties between the United States and Mexico to thrive, given that Mexico is the United States' second largest trading partner and its largest source of foreign-born residents. At the same time, the openness to entry and exit inherent in their filtering role represents a substantial gap in the outward security (in its own terms) of the nation. Probably the bulk of illegal drugs enters through commercial shipments at land, air, and sea ports, whereas the 9/11 hijackers entered through airports (notably, not through the US-Mexico ports). Forty to fifty percent of all unauthorized residents are estimated to have entered via ports of all kinds on legitimate visitor visas, but to have violated the terms of the visa either by overstaying its time period or working without authorization (or both) (Pew Hispanic Center 2006a). The ideal port would have an efficient, rapid detection process that sorted out law-violating from non-law-violating entries, that registered entries, and that assigned them regulations and tariffs as appropriate. Ports are far from this ideal, but their operations and technologies have strengthened in the last decade (e.g., the documentation required to enter the country has become more rigorous and secure).

Fundamentally, however, ports are underfunded and overworked. The United States Government Accountability Office (2007) has identified serious problems of understaffing, related to patterns of inadequate performance by inspectors. Yet ports continue to be neglected; in the Obama administration's 2012 budget request, overall port personnel is planned for an increase of fifty officers, whereas the Border Patrol is projected for an increase of one thousand officers (L. Graber, personal communication, files of author, 2010). The result is delayed and dysfunctional ports, especially at the Mexican land border. This is a key fact that political economy interpretations of the border need to grapple with. Ports are central to the functioning of the transnational capitalist economy; delays waiting in lines for inspections cost billions to manufacturers (especially those who have offshored production to Mexico), commercial shippers, commuters (some of them well-paid professionals), and non-commercial visitors, such as shoppers (see San Diego Association of Governments 2006). The constituency for ports is well connected, in classic power elite terms. Yet investment goes not to this critical infrastructure/bureaucracy, but to powerful displays of political symbolism, the Border Patrol and the border wall. This points in the direction of the analysis we must take.

To understand this, we must first look at stereotypes and realities of unauthorized border crossing outside of ports. Many non-borderlanders think of unauthorized migrants as nearly purely Mexican (when perhaps 60 percent are [Passel and Cohn 2008]) and as almost entirely crossing the land boundary outside of ports (the reality is discussed above). Such images must be explained, a task undertaken later; here I discuss its consequences. In such discourses, the key symbol "border" is reduced to just those segments that are fenced or otherwise closed off, and not open places of interchange. It is illegal to cross the border outside the ports of entry, and the Border Patrol works to detect and interdict such entries, including unauthorized migrants and drugs. The Border Patrol can either deter crossings by making the entrance too risky, or apprehend law violators, seizing contraband and returning or deporting migrants.

The land border between ports can be roughly divided into two tactical zones: in or near densely populated areas and away from such areas. In the former, such as the boundary in San Diego County from the Pacific Ocean to the Otay Mountains; at and near Nogales and Douglas, Arizona; and so forth, the government has already implanted walls of solid iron plates or razor-wire-topped chain-link fence, accompanied by high-intensity outdoor lighting and constant air surveillance. Since late 1993 in these locales the Border Patrol has stationed units in close proximity to the boundary and in tight spacing relative to one another, which has had the effect of discouraging most unauthorized crossers from entering there. This has not, however, stopped or slowed the flow of undocumented migrants, but rather has displaced that flow along the border to more remote desert and mountain crossing areas. The concomitant rise in injuries, deaths, and smuggling costs will be discussed below.

Remote border areas have long witnessed smuggling of high-value drugs and people (i.e., non-Mexicans). After the change in migration policing tactics in late 1993, undocumented Mexican and Central American crossing rose dramatically in those areas. The government raced to catch up by deploying large numbers of patrol officers and extensive surveillance systems into the expanses of rural border. Such areas are too large for massed policing, however; urban deterrence strategies do not work in rural areas. Rather, people cross the boundary in these areas and move northward, while the Border Patrol attempts to detect their movement at or shortly after entrance, cut off southward escape routes, trap them, and effect arrests and seizures. This takes place over wide swaths of small settlements, farms, and deserts (including badlands and mountains), usually shot through with roads and trails.

Nearly seven hundred miles of pedestrian-obstructing "fence" (effectively, a border wall) has been constructed along the 1,969-mile US-Mexico border; much of the rest is remote and rugged (which does not mean that such difficult and dangerous places are not crossed by would-be migrants). This was mandated by Congress in the highly politicized Secure Fence Act of 2006. The US government also sought an advanced electronic surveillance system on the border, but has cancelled those plans (for the time being) due to the failure of the prototype system (United States House of Representatives 2010, especially testimony of Hite and Borkowski). However, lower technology surveillance systems are widespread at the border, including fixed-wing aircraft, heavily instrumented balloons, helicopters, and unmanned aerial vehicles ("drones") that carry surveillance cameras over the boundary. Buried electronic motion sensors are pervasive on the border, as are stadium lighting, surveillance cameras, and low-light vision technology. Still, whether we consider walls, drones, or sensors, ground units are still needed to handle encounters in the field; to arrest people; to deal with emergencies; to transport people and contraband back to be processed; and to do the processing for seizure, voluntary departure, or deportation. We thus do not have to accept the "technologically perfect" border discourse at face value; Jason Ackleson (2005, 2003; also Koslowski 2006) has demonstrated that such claims are overstated and face significant limitations in implementation.

The border has been partially militarized since the late 1970s, even though US relations with Mexico are quite peaceable. Well-publicized deployments of National Guard units to the border respond to peaks in domestic political debate over migration (2006, 2010), as past deployment of regular forces responded to drug-control politics (late 1980s–1997). Military units do construction and maintenance, rear-echelon assistance in training and using surveillance technologies, and frontal listening/observation posts, but not arrests. Joint Task Force North, operating out of Fort Bliss, Texas, coordinates military support to border law enforcement, especially in the areas of intelligence and surveillance. A web of civilian and military intelligence units also operates out of this location. In addition to literal military involvement in law enforcement, the border police organizations themselves have adopted approaches and tactics drawing on or related to military low-intensity conflict doctrine, bringing about the militarization of responses to civilian policy issues such as migration (Dunn 1996).

Some contraband and some unauthorized migrants remain in the borderlands, but mostly they move northward, precisely because these flows are embedded in US society. This movement north requires transiting the roads of the border region, waiting in safe houses, and being transported through interior checkpoints by car, truck, and airplane. There is thus enforcement not only at or near the boundary, but in a heavily policed zone across the entire borderlands, including large cities, small cities and towns, and farm districts. Almost all of these areas count majority Latina/o populaces. Houses are watched, streets cruised, and strip malls and swap meets monitored. Transportation points, such as bus stations, are checked often, and main airports always have officers watching passengers. Roughly twenty-five to fifty miles into the interior, fixed Border Patrol checkpoints halt traffic on all major highways, constituting a second line of questioning and identification before vehicles enter the rest of the nation. The whole border zone virtually becomes a wall (Heyman 2010a, 2009b; Núñez and Heyman 2007).

Qualitatively, federal interior enforcement (sometimes in coordination with state and local authorities) has intensified in the last five years, in visibility and impact on migrant communities (Coleman 2007). The controversial Arizona law S.B. 1070 (see Heyman 2010b) is an extremist tip of a wider trend toward state and local targeting of unauthorized migrants (see Migration Policy Institute 2010). Recently, the law against employing unauthorized workers has been enforced by federal authorities at a greater extent than in the past, where it was largely ignored; however, this has been done by notifying employers of their employees' apparent false documentation, leading to firings, but not by either penalizing business or physically arresting and deporting migrants (Preston 2010). Whether or not this is an effective blow against the unauthorized employment relation is yet to be seen, but certainly it is an effort to find an enforcement tactic that can be publicized during a period of anti-immigrant sentiments while not performing politically touchy mass raids on workers with families or upsetting well-connected employers.

Fundamentally, however, immigration law enforcement remains disproportionately concentrated along the US-Mexico border. In fiscal year 2008 (the most recent year for which data is available), 89 percent of all immigration arrests occurred at or near the US-Mexico border (calculations by the author, based on United States Department of Homeland Security 2009). Likewise, fundamentally, the enforcement process targets the most powerless of law violators, the migrants themselves, especially in places and activities where they have the least political support structure, while in transit (rather than once in communities). The overall unauthorized migration process—including transportation, employment, residence, consumption, and community life, as well as entry—extends far from the boundary and involves not only illegal entrants but also employers, landlords, stores, churches, and so forth. Therefore, a basic fact that any analysis of migration politics must account for is the focus on the Mexican border region and a specific subset of migrants, Mexican and Central American entrants without inspection, by contrast with the many alternative loci, target populations, and policies that might be undertaken (Heyman 1999a).

The character of enforcement itself is in flux. Historically, most unauthorized migrants were removed either through voluntarily agreeing to depart (with no punitive record) or being formally deported (an administrative action that does create a record affecting future legal immigration petitions or enforcement actions). In either case, but especially in the voluntary departure instance, quick removal allows for renewed attempts at entry until the person finally makes it through the border, which in turn allows for the steady influx of undocumented workers into US society in spite of apparently massive efforts at border enforcement. However, recent enforcement policy has utilized harsher legal measures, such as Operation Streamline, in which migrants arrested at some parts of the border are charged with (and mostly plead guilty to) federal criminal charges of illegal entry, with serious future repercussions (Lydgate 2010). Even in non-Streamline cases, the government is making use of formal deportation more often, and voluntary departure less often. A different but also punitive measure is lateral removal, in which persons arrested in one area of the border are removed via another, distant area, designed to make it harder for them to recontact smugglers who will assist them to re-enter.

The buildup of immigration enforcement and the tactical shift toward walls and intensive frontal policing in heavily traveled corridors began in late 1993. The Border Patrol, for example, grew from approximately four thousand to twenty thousand officers in 2009 (Nevins 2010). For a long period, this escalation appeared ineffective, with the buildup essentially throwing good money after bad (Heyman 1999b; Andreas 2000). Surveying likely undocumented migrants in Mexico, for example, Fuentes et al. (2007) found that (1) information about US border law enforcement did not deter them; (2) the rate at which past undocumented entrants reported being apprehended fell during the period of massive Border Patrol buildup; and, (3) the rate of use and cost of smugglers rose dramatically during this period. This belies the notion that enforcement will deter migrants, a crucial assumption of the perfect border-wall vision.

In the period since 2008, the undocumented flow through the border outside the ports of entry has slowed significantly. The Pew Hispanic Institute estimates that the average annual inflow of all unauthorized migrants has decreased by two-thirds from 2000 to 2009 (from 850,000 annually to 300,000 annually; Passel and Cohn 2010). DHS reports a 61-percent reduction in Border Patrol apprehensions—most at the Mexican border—from fiscal year 2005 to 2010 (Sapp 2011). And the government of Mexico recently reported that Mexico's net outflow of migrants has fallen "to almost nothing" (net out-migration of 0.09 percent from March 2010 to March 2011) (Associated Press 2011). The cause of this decline is debated. Perhaps the massive border enforcement buildup is finally having an effect, a change from a long-standing pattern in which enforcement has grown without altering flows (on that, see Cornelius 2006). Alternatively, it could be a product of the sudden decline in U.S. employment, especially in construction (the lower-skill end of this sector having substantial numbers of unauthorized migrants), after the housing bubble burst in 2008. Finally, it could stem from a decrease in the rate of back-and-forth travel (cyclical migration), as unauthorized migrants remain permanently inside the United States, in order to avoid the cost and risk of crossing the border.

The migrants' "success" in crossing the border comes at a cost, sadly. Migrants now pay more money to smugglers, borrow more and thus are deeper in debt, and have higher levels of obligation to moneylenders, labor contractors, and so forth. They have been driven deeper into life outside the law, while smuggling organizations have become richer and better organized. Deaths and injuries at the border have risen dramatically because of the displacement of migration out of relatively safe urban corridors into mountain and desert areas. Conservatively, around four hundred people die each year crossing this border (Eshbach, Hagen, and Rodríguez 2003; Cornelius 2001; Eshbach et al. 1999). Migrants are undeterred, even unto death.

All of these developments mean that an analysis I had previously offered (Heyman 1999a, 1999b, 1998, 1995), that voluntary departure was a mechanism by which migration enforcement can be carried out symbolically (or performatively), without affecting the underlying supply of labor to employers, must be substantially reworked. Border enforcement must now be considered more clearly and substantively directed at its ostensible policy goal of preventing people from entering the national territory. Symbolism/performance analysis is still needed to analyze the politics driving border enforcement actions, but the practical effort itself must be regarded now as genuinely serious, not merely for show. The fact that enforcement arguably is reducing undocumented border crossing, and especially slowing down cyclical migration, indicates that a purely capitalist-functionalist, labor supply analysis is inadequate, and an ideological boundary control analysis should be considered. However, because legally and physically harsh measures have not thoroughly emptied the United States of unauthorized migrants, the underlying pattern of vulnerable labor remains intact, which is central to the perpetuation of the capitalist-functional (economic) side of migration. It has so far remained insulated from obstruction by the xenophobic, territorialistic political side, although we must consider the latter to be demonstrably serious in its intent to obstruct such flows. The self-sacrificing persistence of migrants, in the face of more and more deaths, more and more smuggling costs, and worse and worse legal treatment, means that key contradictions have not yet come fully together to halt the exploitable migratory process, and that genuinely dual economic and political-ideological analyses are both needed to understand the whole.

Although migration is my focal topic, the perfect border also ostensibly halts contraband drugs and terrorists/terror supplies. Drug prohibition policy is less exclusively concentrated at the border than migration policy, but still is extensive there. Price/supply levels suggest that interdiction-based drug policies have failed (e.g., Walsh 2009; Grossman, Chaloupka, and Shim 2002). Interdiction of externally sourced terrorism makes sense, along with prevention of domestic terrorism and reduction of the drivers of terrorism, in light of the horrific events of 9/11, but the US-Mexican border so far has been irrelevant (Leiken and Brook 2006, on the existing record, and Ginsburg 2006, on the low likelihood of terrorists using nonport, overland travel routes). A careful examination of US programs at all boundaries before, during, and after 9/11 indicates that terrorism is quite secondary to anti-Mexican immigration measures (Heyman and Ackleson 2009). Meanwhile, the US neglect, except recently and still at a low level, of outbound interdiction of arms and money, items undeniably linked to many thousands of Mexican deaths, shows that the perfect border focuses on inward sealing of the United States, rather than using the border objectively as a tool to reduce human risks and harms. The constant cycling of media and policy/politics attention between three different border issues—migration, drugs, and terrorism—so that fears always focus on the region in some way or another, suggests instead that border enforcement is driven by some mixture of anxiety specific to the border, stigma of Mexico, and corresponding performances of protection by the state.

In the rhetoric of border buildup, the idea prevails that weak and flawed efforts were made in the past, that the border is in a state of crisis, and that only adding more and more enforcement can address a situation that is out of control. These propositions are clearly wrong. The level of border-control effort has been both large and growing, whether measured in personnel or funding. So why continue to escalate border law enforcement? Shouldn't failure lead to reconsidering this approach? And why does the gap between the ideal of the walled border and the reality of continued flows not lead to rethinking these imagined ideals and their relationship to the realities of the United States, Mexico, and Central America?

Analysis suggests several possible replies to these questions. For example, many advocates of border escalation hold that not enough has been done, and that it has not been done well enough. But, what drives this impulse to do the same thing, over and over again, in the face of failure? Another reading is that border law enforcement has grown and is reasonably competent, but simply cannot succeed in the face of wider social forces, such underdevelopment in Mexico, and demand for immigrant labor in the United States. This may explain why the border enforcement approach is wrongheaded, but it does not explain why a wrongheaded policy is persistent and largely popular. One might posit that the ideal/reality gap is a deliberate failure, because the US power elite actually wants a heavily policed, exploitable undocumented population. There is a thread of truth in this, but it is too simplistic as a whole-cloth explanation, as we shall see. Rather, I will argue, the impulse to fail and fail again at the border emerges from intersecting struggles in the politics, economics, and culture of the contemporary United States.

THE IDEA OF A PERFECT BORDER WALL

The inner circles of US policy-makers envision an ideal border that would be smart and secure (see the Security and Prosperity Partnership of North America 2010, also Andreas and Biersteker 2003). Through advanced technology and tactics, the government would sense and respond to almost all unauthorized incursions. The border would thus function as a hermetic seal against "bad forces" coming into the home space. Also, ports would intelligently and efficiently distinguish among people, vehicles, and shipments to sort out the lawbreakers, or at least those meriting close scrutiny, from trustworthy entrants. In other words, the border would be smart enough to deliver security to the United States while at the same time not impede the cross-border flows crucial to Mexico's serving as a low-wage export platform for US, Asian, and European corporations. The home space would thus be open to "good," or at least profitable, outside forces. The ideal border would be a powerful and intelligent filter.

An underlying ideal of the smart and secure border sharpens the distinction between legal and illegal. The ideal situation is that people with legal and trusted status would be able to move about near or across the border without inappropriate stops, detention, and arrest, because of highly effective systems of surveillance and identification. US citizens and legal immigrants would have nothing to fear, as stated so often in the current immigration debate, because they would not have broken the law. Privileged cross-border commuters and commercial shippers would actually move faster and with less scrutiny and inconvenience because of their high value, command of resources (ability to pay the costs of the program), and trusted status with the government. Only lawbreakers would have reason to fear surveillance, detention, interrogation, and arrest by the border-enforcement apparatus.

With respect to illegality, the smart and secure border would largely resolve three major societal problems: terrorism, psychotropic drug use, and unauthorized migration. This assumption posits that such problems come from outside the national territory. Hence, they would decline or disappear were they prevented from entering the home space. Unauthorized migrants, for example, would be so discouraged by the difficulty of crossing the boundary that they would quit coming in meaningful numbers. The United States would be saved from the illegal immigrant "problem." The assumption states that the United States itself is not involved in the creation and perpetuation of these three issues—for example, that the US domestic economy is not really involved in the employment, housing, and so forth of undocumented immigrants, and that the North American economy does not mobilize them from their homes in Mexico and Central America (see Binford 2005). Rather, bad actors from outside who penetrate an insecure boundary are entirely to blame, and the solution is having a comprehensively smart and secure border (for a broadly parallel analysis of displacement of contradictions from the national interiors to the border, see Santibáñez Romellón 2006).

However, this ideal filter belongs to the inner circles of the public and private power elite, and shares the political field with a more rigidly exclusionary, territorial, and xenophobic vision (Nevins 2010), which arguably has been more influential on actual policies (Heyman and Ackleson 2009). To an important domestic constituency, the ideal border would reverse the tide of social and cultural change that followed from the post-1965 Latin American, Caribbean, and Asian "new" immigration. Specifically, it would stem the so-called brown tide that has "invaded" the United States (Santa Ana 2002; Chavez 2001), the rapid growth in Latinas/os, especially people of Mexican origin, that is no longer just in long-standing Mexican-immigrant settlement areas but throughout the entire nation. It would stabilize socially, culturally, and economically an imagined America[3] of the 1950s, after the cessation of mass European immigration and before both the new immigration and the long decline of many regional economies that began in the 1970s. It would also reverse the forces of sprawl, expense, and degradation in the Sunbelt, restoring the perfect California, Arizona, Colorado, and so forth of the era when just internal US migrants moved there, not these new international migrants. Of course, this vision confuses immigration of all kinds, including millions of legal immigrants, with the specific phenomenon of illegal entry, which a perfect border would prevent; it also neglects unauthorized migration via legal visa overstays. I discuss later the nuances of race, class, citizenship, and legality in the politics of borders and immigration.

Securitization is an important tendency in both elite and popular thinking about perfect borders. This is the process of placing complex societal issues (e.g., migration, drugs, etc.) into the frame of fundamental existential threats to the central state and the civil society that it contains, as if they were equivalent to full-on nuclear warfare (Buzan, Wæver, and de Wilde 1998; Wæver 1995). The formation of a centralized US Department of Homeland Security in 2003 out of more diverse, task-specific agencies, with its most concentrated efforts at the Mexican border, is indicative of securitization. Securitization strengthens the resources, discretion, and ideological reach of the central state, insofar as it is tasked with protecting the fundamental continuity of society (whether real or imagined). It is both a response to and a promoter of absolutist, territorial, and xenophobic political discourses (Huysmans 1995).

The perfect border thus separates rightness, orderliness, and self from badness, disorderliness, and others. This conceptual boundary has been at terrible risk, but an ideal wall will reassert clarity and order. It will reduce the ambiance of illegality and disorder, and renew the sense of protection and control (Tirman 2006). It will reassure a nation that no longer has unquestioned primacy in international relations, is stuck in intractable wars, has enemies that are difficult to discern, receives confusing global headlines from the mass media, and has an economy deeply penetrated by global forces, including both US corporations moving outwards and foreign corporations competitively pushing in. The United States also faces disorderly internal trends, including widening income inequalities and stagnant job creation, for which a perfect wall against lawbreaking outsiders offers a satisfying magic solution. We would all be safe and secure.

The analysis of the perfect border must begin with Mary Douglas's (1966) analysis of the symbolism of external boundaries and of pollution, risk, and danger in crossing them. Douglas proposes that conceptual boundaries are symbolic expressions and materializations of fundamental divisions in social structure. Static contents, internal and external, are normal and pure. Boundary crossing elements are potentially powerful and/or dangerous, as they both highlight and defy these lines of order, and they are thus impure or polluting. The crossing of such thresholds is filled with risk and danger. The relevance of such symbolism to border and immigration issues is evident, as is its considerable motivating power once internalized. But symbols need to be given specific referents (who is inside and outside?), and they likewise need to be communicated across society; they are not self-enacting discourses. That is a matter of political economy, the heart of this chapter.

WHY BUILD A PERFECT WALL?

The fundamental analytical challenge is that several different "perfect" visions all align to escalate enforcement along the border, but they have quite different origins, constituencies, and implications for future arrangement of society. They require several distinct political, economic, and ideological analyses. To one set of interests and perspectives, the virtual wall would be the first step toward a managed, imported labor force, a new Bracero Program made up of people who would labor hard, would be glad (as it were) to receive a modest wage, and would return home when no longer needed or when being too demanding and assertive. Unauthorized migration would cease but well-controlled legal migration—permanent and temporary—would then grow. This is a vision in line with the border seen as a perfect filter of trade, as discussed. An ideal border would thus be open to capital investment, property ownership, commodity trade, information transmittal, and business trips and tourist breaks for the prosperous and well connected, but would tightly control working people—not completely closed to them, but always monitoring them, knowing when they entered and exited, and how they comported themselves while in the United States. Sometimes allied with but also sometimes bitterly opposed to proponents of this approach are the holders of a nationalist-isolationist vision of a restored past and a stable social, cultural, and economic present within the clearly delimited territory of the sacred nation.

There are three distinct networks of agenda-setters at work promoting border escalation, as well as one that is resisting it. The first network is composed of corporate and bureaucratic entrepreneurs in the homeland security industrial complex (see Fernandes 2007), who together with allied congressional representatives constitute the infamous "iron triangle" of budget allocation and public policy-making. Actors in the triangle gain budgets, personnel, technology, and authority by the growth of the virtual border wall. Internally, border enforcement bureaucrats fight over turf, but collectively they constantly feed the press, the Presidency, and Congress with continuous promotion of an intensified security approach. The public appearances on the border of Homeland Security Secretary Michael Chertoff during the 2006–2007 period of rapid escalation of force and infrastructure exemplify the point. Meanwhile, the defense, intelligence, and surveillance industries see a chance to turn modest border construction, maintenance, and equipment contracts into huge contracts for wall construction and implementation of advanced technologies (e.g., Boeing's $2.7 billion contract for the Smart Border Initiative, later partially cancelled, as discussed above). Meanwhile, congressional representatives angle for contracts in their districts and jobs for their kin. Universities and think tanks pitifully lurk underfoot in hopes of a few research crumbs falling from the table.

A second network of border securitization agenda-setters are anti-immigrant ideologues. They have long existed, vocal and vituperative, with congressional allies in districts outside the borderlands (sometimes, however, just north of the border region). This network would have cheerfully led an anti-immigrant wave at any time in the last thirty years, but the particular opportune moment appears to have been provided in 2005–2006, when the Iraq War was turning politically sour and elections were forthcoming. Then, congressional Republicans brought forward immigration as a convenient distraction, putting the anti-immigrant lobby at the front of the media and US political discourse. This is the main frame, continuing to the present, most recently in the context of domestic economic suffering after the collapse of the bubble economy closely connected to Republican business policies. It is worth noting that anti-immigrant networks have had their greatest political and material effects (e.g., in border policing upsurges) during both economic good (late 2005) and bad (2010) times. A simple analysis, tying such policies to the short-term economy either in political terms (e.g., scapegoating) or as a form of regulating the labor supply within capitalism, fails empirically, but a longer-term analysis tying the appeal of anti-immigrationism to long-term decreases in personal economic security in a period of globalization and the retreat of the state, perhaps can be empirically sustained (see Heyman 1998a: 161, on the notion of "long waves of anxiety").

The third key network that promotes the "smart" vision of the border wall is major corporate and central state elites. During 2005–2007 this included Karl Rove, Michael Chertoff, Carlos Gutierrez, and presumably George W. Bush. After the Obama election, this has included Janet Napolitano and Alan Bersin. Outside of the official state, this has included Lee Hamilton, Spencer Abraham, Doris Meissner (all former state actors), and others (see Meissner et al. 2006). Bersin, current Commissioner of Customs and Border Protection, offers a useful illustration. With an elite law school training, and having had a career moving repeatedly between the private sector and government positions under both Democrats and Republicans, he is married into a San Diego family with the most lucrative real estate interests in the entire border region. These center on development of private commercial ports of entry, and related logistical (warehouse, etc.) units, that serve off-shored North American and Asian industries in Mexico (Potter 2009).

Such elites seek two goals: to have an ample, inexpensive, easily disciplined transnational or migrant labor force, preferably one easier to manage than unauthorized migrants; and to have an efficient border-crossing system for people and goods transiting the global economic "highway" between the United States and Mexico. They have so far failed to secure their policy goals, however, especially with the failure of "comprehensive immigration reform" legislation in 2006–2007 and 2009–2010, that would have included large, tightly controlled guestworker programs (versus loose, unauthorized border crossing), and labor market design-based visa programs for permanent migrants. These comprehensive elite redesigns of the border/migration system lurk on the political horizon.

Power elites, while sophisticated and powerful, face an important challenge when seeking to manage and redesign the border. An important electoral base is nationalist, to some extent authoritarian or at least security-/state-oriented, and anxious about social and cultural change (e.g., clearly this frightens the Obama administration into continued border escalation [fieldnotes on Bersin public meeting in El Paso, May 28, 2009]). On the other hand, their agenda actually favors a partially, and inequitably, open border. To remain politically dominant, they must mediate and manipulate lower-order political impulses (anti-immigration activists, iron triangle groupings) for their strategic ends. They aim to keep globalization viable while appearing to please their nationalist following. Securitization of border control helps with their political task, although it threatens the policy agenda of rationalizing migrant labor flows via comprehensive reforms. No one solution is fully rational to them.

Securitization moves are opposed by politically significant pro-immigrant coalitions (here, I draw on participant-observation [see Heyman, Morales, and Núñez 2009]). One network of actors—with roots in Latina/o, Asian, and other post-immigrant groups, some labor unions, and many churches—seeks an overall widening of legal immigration and legalization of current undocumented residents. These agenda-setters and constituents, sometimes termed the humanitarian or human rights coalition, have broadly resisted the securitization of the border. Some, more often based in Washington, DC, accept a law-enforcement approach at the boundary as a rhetorical and policy compromise in order to obtain greater legal migration; others, based in border communities and immigrant communities in the interior, seek de-escalation of enforcement and a change in its philosophy toward community security and respect for rights. Border business, political, and non-governmental leaders, who are historically ambivalent about boundary policing, have largely joined the recent coalition against physical border walls and militarization because they oppose visible symbols of US-Mexico polarization, but they are split over other law enforcement proposals because of the appeal of professional workforces and contracts in the homeland security industrial complex (and despite the factual safety and security of US-side border communities).

A great mass of US voters and media consumers form the constituency courted by these agenda-setters. They are anxious about globalization, fearful of terrorism, suspicious of "illegality," and ambivalent about legal immigration. Public opinion about immigration and border issues is notoriously uninformed, contradictory, and hard to measure, with responses differing according to the exact question asked and the agenda advanced in the mass media at that moment. But, the broad tendency seems to accept comprehensive immigration reform, to be particularly negative about illegal immigration, to express concern over the border being out of control, and to favor border control efforts (see Segovia and DeFever 2010; Keeter 2009; Pew Hispanic Institute 2006b; Espenshade 2001). Hainmueller and Hiscox (2010) have demonstrated that opposition to immigration in the United States is not correlated with directly material variables, either labor market competition or actual fiscal costs and benefits, but rather emerges from broader socio-cultural variables, such as racial attitudes, age, concern with law and order, and concern with change.

To pull together a large number of threads here, border and migration policies are not unified, but rather are the result of a complex set of political contests. Such contests are not simply pluralistic—useful analysis can start from a broadly unified theory of contemporary capitalist economics, politics, and ideology—but they are likewise not cohesive and functional, especially not in terms of the interests of the power elite. The strongest element currently in the struggle is the socio-cultural politics of fear, and the predominant performance of policing is symbolic. So far, the capitalist-functional side of such border and migration policy (the role of the border in producing highly exploitable labor) has muddled through, insulated from ultimate contradictions by the terrible self-sacrifices of the migrants themselves. But regulation of labor and other capitalist system needs is clearly not the thrust of actual state policy, as demonstrated by the implementation of genuine barriers to labor flows, lack of opening and closing actions at the border, the non-economic timing of border escalation peaks, and the neglect of ports of entry (resulting in dysfunctions for transnational movement of commodities and privileged persons). However, extreme nationalism does constitute a useful political and ideological resource for political elites, especially those on the right.

THE PERFECT WALL: BUILT IN MILLENNIAL AMERICA

The current political moment comes from the intersection of a more-or-less global capitalist economy and a particular US capitalist society/culture.[4] Both dimensions need to be understood. The interests of key power elites in cross-border flows of investment, profits, commodities, and vulnerable labor are evident, as are their interests in having strong intelligence, policing, and military tools of the central state. But, to promote various power projects, they must practice politics within and utilize the social and cultural discourses of a specific polity and society. In this regard, the United States' crucial characteristics include widening inequality, a vast central state, and many households with moderate-to-high material prosperity compared to the working poor of the nation and the world. Specific American legacies of racism and citizenship also influence the scenario. The obsession with imposing definite order, and using police and military tools to do it, arises in this context. State and economic elites seek to satisfy a nationalist and xenophobic base while promoting the global economy in the long run.

Our understanding of the mindset of defensive prosperity is imperfect, yet it is crucial to the contemporary United States. We should examine and critique it. One element might be a fear of sharing prosperity with others, including immigrants and their children (let alone the rest of the world). Leo Chavez (2001) has pointed out the concern in anti-immigration rhetoric about women and children coming across the Mexican border. One might also note the strong theme of closing the door to public benefits, including health care, municipal services, and public schooling. (I will discuss citizenship and law as idioms for this shortly.) Another motif is distaste, possibly hiding a sense of guilt and shame, at the hard, sweaty, unremunerative work of immigrant laborers. If such people are racially and culturally foreign, from beyond the wall, one does not need to identify with their struggles. A final thread is the confusion of prosperity with Americanness, and Americanness with a specific kind of post-World War II assimilation to Anglo-American culture and language, together with a distaste for otherness (a once-punitive lesson that descendents of poor rural Americans and past immigrants appear to have learned all too well).

Yet here come new waves of immigrants, some well educated and prosperous and others quite poor but hard working, who through their distinctive languages, cultures, and social networks, threaten the comfortable cultural correlates of the American dream. Intertwined with xenophobic anxieties is disturbing knowledge of domestic and global environmental, economic, and political problems. There is much to be genuinely worried about in America's old age, and US residents can be the bearers of both realistic concerns and paranoid fantasies all at once. Thus, in the virtual and physical wall, a certain selfish hope emerges for unity, uniformity, and prosperity and against insecurity, dialogue, and change.

In the period before 1940–1980, straight-up racism would have served to impose conceptual and material order in places where Mexicans migrated and lived (the historical account that follows draws on Ngai 2004). Public institutions were often segregated, pay rates were unequal, and immigration laws were applied capriciously to allow workers in, keep them in line, and send them home when not wanted. Capitalist economic logic, ethnocentrism, and the selfish defense of prosperity aligned neatly along the boundaries of race. But Mexican Americans had long struggled for social justice and civil rights. Starting around 1940, they began to make real progress against strict racial inequality. The struggle took many years and is by no means completed, but by 1980, a new pattern had emerged. People of Mexican (and other Latin American, Caribbean, and Asian) origin now can often claim resources, rights, and standing in US society as citizens, using that term in both its legal and its cultural senses. A more precarious status is legal permanent residence (still subject to deportation), but even then, the term 'legal' denotes a standing in society as orderly, belonging, and not entirely foreign.

During the same period, however, labor and family-reunification migration from Mexico and Central America has amplified, not only in numbers but also in variety of occupations and locales. This has taken place through both legal and extralegal channels; indeed, the two are often hard to distinguish on the ground. As I discussed earlier, new immigrants, especially Mexicans, are often envisioned as threatening the imagined cultural correlates of prosperity. Yet marking off all Mexicans as outsiders and rendering them powerless is no longer as simple as it was during the period of strict racist hierarchy. A rearrangement of prejudice and victimization has thus emerged. The target now is "illegal immigrants," mistakenly envisioned as always Mexican, with Mexicans often mistakenly envisioned as mainly "illegal" also. "Illegals" are precisely anti-citizens, anti-law, and anti-order. The US-Mexican border distinguishes American law from chaotic outsiderness. The people who cross it without authorization come from a mysterious and disorderly place, and by being in the wrong place for their legal status, they endanger the clarity of the protective categories—hence, the intense concern with an all-knowing, all-seeing virtual wall to ensure the order desired by a wealthy but insecure society. While this begins with social imaginaries, it is possible—but debatable—that the border can be materially closed to unauthorized migration. The current data points this way, but we are still in the midst of a terrible economic recession. Only time will tell what political, economic, and social outcomes emerge from this conjuncture.

It is thus important to take seriously the rhetoric of citizenship and legality as many Americans inchoately express their understanding of who should have jobs, health care, college educations, and so forth. These debates are not simple, and not everyone who uses words like *citizenship* aims to reduce immigration and impose iron-fisted controls, but there is undeniably a thrust in the current language of citizenship toward drawing walls around the sparse sources of redistribution in an era when wealth is becoming more unequal and social benefits smaller and smaller. Struggles over such claims may take place in Pennsylvania or north Texas, but the border is almost always invoked—as having broken down, as needing to be repaired. Symbolic politics is not just a phrase, but a powerful force and massive materialization; the border wall is a giant public symbol for a television and Internet era that differentiates those who belong inside and have claims to public goods (citizens) and those who should remain outside with no such claims (aliens). Nandita Sharma (2006) captures an important insight in her work on global apartheid, as the system that establishes outsiders who may provide labor services but who are denied respect, permanency, and material redistributions, although she examines it in terms of relatively tightly designed temporary labor systems that have largely not been politically viable in the US context (see Spener 2009 for a nuanced, contradictory view of apartheid in the US-Mexico case).

The symbolic or conceptual drive toward apartheid within prosperous capitalism, however, is essential to our analysis. Through the imagined line of the perfect border, applied to people and goods already factually within American society, outside is clearly separated from inside, legal from illegal. The troubling American addictions to drugs and inexpensive labor services are put out of mind—no need for excessive self-honesty here—by displacing them onto the magnificent symbol of a threatened and then defended border. Hypocrisy is an important theme, and we need stronger analytical tools for its analysis as a characteristic product of prosperity within capitalism.

As I made clear above, and as Glick Schiller insists in this volume, migration is a transnational phenomenon, and methodological nationalism as a form of analysis should be rejected (for the US-Mexico case, see Massey, Durand, and Malone 2002). However, it is precisely such bounded national entities as political visions ("imagined communities," in Anderson's [1983] phrasing) that are central to analysis of would-be perfect border policies. The transnational realities of various flows, including migration, lurk within the (otherwise quite different) visions for the future of power elites and migrants and their advocates. But such visions of the present and future are far from being realized, and there is a vigorous struggle afoot to prevent any version of it from becoming open, legitimate public design (hence, the hypocrisy). The frame for what is "society" within capitalism, who is included, and who is excluded, and what material and symbolic resources are collectively distributed, has been and continues to be a central point of struggle. The triangular struggle (elite, nationalist, human rights advocate) over borders and migration is fundamental to such questions, and thus to our collective future.

Politically relevant social science, in my view, should do this sort of analysis. It needs to analyze directly particular scenarios of political contestation. To do that, it needs to be grounded in political economy. But this does not mean simply reducing everything to economic system logics. Nor does it mean reverting to political pluralism or to isolated analyses of discourses, no matter how attentive to power and inequality. Rather, historical, social, and cultural formations are nested in capitalist political economies, but these specific formations are the immediate ground of political analysis. Borders and migration have multiple and contradictory roles in such processes, requiring a number of different but simultaneous explanations, and a sense of how such dimensions interact; a capable and useful analysis for conducting effective struggles will encompass all these elements.

NOTES

1. An earlier version of this chapter was published as "Constructing a Virtual Wall: Race and Citizenship in U.S.-Mexico Border Policing," in the *Journal of the Southwest* 50: 305–333, and is used here with permission. I thank the journal.
2. A Border Crossing Card (sometimes called a local passport or laser visa) allows a Mexican border-city resident with ties to the Mexican side such as a job and

a house to enter up to twenty-five miles into the United States for up to thirty days to visit and shop, but does not allow US employment or residence. A non-immigrant visa (sometimes called a *permiso*) allows the bearer to visit the United States beyond the twenty-five-mile border zone, for a period up to six months, but again not to work or reside in the United States.
3. Properly used, America and Americans include Canada, Latin America, and the Caribbean. I use it on occasion with reference solely to the United States specifically in the context of a nationalistic and xenophobic cultural formation.
4. Purcell and Nevins (2005) parallel my arguments in arguing for multiple forces at the border, and holding that narrowly economic interpretations are insufficient. They perceive the territorial state as having its own, autonomous logic, whereas I see the politics and state logic as nested in a broader cultural formation of contemporary capitalism. Inda (2005) converges with me in foregrounding the discourse of illegality, but as a Foucauldian, he does not locate this meaning formation in political economic processes.

REFERENCES

Ackleson, Jason. 2003. "Securing through Technology? 'Smart Borders' after September 11th." *Knowledge, Technology, and Policy* 16: 56–74.

———. 2005. "Border Security Technologies: Local and Regional Implications." *Review of Policy Research*, 22: 137–155.

Anderson, Benedict. 1983. *Imagined Communities: Reflections on the Origin and Spread of Nationalism*. London: Verso.

Andreas, Peter. 2000. *Border Games: Policing the US-Mexico Divide*. Ithaca: Cornell University Press.

Andreas, Peter, and Thomas J. Biersteker, eds. 2003. *The Rebordering of North America: Integration and Exclusion in a New Security Context*. London and New York: Routledge.

Associated Press. 2011. "Mexico Says Immigration Outflow Drops to 'Almost Nothing'." August 8. Accessed August 16, 2011. http://www.washingtonpost.com/world/americas/mexico-says-immigration-outflow-drops-to-almost-nothing/2011/08/08/gIQAxYJi2I_story.html.

Binford, Leigh. 2005. "A Generation of Migrants: Why They Leave, Where They End Up." *NACLA Report on the Americas* 39(1): 31–37.

Buzan, Barry, Ole Wæver, and Jaap de Wilde. 1998. *Security: A New Framework for Analysis*. Boulder, CO: Lynne Rienner.

Calavita, Kitty. 1990. "Employer Sanctions Violations: Toward a Dialectical Model of White-Collar Crime." *Law and Society Review* 24: 1041–1069.

Chavez, Leo R. 2001. *Covering Immigration: Popular Images and the Politics of the Nation*. Berkeley and Los Angeles: University of California Press.

Coleman, Mathew. 2007. "Immigration Geopolitics beyond the Mexico–US Border." *Antipode* 38(2): 54–76.

Cornelius, Wayne A. 2001. "Death at the Border: Efficacy and Unintended Consequences of US Immigration Control Policy." *Population and Development Review* 27: 661–685.

———. 2006. "Impacts of Border Enforcement on Unauthorized Mexican Migration to the United States." Social Science Research Council. Accessed July 19, 2010. http://borderbattles.ssrc.org/Cornelius/.

Douglas, Mary. 1966. *Purity and Danger: An Analysis of Concepts of Pollution and Taboo*. London: Routledge and Kegan Paul.

Dunn, Timothy J. 1996. *The Militarization of the U.S.–Mexico Border, 1978–1992: Low-Intensity Conflict Doctrine Comes Home.* Austin: CMAS Books, University of Texas at Austin.

Eshbach, Karl, Jacqueline M. Hagen, and Nestor P. Rodríguez. 2003. "Deaths during Undocumented Migration: Trends and Policy Implications in the New Era of Homeland Security." *In Defense of the Alien* 26: 37–52.

Eshbach, Karl, Jacqueline M. Hagen, Nestor P. Rodríguez, Rubén Hernández-León, and Stanley Bailey. 1999. "Death at the Border." *International Migration Review* 33: 430–440.

Espenshade, Thomas J. 2001. "Public Opinion and Immigration." In *Encyclopedia of American Immigration*, edited by James D. Ciment, 560–568. Armonk, NY: M.E. Sharpe.

Fernandes, Deepa. 2007. *Targeted: Homeland Security and the Business of Immigration.* New York: Seven Stories Press.

Fuentes, Jezmin, Henry L'Esperance, Raúl Pérez, and Caitlin White. 2007. "Impacts of U.S. Immigration Policies on Migration Behavior." In *Impacts of Border Enforcement on Mexican Migration: The View from Sending Communities*, edited by Wayne A. Cornelius and Jessa M. Lewis, 53–73. La Jolla, CA: Center for Comparative Immigration Studies.

Ginsburg, Susan. 2006. *Countering Terrorist Mobility: Shaping an Operational Strategy.* Washington, DC: Migration Policy Institute. Accessed July 19, 2010. http://www.migrationpolicy.org/pubs/MPI_TaskForce_Ginsburg.pdf.

Grossman, Michael, Frank J. Chaloupka, and Kyumin Shim. 2002. "Illegal Drug Use and Public Policy." *Health Affairs* 21: 134–145.

Hainmueller, Jens, and Michael J. Hiscox. 2010. "Attitudes toward Highly Skilled and Low-Skilled Immigration: Evidence from a Survey Experiment." *American Political Science Review* 104: 61–84.

Heyman, Josiah McC. 1995. "Putting Power into the Anthropology of Bureaucracy: The Immigration and Naturalization Service at the Mexico–United States Border." *Current Anthropology* 36: 261–287.

———. 1998. "State Effects on Labor Exploitation: The INS and Undocumented Immigrants at the Mexico–United States Border." *Critique of Anthropology* 18: 157–180.

———. 1999a. "Why Interdiction? Immigration Law Enforcement at the United States–Mexico Border." *Regional Studies* 33: 619–630.

———. 1999b. "State Escalation of Force: A Vietnam/US–Mexico Border Analogy." In *States and Illegal Practices*, edited by Josiah McC. Heyman, 285–314. Oxford: Berg.

———. 2004. "Ports of Entry as Nodes in the World System." *Identities: Global Studies in Culture and Power* 11: 303–327.

———. 2009a. "Ports of Entry in the 'Homeland Security' Era: Inequality of Mobility and the Securitization of Transnational Flows." In *International Migration and Human Rights: The Global Repercussions of U.S. Policy*, edited by Samuel Martínez, 44–59. Berkeley and Los Angeles: University of California Press.

———. 2009b. "Trust, Privilege, and Discretion in the Governance of the US Borderlands with Mexico." *Canadian Journal of Law and Society / Revue Canadienne Droit et Société* 24: 367–390.

———. 2010a. "Relationships between the State and Mobile People: The Unequal Construction and Allocation of Risk and Trust at the U.S.-Mexico Border." In *Class and Contention in a World in Motion*, edited by Winnie Lem and Pauline Gardiner Barber, 58–78. Oxford: Berghahn Press.

———. 2010b. "Human Rights and Social Justice Briefing 1: Arizona's Immigration Law—S.B. 1070." Accessed July 19, 2010. http://www.sfaa.net/committees/humanrights/AZImmigrationLawSB1070.pdf.

Heyman, Josiah McC., and Jason Ackleson. 2009. "United States Border Security after September 11." In *Border Security in the Al-Qaeda Era*, edited by John Winterdyck and Kelly Sundberg, 37–74. Boca Raton, FL: CRC Press.

Heyman, Josiah McC., Maria Cristina Morales, and Guillermina Gina Núñez. 2009. "Engaging with the Immigrant Human Rights Movement in a Besieged Border Region: What Do Applied Social Scientists Bring to the Policy Process?" *NAPA Bulletin* 31: 13–29.

Huysmans, Jef. 1995. "Migrants as a Security Problem: Dangers of 'Securitizing' Societal Issues." In *Migration and European Integration: The Dynamics of Inclusion and Exclusion*, edited by Robert Miles and Dietrich Thränhardt, 53–72. London: Pinter.

Inda, Jonathan Xavier. 2005. *Targeting Immigrants: Government, Technology, and Ethics*. Malden, MA: Blackwell.

Keeter, Scott. 2009. "Where the Public Stands on Immigration Reform." Pew Research Center for the People and the Press. Accessed July 19, 2010. http://pewresearch.org/pubs/1421/where-the-public-stands-on-immigration-reform.

Koslowski, Rey. 2006. "Immigration Reforms and Border Security Technologies." Social Science Research Council. Accessed July 19, 2010. http://borderbattles.ssrc.org/Koslowski/.

Leiken, Robert S., and Steven Brooke. 2006. "The Quantitative Analysis of Terrorism and Immigration: An Initial Exploration." *Terrorism and Political Violence* 18: 503–521.

Lydgate, Joanna. 2010. "Assembly-Line Justice: A Review of Operation Streamline." The Chief Justice Earl Warren Institute on Race, Ethnicity and Diversity, University of California, Berkeley. Accessed July 19, 2010. http://www.law.berkeley.edu/files/Operation_Streamline_Policy_Brief.pdf.

Massey, Douglas S., Jorge Durand, and Nolan J. Malone. 2002. *Beyond Smoke and Mirrors: Mexican Immigration in an Era of Economic Integration*. New York: Russell Sage Foundation.

Meissner, Doris, Deborah W. Meyers, Demetrios G. Papademetriou, and Michael Fix. 2006. *Immigration and America's Future: A New Chapter*. Washington, DC: Migration Policy Institute.

Mendoza, Martha [Associated Press]. 2010. "US-Mexico Border Isn't So Dangerous." Azcentral.com. June 3. Accessed July 12, 2010. http://www.azcentral.com/news/articles/2010/06/03/20100603mexico-border-not-so-dangerous.html.

Migration Policy Institute. 2010. "State Responses to Immigration: A Database of All State Legislation." Accessed July 19, 2010. http://www.migrationinformation.org/datahub/statelaws_home.cfm.

Nevins, Joseph. 2010. *Operation Gatekeeper and Beyond: The War On "Illegals" and the Remaking of the U.S.-Mexico Boundary*. 2nd ed. New York and London: Routledge.

Ngai, Mae M. 2004. *Impossible Subjects: Illegal Aliens and the Making of Modern America*. Princeton, NJ: Princeton University Press.

Núñez, Guillermina Gina, and Josiah McC. Heyman. 2007. "Entrapment Processes and Immigrant Communities in a Time of Heightened Border Vigilance." *Human Organization* 66: 354–365.

Passel, Jeffrey S., and D'Vera Cohn. 2008. "Trends in Unauthorized Immigration: Undocumented Inflow Now Trails Legal Inflow." Pew Hispanic Center. Accessed July 19, 2010. http://pewhispanic.org/files/reports/94.pdf.

———. 2010. "U.S. Unauthorized Immigration Flows Are Down Sharply since Mid-decade." Pew Hispanic Center. Accessed August 16, 2011. http://pewhispanic.org/reports/report.php?ReportID=126.

Pew Hispanic Center. 2006a. "Modes of Entry for the Unauthorized Migrant Population." Accessed July 12, 2010. http://pewhispanic.org/files/factsheets/19.pdf.
———. 2006b. "The State of American Public Opinion on Immigration in Spring 2006: A Review of Major Surveys." Accessed July 19, 2010. http://pewhispanic.org/factsheets/factsheet.php?FactsheetID=18.
Potter, Matt. 2009. "Obama Taps Alan Bersin to Oversee the Border." *San Diego Reader*, November 18. Accessed July 16, 2010. http://www.sandiegoreader.com/news/2009/nov/18/cover/.
Preston, Julia. 2010. "Illegal Workers Swept from Jobs in 'Silent Raids'." *New York Times*, July 9. Accessed July 19, 2010. http://www.nytimes.com/2010/07/10/us/10enforce.html.
Purcell, Mark, and Joseph Nevins. 2005. "Pushing the Boundary: State Restructuring, State Theory, and the Case of U.S.–Mexico Border Enforcement in the 1990s." *Political Geography* 24: 211–235.
San Diego Association of Governments and California Department of Transportation, District 11. 2006. "Economic Impacts of Wait Times at the San Diego–Baja California Border: Final Report." Accessed July 16, 2010. http://www.sandag.org/programs/borders/binational/projects/2006_border_wait_impacts_report.pdf.
Santa Ana, Otto. 2002. *Brown Tide Rising: Metaphors of Latinos in Contemporary American Public Discourse*. Austin: University of Texas Press.
Santibáñez Romellón, Jorge. 2006. "Migration and Borders: The Space for Contradiction." Social Science Research Council. Accessed July 19, 2010. http://borderbattles.ssrc.org/Santibanez/.
Sapp, Lesley. 2011. "Apprehensions by the U.S. Border Patrol: 2005–2010." Accessed August 16, 2011. http://www.dhs.gov/xlibrary/assets/statistics/publications/ois-apprehensions-fs-2005-2010.pdf.
Security and Prosperity Partnership of North America. Accessed July 16, 2010. http://www.spp.gov/.
Segovia, Francene, and Renatta DeFever. 2010. "The Polls—Trends: American Public Opinion on Immigrants and Immigration Policy." *Public Opinion Quarterly* 74: 375–394.
Sharma, Nandita. 2006. *Home Economics: Nationalism and the Making of 'Migrant Workers' in Canada*. Toronto: University of Toronto Press.
Spener, David. 2009. *Clandestine Crossings: Migrants and Coyotes on the Texas-Mexico Border*. Ithaca: Cornell University Press.
Tirman, John. 2006. "Immigration and Insecurity: Post-9/11 Fear in the United States." Social Science Research Council. Accessed July 19, 2010. http://borderbattles.ssrc.org/Tirman/.
United States Department of Homeland Security, Office of Immigration Statistics. 2009. "Immigration Enforcement Actions: 2008." Accessed July 19, 2010. http://www.dhs.gov/xlibrary/assets/statistics/publications/enforcement_ar_08.pdf.
United States Government Accountability Office. 2007. *Border Security: Despite Progress, Weaknesses in Traveler Inspections Exist at Our Nation's Ports of Entry*. Report GAO-08-219. Washington, DC: Government Printing Office.
United States House of Representatives, Subcommittee on Management, Investigations, and Oversight and the Subcommittee on Border, Maritime, and Global Counterterrorism. 2010. "SBInet: Does It Pass the Border Security Test? Hearings, June 17." Accessed July 16, 2010. http://hsc.house.gov/hearings/index.asp?ID=259.
Wæver, Ole. 1995. "Securitization and Desecuritization." In *On Security*, edited by Ronnie Lipschutz, 46–86. New York: Columbia University Press.
Walsh, John. 2009. "Lowering Expectations: Supply Control and the Resilient Cocaine Market." Washington Office on Latin America. Accessed July 19, 2010. http://www.wola.org/media/Lowering%20Expectations%20April%202009.pdf.

9 The Aftermath of a Rape Case
The Politics of Migrants' Unequal Incorporation in Neoliberal Times

Bela Feldman-Bianco

On March 8, 1983, under the headline "Men Jeered as Woman Was Gang Raped," the New Bedford's *Standard Times* reported on a gang rape which took place on a pool table of the Big Dan Tavern, a barroom of ill repute located in a Portuguese working-class neighborhood of the South Coast region of this Massachusetts depressed city. The victim was a third-generation young Portuguese-American woman and the alleged rapists were a handful of unemployed Portuguese immigrants from the Azores. Exacerbated by intense media coverage and a televised trial, that dramatic event exposed different cultural codes about gender, bringing to the fore, on the one hand, increasing xenophobia and discrimination against the "Portuguese" and, on the other, a heightened politicization of Portuguese (collective) ethnic identity. New Bedford, a city portrayed by Melville in *Moby Dick* and also known as the Portuguese capital of America, came to be redubbed after this incident as the "Portuguese gang-rape capital of America."

The Big Dan gang rape was cited among the thirty most memorable cases of the last thirty years by the Massachusetts Lawyers Weekly. In addition to the extensive examinations on its legal aspects (Knappman 1994; Bumiller 1990), this gang rape was also among the cases chosen for inquiries on the roles mass media have played in constructing rape (Cuklanz 1996) and covering sex crimes (Benedict 1992). The media's responsibility in overplaying the events and heightening the tensions and divisions in New Bedford and the surrounding region was invariably highlighted by Portuguese transmigrants and local feminists as well.[1] This incident formed the basis for *The Accused*, a Hollywood movie starring Jodie Foster, whose performance in the film won her an Oscar. Under these circumstances the movie was purposefully silent about the national origins and ethnicity of the main protagonists. The erasing of the ethnic features of the rape and its occurrence in New Bedford was an outcome of negotiations with the movie producers pursued by both local public officers and the Portuguese Continental Union.

In this chapter, I focus on this international social drama and its aftermath as a way of unveiling the conjuncture between gender, race, and class in the processes of transnational migrants' unequal incorporation in

New Bedford. Towards this end, I critically examine the relations between multiculturalism, the reconstruction of identities, and their symbolic productions during the rescaling of this gateway city, in the light of changing structures of capitalism in the last thirty years. By adopting a global perspective on migration (Glick Schiller, this volume, 2009, 2009a; Glick Schiller and Faist 2009; Glick Schiller and Caglar 2008) and viewing migration as part of the dynamics of capital formation, which is simultaneously global, national, and specifically local, I pay attention to both the global processes restructuring the locality and migrants' political mobilization and their local and transnational practices through time. From this standpoint, I further attempt to underscore the changing positioning of the Portuguese in New Bedford since that 1983 dramatic episode, as their history, gastronomy, and folklore have been more recently incorporated as a "Taste of Portugal" in the marketing of the local historical heritage in present neoliberal times.[2]

As I will indicate throughout this chapter, the global perspective on migration allows me to highlight the dynamics of unequal power as they have been shaped and contested at the local level at specific times. It also enables me to discern how the global, national, regional, and local have been constructed on the ground through networks and unequal social relations. It further led me to study migrants not as discrete ethnic or transnational communities, but as actors whose life trajectories and identities are shaped and shape the locality. By engaging with place, political economy, and time, I attempt to examine critically the tensions of multiculturalism, the ongoing multiplicities and reconstruction of identities, and the related symbolic productions of locality, region, and nation in the context of transnational migration.

It is important to remember that multiculturalism has emerged in the context of social movements of so-called "minorities" as an attempt to challenge the cultural hegemony of the dominant groups (Turner 2008). Yet, in the present conjuncture of global capitalism, the relations between neoliberal policies and multicultural ideologies rest upon "the formulation of a *rule of exclusion, of visible borders*, materialized in laws and practices", (emphasis in the original, Balibar 2004: 23). This outlook normalizes a differentiation between nationals and foreigners, imposing exclusion, or at least unequal preferential access to goods and rights, as constitutive of specific national projects. Therefore, there are a variety of multiculturalisms directed to different segments of the population.

In the US, multiculturalism is an offspring of cultural pluralism. Formulated in the 1960s by the US government and powerful charity institutions to control and depoliticize the black movement (Basch, Glick Schiller, and Szanton Blanc 1994), the focus of cultural pluralism was expanded to incorporate the urban poor through the channeling of resources along ethnic lines (Glick Schiller 2010). Either in its pluralistic version or as present-day multiculturalism, this ideology rests upon a "divide to control logic" revealed through grants to celebrate ethnic identities. In the present neoliberal governance, based upon flexible labor and the criminalization of immigrants, the interrelation between the politics of investments and the politics of culture have further stimulated the marketing of multiculturalism and, thus, the celebration of ethnic identities with the purpose of attracting tourism and aiding the renewal of cities (Feldman-Bianco 2011, 2010).

In this essay, I emphasize the importance of examining the relations between multicultural ideologies as constitutive of national projects and the political and transnational practices of transmigrants in specific localities and situations. From this viewpoint, I place the Big Dan gang rape and its aftermath into the social history of New Bedford and dedicate attention to the processes of incorporation and exclusion of immigrants as well as to their local and transnational mobilizations and practices.

TRANSNATIONAL MIGRANTS AND THE TRANSFORMATIONS OF THE CITY OF NEW BEDFORD: AN OVERVIEW

Once at the vanguard of the global whaling (1815–1860) and textile (1880–1925) economies, New Bedford has been striving ever since to attract manufactures, services industries, and more recently tourism. In the whaling era, Azorean and Cape Verdean sailors provided labor in eighteenth- and nineteenth-century whaling expeditions thereby creating the capital invested in the early New Bedford textile mills. Both its whaling industry and its subsequent textile production meant that capital formation located in the ports and streets of New Bedford reflected a process that was regional, national, and global. Many of the whalers, as well as the subsequent labor for the mills, came from Portugal and the Azores, and Cape Verde. During its nineteenth-century prominence as a textile city, the Portuguese workforce, whose labor contributed to the global wealth and power of the city, was racialized and disempowered within the leadership of the labor movement and the city.

Paradoxically, it was only as the international position of the mills in the beginning of the twentieth century was lost that efforts made to compensate for falling profits by a more intensive exploitation of labor were met by fierce labor struggles on the part of Portuguese migrants. This included, in 1928, a six-month strike against wage reductions occurring in a historical conjuncture of economic rescaling of the city, when local textiles had progressively closed their activities and/or moved to the American South where workers' wages were lower. At that turning point, return migration deepened and strengthened the transnational social fields that linked the city to continental Portugal and the Azores, and Cape Verde as well.

New Bedford never recovered its position of prominence in the United States and globally but the textile mills, while reduced in size and significance, continued to attract immigrant workers. Certainly, the global marketing of US prosperity in the 1960s, the international development nexus fueled by loans, which led to the debt crisis of the 1970s, the US and Western European support for dictatorial regimes that maintained extractive labor regimes, and the growth beginning in the 1970s and more ferociously in the 1980s, of neoliberal reforms worldwide, were all part of the mix that led to a massive increase in rural urban and international migration. Central to the institution of neoliberal agendas worldwide has been the stripping of trade protections and of state protection for workers' rights.

In the US in the 1960s, workers were briefly recruited into labor regimes in old industrial cities, where they often confronted new and growing sweatshop regimes. Three decades or so later, when unskilled workers could no longer legally enter the US, their numbers were made up by those without legal permission to work and those entitled to documents through family reunion. With the reopening of the immigration gates in the 1960s and through chain migration, New Bedford continued to receive Portuguese immigrants who were invariably related to the earlier contingents. These new arrivals were confronted with a new regime of intensive factory work developed in the partially abandoned industrial areas. More recently, in a period marked by the retraction of Portuguese immigration and the closing of borders, undocumented migrants from Guatemala, Mexico, Nicaragua, and Brazil have come to New Bedford, replacing the Portuguese as unskilled workers in the remaining industries in the locality. Meanwhile, Portuguese migrants became central actors in the efforts of New Bedford and neighboring towns to reposition regionally as the South Coast of Massachusetts and, at the same time, as a location for investments, commerce, and tourism.

In the present conjuncture of capitalism, the processes of the transformation of Portuguese migrants from racialized others to central actors in ongoing efforts at urban regeneration cannot be understood without reference to the ways in which the city of New Bedford and its workforce has been constantly repositioned and rescaled within larger networks of economic and political power. Within this story, immigrant workers have had to constantly struggle to maintain their identities and their family economies that often stretch transnationally. These struggles often have been part of more broadly ranging social movements for both rights and cultural representation.

The need to place the representations and particular nationalities of immigrants as aspects of urban restructuring as these become a reconstitution of global processes of capital accumulation first became clear to me when I started fieldwork in New Bedford in the late 1980s. I use the phrasing 'representations of culture *as an aspect* of urban restructuring' rather than '*within the context* of this restructuring' to emphasize that identity constructions and cultural representations including ideologies of multiculturalism are central aspects in the constitution of political economies.

THE BIG DAN SOCIAL DRAMA AND
THE POLITICIZATION OF IDENTITIES

Public politicization of identity and the politics of identity happen in specific historical situations. The internationally infamous Big Dan rape case occurred in a period marked by the renewal of Portuguese immigration in New Bedford combined with a new cycle of factory closures and capital relocation to countries where labor was cheaper, which resulted in an increase of unemployment in the locality. It also coincided with the opening of a special unit promoted by the local Woman's Center which was directed to aiding victims of sexual abuse. Permeated by cultural misunderstandings, this social drama turned into a field of struggle in a historical conjuncture when, prior to the establishment of neoliberal policies, multiculturalism (in its state cultural pluralism phase) had replaced the former assimilation project as the main discourse in the United States, and a politics based on class relations was being replaced by a politics of identity with an emphasis on difference.

A chronology of events indicated that as the first news on the rape came out, local communitarian groups formed a coalition against sexual violence and organized a candlelight vigil against sexual abuse, in which three thousand people marched silently. The night vigil, attracting notable feminists such as Gloria Steinem to town, quickly reached the national and international media. Almost at the same time, xenophobic phone calls to a radio station's open line began to denounce the Portuguese background of the alleged rapists. As they became aware that the media was covering the rape as an ethnic crime, Portuguese leaders formed a Committee for justice and a Portuguese American Defense League to fight discrimination against the Portuguese. Later, the decision of a Portuguese-American judge to broadcast the trial heightened the schisms even more and made way for growing cultural misunderstandings. After four of the six accused were found guilty, more than fifteen thousand Portuguese and descendents went to the streets in two public demonstrations. Described by perplexed non-Portuguese observers as a "bizarre protest" (Rosen 1985), the public confrontations challenged the prevalent characterization of the Portuguese as an "invisible minority" and a "case of ethnic disappearance" (Smith 1974). Interpreting the sentences as a judgment of all in the community, the accused were transformed by the demonstrators as symbols of their own oppression and lack of power in the locality. At the same time, the victim was penalized for attracting attention and bringing visibility to the "Portuguese community."

It is important to remember that in the 1980s, in the context of both the renewal of immigrant contingents and vigor within the feminist and black liberation movements, feminists and African American struggles were set at odds. Furthermore, beginning in the 1970s having been 'whitened' in part by accepting the US racial order that placed African Americans at the bottom, older immigrant groups in aging industrial cities rejected their previous claims to having been assimilated and began openly to defend their ethnically based voting blocks with an ideology of cultural pluralism, an early form of multiculturalism. The tensions of race, gender, class, and ethnicity as they were manifest in New York City were portrayed by Spike Lee in *Do the Right Thing*, a movie that came out in 1989.

In New Bedford, the split between gender and ethnicity around the Big Dan case exposed subjacent class and race discrimination and brought to light existing divisions in different spheres of social life, including the workplace and labor unions. Male and female feminists, including some of Portuguese descent, tended to perceive the Portuguese protests as just expressions of male chauvinism. Comparatively, significant numbers of Portuguese and Portuguese-Americans felt they were enacting, through public demonstrations, their emotional reactions to recurrent experiences of discrimination, racism, and second-class citizenship in everyday life.

Ironically, the mobilizations around the Big Dan gang rape were led on both sides by leftists involved with union politics who had recurrently struggled against class and race oppression. In this regard, Liz Bennet, an activist at the local Women's Center, wrote, "We were clear that . . . we were primarily responding to the larger issue of violence against women . . . and that all our education and outreach should draw connection between sexism, racism and class oppression" (Bennet 1985: 11). But at the same time, the Women's Center was at that time very much influenced by *Our Bodies, Ourselves*, a book which appeared in the early 1970s favoring "body politics" as a way of breaking the silence about rape, sexual abuse, and violence against women and girls. On those grounds, there was strong disagreement with the position taken by Alda Melo, an immigrant female labor-union leader, who shared similar political views, but decided to side instead with her Portuguese kin and community. After Alda Melo told "a crowd of 10,000 (Portuguese) that We are here to protest the great injustice done in this case. We cannot let immigrants be scapegoats" (Bennet 1985: 10), Liz Bennet firmly stated that "this is not what happened in New Bedford. These convicted men where not framed scapegoated or railroaded. They are rapists serving time in prison for their crime" (Bennet 1985: 10). Rather, speaking from her experience as an immigrant in New Bedford, for Alda Melo the "ethnic march arose the consciousness that, even after a century of work and construction in which Portuguese immigrants built many neighborhoods and even full cities that were in decaying conditions, we have heard that we should go back to our country of origin, we have been discriminated against in schools and jobs" (Gabe 1984).

Portuguese-American anthropologist Steve Cabral (1985:2) also sided with the Portuguese, while recognizing "the contradictions between protesting the convictions and condoning the crime of rape." He stressed that rather than an endorsement of the rapists, the (ethnic) march was a response to ongoing discrimination rooted in the daily lives of immigrants which was further aggravated by the extensive media coverage on the case. Further, he recalled that "on a daily basis, factory workers listened to radio shows where the defendants were denigrated as animals, aliens and ignorant greenhorns" (Cabral 1985: 3). In addition to "calls for castration and deportation, callers argued that all *Portagees* should be sent back to the old country" (Cabral 1985: 3).

While successive generations of Portuguese-Americans had suffered the pressures of assimilation and were forced to disguise their Portuguese ancestry to gain upward social mobility and avoid the stigma of 'Black Portagee,' recent immigrants and their children, stigmatized as "(ignorant) greenhorn(s)," were exposed to discrimination in their everyday life. As a school teacher born of immigrant parents stated in an interview to the press: "There is discrimination against Portuguese people. I was born here. I am educated. I could easily sit back and avoid things like this, but I can't. I think that we have responsibility to stand up against bigotry no matter against whom it is directed. I grew up ashamed of my background. No more."[3]

By and large, the Big Dan social drama and its polarizations revealed the complexity of identity politics and that, underneath the schisms between gender and ethnicity, there were different cultural codes and perceptions of gender. It must be remembered that in the everyday life in New Bedford and the surrounding region, Portuguese cultural constructions of gender and gender roles, marking difference and otherness, have often made way for conflicts between older and younger generations of Portuguese men and women. Yet, misinterpretations of these discrepant gender codes became politicized and highly publicized with the outbreak of the gang-rape affair. The politicization further exposed the entanglements between gender and ethnicity in the ongoing clashes between generations and the ambiguities, negotiations, and radicalization of younger Portuguese and Portuguese-American females.

THE BIG DAN SOCIAL DRAMA: UNVEILING THE POLITICAL ENTANGLEMENTS OF GENDER AND ETHNICITY AMONG PORTUGUESE IMMIGRANTS AND DESCENDENTS

In a historical period marked by the continuous renewal of immigration from continental Portugal and the Azorean Islands, the deciphering of the apparently bizarre demonstrations of the Portuguese requires understanding of the ways in which the emotional and painful reactions were embedded in their varied everyday experiences of discrimination and second-class citizenship in the locality. As I have shown elsewhere (Feldman-Bianco 2010, 1992, 1991), as a pattern, successive contingents of male and female immigrants from rural backgrounds who had entered industrial work have recurrently tended to reconstruct their memories and social practices of their homeland's past in their everyday life in reaction to the time discipline of industrial capitalism in New Bedford.[4] The symbolic representations and social practices of their past of non-industrial labor provided the basis for self-reconstitution as Azoreans, Madeirans, and mainlanders, thus demarcating, in the context of renewed migration, their strong regional identities. These re-elaborations of regional and national identities were accompanied by exacerbated reconstructions of cultural codes for gender. Against this background, for many Portuguese women and men the feminists' concerns with body politics voiced at the outbreak of the Big Dan social drama did not make sense at all.

Different perceptions of gender roles and gender relations represented different forms of resistance and negotiation of female identity in the context of immigration. Above all, these perceptions expressed how the women's condition and the reconstruction of Portuguese regional and national identities were differentially intertwined in the subjectivities of female immigrants. In this regard, my research indicates that women who emigrated as adults and whose history of immigration encompassed the transition from pre-industrial task-oriented activities in the homeland to industrial work in the United States, tended to reconstruct their "selves" fragmented by emigration through the (re-)creation of imageries and social practices of their past of non-industrial labor. Since childhood they had been subjected to an apprenticeship in domestic chores, and this was associated with the construction of the "virtuous woman" and a rigid demarcation between (unequal) female and male roles. These women learned to accept, or to simulate that they accepted, their submission to a male authority and to distinguish themselves from the "biblical Magdalene" type of sinner. Faced with dramatic changes in their conditions of existence that were caused by immigration, these women reterritorialized themselves to the ways of life of their regions and villages of origin. Thereby, they tended to mask the effective transformations of power relations between the sexes and generations caused by women's entrance into the American labor market and (because they tended not to speak English) by their constant dependence on the cultural brokerage of bilingual offspring. At the same time, along with their husbands, they tried to indoctrinate the same values in their daughters as a form of social control.

In particular, older immigrant religious women tended to act as the more extreme arbiters of the moral values modeled on the "myth of Adam and Eve,"[5] which were, prior to the 1974 Revolution of the Carnations, constantly reinforced by the traditional Catholic Church and Salazar's national ideologies. Against the background of their everyday lives in New Bedford and the surrounding region, marked by discrimination and confrontation with new structures of domination, these women tended to (re)interpret the moral values related to gender roles and gender relations and act as the bastions of "Portugueseness" in the diaspora. While their local and transnational spatial-temporalities tended to be stronger in their everyday social practices (Feldman-Bianco 1995; Santos 1993), in situations of discrimination, gender issues were transformed into the main symbols of a certain type of Portuguese nationalism, reminiscent of Salazar's era of immigrant labor. Thus, at the outbreak of the Big Dan social drama, the traditional moral values related to gender and gender roles were equated with Portuguese nationalism and ethnicity.

By contrast, the defense of equal rights for women and men among younger women represented a response to the repression, prohibitions, and social control they were subjected to by parents—either in the homeland or in somewhat more heightened ways in the context of immigration—and in their (diverse) social locations in between diverging cultural codes. Young women, who experienced the social changes provoked by the Revolution of the Carnations in Portugal and who challenged while still in the homeland the prevailing (traditional) gender roles, confronted with (double) perplexity the (re-)elaboration of these very values in the Portuguese enclaves of New England. Women who were in their teens (or younger) when they came to the United States reacted to the "myth of Adam and Eve" from the background of their experiences, that is, of lives fragmented by simultaneous exposure to Portuguese and American values. While their parents tended to reinvent Portuguese times and spaces in their everyday lives in America, these women tended to construct dual identities that emphasize the subjectivity of experiences lived on the borders of discrepant worlds, as well as diverse Portuguese nationalist projects.

This political entanglement of differential constructions of gender was imbued in the painful emotional decisions that led women and men of Portuguese descent to mobilize either as members of an ethnic group or against sexual violence at the time of the Big Dan social drama. While criticizing the prevalent male chauvinism, many of the women who acted as brokers for their families and community choose to align themselves as members of the Portuguese ethnic group. Other women, reacting to the exacerbated reconstructions of Portuguese cultural codes related to gender and generation, repudiated their Portuguese identity, positioning themselves as feminists fighting against sexual violence. Still others allied themselves in favor of the ethnic group, but, articulating their Portugueseness and feminism, subsequently also became active in the local Women's Center.

This political entanglement ultimately heightened the rape victim's personal drama. Caught in between contested domains she managed to disguise herself throughout the televised trial, covering her face with a black veil before her identity was inadvertently disclosed by one of the prosecutors. Accused for exposing the "Portuguese community," she was unable to remain in New Bedford and, after the trial was over, decided to move to Florida with her two children, only to die in a car accident just four years after being gang raped.

FROM A 'WHALING CITY' TO A 'PORTUGUESE GANG-RAPE CAPITAL OF AMERICA': THE BIG DAN SOCIAL DRAMA AND THE DOWNSCALING OF NEW BEDFORD

Characterized as the "Portuguese gang-rape capital of America," the city of New Bedford together with Portuguese immigrants were pejoratively portrayed by the local, national, and even international media. Not by chance, independently of their positioning with regards to the polarization between "gender" and "ethnicity" issues, different protagonists invariably associated the explosion of the events related to the Big Dan social drama to the "hard times the city has suffered since the 1928 six-month strike." This strike erupted to contest wage reductions during the historical conjuncture of economic downscaling of the city, when local textiles had progressively closed their activities and/or moved to the American South where workers' wages were lower. In an interview with the *New York Times*, entitled "Barroom Rape Shames Town of Proud Heritage," Mayor John Bullard, whose ancestors helped to build the city's whaling industry, summed up the state of affairs by claiming that "the city has had hard times since the textile strike of 1928. It's been economically depressed for two generations. Expectations have been lowered." Reflecting his interests as a leader of New Bedford's waterfront restoration for tourism purposes, he continued that therefore, "People have become sincerely negative about themselves and about the city," and asserted that the barroom rape "hurts us more than it would a lot of other cities . . . Then we just have to try that much harder to get back up to zero" (Clendinen 1983: 16).

In effect, the textile industry ended in the locality in 1940. Most of the tools and dye operations left the area in the 1970s. In that decade, labor-intensive factories based on piece work began to replace the former textile mills. Ongoing American policies stimulating chain migration enabled these shops to hire a cheap immigrant labor force related by kinship to the older contingents of Portuguese already settled in the region. In the 1980s, local factories were already moving to other countries or were forced out of business due to increased exposure to global competition. In this context, this gang-rape case, symbolically turning the once-celebrated "whaling city" into a "city of bizarre immigrants," marked the beginning of a new economic rescaling in yet another historical juncture, when flexible capital and progressive outsourcing paved the way for a new cycle of local factories' closures and/or their relocations to other countries where labor was cheaper.

When I began fieldwork in the late 1980s, the dramatic Big Dan episode was still a constitutive part of the local social mobilizations. In October 1986, Portuguese demonstrators, carrying "Save the Big Dan five" banners, protested against the fact that, in a quite similar case, a handful of medical doctors accused of gang raping nurses were arrested and convicted with lighter sentences than those given to their compatriots. In the midst of this demonstration, open lines of the Portuguese radio station resorted to biblical rhetoric to blame the victim, portrayed as "Magdalene," for heightening long-standing anti-Portuguese prejudice and xenophobia discrimination.

Cultural misunderstandings were again brought into the open. Even though they reproached the rape, older Portuguese women who were religious and Portuguese males still did not understand the feminists' causes. And many young Portuguese, male and female, felt ashamed of both New Bedford and their Portuguese background. Meanwhile, male and female activists at the local Women's Center persisted in viewing these manifestations as just expressions of male chauvinism. Paradoxically, even though Women's Center activists stated that, "We understand the need to confront issues ranging from poverty, unemployment, and housing to sexual violence and harassment. We understand that oppression affects not only women" (Bennet 1985:13), local feminists, apparently, still failed to grasp that the seemingly bizarre Portuguese manifestations were against racism and class oppression in everyday life.

Still in 1988, five years after the Big Dan gang rape, strikers at Carol Cable perceived the company's attempt to impose wage cuts and cancel workers' health insurance as discrimination against the Portuguese. Like other local factories, Carol Cable was built on the new immigration process but subsequently its management had to confront the fact that the very forces that had brought the industry to New Bedford were poised to relocate it to other sites where the conditions of profitability for operating such a plant were greater. In their meetings, the Carol Cable Portuguese workers were aware of this global trend. At the same time, transforming their demands as workers into an ethnic mobilization, they also claimed that their salaries were already lower than those of the workers of other Carol Cable plants. In the end, the workers won the strike, but one year later Carol Cable closed its plant in New Bedford. Since then, and particularly after the signing of the NAFTA agreement in 1993, numerous other plants have closed their operations in the city.

The processes of economic restructuring experienced by New Bedford were statewide in scope. Both individual cities and the state of Massachusetts as a whole were strongly affected by the 1993 NAFTA trade agreement. Between 1993 and 2000 Massachusetts lost an estimated total of seventeen thousand jobs. The apparel industries were dramatically affected by the NAFTA protocol throughout the 1990s. Local manufacturing employment fell drastically by 55.1 percent from 20,528 in 1985 to 9,212 jobs in 1999 (Barrow and Borges 2001). If the twenty-year period from 1985 to 2005 is considered, the overall loss of manufacturing jobs was even greater, reaching a total of 61 percent (Sá and Borges 2009). However, whereas other regions within the state were able to cope with the global structural changes of the 1980s by diversifying their local economies and/or attracting "new technology" industries, New Bedford and neighboring Fall River continued to depend heavily on older forms of industrial production and fishing. Since the 1990s, commercial fishing shrank because of changing laws, and as a result the local fishing workforce was reduced (Georgeanna and Shrader 2008: 188).

Consequently, in 1995 the state designated New Bedford an "economically distressed" area, after a Department of Housing and Urban Development report had characterized the city as being "double burned" by population loss and high unemployment and poverty rates (United States Environmental Protection Agency 2000). Total employment rates decreased from 65 percent in 1985 to 50 percent in 2001. In that same year, the locality was ranked as the 348th lowest income community among the 351 municipalities in Massachusetts (Barrow and Borges 2001: 2). These were the clear signs of New Bedford's further downscaling.

Like laborers around the world, New Bedford's working class has had to cope with the restructuring of global capitalism and the reorganization of workforces as "flexible labor" without long-term job security, benefits, unions, or grievance procedures. In this situation, many local citizens started to look for alternatives elsewhere. Accordingly, the city's population dropped from 99,222 inhabitants in 1990 to 93,768 in 2000. While some Portuguese decided to migrate to other regions of the United States, especially Florida where they believed the cost of living was lower, others opted to return to the homeland, where economic conditions had improved after Portugal joined the European Community. For those who remained in New Bedford, the growing service sector, together with the declining manufacture industry, were the major employers in the city. Those who lost their factory employment because of NAFTA were forced to learn new skills, including the English language. Most began looking for employment in the service sector in the city and surrounding region. The majority of the men went into blue-collar trades, especially construction work, while women tended to move into pink-collar occupations like office work, child care, elderly care, and social work (Sá 2008).

Thus, Portuguese laborers, along with workers elsewhere, are now exposed to even greater economic vulnerability, as they have entered flexible labor employment which does not offer either job stability or social benefits. However, in a seeming paradox, they have advanced their position within the local working class. Upon the drastic decrease of immigration from the Azores and continental Portugal to New England, new contingents of immigrants from Latin America and the Caribbean have settled in the city and taken the unskilled jobs in the remaining factories and fish-processing plants. Since most of these new arrivals from Guatemala, Mexico, and Nicaragua and, to a lesser degree, Brazil are undocumented migrants, they have become the local underclass, exploited by their employers and exposed to the stringent post-9/11 immigration policies, which make them victims of the increasingly frequent Homeland Security and workplace raids.

"A TASTE OF PORTUGAL": NEW BEDFORD'S DOWNSCALING, PORTUGAL'S UPSCALING, AND THE CHANGING POSITIONS OF THE PORTUGUESE IN THE LOCALITY AND REGION

Against the background of New Bedford's downscaling, the Portuguese seem to have enhanced their structural location in the locality and region, including within the realm of local politics. While most members of the successive contingents of immigrants from the Azores and continental Portugal settling in the city and surrounding regions since the late 1950s began their lives as factory workers or fishermen, they have experienced a gradual process of differential social mobility and unequal incorporation. Many have managed to attain retirement in the US and thus access to the American structure of social benefits. Also, their sons and daughters were able, at least since the 1970s, to pursue an education. Some offspring who earned a college degree began to serve as cultural brokers between immigrants and American institutions. They benefited from the prevailing ideologies of multiculturalism and from their bilingual and bicultural skills by entering occupations within the local government structure, the bilingual educational system, and local and regional Portuguese institutions created in the 1970s with the aid of federal grants (Feldman-Bianco 1992). Others managed to open businesses or became professionals in various fields. And a few immigrants and descendents even became millionaires (Sá 2008).

Above all, their improved position in the city is a result of an interplay of complex factors, including the drastic reduction of immigration from continental Portugal and the archipelagos of the Azores and Madeira, the gradual process of incorporation of immigrants and their descendents in the region, the corollary process of upward mobility and suburbanization, and the fact that for the first time in over a century, the newest contingents of immigrants settling in the locality are not Portuguese. In this context, it is important to take into account the shifting position of the Portuguese post-colonial state in the global economy and the increasing role played by a long-distance nationalism activated by bilingual and bicultural brokers to change the image of Portugal and the Portuguese in the region. This process began in 1985, when the post-colonial Portuguese state entered the European communitarian space, just a couple of years after the Big Dan affair (Feldman-Bianco 2011, 2001).

After the Portuguese state recognized and incorporated the diaspora as part of the nation, immigrants and descendents were given dual nationality and citizenship rights—rights that became valuable resources in localities such as New Bedford. At the same time, Portuguese governmental authorities have intensified their relations with the leading citizens of the diaspora who have been able to gain positions of power in the localities and countries of residence, as well as playing brokerage roles in favor of the Portuguese politics of culture and investments. This long-distance nationalism has also helped these transnational brokers to increase their political power as an ethnic group in US politics.

In the past, Portuguese immigrants and their descendents were confronted with the choice of continuing to be part of Portuguese immigrant communities or assimilating and becoming American (Feldman-Bianco 1992). Despite their association with Cape Verdeans migrants—who were, until the one-time colony's independence in 1975, part of the Portuguese community of New Bedford—the rejection (and, thus, invisibility) of Portuguese identity eluded the issue of race (and, thus, the stigma of "Black Portagee") providing them with the possibility of "passing" into the mainstream society, even though in many cases they retained the Portuguese language and traditions. Later, in the 1970s, as part of continued efforts to establish themselves as part of the majority, affluent and influential Portuguese-Americans decided not to make use of the affirmative action program (Moniz 2009) and distanced themselves from a racially defined minority status—a path chosen by immigrants from the newly independent Cape Verde. In the last two decades and a half, newer generations of upwardly mobile immigrants and descendents joined an already-established stratum of Portuguese-Americans, some of whom had reasserted their Portuguese-American identities after the shift from assimilationist to multiculturalist ideologies in the US. Members of this stratum have revived the historical memory of the discoveries and promoted the politics of high culture supported by the Portuguese state in order to enhance their own position as representatives of a "modern" Portugal—as opposed to the entrenched images of Portugal as consisting entirely of traditional and culturally conservative peasants. At the local level, these strategies further aimed at erasing memories about the Big Dan social drama.

As part of the politics of high culture of the post-colonial state, the Center for Portuguese Studies and Culture was formed in the mid-1990s at the University of Massachusetts Dartmouth. This center has played a major role in changing the image of Portugal and of the Portuguese in the region through a multiplicity of educational and cultural programs and activities including: summer language programs; the establishment of a Department of Portuguese; the publication of English translations of Portuguese literary and scholarly work; the organization of seminars and conferences with renowned scholars and writers; the creation of an endowed chair; the formation of Portuguese-American archives to document the history of the Portuguese in the US; and the launching of a new graduate program in Luso-Afro-Brazilian Studies. Indicative of the active transnational fields characterizing the region, the academic programs and the Center have received financial support from the state of Massachusetts, the Luso-American Development Foundation, the support of affluent Portuguese-Americans, as well as the Portuguese state. The University of Massachusetts Dartmouth has been one of the primary academic institutions facilitating the higher education of successive generations of Portuguese immigrants and descendents and the Portuguese Department and Center have greatly contributed to the enhanced image of Portugueseness in the region.

Portuguese and Portuguese-American professionals and business people have used their transnational social fields and practices (see Glick Schiller, this volume) to become involved in "the concerted efforts by local governance in partnership with state and federal governments, citizens and business organizations, non-profit agencies and institutions of higher education regarding the implementation of economic development policy" towards meeting, in the words of the incumbent mayor, "the twenty-first century challenges" (Lang 2008). By 1997, efforts to fund local initiatives at urban reinvention through attracting international investment bore fruit. Facilitated by leading Azoreans from New Bedford, Portugal's Ministry of Foreign Affairs (then headed by an Azorean) provided a $500,000 grant to the Whaling Museum for the construction of a special wing to portray the cultural heritage of the Azorean whalers of the city. This donation enabled the Azorean whalers to be finally incorporated into the historical heritage of the city's elite.

Before the recent debt crisis in Portugal, there had also been attempts by the New Bedford Economic Council to attract Portuguese enterprises to the city's business park and free-trade zone resulting in, for example, the opening of Portuguese banks in the city, one of which had already closed down in 2010. Directors of the Council have visited Portugal in search of investments and in 2008 a delegation of government, education, and business leaders went to the Azores on a trade mission designed to strengthen its educational, culture, and economic ties with the South Coast. It is important to note that access to the Azores also means access to European markets.

Promoting New Bedford as a tourist destination—with multicultural and multi-ethnic attractions—has been another cornerstone of the city's economic revitalization efforts. And the Portuguese identity, which was previously racialized and then linked to the moniker of "rape capital of America" in the context of the highly publicized Big Dan case, has become a component of the cultural heritage of the city. As part of the city's Office of Marketing and Tourism strategy to attract tourists, Portuguese restaurants, bakeries, and summer festivals have been promoted as "A Taste of Portugal" and, as such, have become a constitutive part of the city's intangible yet highly marketable cultural diversity. The more public identification of New Bedford with Portuguese immigration and Portugal ironically thus became an asset in the struggle of New Bedford to become more competitive regionally and globally. Migrants proved to be able to play a crucial role in securing the transnational reach of the city. The entrance of Portugal into the European Union was crucial to the new positioning of Portuguese migrants in New Bedford as social, economic, and political actors both within their place of settlement and vis-à-vis Portugal and the Portuguese state.

With the aim of counteracting restrictive immigration laws, bicultural community leaders started an extensive "naturalization" campaign in 1997 as a way of insuring that immigrants living in the US had access to social benefits and political voice. The naturalization campaigns resonated with the politics of dual citizenship rights promoted by the post-colonial Portuguese state. These politics emphasized the incorporation of the Portuguese abroad in the localities of settlement while continuing to act as representatives of Portugal. Accordingly, the motto "To be a good Portuguese, it is necessary to be a good American," which had been employed during the Americanization campaign of the 1930s to persuade immigrants to assimilate into American society, was redefined by then-President Mario Soares in the 1980s to stimulate biculturalism (Feldman-Bianco 2011).

The Luso-American Development Foundation (FLAD), a private, financially independent institution created by the Portuguese government in 1985 "to contribute towards Portugal's development by providing financial and strategic support for innovative projects thereby fostering cooperation between Portuguese and American civil society,"[6] also supported the ongoing naturalization campaign. In 1999, they launched a Portuguese-American Citizenship Project to promote citizenship and civic involvement in Portuguese-American communities across the US. Presently, seven of the eleven town councilors of New Bedford are of Portuguese descent and an eighth is the widow of a deceased Portuguese member of the Board of Election Committee.

Precisely because of the historic and contemporary deterioration of the regional and global positioning of New Bedford, the transnational reach of Portuguese migrants and especially their reach to the European Union were especially significant for both the migrants and the city. Their connections position them more centrally in the political and economic landscape of the South Coast as they facilitate educational and economic partnerships in their homeland, particularly with the Azores. They also are brokers who channel the much-desired Portuguese funds to New Bedford and the region. They have become part of the repositioning efforts of both New Bedford and the Portuguese state within the neoliberal global order.

However, with the gain in social position and cultural capital of these migrants in New Bedford and in their homelands have come significant losses for the quality of life and future aspirations of those who labor and must migrate to seek work. The neoliberal regime of flexible capital and labor, together with the stringent immigration policies which criminalize undocumented migrants and approach immigrants from the perspective of national security, has meant not only the end of safe and secure working conditions won by the labor mobilizations of the early twentieth century, but also increased exploitation and economic vulnerability.

The ongoing interplay between the politics of culture and the politics of investments seems to mask the current stringent American immigration policies and the continuing immigration raids by Homeland Security officers against undocumented workers. In 2004 and 2007, New Bedford attracted national news coverage because of Homeland Security raids. Thirteen undocumented immigrants working at a fish-processing industry were detained in

2004. Homeland Security agents arrested three hundred women and men, mostly from Guatemala, Nicaragua, and Mexico, in 2007. Although in smaller numbers, Brazilians and Azoreans were also among the detained. Yet, since the "Mayans" have become the new scapegoats, the media largely ignored the Azoreans under arrest. As a considerable number of mothers were separated from their small children when they were arrested, their drama caught the attention and sympathy of local and state authorities including US Senators Ted Kennedy and John Kerry. This incident, which brought attention once again to gender issues, mobilized (this time without schisms) the citizens of New Bedford, including the leaders of labor unions and other community leaders. This local and state support also acknowledged the significant role of unskilled female and male labor in maintaining the economic base of the reinvented and restructured city of New Bedford. It also made apparent that, among the New Bedford residents who were subject to these raids and were deported, there were people who had permanently settled in the area and were contributing to the revitalization of neighborhoods and commerce in the city. However, despite the considerable social solidarity displayed and the reliance of the city on its immigrants, the stringent federal immigration laws did not leave room for appeal.

In this regard, the social solidarity calls attention to the ongoing mobilization of different segments of civil society (as labor unions, feminists, NGOs, churches, intellectuals, among others) in favor of the citizenship rights of these immigrants and their struggle for a world without borders—not just in the case of New Bedford, but also in other localities. Therefore, side by side with the marketing and consumption of identities that have reinforced ethnic groups and provided strategies for access to political and social resources, there have emerged mobilizations that reunite different segments of civil society in favor of undocumented immigrants who have been systematically criminalized and excluded from neoliberal policies and their multiculturalism ideologies. From the viewpoint of transnational migrations, the emergence of these movements seems to signal a new type of social mobilization in contemporary globalization.

CONCLUSIONS

Since transnational migrants are protagonists and yet a constitutive part of the social fabric both in their localities of origin and residence, I inserted the Big Dan gang-rape case into the social history of New Bedford and dedicated attention to the processes of incorporation and exclusion of immigrants as to their local and transnational mobilizations and practices. In so doing, I delineated the geographies of incorporation, unequal access, and participation of immigrants through time, which allowed me to discern the changing position of the Portuguese in the city, as well as the role they have played throughout local and global restructuring processes.

I emphasized the importance of examining the relations between multicultural ideologies as constitutive of specific national projects in neoliberal times and the political and transnational practices of transmigrants in specific localities and situations. But while multicultural ideologies emphasize belonging to only one nation-state, transnational migrants are part of at least two countries and develop transnational social fields. In this sense, it was necessary to take into account the new conceptions of nations emerging in the mid-1980s through which, either by way of legislation or rhetoric, both former imperial metropolis and former colonies have incorporated their emigrant populations. These new conceptions of the nation, based on long-distance nationalisms, have stimulated and reinforced the connections and the transnational practices of transmigrants with their localities and countries of origin and particularly the role of transmigrant leaders as transnational brokers for both locality and region of origin and those of residence (Feldman-Bianco 2011, 2001; Glick Schiller and Fouron 2001).

Starting my analysis by focusing on the New Bedford 1983 Big Dan rape, I argued that public politicizations of identity and the politics of the identity happen in specific historical situations and conjunctures that are molded by the continuing global repositioning of cities and their populations. I showed that such a conjuncture was this infamous gang rape which occurred in a period marked by renewal of Portuguese immigration and a new downscaling of this gateway city, when class-based politics was being replaced by identity politics that emphasized cultural difference.

Since then, concurrently with the continuing economic downscaling of the city, local laborers have confronted the increasing institutionalization of neoliberal agendas world wide, including the stripping of trade protections and of state protection for workers' rights. I discerned the multiple factors that led, in this new conjuncture, people of Portuguese descent to become central actors in the efforts of New Bedford and neighboring towns to reposition regionally as the South Coast of Massachusetts and, at the same time, as a location for investments, commerce, and tourism. Among the main factors was the relevance of the entrance of the Portuguese post-colonial state in the European communitarian space and the increasing role played by a long-distance nationalism activated by bilingual and bicultural brokers for both changing the image of Portugal and the Portuguese in the region and, at the same time, providing investments and access to the European Union to local officers.

I further unveiled how multiculturalism in neoliberal times has stimulated the marketing and consumption of identities that have reinforced ethnic groups and provided strategies for access to political and social resources. At the same time, in the context of draconian immigrant policies, there have emerged mobilizations that reunite different segments of civil society in favor of undocumented immigrants who have been systematically criminalized and excluded from the neoliberal policies and their multiculturalism ideologies. I argue that these mobilizations signal a new type of social movement in contemporary globalization.

NOTES

1. For an analysis of the role of the media in covering the Big Dan rape from the perspective of the Portuguese the reader is referred to Almeida (2009) and, from the perspective of local feminists, to Bennet (1985).
2. I thank Nina Glick Schiller for her input in the writing of this paper. Her global perspective on migration has been crucial for framing my analysis of the Big Dan rape (Glick Schiller 2010, 2009, 2009a, Glick Schiller and Faist 2009; Glick Schiller and Caglar 2008).
3. Interviewed by *Providence Journal*, reported by Cabral (1985).
4. This analysis is based on E.P. Thompson's distinction between "natural time" and the "time-discipline of industrial capitalism" (1967: 56–57).
5. On the myth of Adam and Eve, see also Pina-Cabral (1986).
6. In http://www.flad.pt/?no=1010002

REFERENCES

Almeida, Onésimo T. 2009. "Media-Made Events: Revisiting the Case of Big Dan's." In *Community, Culture and the Making of Identity: Portuguese-Americans along the Eastern Seabord*, edited by Kimberly Da Costa Holton and Andrea Klimt, 247–264. North Dartmouth: University of Massachusetts Dartmouth, Center for Portuguese Studies, Portuguese in the Americas Series.

Balibar Étienne. 2004. *We, the People of Europe? Reflections on Transnational Citizenship*. Princeton and Oxford: Princeton University Press.

Barrow, Clyde, and David R. Borges. 2001. "Greater New Bedford Economic Base Analysis: Critical and Emerging Industries and Work Force Development Target." Economic Research Series 29. University of Massachusetts Dartmouth, Center for Policy Analysis.

Basch, Linda, Nina Glick Schiller, and Cristina Szanton Blanc, eds. 1994. *Nations Unbound: Transnational Projects, Postcolonial Predicaments, and Deterritorialized Nation-States*. Amsterdam: Gordon and Breach.

Benedict, Helen. 1992. *Virgin or Vamp*. Oxford: Oxford University Press.

Bennet, Liz. 1985. "New Bedford: Bigotry Misnamed." *Inside Aegis* 39: 10–16.

Bumiller, Kristin. 1990. "Fallen Angels: The Representation of Violence against Women in Legal Culture." *International Journal of the Sociology of Law* 18: 125–142.

Cabral, Stephen. 1985. "Big Dan: A Bad Case of Victimization." Unpublished manuscript.

Clendinen, Dudley. 1983. "Barroom Rape Shames Town of Proud Heritage." *The New York Times*, March 17.

Cuklanz, Lisa M. 1996. *Rape on Trial: How the Mass Media Construct Legal Reform and Social Change*. Philadelphia: University of Pennsylvania Press.

Feldman-Bianco, Bela. 1991. *Saudade*. Ethnographic video documentary (58 minutes). Watertown, MA: D.E.R.

———. 1992. "Multiple Layers of Time and Space: The Construction of Class, Ethnicity and Nationalism among Portuguese Immigrants." In *Transnational Perspective on Migration: Race, Class, Ethnicity and Nationalism Reconsidered*, edited by Nina Glick Schiller, Linda Basch, and Cristina Szanton Blanc. New York: Annals of the New York Academy of Sciences.

———. 1995. "The State, Saudade and the Dialectics of Deterritorialization and Reterritorialization." Oficina do CES. Centro de Estudos Sociais, Universidade de Coimbra 46 (January).

———. 2001. "Colonialism as a Continuing Project: The Portuguese Experience." *Identities: Global Studies in Politics and Culture* 8(4): 477–482.

———. 2010. "Migración, Enfrentamientos Culturales y Reconstrucciones de la Identidad Femenina: El Caso de las Intermediarias Culturales Portuguesas." In *Diasporische Bewegungen im transatlantischen Raum. Diasporic Movements—Movimientos diaspóricos*, (org) Kron, Stefanie/zur Nieden, Birgit/ Schütze, Stephanie/Zapata Galindo, Martha. Berlin: Edição Tranvia.

———. 2011. "Remaking Locality: Uneven Globalization and Transmigrants' Unequal Incorporation." In *Locating Migration: Rescaling Cities and Migrants*, edited by Nina Glick Schiller and Ayse Simsek-Çaglar, 213–234. Ithaca and London: Cornell University Press.

Gabe, Catherine. 1984. "Women's Rights, Justice, Bias Issues Cloud Rape Case." *The Standard Times*, March 24.

Georgeanna, Daniel, and Debra Shrader. 2008. "The Effects of Days at Sea on Employment, Income and Hours of Work: Some Preliminary Evidence." *Human Ecology Review* 15(2): 185–193.

Glick Schiller, Nina. 2009. "A Global Perspective on Migration and Development." *Social Analysis* 53(3): 14–37.

———. 2009a. "Towards a Comparative Theory of Locality in Migration Studies: Migrant Incorporation and City Scale." *Journal of Ethnic and Migration Studies* 35(2): 177–202.

———. 2010. "A Global Perspective on Transnational Migration: Theorizing Migration without Methodological Nationalism." In *Diaspora and Transnationalism: Concepts, Theories and Methods*, edited by R. Bauböck and T. Faist, 109–130. University of Amsterdam and IMISCOE.

Glick Schiller, Nina, and Ayse Caglar. 2008. "Beyond Methodological Ethnicity and Towards the City Scale: An Alternative Approach to Local and Transnational Pathways of Migrant Incorporation." In *Rethinking Transnationalism: The meso-links of organizations*, edited by Ludger Pries, 40–61. New York: Routledge.

Glick Schiller, Nina, and Thomas Faist. 2009. "Introduction: Migration, Development, and Social Transformation." *Social Analysis* 53(3): 1–13.

Glick Schiller, Nina, and Georges Fouron. 2001. *Georges Woke Up Laughing: Long Distance Nationalism and the Search for Home*. Durham: Duke University Press.

Knappman, Edward W., ed. 1994. *Great American Trials*. Detroit, MI: Visible Ink Press.

Lang, Scott W. 2008. "State of the City Address." *City of New Bedford*, March 1.

Moniz, Miguel. 2009. "The Shadow Minority: An Ethnohistory of Portuguese and Lusophone Racial and Ethnic Identity in New England." In *Community, Culture and the Makings of Identity: Portuguese-Americans Along the Eastern Seaboard*, edited by Kimberly DaCosta Holton and Andrea Klimt, 409–430. North Dartmouth: University of Massachusetts Dartmouth, Center for Portuguese Studies, Portuguese in the Americas Series.

Pina-Cabral, João de. 1986. *Sons of Adam, Daughters of Eve: The Peasant Worldview of the Alto Minho*. Oxford: Clarendon.

Rosen, Ellen I. 1985. "Rape Trial in New Bedford: New Thought on an Old Problem." *Dissent* Spring: 207–212.

Sá, Maria Gloria de. 2008. "The Azorean Community on the East Coast." In *Capelinhos: A Volcano of Synergies-Azorean Emigration to America*, edited by Tony Goulart. San Jose: Portuguese Heritage Publications of California, Inc.

Sá, Maria Gloria de, and David Borges. 2009. "Context or Culture: Portuguese-Americans and Social Mobility." In *Community, Culture and the Makings of*

Identity: Portuguese-Americans Along the Eastern Seaboard, edited by Kimberly DaCosta Holton and Andrea Klimt, 265–290. North Dartmouth: University of Massachusetts Dartmouth, Center for Portuguese Studies, Portuguese in the Americas Series.

Santos, Boaventura de Sousa. 1993. "Modernidade, Identidade e a Cultura de Fronteira." *Revista Crítica de Ciências Sociais* 38: 11–42.

Smith, Estellie M. 1974. "Portuguese Enclaves: The Invisible Minority." In *Social and Cultural Identity: Problems of Persistence and Change*, edited by Thomas K. Fitzgerald, 81–91. University of Georgia: Southern Anthropological Society Proceedings.

Thompson, E.P. 1967. "Time, Work-Discipline and Industrial Capitalism." *Past and Present* 38: 56–57.

Turner, Terry. 2008. "Anthropology and Multiculturalism: What is Anthropology that Multiculturalism Should Be Mindful of it?" *Cultural Anthropology* 8(4): 411–429.

United States Environmental Protection Agency. 2000. *Brownfields Showcase Community Fact Sheet: New Bedford, Massachusetts*. Accessed February 12, 2012. http://epa.gov/brownfields/success/showcase/sc_newbed.htm

10 Gender, Migration, and Rural-Urban Relations in Post-socialist China

Yan Hairong

> People [*dajia*, referring to migrants] don't understand, but people escape from the countryside like fleeing from death. This really is worth analysis. Why is it like this to such an extent? Even if we die, we want to die outside! It's not that we don't miss home. We miss home. Time and again, we return home, but time and again we come back out. It's not a single person doing this, but a whole generation. Coming out is to meet suffering [*zao zui*], but [we] still want to come out, knowing that there is almost no hope [outside].
>
> Hua, migrant woman and veteran organizer

In recognition of Chinese workers' contribution to "leading the world to economic recovery," the American magazine *Time* had the nameless "Chinese worker" as the runner-up for its "person of the year" for 2009 (Ramzy 2009). The top prize went to US Federal Reserve Bank Chairman Ben Bernanke. The irony of juxtaposing a banker with a worker aside, this is acknowledgment enough of how Chinese workers, particularly migrant workers, have been at the heart of global capitalism and underscores the perception of China as a rising global power. Yet in moving beyond such popular perceptions and mediated imagery, we find that in China 168 million persons make a living in the informal sector—that is, without a labor contract, employment protection or benefits. This represents 59.4 percent of its total urban workforce and this proportion is on a par more with developing regions rather than global powers. In South and Southeast Asia 65 percent of the labor force is informal, while in North Africa 48 percent and in Latin America 51 percent of workforces are similarly informalized (Huang 2009: 52). In China, some 120 million rural migrants make up most of the informal urban workforce, employed mainly in manufacturing, construction, and the service sector (Zhongguo 2006).

The post-Mao rural-to-urban migration has fed the engine of regional and global accumulation since the early 1980s. Marx long ago wrote of this process as one that revealed the inherent contradiction in primitive accumulation, which is simultaneously a process of laborers' emancipation from serfdom and guilds, and a history of expropriation and violence "written in the annals of mankind in letters of blood and fire" (1977: 875). But China's rural-to-urban migration is not based on the forced expropriation of land, as described by Marx. It is, ironically, conditioned on a rural reform of decollectivization and a re-establishment of household farming.

Around 1978, rural reform broke up collective production and reapportioned land use rights to individual households. This reform retained the tail of socialism—reflected in the continuing collective ownership of land and the egalitarian distribution of its use rights—but it created a fragmentation and de facto privatization of land use rights. While seemingly different from the classical model of concentration and enclosure, the new land system in China provided a necessary condition for unfettering the mass of peasant labor power to feed a flexible accumulation. In the 1990s land had become a source of welfare—absorbing ill, injured, and unemployed bodies, enabling a cheap reproduction of the next generation of migrant workers. It is the socialist legacy subsidizing capitalism.

The entry of migrant labor into the city for China's post-socialist accumulation also required establishing a new flexible labor regime based on a commodification of labor. With the completion of the rural reform, the launch of the urban reform in 1984 saw a steady push for a market in labor and the move to "smash the iron rice bowl"—life-long employment typically provided by state-owned enterprises until then. In the general context of labor commodification, millions of migrant workers, as the new urban workforce, experience the most brutal form of exploitation, with no contracts and little protection and benefits.

The "silent compulsion of economic relations sets the seal on the domination" of capital (Marx 1977: 899), and mainstream media and capitalist institutions in the West and China more or less take for granted China's large supply of migrants toiling for the world economy. It may even appear to some that rural youth are naturally attracted to working in the city. Yet Hua's words (above) call this very assumption into question. To probe this question is to further unravel what Marx called silent compulsion: what has compelled the migration of the rural young from the countryside to the city and how do migrants themselves see their processes of migration? This probing is not about trying to get to the human side of the story by collecting sample voices, but to examine one important foundation of the post-socialist transformation.

This chapter will retrace how the theater of migration had its stage constructed. I particularly track how the tectonic shift in rural-urban relations, with political, economic, cultural dimensions, had transformed how rural youth came to see the countryside and themselves, and to ask why the countryside in the 1990s was often invoked by rural young women as a symbolic field of death compelling them to seek a modern subjectivity elsewhere. Encapsulating the widespread ethos among rural youth to "see the world" (*jian jian shi mian*), migration to the city enabled and was enabled by China's joining the capitalist world system.

Pursuing this question requires us to link the political economy of development and the processes of subjectivity formation. Thus I compare two cohorts of rural women who migrated to Beijing from Wuwei County, in southeast Anhui Province, north of the Yangtze River.[1] One consisted of women who migrated in the late Mao era of the 1970s and the other of those who migrated in the post-Mao era of the 1980s–1990s.[2] Although both cohorts are migrant wage laborers, a comparative analysis reveals the radical shift in rural-urban relations that has impressed itself upon rural young women's subjectivity.[3]

MIGRATING IN THE MAO ERA: STATE, PATRIARCHY, "RURAL WOMEN" IDENTITY

Unlike their post-Mao counterparts, migrant women in the Mao era positively asserted an undiminished "rural women" identity and continued their participation in agriculture. This prevailed despite the double burden of gender and rural origins shouldered by these women during the Mao era. Here I examine the nature of this double burden and the role of patriarchy and the state in the construction of the subject position *nongcun funü* (rural women).

Wuwei was once a Communist base that resisted Japanese invasion during World War II. It was said that some Communist officers left their children in the care of local women during the war. After the founding of the PRC in 1949, some of these women were asked by veterans to continue to look after their children who had moved to Beijing. This established the link for later migration.[4] Three to four thousand rural women from Wuwei had worked as domestics in the cities up to the 1970s (Wang and Li 1996: 23).[5] One of these women was Great Aunt who was sixty-five years old when I met her in Beijing in 1999. Living with her son and daughter-in-law in a single-room house in the suburbs of Beijing, she looked after her one-year-old grandson and cooked for the young couple while they went out every day to sell processed chicken in the market. A mother of four children, Great Aunt first came to Beijing more than twenty years ago to work as a *baomu* (maid or servant). Sitting in the courtyard, she told me about her daily labor and life during the collective era and her experiences of being a migrant.

Great Aunt spoke with excitement and sighs of frustration about the endless work and sometimes-insufficient food. She remembered the days of collective labor as bustling with communal activities in the field and in the village, with women's labor contribution publicly recognized and compensated in terms of work points, which gave women some standing in the public arena. In the post-Mao era, when production became a "household responsibility," rural women in Great Aunt's village witnessed a loss of the limited ground they had gained in the public arena. With the demise of collective life, rural women's status has substantially contracted, and the public sphere belongs more exclusively to men.

With three small children, Great Aunt's family experienced food shortages then. To earn a bit more money, she went to work for families in Beijing in the late 1970s. The predicament for rural women like Great Aunt during the Mao era was that they were subjected to the double burden deployed in the discursive category of "rural women."[6] The Mao-era state was determined to achieve rapid industrialization and nationwide accumulation and regarded it as a necessary step toward eventually resolving the rural-urban gap and the "price scissors" (differential) between industrial and agricultural products. In the meantime, to maximize the surplus of industrial output for expanded reproduction, the state practiced price controls through a unified procurement system. This system established a state monopoly over surplus agricultural products, enabled egalitarian grain distribution policies, but kept prices for agricultural products at a consistently low level.[7] The peasantry shouldered the burden to provide surplus for industrialization, although the leadership imagined that industry would subsidize agriculture before long.[8]

For rural women, this burden was accompanied by another burden created by a persistent, albeit restrained, patriarchy in the domestic division of labor and in the organization and rewarding of collective labor. With gender liberation and equality based on women's participation in public labor, the gender politics in the Mao era certainly enabled women like Great Aunt to draw a new sense of pride from their active performance in collective labor. The liberation of women from the burden of housework, however, was expected to be realized through the eventual socialization and mechanization of domestic labor rather than by challenging the gendered division of labor. One may argue that the surplus labor performed by a woman—on top of her own participation in public labor—to put food on the table to enable her husband's full participation in production, mirrored the peasantry's contribution of surplus labor to enable the nation's accumulation and industrialization. The final liberation of "rural women" from their burdens, presumed to be contingent upon further industrialization, made the expansion of industrialization all the more compelling in the national agenda and women's labor contribution all the more necessary.[9] Thus the subject position of rural women in the post-liberation period was, on the one hand, highlighted by active participation in collective labor and surplus production for the state's industrialization and, on the other hand, marked by a continuation of the patriarchal structure that circumscribed the nature and value of women's labor.

Writing of the genealogy of *funü* (women) as the principal subject position available to women in Chinese socialism, Tani Barlow argues that "the Revolution restituted *funü*/women inside *guojia*/state (and thus by synechdochic logic, inside *jiatiing*/family) under Maoist inscription" (1991a: 132). Although women were encouraged and recognized for their participation in collective labor and gained a visibility and a limited degree of equality (Davin 1975), the continued patriarchal culture defined the work performed by women as *nei* (inside) and hence categorically worth less than the work performed by men, which was deemed *wai* (outside) (Harrell 2000; Jacka 1997). During the time of collective labor in Wuwei villages, as elsewhere, the highest number of work points for a man was ten per day, whereas that for a woman was typically eight, even when she performed the same task as a man.

It was, then, perhaps no coincidence that in the radical years of the Cultural Revolution (1966–1976), the proto-image of women's liberation was found in female youth groups, the Iron Girl teams.[10] The sprouting across the nation of Iron Girl groups, which were modeled after a group of rural adolescent girls of the Dazhai production brigade, became a sign of the liberated productivity of Chinese women outside the domestic closure, on whose base gender equality was claimed (Honig 2000). The rise of the Iron Girls to legendary national prominence obliterated the *funü*, which was situated in reformed patriarchal domestic relations and was working under a double burden. Aunt Lu, who is related to Great Aunt and who also went to Beijing as a *baomu* in the late 1970s, came of age during the Cultural Revolution, when she was active in her village's performance troupe. Her migration began after her first child was born. In her narrative she portrayed herself as a spirited activist, dynamic and mobile in her community during her teens, and as a burdened woman after she was married and became a mother.

It was in the context of this disjuncture and of the double burden borne by married women that there occurred a small exodus of women from Wuwei to big cities. There they worked as domestics and sought redress by their own means to the problem of double undervaluation of their labor. Great Aunt worked in Beijing to get more return for her labor, undervalued in agriculture once by the state as "peasant" labor and again by patriarchy as "woman's" labor. Almost all of the rural Wuwei women who went to work as domestics in the cities then were married with children. Most of them were illiterate or semi-illiterate. In the 1970s the monthly wage for a domestic was eighteen to twenty-five yuan, or ten to fourteen US dollars. At a time when the annual income for a rural household was about one hundred to two hundred yuan a year, migrant women's earnings were an important subsidy to the family income.[11]

Yet the income contribution of these women was vaguely associated with the socially transgressive meanings of this particular form of labor. The local term for a hired domestic was *zai ren jia bang gong* (helping out in someone else's home), and it was sometimes uttered with a slight tinge of embarrassment by such workers themselves. They use these words only when they have to. When they do, their voices seem to lose their usual substantiality and become hesitant.

Where is the source of the shame that makes these women embarrassed to speak of their labor? If this shame circumscribed the narration of the migration experiences of married women, it made it almost unthinkable for unmarried women to migrate before the early 1980s. On why no young women "went out" in the 1970s, a woman cadre in a local township government remarked, "At that time people's minds were closed [*fengbi*] and feudal [*fengjian*]. If girls had gone out, they would have had problems in getting married." A young woman's chastity was not just a matter of sexual purity but was also linked with the location of her labor. If a woman performed domestic labor away from kin and home, the sphere of local patriarchy, her chastity may be called into question as it could not be locally scrutinized.

These women also experienced a vague sense of shame on the urban front: they embodied a trace of the past in the socialist present. Although the Mao-era state had no problem with elites hiring domestics, such employment could potentially signify a specter of class oppression. This became the very point of attack by rebels in the Cultural Revolution against the elite bourgeois lifestyle. Although the state subsidized such employment in some elite's salaries, it never attempted to incorporate this service openly into the socialist relations of production by making domestics state or collective employees. Hiring and firing were carried out in the private sphere of employers, invisible from the public relations of production. With urban women's unprecedented participation in public labor in factories, schools, hospitals, department stores, etc., rural women working as domestics, who appeared and disappeared now and then around the corners of the residential alleys, could not fit into that new subject position for women and were like fragments of the old society within socialism.

In both the city and the countryside, these rural migrant women were transgressors. This notion of transgression constitutes a vague source of shame for these women, who were cornered by a triangulation of discourses: the undervaluation of "rural women's" agricultural labor, the circumscriptive power of local patriarchy to define the propriety of their labor, and the invisibility of domestic service in public discourse.

In this cornered space, the state thus colluded with local patriarchy in making the position of rural migrant women unclear. The wage a woman brought home could be denigrated by her husband or others as *bu qingshuang*, illegible, unclean. Women's migrant domestic labor therefore seemed to lack discursive accountability and interpretive clarity, rendering these women ambiguous in personhood.[12] And women could not speak for themselves in this discourse. On the one hand, within the state discourse, there was no space for rural women to speak about the double burden on their backs. On the other hand, within local patriarchal culture, these women found it shameful to speak bitterness about their labor in the cities. The women often sighed when reminiscing about their migration: "If it had not been so hard at home, who would have wanted to take the suffering outside?" Lin, a woman in her late forties, ended her narrative in tears: "It's bitter to be outside. Yet with the bitterness we took outside, it is also embarrassing [lit. it also makes me look ugly] to speak of it at home [*zai wai mian shou de ku, hui lai jiang hai chou*]."

The embarrassment in their narratives was counterbalanced by assertions of their contributions to the family economy and by detailed and sometimes sobbing descriptions of how much they worried about their young children at home. Through such recitations, they assertively located the place of their belonging and their identity in the family and the community. Most of the early migrant women returned home after decollectivization, when their labor was needed to farm the land distributed to their households.

When I was in Wuwei, seventy-six-year-old Grandmother Four returned to her village for good after working as a domestic in Beijing since 1951. When I asked her and several women whether they found themselves changed after working in the city so that it was difficult to get back to rural life, they replied, "We didn't have a comfortable life [*xiangfu*] when we were working outside. Why wouldn't we be happy to return to [village life]?" Grandmother Four described returning to her village as a homecoming. Lin replied to my question as she picked up her shoulder pole, preparing to leave for the field, "I'm farming twenty mu of land with my husband. Had I changed, how could I have done this?" Giving rhetorical questions as a reply, these women demonstrated their linkage with rural life and agricultural labor and affirmed their continuing identity as "rural women." They subtly contested the propriety of my question and rendered any questioning about their personhood improper and irrelevant, including questioning from the power of local patriarchy.

NEW RURAL-URBAN RELATIONS: THE RISE OF THE CITY AND THE EMACIATION OF THE COUNTRYSIDE

The urban reform intensified the work pace and increased urban demand for paid domestic service. A rhyme circulating in the 1980s Beijing highlighted Wuwei as the single most important source of domestic workers in the capital: *Beijing baomu chu Anhui, Anhui baomu chu Wuwei* (Baomu in Beijing are from Anhui, Anhui *baomu* are from Wuwei). In Wuwei it is generally acknowledged that young rural women in the 1980s were the pathbreakers for a migration in the 1990s that involved an army of over 200,000 men and women from the county, making Wuwei one of the most active labor-exporting counties in Anhui. The media in Anhui are fond of contrasting those migrating before and after the post-Mao reforms: The older generation sought "survival;" those in the younger generation seek "wealth and knowledge" because their minds have been enlivened and activated (*sixiang huoyue*) by the reforms (e.g., Jin and Xu 1994). Released as "surplus labor" by the breakup of collective farming, young women now respond to the urban labor market through market "push-pull" mechanisms. This mainstream interpretation celebrates an epistemic shift brought on by the reform and an ontological rectification that finally steers the nation onto the normal path to Progress. Just as primitive accumulation was perceived by Marx's bourgeois economist contemporaries only as a form of freedom, the current labor migration is perceived by the liberal media and scholarship as a process in which the individual comes into her own in post-Mao modernity.

While migrants were viewed as "blind drifters" (*mang liu*) and "errant waters" (Solinger 1999: 1) in need of social control, they were also increasingly seen as the flexible individual agents of the market economy. This positive perception was offset by a new angst over the lack of such flexibility among the growing number of unemployed urban workers shed by the restructured state-owned enterprises. Between 1991 and 2005, the urban workforce employed in the public sector dropped from 82 percent to about 27 percent (Andreas 2008: 130). New social value was then invested in the sign of the migrant in contrast with the laid-off urban worker, just as the "dynamic" market economy, growing in volume and volubility, was positively paired against the "inflexible" planned economy.

Rather than framing migration as "individuals" responding to "push-pull" forces, I interpret it as a troubled process of subject formation for rural youth, particularly rural young women. Migrant young women often opened their stories to me with a despondent judgment of their situation, "There is no way out in the countryside" (*zai nongcun meiyou chulu*). The context in which rural young women found themselves in the 1980s–1990s represents an epistemic shift from that of their forerunners. Below I analyze how post-Mao development has reconfigured the rural-urban relationship in its imagining of modernity.

The rural-urban relationship has figured quite differently in the modernization projects of the Mao and post-Mao eras, with the former based on improved national self-sufficiency, and the latter aiming for the nation's relinking with the global capitalist market. Shortly after the Communists took over the cities, the Maoist development strategy was to quickly transform colonial consumer cities (*xiaofei chengshi*) into purposeful production cities (*shengchan chengshi*) (Kirkby 1985: 14–15). Moreover, planning policies de-emphasized the growth of cities and avoided focusing resources into existing cities, especially large coastal cities (Naughton 1995: 61). The Great Leap Forward (1958–1960) marked a shift away from Soviet-style central planning to reliance on urban and rural local initiatives for speedy social transformation, with the rural "People's Commune" carrying the vital agency (Kirkby 1985: 5). During that period, small-scale industries in the rural communes took precedence over large-scale Soviet-style urban factories (Buck 1984: 5). The "Third Front" construction (1965–1971) saw a massive relocation and construction of defense industries in interior provinces for national security reasons, allowing a more balanced distribution of industry throughout the country (Ma and Wei 1997: 219–221). The new oil city of Daqing was touted by the government as a socialist utopian city: a ruralized city or urbanized village, integrating rural, industrial, and residential sectors within its bounds (Lo 1986: 446–447). In the period of the Cultural

Revolution, the countryside figured as the ideological high ground, functioning as a vast classroom where sent-down urban youth could be reacquainted with the revolutionary spirit of the peasantry; as Kirkby observes, "It was the farms rather than the factories that dominated the self-advertisements of Cultural Revolution China" (1985: 5). Although scholars debate whether the development policies of the socialist period carried an anti-urbanism (e.g., Naughton 1995; Chan 1994; Kirkby 1985), there seems to be agreement that the development policies at that time unlinked the symbiotic connection between industrialization and the privileges assumed by the city in liberal market economies; both the cities and the countryside were enveloped in "hard struggle, plain living" (*jianku pusu*).

The rural population perceived the difference between the countryside and the city as that between peasants and workers (Potter 1983). The city signified a secure and desired welfare in the arms of the state; it was also a site associated with modern industrial production. I argue later that in the post-Mao development strategy the city commands a different signifying power for rural young women.

The post-Mao policies of "reform and opening" (*gaige kaifang*) ushered in a new form of modernity based on the nation's insertion into the global capitalist economy. The flow of foreign direct investment to China, the growth of exports from China to the world market, and the rapid expansion of the domestic service sector have been underpinned by China's access to cheap migrant labor. This economic reorientation and restructuring underlies the process by which the rural is emaciated in relation to the urban telos. In what follows, I examine this post-Mao shift in rural-urban relations—the rise of the city and the decline of the countryside—in economic, ideological, and cultural dimensions.[13]

Beginning in 1978, the cities began to emerge as the engines of economic growth, occupying the central place in the post-Mao development discourse of constructing a commodity economy (*shangpin jingji*), marking a radical departure from the Maoist policy line. This switch from "production city" to "entrepreneurial city" in China's development strategy (Solinger 1993) paralleled what David Harvey (1989) has described as a recent transformation in advanced capitalism from "managerial cities" (managing social services) into "entrepreneurial cities" (fostering investment and development)—a change in urban governance corresponding to the new logic of flexible accumulation. In a speech in December 1982, Premier Zhao Ziyang made one of "ten great principles for the development of the economy" reliance on big cities to construct economic centers (Solinger 1993: 208). As Kirkby observed about this tendency toward agglomeration, "There is no reluctance to admit that the chief purpose of this arrangement would be to strengthen the hierarchy of cities and regions. The prevailing view among China's economists today is that the institutionalising of such inequalities will accelerate national economic growth" (1985: 225). Beginning in 1983, the administrative hierarchy was restructured so that cities were free from the prefectural government (*qu*) to administer directly their surrounding counties (*shi guan xian*) and their agricultural and peasant labor resources (Chan 1994: 105).

Along with this economic and administrative restructuring, the city has also been renewed as the privileged space of modern civilization or civility (*xiandai wenming*), gesturing toward elusive capital and development.[14] In this discourse, it appears that Modernity and Progress, themselves post-Mao ideological constructs, are given their permanent residence in the city. As Louisa Schein observes, "The city, however conceived, has become an object of increasingly intense desire in the era of reform" (2001: 225). A directive was issued in 1978 channeling 5 percent of the total profits of all urban industrial and commercial enterprises into housing, roads, and other urban infrastructure projects (Buck 1984: 9). Whereas previously all such funds were distributed to state-owned factories for reinvestment, this new tax money given to the city fueled an urban construction boom beginning in the early 1980s. At the same time, cities also saw a campaign for urban beautification (*meihua chengshi*), with special attention to parks, landscaping, and cleanliness (Buck 1984). The urban beautification campaign paralleled the *wujiang simei* (five advances and four beautifications) campaign by targeting urban citizens as subjects of modern civility. It did so through what Foucault termed "biopower," operating on each citizen's language (*yuyan mei*), behavior (*xingwei mei*), mind (*xinling mei*), and agency in improving the urban environment (*huanjing mei*) through the citizen's advancement in levels of civility (*jiang wenming*), etiquette (*jiang limao*), hygiene (*jiang weisheng*), scientific outlook (*jiang kexue*), and morality (*jiang daode*).

At the same time that the city occupied the high ground in the state's development strategy, agriculture's share in state capital investment plunged. State capital investment in agriculture, which had been 10.5 percent in 1976–1980 plummeted to 5 percent in 1981–1985 and dropped further to 3.3 percent in 1985–1990 (Chan 1994: 61). Agriculture's share of capital investment dropped from 10.6 percent in 1979 to 1.7 percent in 1994 (Li 2000: 41), remaining below 2 percent throughout the 1990s. For a brief period between 1979 and 1984, there was a significant increase in agricultural production and rural income, inspired by the rural reform, particularly the raising of procurement prices for agricultural goods and the relaxed state monopoly on agricultural products,[15] but rural income has stagnated since the mid-1980s, which was openly confirmed by a rural township party secretary in Wuwei. The prices for fertilizers and pesticides increased by 43 percent and 82.3 percent in 1985 (over 1983 prices) because of their marketization. The state also lowered procurement prices in 1985 by 28 percent below those of 1984. In 1998, the income from growing one mu of rice in Wuwei was only around 200–300 yuan, and from one mu of cotton around 500 yuan. According to internal government statistics, the Gini coefficient for rural and urban incomes had reached 0.59 in 2002

(Ma 2002), beyond the 0.4 danger level. Although the rural-urban income disparity narrowed between 1978 and 1985, the gap began to widen again after 1985 and was larger in the 1990s than before 1978 (Li 2000: 32–33; World Bank 1997: 15–17). In the meantime, the limited welfare and medical care supported by the production collectives were dismantled when the rural reform privatized production.[16]

The making of the countryside as a wasteland in the economic strategy of state investment was symbiotic with the ideological construction of the countryside as a wasteland of "backwardness" and "tradition." To borrow from Walter Benjamin, one might say that "tradition," negatively defined against modernization and development, is a signifier whose signified cannot be fixed, growing like the "piling of wreckage upon wreckage" that the storm of Progress keeps hurling back as its antithesis (1992: 249). China's opening toward Western culture and overseas investment not only opened a new vision of modernity but also furnished a new frame of reference that has reorganized narratives and interpretations of history. The euphoric meaning of the present, previously derived from the present's juxtaposition with the pre-liberation past, vanished and was displaced by an urgent sense of crisis when the elite and educated youth refracted the gaze of the West to see peasant China as "backward and poor."[17] As a mother commented in the 1980s on how urban youth look at the present, "Instead of comparing China with what it was like before liberation, they contrast it with Japan and the West. They don't appreciate how much better things are now than they were in the old society" (Hooper 1985: 35).

The urban telos appropriates the rural into its system of representation by devalorizing the rural as its moribund other. The 1980s discourse of enlightenment, epitomized in the iconoclastic TV series *Heshang* (Deathsong of the River), links China's backwardness with its agrarian roots and the peasant mentality of its population (Bodman 1991). *Heshang* urges intellectuals to fulfill their historical agency in the task of national regeneration. Critiquing *Heshang*, Jing Wang observes that "tradition" and, synonymously, the countryside, are not treated as "an autonomous system of representations" but become "derivative" when they are evaluated in a new epistemology in which a hostile modernity has appeared as dominant and unmarked (1996: 130). The discourse of enlightenment, reconstructing the countryside as the wasteland of "tradition" while development policies opened up the coastal cities as special portals for overseas connections and investment, harkens back to a semi-colonial discourse of the early twentieth century that similarly produced the city and the countryside as the two poles of a primary contradiction in its modernization project. Tani Barlow (1991b) points out that both old and new nationalist enlightenment projects borrowed the authority and power of an imagined Western (read: universal) modernity and produced remarkably similar representations of "Chinese tradition."

The emaciation of the rural is much more deeply articulated in the relationship between peasants and land in many rural areas, where the land of production has practically become a land of subsistence (*bao kouliang*). Labor migration from the countryside to the cities is termed by scholars and the Chinese government as "the transfer of surplus rural labor power," but the irony is that the migrants, rather than "surplus" labor, consist mostly of better-educated rural youth who are most needed for innovative agricultural production. Those who stay behind to continue farming constitute what is often called the "773861 army"—"77" refers to the old (i.e., seventy-seven-year-olds), "38" refers to women, typically married women ("38" is March 8, International Women's Day), and "61" refers to children (June 1, International Children's Day).

Private enterprises, domestic and transnational, draw millions of able-bodied migrants to work in sweatshop conditions with little labor protection. The injured, debilitated, the ill, and the unemployed are thrown back to the countryside each year in the tens of thousands.[18] The countryside has become a reservoir releasing and absorbing labor according to the capricious needs of the market, supplying a flexible army of migrant laborers for a carnival of accumulation in which Chinese and transnational businesses share in the banquet of profits.[19] The process of emaciation is a process of violence that appropriates economic, cultural, and ideological value from the countryside, where rural youth can no longer find a path to the future.

RURAL YOUTH IN THE POST-MAO ERA: DISCONNECTION, DOMESTICATION, AND THE CRISIS OF SUBJECTIVITY

The post-Mao project of development has thus produced the countryside both materially and ideologically as a wasteland stripped of state investment and inhabited by moribund "tradition," with the two dimensions mutually reinforcing each other. It was in this discursive context that the countryside could not function as the locus of a modern identity for rural young women, and their despondent remark, "There is no way out in the countryside" meant "There is no path to modernity in the countryside." As Anthony Cascardi argues, "The culture of modernity is given shape as a divided whole that can only be unified through the powers of an abstract subject, or its political analogue, the autonomous state. Indeed ... the state ... provides the means through which the divided subjects of modernity can be made whole" (1992: 179). Yet, we also need to be attentive to what happens when the post-Mao era severs the Mao-era discursive linkage between rural youth and the state—especially the linkage to rural young women, which used to be the ideological icon of "Iron Girls."

What is at issue here is not simply how bad rural life is for young women and how much better urban life is. What is critical is how the ideological and material rise of the city and the emaciation of the rural reorganize how rural youth imagine the future and modernity. In this section, I analyze the experience of Liu Li who went to Beijing from Henan. I choose Liu Li's case because her narrative reinforces the data I have collected from my interviews in Wuwei and demonstrates common problems facing many rural young women today, despite the women's different origins.

Liu Li's Narrative: Leaving Home

> I remember that day to be the 13th. My elder cousin would accompany me to the county bus station. My younger brother stood by the door of our house. I was so saddened that I felt like crying. Tears fell, but I didn't turn my head around. My parents were weeping too. They didn't approve of my leaving home. I'm one of the two junior high graduates among the girls of my age in the village, and I'm the first one in my village to be a migrant . . . My family's economic situation is not good and I want to help out. People in my village do not allow their daughters to come out. They say that girls who go out will become bad, just like those women on TV. . . . People in my village just think that after daughters grow up, parents should find them a mother-in-law's family [*po jia*]. So the parents would save money and prepare new clothes and things like that [for a wedding]. Then there is the marriage and childbirth and raising the family. Just like that . . . But I don't think this way. I don't want to get married this early. I don't want to be like my parents—their life is going nowhere . . . What matters to me is that I want to achieve something. I want to live like a human [*huo de xiang ge ren yang*]. (Excerpt from interview with the author)

"Rural youth" live awkwardly and uncomfortably in the post-Mao era, trapped as modern subjects in a space in, but not of, the culture of modernity. When they are in school, rural youth are alienated from their rural livelihood and context by post-Mao urban-oriented education. This role of education is termed "educational colonization" by Dale Jiajun Wen (2008) and as "mental enclosure" (*jingshen quandi*) by Pun Ngai, Lu Huilin et al.(2009: 19). When rural youth are off-school, they are domesticated by the post-Mao system of family farming. Almost all the fifty-nine young women migrants I interviewed in Wuwei left home on their own initiative, and almost half did not have their parents' approval to migrate, at least initially. Although some were able to change their parents' minds, a fair portion of them simply fled home (*tou pao*), often with friends. The young women of Wuwei overwhelmingly said that everyday life at home was *meijin* (inert) and *meiyisi* (meaningless or boring). The description "inert and meaningless" was also given to me as a self-evident reality in the discursive context of rural-urban relations—the city is where everything happens, whereas the rural constitutes only a lack. My observation in rural Wuwei coincided with that of Mobo Gao in rural Jiangxi that "there is no longer any focal point for public life in the village" (1999: 174).

Not only did public life largely disappear in many rural areas after post-Mao decollectivization, rural youth also became marginalized in agrarian relations of production. Most of the young women I interviewed have never had firsthand experience in agriculture. Everyday life entails what might be termed the "domestication of youth." Whereas rural youth, including rural young women, actively participated in collective farming during the Mao era and were mobilized for public projects such as building dikes along the Yangtze River, repairing water control and irrigation systems, and taking part in performance troupes, since decollectivization they have been domesticated and subjected to parental authority, which has replaced the production team as authority in labor management.

Domestication for many rural young women forebodes an imminent snare that threatens to seal them off from the possibility of a modern identity. Domestication in their natal homes delivers them into their future households through engagement and marriage, trapping them in a snare in which a married woman's place and activity of identity is typically described as "moving around the stove" (*weizhe guotai zhuan*). The aspirations of Liu Li and many other young Wuwei women conflict with their experience of everyday life in the post-Mao countryside as a site of inertness. However, "inert experience" should be taken not as a natural, given fact, but as a product of the discourse of modernity itself, which has redefined "peasant" and rural life in both material and ideological aspects.

The "inert and meaningless" life in rural young women's narratives today contrasts with narratives of older migrants about their dynamic and bustling lives as young unmarried women in the collective era. The discursive connection between rural youth and the state, embodied in the heroic agency of the Iron Girls, has been severed.

Youth is thus the only possible crevice in the life cycle through which a rural woman might take a leap to create a modern identity and rearrange her life. My informants often said that "everything is finished once a woman is married." Sociologist Tan Shen similarly observes how gender defines marriage expectations for men and women in rural China: "According to the gender roles in a traditional marriage, a man's marriage prospect depends largely on his individual achievement ... but for a woman, the gender role 'designated' for her in a traditional marriage has almost nothing to do with her individual achievement. Her development is to a great extent restrained by her marriage. For many women marriage means the ending of individual development" (1997: 45). "Youth" is therefore a strategic site for action. Liu Li left home not only to help her parents but also because she felt she was in danger of losing the possibility of having a (modern) personhood (*huo de xiang ge ren yang*).

Rural youth experience a crisis of subjectivity. While the Mao-era generation of migrants returned to the countryside with asserted rural identity, for the post-Mao rural youth how to have a modern subjectivity has become an issue of whether life is worth living at all in the countryside. The countryside is invoked as a field of death where a woman's modern subjectivity is smothered so that she "always moves around the stove."

Rural youth continue to feel disconnected from rural livelihood and leave the countryside. With increased commodification of agricultural inputs, daily necessities, education, and medical care, rural households have growing dependence on remittances. By 2006 remittances contributed 15 to 30 percent of net rural income in interior sending provinces (Bramall 2008: 46). In interior rural provinces, migration has become a norm for rural youth, so much so that those who do not leave are seen by their peers and villagers as "incompetent" (*mei benshi, mei you yong*). Rural sociologists term the emptying out of rural areas *kong chao hua* (literally "emptying the nest").

Does migration resolve the crisis of subjectivity for rural youth? In the volatile global capitalist system, China being the workshop of the world is predicated on migrants being "rational" individuals who respond to push-and-pull factors. Yet in a recent survey of some six hundred migrants in the city, many report that they not only miss home, but also deem their migrant life as "unfree" and "meaningless" (Pun, Lu et al. 2009: 18). Neither in the countryside nor in the city can migrant youth resolve their crisis of subjectivity and locate the meaning of their life.

To conclude, my thesis is that labor mobility cannot be singularly celebrated, as many have done, as a new form of freedom to be realized in the transition from a planned to a market economy. The unraveling of what Marx called "compulsion" revealed how post-Mao development has robbed the countryside of its ability to serve as a place for rural youth to construct a meaningful identity and how the post-Mao shift in rural-urban relations is constitutive of rural youth's desire for the city. Embedded in the post-Mao culture of modernity is an epistemic violence against the countryside that devalorizes the rural in both material and symbolic practices. My analysis implies a critique of the dominant discourse of development in many developing countries and beyond.[20] The experiences of two cohorts of migrant women illustrate modernities in the plural, not in terms of essentialized cultures to argue for a Chinese brand of modernity, but in terms of historicity to examine the tension and discontinuity in social processes, and thus to offer a critique of the teleology of capitalist modernity. It thus contributes to what Dirlik has called "the identification of alternative modernities, not in terms of reified cultures, but in terms of alternative historical trajectories that have been suppressed by the hegemony of capitalist modernity" (1997: 123).

ACKNOWLEDGMENTS

Adapted and reproduced by permission of the American Anthropological Association from *American Ethnologist* 30, no. 4 (2005): 587–596. Not for sale or further reproduction.

NOTES

1. According to my interview with Wuwei government officials, Wuwei is a base for rice and cotton cultivation. In 1990s it had 1.34 million mu (1 mu = 0.165 acre) of agricultural land and a rural population of 1.2 million, about 92 percent of its total population.
2. The interviews with migrants were conducted in Anhui and Beijing from 1998–2000, followed by visits and communications via phone and mail in the ensuing years. My interviews in Wuwei included 104 women in twelve villages. Only sixteen had never migrated, citing family reasons or illiteracy as their obstacles. Among eighty-eight who experienced migration, thirteen were over forty years of age and migrated by themselves in the Mao-era and seventy-five were between their late teens and early thirties and migrated in the 1980s or 1990s, on their own initiative (fifty-nine) or with kin (sixteen).
3. Yan Hairong (2006) compared their work experiences in detail.
4. According to Wuwei Xianzhi Bangongshi (1993), before 1949, floods often caused men and women to seek livelihood as hired hands in cities like Shanghai. Women often worked as maids.
5. Rural-urban migration had been very strictly regulated by the government until the early to mid-1980s. Rural women who migrated outside the state plan worked mainly as domestic workers then.
6. See Cohen (1994) and Kelliher (1994) for analyses on the political category of peasant.
7. Tim Oakes notes that, in the Mao era, up to one-third of the state's procurement of grain was transferred to grain-deficient rural areas at subsidized prices and contributed to China's remarkable success in reducing its mortality rate by more than half in less than two decades (2000: 308).
8. Perkins and Yusuf (1984) show that, in the late 1970s, value flow into the countryside exceeded outflow, thereby beginning to reverse the trend in the previous decades of agriculture heavily subsidizing urban industrialization. See Ching (2008) for a comparison about conditions for agriculture during and after the Mao era.
9. It is noteworthy that Mao spoke of a more profound transformation of Chinese women in an episteme yet to come that would specifically unlink gender equality from mechanization (Malraux 1968: 373–374).
10. Andors (1983: 125) credited the campaign against Lin Biao and Confucius in 1973 with inspiring more efforts to promote women's equality, including women gaining parity in work points with men.
11. Drawn from my own field notes and Gao (1999).
12. Rofel (1999) shows how, before socialist liberation, the labor of factory women performed under a male gaze marked such women as similar to prostitutes ("broken shoes").
13. Collectively owned rural industry in the coastal areas thrived in the 1980s, but has declined since the 1990s, as the post-Mao state, focused on the city since the late 1970s, provided neither direct investment nor long-term planning regarding rural industry.
14. See Anagnost (1997: 75–97).
15. See Mobo Gao (1999: 177–179) for a detailed discussion of how the reform has influenced rural income.
16. See Potter and Potter (1990: 132–134) and Gao (1999: 72–79) on the function of the village-level medical care system before the rural reform. Gao's work also compares rural health before and after the reform.
17. See Hayford (1998) for a good analysis of the Orientalist discourse of "peasant China."

18. A 2006 report reveals that in Guangdong province, incidents of work-related injury reach 120,000 times every year (Wang Xiaohai 2006).
19. In 2005, foreign-funded enterprises accounted for China's 58 percent of exports, 59 percent of imports, and 84 percent of the processing trade (Zhao Min 2006: 22).
20. Becoming hegemonic since the 1960s and offering an unrestrained freedom of capital, this pro-market developmentalism finds its supporters among the political and business elites in China and other countries in the South. Escobar (1995) and Crush (1995) provide incisive critiques of the discourse of development.

REFERENCES

Anagnost, Ann. 1997. *National Past-Times: Narrative, Representation, and Power in Modern China*. Durham: Duke University Press.
Andors, Phyllis. 1983. *The Unfinished Liberation of Chinese Women, 1949–1980*. Bloomington: Indiana University Press.
Andreas, Joel. 2008. "Changing Colors in China." *New Left Review* 54: 123–143.
Barlow, Tani E. 1991a. "*Zhizhifenzi* [Chinese intellectuals] and Power." *Dialectical Anthropology* 16(3–4): 209–232.
———. 1991b. "Theorizing Women: *Funü, Guojia, Jiating* [Chinese women, Chinese state, Chinese family]." *Genders* 10: 132–160.
Benjamin, Walter. 1992. "Theses on the Philosophy of History." In *Illuminations*, edited by Hannah Arendt, 245–255. London: Fontana Press.
Bodman, Richard. 1991. "From History to Allegory to Art." In *Deathsong of the River: A Reader's Guide to the Chinese TV Series Heshang*, edited by Su Xiao Kang and Wang Luxiang, translated by Richard W. Bodman and Pin P. Wan, 1–62. Ithaca: East Asian Program, Cornell University.
Bramall, Chris. 2008. "Rural Industrialization and Spatial Inequality in China, 1978–2006." *Economic and Political Weekly* 43(52): 43–50.
Buck, David D. 1984. "Changes in Chinese Urban Planning since 1976." *Third World Planning Review* 6(1): 5–26.
Cascardi, Anthony J. 1992. *The Subject of Modernity*. Cambridge: Cambridge University Press.
Chan, Kam Wing. 1994. *Cities with Invisible Walls: Reinterpreting Urbanization in Post-1949 China*. Oxford: Oxford University Press.
Ching, Pao-Yu. 2008. "How Sustainable is China's Agriculture: A Closer Look at China's Agriculture and Chinese Peasants." Special release published by the People's Coalition on Food Sovereignty (PCFS) and the Pesticide Action Network Asia and the Pacific (PAN AP). http://www.foodsov.org/resources/resources_000009.pdf.
Cohen, Myron L. 1994. "The Cultural and Political Inventions in Modern China: The Case of the Chinese 'Peasant'." In *China in Transformation*, edited by Tu Wei-ming, 151–170. Cambridge, MA: Harvard University Press.
Crush, Jonathan S., ed. 1995. *Power of Development*. New York: Routledge.
Davin, Delia. 1975. "Women in the Countryside of China." In *Women in Chinese Society*, edited by Margery Wolf and Roxane Witke, 243–273. Stanford: Stanford University Press.
Dirlik, Arif. 1997. "Chinese History and the Question of Orientalism." In *The Postcolonial Aura: Third World Criticism in the Age of Global Capitalism*, edited by Arif Dirlik, 105–128. Boulder: Westview Press.

Escobar, Arturo. 1995. *Encountering Development: The Making and Unmaking of the Third World*. Chichester, West Sussex: Princeton University Press.
Gao, Mobo C.F. 1999. *Gao Village: A Portrait of Rural Life in Modern China*. Honolulu: University of Hawai'i Press.
Harrell, Stevan. 2000. "Changing Meanings of Work in China." In *Re-Drawing Boundaries: Work, Households, and Gender in China*, edited by Barbara Entwisle and Gail E. Henderson, 67–76. Berkeley: University of California Press.
Harvey, David. 1989. "From Managerialism to Entrepreneurialism: The Transformation in Urban Governance in Late Capitalism." *Geografiska Annaler* 71B(1): 3–17.
Hayford, Charles. 1998. "The Storm over the Peasant: Orientalism and Rhetoric in Constructing China." In *Contesting Master Narrative: Essays in Social History*, edited by Jeffrey Cox and Shelton Stromquist, 150–172. Iowa City: University of Iowa Press.
Honig, Emily. 2000. "Iron Girls Revisited: Gender and Politics of Work in the Cultural Revolution, 1966–76." In *Re-Drawing Boundaries: Work, Households, and Gender in China*, edited by Barbara Entwisle and Gail E. Henderson, 97–110. Berkeley: University of California Press.
Hooper, Beverley. 1985. *Youth in China*. Victoria, Australia: Penguin Books.
Huang, Zongzhi. 2009. "Zhongguo bei hushi de feizhenggui jingji: xianshi yu lilun." *Kaifang shidai* 2: 51–73.
Jacka, Tamara. 1997. *Women's Work in Rural China: Change and Continuity in an Era of Reform*. Cambridge: Cambridge University Press.
Jin Yuanju, and Xu Deyuan. 1994. "Baomu xiaoying—laizi Wuwei de diaocha baogao [Baomu agency—An investigation report from Wuwei]." *Anhui ribao* [Anhui daily], May 15: 2.
Kelliher, Daniel. 1994. "Chinese Communist Political Theory and the Rediscovery of the Peasantry." *Modern China* 20(4): 387–415.
Kirkby, Richard. 1985. *Urbanization in China: Town and Country in a Developing Economy, 1949–2000 AD*. London: Croom Helm.
Li Zuojun. 2000. *Zhongguo de genben wenti: jiuyi nongmin hechuqu* [China's fundamental problem: Where would nine hundred million peasants go]. Beijing: Zhongguo Fazhan Chubanshe.
Liu, Lydia. 1993. "Translingual Practice: The Discourse of Individualism between China and the West." *Positions: East Asia Cultures Critique* 1(1): 160–193.
Lo, C.P. 1986. "Socialist Ideology and Urban Strategies in China." *Urban Geography* 8: 440–458.
Ma, Josephine. 2002. "Rural Cash Crunch Taxes Reformers." *South China Morning Post*, January 8: 8.
Ma, Laurence J.C., and Yehua Dennis Wei. 1997. "Determinants of State Investment in China, 1953–1990." *Tijdschrift voor Economische en Sociale Geografie* 88(3): 211–225.
Malraux, Andre. 1968. *Anti-Memoirs*. New York: Holt, Rinehart and Winston.
Marx, Karl. 1977. "The Secret of Primitive Accumulation." In *Capital*. Vol. 1, edited by Karl Marx, 873–940. New York: Vintage Books.
Naughton, Barry. 1995. "Cities in the Chinese Economic System: Changing Roles and Conditions for Autonomy." In *Urban Spaces in Contemporary China: The Potential for Autonomy and Community in Post-Mao China*, edited by Deborah S. Davis, Richard Kraus, Barry Naughton, and Elizabeth J. Perry, 61–89. Washington, DC and Cambridge: Woodrow Wilson Center Press and Cambridge University Press.
Oakes, Tim. 2000. "China's Market Reforms: Whose Human Rights Problem?" In *China Beyond the Headlines*, edited by Timothy B. Weston and Lionel M. Jensen, 295–326. New York: Rowman and Littlefield.

Perkins, Dwight, and Shahid S. Yusuf. 1984. *Rural Development in China*. Baltimore: Johns Hopkins University Press.

Potter, Sulamith Hein. 1983. "The Position of Peasants in Modern China's Social Order." *Modern China* 9: 465–499.

Potter, Sulamith Hein, and Jack M. Potter. 1990. *The Anthropology of a Revolution*. Cambridge: Cambridge University Press.

Pun Ngai, Lu Huilin et al. 2009. "Nongmingong: wei wancheng de wuchanjiejihua." *Kaifang shidai* 6: 5–35.

Ramzy, Austin. 2009. "Runners-up: The Chinese Worker." *Time*, December 16. http://www.time.com.

Rofel, Lisa. 1999. *Other Modernities*. Berkeley: University of California Press.

Schein, Louisa. 2001. "Urbanity, Cosmopolitanism, Consumption." In *China Urban: Ethnographies of Contemporary Culture*, edited by Nancy N. Chen, Constance Clark, Suzanne Gottschang, and Lyn Jeffrey, 225–41. Durham, N.C.: Duke University Press.

Solinger, Dorothy J. 1993. "The Place of the Central City in China's Economic Reform: From Hierarchy to Network?" In *China's Transition from Socialism*, edited by Dorothy J. Solinger, 205–222. Armonk, NY: M.E. Sharpe.

———. 1999. *Contesting Citizenship in Urban China: Peasant Migrants, the State and the Logic of the Market*. Berkeley: University of California Press.

Tan Shen. 1997. "Nongcun laodongli liudong de xingbie chayi [Gender differences in rural labor mobility]." *Shehuixue yanjiu* [Studies of Sociology] 1: 42–47.

Wang, Jing. 1996. "Heshang and the Chinese Enlightenment." In *High Culture Fever: Politics, Aesthetics, and Ideology in Deng's China*, edited by Jing Wang, 118–136. Berkeley: University of California Press.

Wang Shucheng, and Li Renhu. 1996. "Wuwei: Baomu xiaoying [Wuwei: The effect of migrant domestic workers]." *Banyuetan* (half-monthly forum) 8: 23–25.

Wang Xiaohai. 2006. "Yue ni tou 3.1yi kuojian gongshang kangfu zhongxin" [Guangdong plans to invest 310 million yuan in expanding the Rehabilitation Center]. *Nanfang ribao*, October 31.

Wen, Dale Jiajun. 2008. "China's Rural Reform: Crisis and Ongoing Debate." *Economic and Political Weekly* Vol. 43(52): 86–96.

World Bank. 1997. *Sharing Rising Incomes: Disparities in China*. Washington, DC: World Bank.

Wuwei Xianzhi Bangongshi [The Office of Wuwei Annals]. 1993. *Wuwei xianzhi* [Wuwei annals]. Beijing: Shehui Kexue Wenxian Chubanshe.

Yan Hairong. 2006. "Rurality and Labor Process Autonomy: The Question of Subsumption in the Waged Labor of Domestic Service." *Cultural Dynamics* 18(1): 5–31.

Zhao Min. 2006. "External Liberalization and the Evolution of China's Exchange System: An Empirical Approach." Washington: World Bank. http://efinance.org.cn/.

"Zhongguo nongmingong wenti yanjiu zong baogao." 2006. *Gaige* [Reform] 5. http://www.ncwt.net/Article_Show.asp?ArticleID=327.

11 "Value Plus Plus"
Housewifization and History in Philippine Care Migration

*Pauline Gardiner Barber
and Catherine Bryan*

Philippine care-labor migration is situated within a historical context of regional and global inequalities fuelled through the indelible expansion of capitalist modes of organization and accumulation. Interconnected, these facets of capitalism continuously alter social reproduction in order to stimulate capital growth. In this way, while capitalism represents a powerful mode of cultural and social organization, it is both adaptive and transitory. This is particularly true where women are concerned. For example, in many contexts we see a historical confluence of social and economic processes which redefined and repositioned women's labor in the household, a process Maria Mies (1986) captured in an earlier period of ambitious feminist theorizing with the concept of "housewifization."[1] The processes characterized in this earlier, pre-post-modern phase of feminist scholarship are now seen to have partially given way to the feminization of labor, the new international division of labor, and the feminization of labor migration itself (Piper 2007).

International care-labor migration emerges as a means of maximizing capital accumulation for both employers and states. It can be understood as an outcome of capitalism's insatiable drive for profit. It can also be used as a lens through which to understand capitalism—and increasingly neoliberal capitalism—as casting and recasting social identity. In an era of neoliberal capitalism, care labor migration becomes a central feature of the dispersal and reorganization of social reproduction labor globally. At once it affirms and alters what Mies and other feminist and Marxist scholars described as "the sexual division of labor," as it emerged under prototypical capitalism; gender is partially recast to meet the emerging demands of capital accumulation, while earlier ideological models are retained. Women are encouraged to migrate for paid employment, yet their paid employment is directly connected to conventional understandings of gender both in terms of the kind of employment they can access and in terms of the reasons why they seek out this employment. When situated in a historical and gendered account of capitalism, care migration represents a global reinitiating of a gendered (and increasingly racialized) process of "housewifization."

So calibrated, migrant women's labor is not valued for the multiplicity of learned skills it demonstrates, nor its critically important social and economic contributions.

Central to this process is the continual adjustment and readjustment of social reproduction within both the Philippines and the labor markets to which care migrants travel. Hence, our theoretical contribution is to suggest that care labor migration cannot be viewed as epiphenomenal, the by-product or secondary effect of failed capital investment or short-sighted structural adjustments (although it is influenced by both). Nor can it be regarded as simply the individual undertaking of a growing number of women. Rather, care labor migration is central to the processes of contemporary global capitalism, a means of reorganizing social relations and reproduction in multiple sites, sharing some similarities in the organization of social reproduction and gender divisions of labor, and connected through the transnational social networks of migrants and migration industries. From this vantage point, care migration can also be seen as a strategy to redress the drawbacks of unfettered accumulation under neoliberal capitalism and its antecedents. Since the value accorded social reproduction is continually undermined (as Nonini argues, this volume) care labor and those who produce it for wages see their work "cheapened," if not degraded (Anderson 2000; Bakan and Stasiulis 1997). This occurs through a combination of the stigmatization associated with the nature of the work itself and the gendered cultural performances associated with particular kinds of migrants and migration flows (Barber 2008a).

The title for this chapter most obviously references value drawn from social reproduction labor. But "value plus plus" also plays on a Filipino idiom for signaling the taxes added to the price of goods and services at the point of purchase. Hence our title emphasizes the unforgiving market logic whereby Filipinos, as exemplary global care migrants, obtain tertiary-level education to be competitive in select labor markets. They do so encouraged by the state, unscrupulous recruiters, and assorted migration industries all of which promise more and better opportunities will result from their products, and because normative practices change through migrants' word-of-mouth stories. And so it becomes self-fulfilling that care migrants set a higher bar by seeking levels of post-secondary training, even when this is known to be politically problematic among migrant advocacy groups. Employers benefit from but do not credit the additional levels of skill in the wage calculations; in effect they receive *value plus plus* from their employees. Thus our analysis probes the social complexity and value distortion underlying contemporary processes of deskilling in Philippine care migration.

Later in the chapter, examples of individual migration histories, historical and contemporary, drawn from Barber's sixteen years of Philippine-based ethnographic fieldwork illustrate the social complexity of care migration, both in terms of the shifting directions and volumes of migration flows, and in terms of the systemic deskilling and skewed class dynamics that confound even the best staged migrants' journey.[2] However, in order to better contextualize the ethnographic setting, we first draw upon Mies's concept of "housewifization" to sketch the sexual division of labor and address the historical tension between productive and reproductive work under global capitalism. This first section highlights the ephemeral yet immutable character of capitalism. It establishes the conceptual and theoretical context informing the migration histories presented in the second section. In concluding, we bring together the theory and migrants' stories, highlighting the complexity of care labor migration in relation to shifting patterns of gender and reproductive labor. Overall we contribute to the ongoing conversations about the how and why of gendered systemic inequalities defining contemporary global migration but we do so with full attention to the complexities of migrant agency. As the third top source country for global migrants in 2010, the Philippines provides an important case to address these questions.

HOUSEWIFIZATION, CARE AS A COMMODITY, AND FICTIONS OF SOCIAL REPRODUCTION

The formation of the European working classes in the eighteenth century required a departure from previous patterns of livelihood and subsistence, and a separation of reproduction and productive tasks. This was achieved over the course of several generations, beginning with expropriation of common lands during the sixteenth century, and culminating in the commodification of labor and the establishment of the wage-nexus. Under these conditions, access to wages, and subsequently survival, became dependent, case by case, on the demands of capital accumulation; demands created, sustained, and modified by the capitalist class and the states that supported them. These couplings, capital with wage-dependent labor, and the capitalist class with the state, resulted in the emergence of a prototypical complex and stratified social order premised on the availability of exploitable, wage-dependent labor. In this context, European working-class men and women fared differently, as certain types of labor were allocated to certain categories of people.

Biological difference—or more precisely, the values assigned to perceived biological difference—became a central organizing feature of early capitalist production. This is illustrated by the relegation of women to specific types of low-wage, low-status occupations (Mackintosh 1981), and by the complementary processes of "housewifization": the means by which capitalism creates particular kinds of subjectivities conducive to capital accumulation. Women's status within the varying permutations of capitalism's economic ordering is illustrated by their relegation to specific types of unpaid or low-wage, low-status occupations. Their labor within the domestic sphere is trivialized and obscured, reduced to natural inclination and intuitive duty, and their paid productive labor becomes regarded as supplemental. Both are legitimated and sustained through gender ideologies, rather than compensated through adequate wages (Stolcke 1981). This ideological sleight of hand deprives social reproductive labor of economic consideration. As a result, social reproduction is considered largely tangential to economic growth (Yeates 2005; Lutz 2004; Wichterich 2000), and economic concerns are prioritized over human needs to the extent that capital accumulation often runs counter to those needs (Li 2009; Harvey 2005; Wolf 1982).

Historically then, under capitalism, European women (and their counterparts in the colonies, under the tutelage of colonizing agents) emerge as housewives, as caregivers, as non-productive entities, or as labor reservists, not because they are these things, but because they have been constituted as these things,—their reproductive labor, unlike the productive labor of men, construed as natural rather than human, ancillary at best, and immaterial at worst (Mies 1986). This has become even more salient under neoliberal capitalism. As Li (2009) points out, as national regimes are reconfigured by decentralization and privatization efforts, it has become increasingly difficult for governments to deliver on national commitments related to social and human needs. This gap in care provisioning following neoliberal rationalization necessitates that women, whose paid labor is undervalued and whose domestic labor is regarded as infinitely flexible, take up this social intervention. However, how this occurs varies by class and context as different women respond to correlated yet diverse neoliberal outcomes. While for some women this means committing all their energies to social reproductive tasks, for others it means working a double-day, and for others still it means employing and managing a domestic care laborer. For those women employed as domestic care laborers, their work represents a convergence of women's undervalued productive roles and their unvalued reproductive roles. Their labor is simultaneously informed by the logic of the labor market and the emotional and relational underpinnings of care provision.

The transaction between labor and capital requires a market in which the human capacity to work can be bought and sold. Facilitating this is a fiction that postulates an equal relationship between those who sell and those who buy labor. This fiction obscures asymmetrical class relations by effectively concealing a key mechanism of capitalist accumulation, surplus value; workers are paid for only a portion of the product of their labor, surrendering the rest to the capitalist class. Where domestic—and more precisely care—labor is concerned, these aspects of labor/capital relations are present, yet reconfigured. The fiction of equal exchange (wages for labor) is both harnessed and undermined in the context of care labor. Here, care emerges ambiguously as both commodity and relationship.

The commodity of care embodies only a small fraction of the labor necessary to produce it. Hidden are costs to the individual care provider, as well as structural inequalities that facilitate the accumulation of surplus value. Employers of care laborers, often paying low wages and demanding long hours, are able to benefit from these hidden costs or additional values. At the same time, they are also able to appeal to the fiction of the equal exchange of wages for labor, with the employer able to terminate the labor "contract" without any responsibility to the care laborer. While this may be true of the wage relation in general, for domestic workers employment is located in the household, a workplace structured by further "fictions"—those of kinship and family. This location of employment also influences the relationship between laborers and employers, whereby the latter may invoke a rhetoric of shared interest and personal ties to limit the bargaining power of domestic care laborers. In this way, the dynamic of household-based labor is characterized by a profound ambiguity, with the employer able to simultaneously draw on fictions of equal exchange and those of kinship and care. In the context of care labor, surplus value must, as such, be understood as encompassing both the economic, as described by Marx, and the emotional, labeled "emotional surplus value" by Hochschild (2000).

Just as the ability of capital to mobilize labor is contingent upon a market in which the capacity of human beings to work can be purchased as a commodity (Wolf 1982), the capacity of human beings, and more precisely of women, to care must also be commodified. It is not, however, merely the provision of care that is commodified. In light of the intrinsic humanness of care, the producer of care and the product of care are conflated, and "exchanged without reference to the social matrix in which they [are] produced" and reproduced (Wolf 1982: 310). This becomes all the more relevant where migrant care labor is concerned. Here, employers are able to access the benefits of domestic labor, as well as those of migrant labor.

Care labor migration is thus rooted in a global political economy characterized by intensive capital accumulation and increasingly diametric class structures. In addition to redressing limited state-funded social services, the availability of feminized migrant care labor represents one of the ways in which capital accumulation is facilitated by the state. Again, the rhetoric of balance and osmosis between two equal partners is salient; while "the [domestic] worker who moves across continents may seem the logical result of capitalism's individual subject, the juridical person, torn from all social contexts, selling her labor power in the global market place" (Anderson 2000: 108), she is, in fact, herself a commodity. She does not just complete tasks, she fulfills a role.

Once the migrant care laborer is commodified, made an object to be "exported-imported, bought-sold, and controlled in the most demeaning ways" (Chin 1998: 94), surplus value is extracted by both individual employers and the state. Even where the state provides some protection to workers, through work permits and regularized status, the ambiguities of paid care are frequently—if not deliberately—exploited by individual employers. Here, surplus value, both monetary and emotional, is extracted.

At the same time, the receiving state maximizes "indirect surplus value," or the surplus value accumulated through taxes and managed by the state. Migrant care labor serves to supplement the "indirect surplus value" available to states. Here, the conflict of "who gets what when" (Wolf 1982) is mediated through the private provision of care, and "indirect surplus value" is invested into industry, rather than social reproductive services. This surplus is further augmented by the status of care labor migrants in receiving countries; unable to access state supports, they (unlike local-born workers) generate direct and indirect surplus without costing the state anything. In light of the hegemonic status achieved by neoliberal doctrine and discourse, such an arrangement, satisfactory to some but not all, remains largely unproblematized.

The disjunction between reproduction and production has both intensified and abated under neoliberalism. This has had direct implications for the understanding and expression of gender in myriad social and cultural contexts, as women meet their social reproductive responsibilities in new ways (Barber 2008a; Yeates 2005; Sarvasy and Longo 2004). While varied, dependent on class, ethnicity, and nationality, the contemporary strategies employed by women are in effect responses to a singular—albeit it nuanced—global reality, that of neoliberal capitalism.

For most sending states, the anticipated outcome of care labor migration, and labor migration more generally, has not materialized. Instead, as is the case in the Philippines, development objectives have been delayed rather than hastened (Chin 1998) and debates have flourished over the "fate" of children "left behind" (Asis 2008). In spite of this, labor migration has been established as a long-term rather than short-term solution to the consequences of structural adjustment, liberalization, and stabilization programs (Barber 2008b). This has occurred in part because labor migration meets the objectives of both international capital (the continuous flow of cheap, pliable labor) (Wichterich 2000) and sending states that rely on remittances as a source of foreign capital. Meeting these objectives necessitates the vigorous promotion of labor migration by sending-states. As the Philippine case demonstrates, this includes the mobilization of those segments of national populations regarded as most likely to remit income and, as Kunz (2008) has demonstrated for Mexico, the reconceptualization of that segment as particularly well suited to migration. In light of the caring roles culturally assigned to women, mothers and daughters emerge as ideal candidates. Gender, then, becomes central in the discourses surrounding care labor migration and women's migration more generally. Individual migrants are resocialized according to the needs of capital as embodied in the actions and objectives of states and employers. In essence, they are subjected to a global process of housewifization and the cultural and social meanings embedded within it.

To recap, the reconceptualization of women as labor migrants and remittance senders happens at three interconnected levels: i) at the level of the state through numerous bureaucratic techniques and efforts; ii) at the level of cultural discourse; and iii) at the level of individual agency as women evaluate their options and make decisions. The belief that women will remit more of their foreign income to non-migrant family members relative to men, while challenged by a number of ethnographic studies (Kunz 2008; Binford 2003), fuels government initiatives to recruit women. Women are posited as best suited to care for their own families and the families of their employers. And while the services they offer to their employers typically remain conventional (cooking, cleaning, child and elder care), the care they offer their own kin is transformed. Mothers and daughters become increasingly defined in terms of their capacity to remit money from abroad even as their own social reproductive work is rendered more elastic as it stretches between the two households who claim their emotional and physical labor. Such elasticity is technologically enabled by the immediacy of new global systems of communication (Barber 2008a).

Framed by discourses of familial obligation, remittance-sending is increasingly regarded as an extension of women's responsibility towards their families. As Kunz maintains, the conflation of care, migration, and remittances directly "contribute[s] to the reproduction of social expectations of women's roles and behaviors in the remittance process, and the social pressure that goes with it" (Kunz 2008: 1404). Such social pressures are evident in state recruitment strategies that link labor migration to national identity and loyalty, a trend that has been particularly marked in the Philippines.[3] They are also manifested in local and inter-personal dynamics (Fouron and Glick Schiller 2001), and experienced directly by individual women as livelihood opportunities are considered and embarked upon (Gamburd 2000; Wichterich 2000; Chin 1998). It is to these women that we now turn in our example of the Philippines.

PHILIPPINE CARE-MIGRATION HISTORIES

Migration has a lengthy and complex history both within the Philippines and beyond its shores. Found in over 190 countries, Filipinos work in varied labor markets but primarily in gendered in-demand slots in service work, including care. In 2009 there were 1,236,013 Filipinos deployed overseas, an increase of 15 percent over the previous year. The top six occupational categories posted by the Philippine Overseas Employment Administration for new hires in 2009 were: i) household service workers; ii) nurses; iii) waiters, bartenders, and related workers; iv) charworkers, cleaners, and related workers; v) wiremen electrical—the only male dominated category; and vi) caregivers and caretakers.

Much of the literature on Philippine migrants has focused on women as caregivers who are sometimes nurses working in deskilled employment (Stasiulis and Bakan 2005; Pratt 2004). But in certain migration flows, such as to the US, Philippine nurses are also recruited to work as nurses (Choy 2003). Indeed responding to this, the Philippines deliberately produces an oversupply of nurses for the global market place. Given the promise of work abroad for nurses and caregivers, many potential migrants commence but do not complete nursing education and board examinations. This has led to a pernicious cycle of deskilling whereby employers favor care workers with some medical training so women contemplating care migration feel compelled to get some. High failure rates for Philippine nursing board exams—as high as 57 percent in 2007—in part reflect the entanglement of migrant ambition and state deficiencies in regulating migration-related industries, including educational institutions. Thus the cycle of preparation for migration and the indebtedness that typically accompanies it now includes money spent on educational qualifications that have become the new norm. This pattern was apparent in the late 1990s but it has intensified through the early years of the twenty-first century. While both women and men work in nursing and care provision, these occupations are feminized as is the overall migration flow out of the Philippines. This pattern first emerged in the mid-1980s when Middle Eastern markets for male labor became less reliable.

But there are historical precursors within the Philippines itself both for state-sponsored labor export and contemporary care migration. Barber's research in the Visayas during the 1990s identified four types of care work which can be seen to set the stage domestically for care migration. Each set of relationships holds class-, gender-, and age-specific properties that are translated across the various forms of care work described and reflected in the subjectivities associated with the normalization of care migration in daily life. The examples also illuminate the fine calibrations of production and social reproduction—the gender and class distinctions between labor providers and those benefiting from such labor. Processes of housewifization and the grooming of women and their daughters for careers in social reproduction made ever more flexible and geographically mobile through migration are made evident through these examples. Men's relations to women's social reproductive labor are also seen to vary through the drawing of value class by class in each example.

First, in the most clear-cut example of historical class divisions, in the sugar-producing regions of Negros, people recalled how workers on haciendas had capitalized upon the labor of daughters who worked in household servitude for their landlords. This was one means of response to the interminable burden of the sugar laborer's debt cycle; interminable because the relationship was quasi-feudal. Hacienda workers were "born" into the work, with whole families participating in the production cycle during the busiest seasons. They were typically landless, dependent on landlords for daily necessities and without access to resources for subsistence farming or other means of supplemental but essential cash income. Indebtedness to one's landlord was fundamental to the class relationship, yet was sometimes smoothed over by kindly patronage and generous social provision on the part of property owners. In some cases, workers were able to grow modest agricultural crops on hacienda lands, a practice that became contested as a basis for land claims in the post-Marcos period (after 1986). Even in the 1990s, some schools were hacienda-based and different haciendas had different reputations for their treatment of resident workers' families. Still, indebtedness was pervasive, and women's and girls' social reproduction labor, in addition to their field labor, was subject to the command of male kin, patriarchs, and patrons alike.

In the second example, still practiced during the 1990s, children (boys and girls) as young as ten years old from poor rural households were sent to "board" with households in nearby towns. No money changed hands. Rather, in return for food, clothing, and school supplies, the children were expected to serve the households as "helpers." These young helpers performed such daily tasks as sweeping inside and outside the residence, running errands to the local market visited daily, and caring for livestock, particularly pigs which are labor intensive, but also goats, chickens, and occasionally one or two cattle. More often than not, the helper's labor was all the more intense because the households where they took up residence were not well-off so the chores associated with sustaining those households were time-consuming and diverse, sometimes without benefit of electrical appliances or a reliable supply of potable water to the household. Any emotional bond forged between the child helpers and their "patrons" was mostly incidental to the functionality of the arrangement. Parents were relieved from the responsibility of feeding and educating the child; patrons received labor at a relatively low cost which they could factor into their own class ambitions, usually in terms of petty entrepreneurship. For example, women could draw on the labor of their helpers to attend to chores otherwise gendered wifely while they themselves attended to buying and selling goods for their own small roadside stalls (*sari sari*) stores). Such stores are ubiquitous in Philippine towns and villages. Modest profits are made from reselling small quantities of such daily essential commodities as pop and candy, small packaged snacks popular with school children, cigarettes by the piece, soap, cooking oil, dried fish, and rice. In larger centers there may be more specialization, for example in prepared foods and/or fruits and vegetables. The potential for exploitation in the helper-patron relationship is great. However, there is usually some social connection between the two households which, potentially at least, may curb abuse, although not the troublesome burden of emotional gratitude the helper must carry forward in life. The relationship best fits the mode of domination described by Bourdieu as symbolic, namely, "the gentle, hidden form which violence takes when overt violence is impossible" (Bourdieu 1977: 196). The varieties of violence embedded in the relationship exclude "overt violence" such as that comes to be defined in situ, because the child could flee if conditions became intolerable in comparison with those in the parental household.

In one example, an eleven-year-old boy lived with an older couple in a modest two-bedroom dwelling. The boy was a distant relative and had moved to the town because, it was explained, the school in his mountain village kept unpredictable hours as a result of the teacher's long commute. The boy slept on a portable cot in the couple's kitchen. When not at school, he was summoned by the clapping of hands and sometimes scolded and cuffed about the ears for being lazy. But he was also given special foods and fruits, and required to attend school. Although not entirely free to seek the companionship of other children his own age, he was curious rather than timid and showed no signs of distress or ill health. His chores were not so different from those assigned to others in his age range, although typically daughters were preferred household assistants and child minders. Sons were more likely to be given responsibility for livestock and errands. Always, child labor was described as a familial obligation, with more responsibility assigned to daughters than sons. These cultural prescriptions for gendered labor echoed adult divisions. Women's labor was expended over more tasks for considerably more hours of the day than men's (see Barber 1995). Resignation on the part of girls and women to the cultural scripting of housewifization's gendered tasks was pervasive. But women also recognized the challenges associated with managing their household economies and men acknowledged women's role as "holders of the purse strings." Here we see the direct economic functionality of the multilayering of gendered tasks in social reproduction; as Nonini also argues (this volume), capitalism depends upon the reproduction of all forms of labor. Care labor underpins capitalism in its daily unfolding, location by location, class by class.

The third example of adult "domestic helpers" is equally long-standing and widespread throughout the country. It lays the foundation for the global export of Philippine care labor which proliferated when migration became feminized (and racialized) during the 1980s (Barber 2008b). Domestic help, as it is institutionalized within the Philippines, is typically provided by live-in workers and takes two forms. Most households with the capacity to do so utilize some sort of domestic help, typically women's live-in labor but also men's to a lesser degree. For example, middle-class households are likely to employ one or two helpers whose working days are not unlike those of their counterparts abroad. In return they receive wages in addition to the promise of long-term support for themselves and family members should the need arise. Unlike their counterparts abroad and because the Philippine relationship occurs within a decidedly familial cultural idiom (fictionalized as that may be), they are also in a position to negotiate some flexibility relative to hours worked and tasks performed. It is not uncommon for the relationship between helpers and employers to span several generations, adopting a kin-like quality barely discernable to visitors unfamiliar with the household composition. Here again, symbolic violence is present in terms of Bourdieu's (1977) insight that reciprocity can never be devoid of power. Helpers in as much as they are dependent on the wage relationship and employer beneficence remain employees despite the fiction of their quasi-kin status.

Alternatively, some helper-employer relationships are more "professionalized," the classed power differences more obviously marked. This was the case of one well-off household we visited in 2010, where two helpers with a nursing education each worked a twelve-hour shift to care for an elderly woman whose daughter had migrated to Europe. Their care work was in addition to the labor of a male worker. He served as the gardener and driver, in addition to running errands and performing various kinds of heavy work and household maintenance. In this example, the house was well situated and had sufficient rooms to enable separate sleeping quarters for all the household workers. In another example, university students lived with professors and served as household helpers running errands, marketing, cooking, and cleaning in return for free accommodation. Again, these relationships were often established through social networks enabling both the introductions and references necessary to gain credibility for both the labor providers and receivers. Kin-like ties smoothed over the harsh edges of the long hours, the poor wages, and the wealth and social disparities. The calibrations of value and skill become further distorted as more and more migrants' capital is expended on staging migration to global care markets. The familial idioms are, we maintain, fictionalized relationships which disguise care labor and the skills demanded for such labor.

In the final example, child care is provided by Philippine *ya yas* (nannies)— young women who, because they are paid less than a subsistence wage and live-in under conditions that are not subject to labor standards governing wages, working hours, and such, are necessarily dependent upon their employer. As with most ethnographic examples of nanny employment, *ya yas* often do various other household tasks. The scenario is a cultural variation on the emotionally fraught outsider/inside relation of caregiving/service work, for example in Hong Kong (Constable 1997), or indeed in Canada (Bakan and Stasiulis 1997; Macklin 1994). There are class variations to the proper conduct of employees in this line of work. Unlike in Canada or in Europe, where the identity of the nanny is often visibly marked by ethnic and/or cultural difference, many Philippine middle-class employers insist upon marking the insider-outsider roles through comportment. So in public spaces, it becomes apparent just who is kin and who is not from the deferential demeanor of the female worker and the spatial discretion she observes. Always proximate to the family group, whether walking behind or discreetly parallel, she waits for the signal, sometimes quite ostentatiously ordered with a slap of the hands, or a brisk command, to assume responsibility for her charges. Sometimes, she wears a uniform signaling publicly that, potentially at least, she is educated as a health-care professional. And our research shows that indeed she may be. Hence the uniform serves as status marker for her employer but it is also a matter of ambivalence, sometimes deeply felt, for the worker herself. She may find the uniform practical and she is definitely proud of her educational accomplishments. At the same time, the situation is potentially humiliating, a condition she is resigned to and accepts, but not so completely she cannot grumble to relatives and friends even as she takes pride in her work.

The case bears resemblance to the subjective rendering, nationally, accompanying the placement of Philippine women workers in global care work. In the example just given, the nanny's subordinate status is publicly marked so she contributes to but is herself socially distanced from the class aura of her employers. Patronage may, however, provide benefits inasmuch as she moves through the city on the periphery of elite consumption. Hence, we see the unfolding of housewifization in the present; the coming together of the subjective, the material, and the symbolic logics of gendered class expression underlying Philippine care-worker labor export. These tensions are particularly marked in wealthier urban centers, such as in Makati, Manila's first financial district which hosts high-end retail malls and restaurants. In the provinces, the social markers are less visible but the fundamentals of the relationship remain the same; women provide undervalued and feminized social reproductive labor to replace the labor of their more economically and socially privileged female employers. This class scenario is played out across the global markets of Philippine gendered-labor export.

By 2005 when Barber's fieldwork was focused more specifically on the classed aspects of migration, it was becoming much more difficult for middle-class women to recruit working-class women willing to work as *ya yas*. This was as true in Manila as it was in the provinces where there had previously been a rural-to-urban migratory pattern. Increased opportunities for overseas migration were blamed for this labor shortage. Wages for *ya yas* in 2005 varied significantly by geographic and class context and ranged from a low of 1,000 to 10,000 pesos per month, supplemented by room, food, and occasional gifts. (The rate of conversion then was approximately thirty-two pesos to one US dollar.) In 2005, the legal wage for a maid in Hong Kong was P23,100 reduced from P25,859 in 2003 because of a recession. This wage difference, in part, explains the material equation that is calculated each and every time Philippine women seek employment abroad.

As can be seen from the above examples, women from poor fishing and farming households have long been accustomed to migrate to regional centers for service sector work. Through the lens of one migrant's journey, we will now show in more detail how migration pathways are forged and situated in shifting global economics.[4] Maria Perez met up with Pauline Barber when they were both visiting Maria's home village (*barangay*) in a coastal area of Negros in the early 1990s. Because of the degraded environmental conditions along the Philippine coastline, households that once subsisted upon combinations of fishing and small-scale agriculture have increasingly become dependent upon income from remittances. Nonetheless, the economies are still described as coastal, the households as sustained by fishing (Barber 1995). This reflects the pervasive reach of historical processes of housewifization whereby women's economic contributions through waged and unwaged labor are rendered invisible, and secondary to those of men. Yet they are also more 'elastic' both in terms of skill sets and contributions to quite varied labor markets gendered female and thereby devalued, and also in terms of geography. Maria was one of the first women to leave her *barangay* in the late 1970s. She did so leaving behind her infant son in the care of her parents while she travelled to Manila to work in the retail and the garment industries. With the boy's father no longer in the picture she relied upon friends who helped her secure employment abroad. Here is Maria commenting on her decision to leave the village on a journey which saw her transiting through various low-waged feminized jobs to care migration abroad:

> My relatives were very poor so I decided then that it was my role to help my family . . . In the 1970s, domestic work was frowned upon. It was a matter of pride. It's a low status job. Now so many do it and it's accepted. I ignored criticism and did what I had to do. What use is pride if people are hungry? Now, when I come home, people ask me for advice and even high school graduates cannot get jobs here [in the Philippines]. To get a job in government you need *compadres*. It's not *what* but *who* you know. But today also, more girls are keen on education and there is a shift in values. The young generation doesn't respect elders' values any more. This is a new thing. It's because of TV. Also some young ones travel overseas for work and they tell their friends about values they see overseas. (Interview with Maria Perez, 1993)

Assuming economic responsibility for the family (again demonstrably linked to housewifization in complex ways) is one of the facilitating cultural practices for Philippine women's migration and is raised in most accounts of migrants' lives. It is also widely referenced in the literature. When Maria first left home, her parents assumed responsibility for her son assisted by Maria's siblings who lived in adjacent houses on the same plot of land. Such household clusters are common because both land and finances are in short supply. They are also convenient for co-operative child-care practices now essential to family life in households with family members working abroad. Maria practiced transnational parenting (Parreñas 2008) through letter writing and occasional phone calls made to and from public telephones because land lines were scarce in the 1990s. Since then, the flourishing of cellular technologies has enabled greater contact between migrants and kin but with complicated results for their geographically stretched social reproductive labor in their Philippine family settings (Barber 2008a). Communication often includes talk of economic woes at home, compounding the difficulties of transnational living arrangements.

In Maria's case, migration supplemented her extended family's meager livelihood from artisanal fishing and subsistence agriculture. But, her primary goal was to provide a good education for her son, followed by contributions to her parents' household needs. Her ambitions for her son's upward class mobility were not realized. Not only was he disinterested in post- secondary study, but, she reported, he also became overly invested in material goods and "girls." Here again, Maria's circumstances mirror a common pattern indicative of class and consumption dynamics fuelled through migrant remittances. Migrants understand very well that many people anticipate some material benefit from their earnings abroad. Indeed most workers factor this into their homecoming, planning for months in advance by purchasing consumer durables to serve as the customary gifts (*pasa lubong*) given when travellers return. This is in addition to their relentless struggle to tackle migration debt and to save for the various household projects that occasioned the migration in the first instance. Greater earnings and remittance levels fuel higher material aspirations, hence indebtedness remains even as consumption levels provide the illusion of class mobility—a further fiction. Women care migrants become subject to intensified economic and emotional pressure from Philippine kin to earn more, work harder, save more. In these ways, the emotional and actual economies of kinship relations are recalibrated through care migration to introduce new tensions, and power differentials.

After a second two-year contract as a domestic worker in Hong Kong Maria secured a third contract, this time with a Canadian couple, parents of a one-year-old child. Maria remained with this family as the number of children increased. When the family returned to Canada they arranged for Maria to travel with them under the terms of a live-in caregiver contract. Maria was conflicted, partly because of geographic distance but described the employment offer as "too good to refuse." Under the terms of her visa, after three years of live-in employment, Maria became eligible to apply for permanent residency in Canada. At this time, she commenced night classes to gain a practical nursing certificate. With this qualification she sought employment in a facility providing care for the aged; commodified domestic labor is transferable but in circumscribed labor niches that maintain the diminished gender and value profile of care labor despite the workers' skill sets. Practical nursing is one of the care-related occupations where Filipinos predominate in Canada and in many other countries, most often through a career trajectory not unlike Maria's. However, in recent years, the care workers are more likely to have even higher levels of relevant tertiary education than Maria did (Barber 2008b). Indeed, the burgeoning institutional-care industry's reliance upon Filipinos is tied to a set of cultural stereotypes (associated here with housewifization) that similarly captures attention from employers and workers (Bakan and Stasiulius 1997). In a common pattern of staged familial migration, when Maria launched her Canadian career as a permanent resident, she secured employment for her sister with her initial Canadian employers.

Maria's story of resilience, strategizing, and ongoing geographical and occupational mobility, though not actual class mobility, either for herself or her family, is characteristic. With very few exceptions, the approximately sixty women interviewed by Barber described their work abroad, even with all its hardships, as an essential component of survival in their household's livelihood. For a few, however, it was a means to accomplish personal projects unrelated to the needs of kin. Most described their work abroad with pride even though indebtedness and sometimes sheer bad luck may have left them no farther ahead economically. For this reason, despite their initial desire for one or two contract cycles, many women engage in protracted circular migration.

Maria's story also reflects transnational ambivalence inasmuch as her attention remains divided between people and places in the two countries of her citizenship. In 1993, as a Canadian citizen, she mused about retiring in the Philippines. During 2002, she again travelled to the Philippines to research property options for a retirement home. The "dream" of return is shared by many in the Philippine diaspora. It is also a debate that carries over to the next generation when the children of emigrants question their relationship to Filipino identity. Ignacio's (2005) study of Internet dialogues among the children of immigrants to the US also affirms the ideal of the Philippine homecoming as an important feature of life in diaspora families. Yet, given the degree that "homecoming" depends upon Philippine economic stability and this, in turn, is linked to migration and its deterritorialized gendered labor markets, this seems improbable. A further aspect of transnational ambivalence is the question of the long-term effects of family fracture through geographic displacement upon both migrant's children and their aging parents who would normally look to female kin for care labor as they age. As Maria's example demonstrates, there were clearly emotionally painful consequences from her best efforts at transnational parenting. Her son's material circumstances were much improved through her work abroad but their relationship was frayed. There is now considerable evidence from the Philippines to outline that material benefits for children result from parental remittances (better education, housing, nutrition, and such) but the emotional consequences for the children of migrant parents remain incalculable (for example, Asis 2008). Even as female kin step up to provide social reproduction labor support to replace that of mothers (and to a lesser extent, fathers) working abroad, the calculations made by women migrants force a cruel measuring of economy versus emotion. For Maria and her migrant compatriots, the emotionally complex repercussions will ripple through several generations as social reproductive labor is substituted, sold, purchased, and sometimes denied for the younger and older generations of kin in their families. These tensions are gendered and experienced most acutely by women given the housewifely expectations afforded their social reproductive duties.

As demonstrated by Maria and subsequent generations of care migrants, gender subjectivities are once again altered under neoliberalism—transformed to meet the demands of states, both sending and receiving, and more broadly of global capital accumulation.

CONCLUSION: SOCIAL REPRODUCTION AND CARE LABOR MIGRATION UNDER NEOLIBERALISM

While neoliberalism is a global force "shaping all aspects of human life according to market criteria of efficiency and rationality" (Bakker 2007: 553), as we have seen, its processes and outcomes are experienced differently dependent upon social location, nationality, and gender. Women, then, are affected by neoliberal discourses and policies in a variety of ways, and as such the effects of these discourses and policies are redressed in a variety of ways. In relation to care labor migration we can identify, at minimum, three groups of women who contend with neoliberalism in related, yet divergent ways: those who employ care laborers, those who migrate as care laborers, and those who remain in their country-of-origin, caring for the children of those who left and engaging in a variety of other survival strategies. These three groups are connected in their social reproductive efforts (Mattingly 2001; Hochschild 2000). That said, their diverse positions within global hierarchies inform the strategies they employ in mediating the challenges of neoliberalism. In essence, as different women assume different aspects of social reproductive work globally, neoliberal capitalism initiates a new process of housewifization. The sexual division of labor is confirmed yet divided; it remains obscured and its ideological underpinning retains saliency.

While some individuals, by virtue of their social locations and positions within global hierarchies, are unable to migrate, others, by virtue of theirs, do not need or wish to. Nonetheless, their lives are shaped by migration, and they belong (knowingly or not) to vast linkages of individuals, families, communities, and states. These linkages, defined by Hochschild as "global care chains" express "an invisible human ecology of care, one kind of care depending on another and so on" (Hochschild 2000: 131). They are embedded in transnational social relations established under capitalism and neoliberalism. They embody the global reorganization of social reproductive tasks, a current manifestation of capital's ability to cast and recast social relations and subjectivities. In all of this, the woman in the middle, the care labor migrant, is pivotal. She is, in essence, the transnational link. Through her, migration becomes a central component of the social reproductive strategies of different groups of women (migrants and non-migrants alike)—those who depend on her to provide direct care through labor, as well as those who depend on her to provide indirect care through remittances. In this way, an extended group of non-migrants are integrated in and connected to transnational social fields.

While the care chain concept is a useful analytic tool, highlighting the international division of social reproductive tasks, it fails to address issues of simultaneity, it ignores broader issues of transnationality, particularly in relation to networks, and it neglects the gendered political economy in which social reproductive tasks are rearranged and dispersed. With this in mind, it seems useful to broaden the concept, moving beyond the linear transference of private care responsibilities between women globally, to a more nuanced and situated understanding of the redistribution or dispersal of care labor and social reproduction under neoliberal capitalism.

If we view the global care chain as a dispersed network of social reproductive tasks and objectives, myriad spatial scales emerge (Pessar and Mahler 2003): the households both in the sending and receiving countries, the communities of the women involved, and the sending and receiving states. Conventional notions of femaleness are upheld as female employers actively seek out other women to perform gendered work, as migrants are propelled into this gendered work and away from other types of employment, and as migrants rely on female family members or other women to care for their own children. These are reinforced socially at different scales: at the level of the state through migration policies, community in both the sending and receiving states, layered transnational relations between family and friends, and the dynamics between laborers and employers. In addition to these, the links between migrants and non-migrants, those who remain in the country of origin, are particularly vital.

Migrants are connected to non-migrant kin in the Philippines in multiple ways. These connections are facilitated by the relative ease of international travel, the increasingly important role of migration in both sending and receiving contexts, and the perpetual evolution of communication technology (Levitt 1998). In particular, as we have mentioned, the availability of technology such as cell phones, email, and instant messaging means that the transfer of social reproduction does not occur in a linear fashion, but rather that it filters and shifts through transnational spaces as care labor migrants engage in the daily activities and routines of both their employer's household and their own in the Philippines. The very act of sustaining social reproduction simultaneously and over distance serves to further obscure the value distortions involved in social reproduction labor whether performed on behalf of kin, or as commodified labor. Women migrants struggle with ambivalence about their dual obligations and loyalties, the paid work being more immediate and pressing in its demands, while the kin work and family concerns also remain ever-present and wearying emotionally yet are also powerfully instrumental in decisions to migrate, to tolerate, and sometimes confront (Barber 2008a) whatever employment abroad brings.

The possibility of international communication thus adds to the complexity of the lives of migrant care laborers. Technologies such as cell phones and instant messaging results in the "stretching of intimacy" and the establishment of "an absent presence" over the distances that physically separate migrant women from the children and kin (Barber 2008a; Parreñas 2008).

In this context, care for children and kin in the country of origin is not entirely displaced onto other family members or paid labor. Rather, the migrant woman, responding to obligations to provide support that is both financial and emotional, remains available to children and kin via these technologies. And while more regular contact may momentarily relieve stress and guilt, it may also produce anxiety when face-to-face intervention is impossible (Barber 2008a). Migrants' children also experience (and communicate) a sense of longing for a "complete" family life (Asis 2008: 91). In addition to and because of these anxieties, migrant women are forced, or feel compelled, to carry the social reproductive tasks of two households; doing physical work in the employer's house, while managing and supervising her own (Parreñas 2005). The result is transnational "double duty." Hence, despite their productive reproductive labor, cultural and gendered scripts in the country of origin necessitate that migrant women—when possible—attend to the social reproductive needs of their own children and kin. In this way, filtered through migration and communication technology, social reproductive labor is not always merely transferred. Rather, it is reorganized and rearranged, spatially, emotionally, and so on.

The global care chain represents, then, a transnational site where "gender is imagined and lived across multiple social and spatial scales. The disciplining force and seeming immutability of any given gender regime is reinforced through repetitions in the ways in which gender is embedded and re-enacted between and among these scales" (Pessar and Mahler 2003: 818–819). Here, migrant care laborers often depart from a system of gender stratification to enter another one in the receiving country (Parreñas 2008). Where gender hierarchy is less visible, for example in advanced capitalist states where there are high levels of female labor-market integration, the propensity to hire female care-labor migrants elucidates gender hierarchy, while simultaneously obscuring it. This follows from the "social location" of migrant care laborers in the receiving county, and the intersection of gender, class, ethnicity, and nationality.

"Social location" refers to a person's positions within interconnected power hierarchies. These are created and sustained through historical, political, economic, kinship-based, and other socially stratifying factors. An individual's social location confers upon them, in particular times and locales, certain advantages or disadvantages. "Social location" is not merely dependent upon nationality; rather, it includes complex hierarchies of class, ethnicity, sexuality, and gender. These variants operate at multiple scales; they make up a person's identity, shaping, informing, and positioning people, their points of views, their activities, and their relations. Social location shifts within the context of the global dispersal of social reproduction. Rather than a static outcome of migration, these shifts are ongoing; they are both physical, reflected in the act of relocation, and conceptual, related to how people understand themselves and how they present themselves. Here, issues of class and ethnicity are particularly salient. Care labor migrants may engage in a variety of actions and behaviors that can be understood as performances of class subordination and complicity (Barber 2008a). These performances, in some instances, are premised on cultural stereotypes pertaining to particular ethnic groups. These stereotypes are harnessed by migrants, employers, and sending and receiving states alike (Barber 2008a; Gamburd 2000; Chin 1998).

Care labor emerges not only as a set of social reproductive tasks (cooking, cleaning, caring), but as gendered performances of subordination "that [are] produced knowingly, in order to accomplish not just employment but a position with the most desirable employer under the circumstances. This can be read as a classed performance of what we might also call an *economic subjectivity* responsive to new gendered geographies of class and power in commodified domestic labour" (Barber 2008a: 30). Such performed subordination includes compliance with gender scripts, minimizing assertiveness, downplaying aspects of identity that might suggest class advantages, constraint of body language, and the depiction of a "subordinated self" that draws on cultural perspectives of Filipinos as subservient (Barber 2008a).

Responding to the spatial scales of household and receiving states, and the social and relational scales of employer-employee dynamics and corresponding stereotypes, social location in the country of origin is deliberately recast in the receiving country. Social location is not, then, a condition or an outcome, but a process, a negotiation, and a performance. While this conceptualization appears to prioritize the migrant's agency—her ability to act as a free, rational agent—this agency is relational, predicated upon multiple social and spatial scales, the meanings assigned to particular facets of identity (for example, gender and ethnicity), the value assigned to care labor, and class hierarchy. In this way, the reorganization of social reproductive tasks globally is not just a matter of care transference. Rather it is a matter of pliable social relations, conditional agency, and structural constraints. In the current era, such constraints have been characterized as neoliberalism. Here, we situate them within the history of "housewifization" under capitalism.

NOTES

1. Mies contends that women became the optimal labor force because their redefinition as housewives cheapened their labor. As housewives situated within the domestic sphere and subject to the authority of state-sanctioned male kin, their labor is 'unfree' relative to men's. These processes were particularly acute for women in the colonies where there was "increasing convergence between the sexual and international division of labor" (Mies 1986: 116).
2. Pauline Gardiner Barber gratefully acknowledges the Social Sciences and Humanities Research Council of Canada for two standard research grants. The first project "Beyond Victims and Heroines" (1999) focused on the transnational circuits of Philippine care migration to Hong Kong. The second project was a collaboration with Belinda Leach, "Performed Subordination:

Global Migration and New Economic Subjectivities" (2006), which compared class streamed migration from the Philippines and Trinidad into Canada.
3. For example, in February 2011, the website for the Philippine Overseas Employment Administration shows an image of past president Corazon Aquino against a backdrop of its Manila office at the EDSA intersection. The caption reads "POEA and EDSA where heroes converge." EDSA is the infamous site of the large mass rally in 1986 that provoked the resignation of then president Marcos, reviled for his abuse of power.
4. Maria Perez's migration journey to Canada is also reported by Barber (2011) but is here considerably revised. It bears retelling because it covers an extensive time period and conveys much that is characteristic of how women stage migration. It also encapsulates some key aspects of migration's class effects for care migrants.

REFERENCES

Andersen, Bridget. 2000. *Doing the Dirty Work? The Global Politics of Domestic Labour*. London: Zed Books.

Asis, Maruja M.B. 2008. "The Social Dimensions of International Migration in the Philippines." In *Moving Out, Back and Up: International Migration and Development Prospects in the Philippines*, edited by Maruja M.B. Asis and Fabio Baggio, 78–108. Quezon City: Scalabrini Migration Centre.

Bakan, Abigail Bess, and Daiva K. Stasiulis. 1997. *Not One of the Family: Foreign Domestic Workers in Canada*. Toronto: University of Toronto Press.

Bakker, Isabella. 2007. "Social Reproduction and the Constitution of a Gendered Political Economy." *New Political Economy* 12(4): 541–556.

Barber, Pauline Gardiner. 1995. "Invisible Labour, Transnational Lives: Gendered Work and New Social Fields in Coastal Philippines." *Culture* 37(2): 181–194.

———. 2008a. "Cell Phones, Complicity and Class Politics in the Philippine Labour Diaspora." *Focaal: European Journal of Anthropology* 51: 28–42.

———. 2008b. "The Ideal Immigrant? Gendered Class Subjects in Philippine-Canada Migration." *Third World Quarterly* 29(7): 1265–1285.

———. 2011. "Women's Work *Unbound*: Philippine Development and Global Restructuring." In *Gender and Global Restructuring Sightings, Sites and Resistances*, 2nd ed., edited by Marianne Marchand and Anne Sisson Runyan, 143–162. London and New York: Routledge.

Binford, Leigh. 2003. "Migrant Remittances and (Under)development in Mexico." *Critique of Anthropology* 23(3): 305–336.

Bourdieu, Pierre. 1977. *Outline of a Theory of Practice*. London: Cambridge University Press.

Chin, Christine B.N. 1998. *In Service and Servitude: Foreign Female Domestic Workers and the Malaysian "Modernity Project"*. New York: Columbia University Press.

Choy, Catherine C. 2003. *Empire of Care: Nursing and Migration in Filipino American History*. Quezon City: Ateneo de Manila University Press.

Constable, Nicole. 1997. *Maid to Order in Hong Kong: Stories of Migrant Workers*. New York: Cornell University Press.

Fouron, Georges, and Nina Glick Schiller. 2001. "All in the Family: Gender, Transnational Migration, and the Nation-State." *Identities: Global Studies in Culture and Power* 7: 539–582.

Gamburd, Michelle G. 2000. *The Kitchen Spoon's Handle: Transnationalism and Sri Lanka's Migrant Housemaids*. London: Cornell University Press.

Harvey, David. 2005. *A Brief History of Neoliberalism*. Oxford: Oxford University Press.
Hochschild, Arlie. 2000. "Global Care Chains and Emotional Surplus Value." In *On the Edge: Living with Global Capitalism*, edited by A. Giddens and W. Hutton, 130–146. London: Jonathan Cape.
Ignacio, Emily. 2005. *Building Diaspora: Community Formation on the Internet*. New Brunswick, NJ: Rutgers University Press.
Kunz, Rahel. 2008. "Remittances Are Beautiful? Gender Implications of the New Global Remittances Trench." *Third World Quarterly* 29(7): 1389–1409.
Levitt, Peggy. 1998. "Social Remittances: Migration Driven Local-Level Forms of Cultural Diffusion." *The International Migration Review* 32(4): 926–948.
Li, Tania Murray. 2009. "To Make Live or Let Die? Rural Dispossession and the Protection of Surplus Populations." *Antipode* 41(6): 1208–1235.
Lutz, Helma. 2004. "Life in the Twilight Zone: Migration, Transnationality and Gender in the Private Household." *Journal of Contemporary European Studies* 12(1): 48–55.
Mackintosh, Maureen. 1981. "Gender and Economics: The Sexual Division of Labour and the Subordination of Women." In *Of Marriage and the Market: Women's Subordination Internationally and Its Lessons*, edited by Kate Young, Carol Wolkowitz, and Roslyn McCullagh, 3–17. London: Routledge.
Mattingly, Doreen J. 2001. "The Home and the World: Domestic Service and International Networks of Caring Labour." *Annals of the Association of American Geographers* 91(2): 370–386.
Macklin, Audrey. 1994. "On the Inside Looking In: Foreign Domestic Workers in Canada." In *Maid in the Market: Women's Paid Domestic Labour*, edited by W. Giles and S. Arat-Koc, 13–38. Halifax: Fernwood Publishing.
Mies, Maria. 1986. *Patriarchy and Accumulation on a World Scale: Women in the International Division of Labour*. London: Zed Books.
Parreñas, Rhacel Salazar. 2005. *Children of Global Migration: Transnational Families and Gendered Woes*. Stanford: Stanford University Press.
———. 2008. *The Force of Domesticity: Filipina Migrants and Globalization*. New York: New York University Press.
Pessar, Patricia, and Sarah Mahler. 2003. "Transnational Migration: Bringing Gender In." *International Migration Review* 37(3): 812–843.
Piper, Nicola. 2007. "International Migration and Gendered Axes of Stratification: Introduction." In *New Perspectives on Gender and Migration: Livelihood, Rights and Entitlements*, edited by Nicola Piper, 1–18. New York: Routledge.
Pratt, Geraldine. 2004. *Working Feminism*. Philadelphia: Temple University Press.
Sarvasy, Wendy, and Patrizia Longo. 2004. "The Globalization of Care." *International Feminist Journal of Politics* 6(3): 392–415.
Stasiulis, Daiva K., and Abigail Bess Bakan. 2005. *Negotiating Citizenship: Migrant Women in Canada and the Global System*. Toronto: University of Toronto Press.
Stolcke, Verona. 1981. "Women's Labours: The Naturalization of Social Inequality and Women's Subordination." In *Of Marriage and the Market: Women's Subordination Internationally and Its Lessons*, edited by Kate Young, Carol Wolkowitz, and Roslyn McCullagh, 159–177. London: Routledge.
Wichterich, Christa. 2000. *The Globalized Woman: Reports from a Future of Inequality*. London: Zed Books.
Wolf, Eric. 1982. *Europe and the People without History*. Berkeley: University of California Press.
Yeates, Nicola. 2005. "A Global Political Economy of Care." *Social Policy and Society* 4(2).

12 Migration, Political Economy, and Beyond

Pauline Gardiner Barber and Winnie Lem

> Marxism is finished. It might conceivably have had some relevance to a world of factories and food riots, coal miners and chimney sweeps, wide spread misery and mass working classes. But it certainly has no bearing on the increasingly classless, socially mobile, postindustrial Western societies of the present.
>
> Eagleton 2011: 1

So begins Terry Eagleton's recent polemic in which he records and challenges some of the most common objections to Marxism and Marxist analysis. Working from the premise that Marx's insights were plausible, Eagleton suggests that the death knell of Marxism was sounded precisely because of feelings of political impotence on the part of the left, who grappled with how intractable and intensified capitalism had become in the post-1970s period. Yet it is clear from our discussion that the same problems of the amassing of wealth alongside widespread poverty remain and shape mobile populations under capitalism. In this volume, our project has been to demonstrate how and why Marxist analysis and the political economy of Marx are not only relevant but indispensible for understanding the configurations of migration.

It is generally proclaimed that the study of migration requires an interdisciplinary lens (Brettell and Hollifield 2000). While acknowledging that within each discipline there is a varied range of theoretical and methodological orientations which produce different insights and conclusions, some researchers have suggested that each approach has its place so long as there is no claim to correctness. They also propose that a full understanding of migration requires a theoretical open-mindedness (Castles and Miller 2009). It is not our intention to lay claims for correctness or to make calls to restrict the theoretical imagination. We do nonetheless argue for the primacy of a critical political economy as a means of contending with the imbrications of migration in the complex context of capitalist transformation.

In this volume, we have detailed how and why a political-economy perspective provides migration scholarship with a cogent and coherent framework for problematizing the complexity of the migration-capitalism nexus. Our discussions have focused on the question of how migrants as distinct populations in particular localities are produced, sustained, transformed, and reproduced—even as they remain socially differentiated among themselves—within contemporary and historical transformations of capitalism. We have suggested that deploying the framework of political economy to analyze migration yields significant insights into the forces that create differences and class inequalities both within as well as between migrants and other populations in the societies in which they relocate.

As anthropologists, our concerns lie with the realities of migrants' everyday lives and livelihoods. Our ethnographic methodologies secure us the privilege and responsibilities of sustained access to the social realities—the promise and hardships—of emigration, migration, and immigration. Informed by political economy, our insights on the dynamics of the mundane are set against the everyday complexities of capitalism in terms of power relations and accumulation processes. In this sense our engagement as anthropologists with a political economy of migration is dialectical. Each of the authors in this volume has employed this method of intellectual inquiry as they illustrate the productive tension between field-derived observations and the theoretical debates that define anthropological ethnography. In this project, they have demonstrated the heuristic value of Marx's critical political economy in the study of migration informed by but not restricted to the field of anthropology. While we have confined our focus to studies of migration generated by anthropologists, we contend that the value of this approach extends beyond anthropology as a discipline. We aim to challenge researchers in other disciplines to undertake an exploration of the question of migration through the analytic optics that we have used here.

We further argue that there is in fact a political immediacy that impels us toward the approach of a critical political economy. This political urgency is defined by changes in the ways in which migration, immigration, and constructs of 'the immigrant' have been imagined over the last few decades in the public and official realms of global centers of immigration. In this public sphere, the *question* of migration has come to be framed increasingly as the *problem* of migration and particularly the problem of immigrants themselves. As an issue, immigration and the need for immigrant citizens, at least in the period of economic expansion in the post-World War II period, was one of many items on the agenda of governing bodies and ministries (as Glick Schiller reviews in her chapter). In the period of global restructuring that followed on the heels of economic downturns and recession in Northern economies, a vociferous consensus began to emerge which defined migration as a *problem*. More recently resident immigrants and migrants are seen not only to constitute a *problem* but they have also been portrayed as a *threat* to the public order and economic well being of Western developed nations. But contradictions abound.

Following the disruptions to global mobility set in motion in the wake of the attacks on September 11, 2001 on the on the World Trade Center in New York, subsequently glossed as 9/ll, struggles over immigration policies have intensified, along with securitization agendas. But the necessity for immigration and the political, economic, social, and cultural conditions that precipitate emigration are unfaltering for all the reasons a political economy analysis exposes. That is, capital interests seek out desirable and malleable labor; people with capital seek opportunities to maximize their returns on investment; and people with little but their labor seek better wages and job and personal security both for themselves and most particularly, for the next generation. Nonetheless, concerns over migrants and their loyalties are reiterated, context by context, through political debates over immigrant alterity, the 'end of multiculturalism,'[1] and immigrant illegality. Copious evidence of variations on these themes is to be found in various political and media campaigns in countries that illuminate the contemporary paradox of the immigration conundrum.

At risk of repeating ourselves, and as authors in this volume demonstrate, demographic scenarios combined with the dictates of capital accumulation necessitate that future economic productivity depends everywhere upon a domestically available class-structured, pliable, and adaptive labor force. Surplus populations and disposable labor are indeed fundamental to capitalism. Immigrants from less robust economies and with aspirations for social and economic improvement are prime candidates for job slots in all the sectors that fuel accumulation and for social reproduction across the class register. Additionally, migrants bearing infusions of entrepreneurial capital offer new transnational social networks and financial possibilities. Such migrants are highly desirable—yet still subject to securitization and the circumscriptions of multiple citizenship agendas—as Nonini's chapter in particular makes clear. Such immigrants provide grounds for competition between immigration countries in Europe, North America, and Australasia. Competition is also accelerating for those migrants who qualify as contributors to the newly demarcated highly skilled knowledge-economy. These migrants, many of whom are first identified as mobile international students, are seen to fulfill neoliberal precepts but still their mobility is securitized.[2] Nonetheless, all classes of immigrants, particularly from non-European regions or subordinate economies within Europe, remain suspect through securitization agendas. And persistent public pronouncements over immigrants' unreliability and divided loyalties nurture fear (social, cultural, economic, and most perniciously about political solidarity) among settled populations in immigration countries. Heyman's chapter exemplifies these contradictory politics of fear at the US-Mexican border. Yet, powerful economies must allow immigration to retain wealth and economic competitiveness.

In the media, in policy statements of political parties, and in government programs addressed to immigrants, contradictory framings of the question of immigration have become so hegemonic that they pervade the social field of migrant lives and everyday public culture. The repositioning of migration in public culture coincides with the conjunctural moment in history which finds national *societies* being restructured as *economies* to respond to the challenges of global competition. Institutions of governance are also being shaped by rationalities that are dedicated to eliding the criteria for citizenship with the perceived needs of the market and the economy (Green 1997). The guiding principles of these transformations are encapsulated in the doctrines of neoliberalism. Thus framed by the discourses and practices of neoliberalism, this elision between society and economy effectively redraws existing rhetorics of exclusion and the criteria for citizenship that are being propagated in different arenas of different national public spheres. Also migrant responses to these changes will be strongly conditioned by the prevailing political and economic conjuncture. Research programs that are dedicated to the investigation of the effects on migrants of the transformations that prevail within the conjunctural moment characterized as neoliberalism, as well as the ways in which migrant agency is conditioned by it, so we contend here, incline investigations toward a critical political economy (Lem 2010, 2007; see also Lem and Barber 2010).

In this contemporary period of continual economic crisis and change, political exigencies have many different valences. In 2011, what has come to be known as the 'Arab spring,' and particularly the attempts made by Middle Eastern powers to contain it, has unleashed significant flows of migrants, escaping from the tumult and repressive militarism of leaders clinging to power. Such conflicts labeled in the press as 'revolutions' were purportedly triggered by the self-immolation of a powerless man in the aftermath of a confrontation against a member of governing elite in Tunisia.[3] These protests began with efforts made by members of subaltern classes to contest the prices of basic items of food. The actions quickly gathered momentum spreading across the Middle East to challenge the authority and authoritarianism of members of political dynasties who had amassed fortunes as beneficiaries of the global imperative to privatize national productive and financial institutions.[4] As the conflicts have escalated, members of the ruling classes who have fled with national assets arrive unimpeded in private planes in the capitals of Western nations such as Britain and Paris. Meanwhile, the same European nations consider ways to block the entry of waves of the divested and dispossessed.[5]

These reluctant migrants and refugees share the fate of other migrant streams. However, the abruptness of the transformation of citizens of a nation into global migrants provides stark reminder of how quickly and intensely the forces of migration act to transform lives and indeed livelihoods. They provide stark reminder of how people, once productive workers and citizens, can become summarily, sometimes violently, transformed into non-citizens and members of surplus populations. The flight of the capital rich and the ways in which such tumult creates capital poor reminds us that the transformation of people into a mobile population is configured and differentiated by class. Toward this end, recent events provide a constant reminder that in order to understand migration we must conceptualize migration as intrinsic in the process of the formation and reproduction of classes in capitalism. The flow of migrants away from this specific conflict and their differential reception in counties of destination is indicative of broader processes of class reformation and further formation in time, as the bulk of migrants globally join the ranks of laborers, service workers, informal workers, domestic workers, and petty entrepreneurs. All chapters in this volume amply illustrate this observation.

Finally, to return to the relevance of Marx, it is through Marx that our consideration of questions about migration can be framed as the "migration question." This phrase is a rendition of the 'agrarian question' in classical Marxism. Classical Marxists were interested in the political question of the role that peasants and various segments of the peasantry would play in facilitating the development of capitalism, or in resisting it. While of course the classical Marxists were concerned with the early development of capitalism, these questions have considerable purchase in the contemporary world of agrarian transformations. Similarly, in framing our discussions in terms of the migration question, our concern is focused on the question of how classes are formed among different migrant populations and particularly their agency as they struggle within and against the terms of their inclusion into the neoliberal order. In this book, we have argued that the perspective of a critical political economy promises cogency about the multiple and varied ways that migration as a process is embedded in capitalism. Our concern with the analysis of class and the trajectories of power are central to the project of grappling with the question of how capitalism is reproduced, transformed, and potentially transcended.

NOTES

1. In 2010, German Chancellor Angela Merkel captured media attention with her declaration that multiculturalism was an "absolute failure." This pronouncement can be seen as a clever move to reconcile competing political factions and thus it can be read as representing political consensus (see Sonnecken 2010).
2. Ley's (2010) study of millionaire migrants details the risk-aversion strategies of parents who situate their children in dispersed countries seeking varied citizenship options as their children become candidates for passports in the countries they study and increasingly work in as post-graduates.
3. See "France Blocks Italian Trains Carrying Migrants," http://www.bbc.co.uk/news/world-europe-13109631.
4. See http://guardian.co.uk, Friday, February 4, 2011, "Mubarak Family Fortune Could Reach $70bn, Says Expert."
5. http://webcache.googleusercontent.com/search?q=cache:18Eu3Hi-4CsJ:www.france24.com/en/20110418-french-decisio.

REFERENCES

Brettell, Caroline, and James Hollifield, eds. 2000. *Migration Theory: Talking across Disciplines*. New York: Routledge.
Castles, Stephen, and Mark Miller. 2009. *The Age of Migration: International Popular Movements in the Modern World*. Basingstoke and New York: Palgrave-Macmillan and Guilford Books.

Eagleton, Terry. 2011. *Why Marx Was Right*. New Haven and London: Yale University Press.
Green, A.D. 1997. *Education, Globalization and the Nation State*. Basingstoke: MacMillan.
Lem, Winnie. 2007. "Chinese Migrants and Belonging in the Age of Global Capitalism: A Critique of Representation." Paper presented at Canadian Anthropology Société Canadienne d'Anthropologie meetings, Toronto, May 8th–14th, session title Cosmopolitanism, Capitalism, Class, organized by Belinda Leach, Pauline Gardiner Barber, and Winnie Lem.
———. 2010. "Making Neoliberal Citizens in Urban France." In *Class, Contention and a World in Motion*, edited by Pauline Gardiner Barber and Winnie Lem, 163–184. New York: Berghahn.
Lem, Winnie, and Pauline Gardiner Barber, eds. 2010. *Class, Contention and a World in Motion*. New York: Berghahn Publishers.
Ley, David. 2010. *Millionaire Migrants: Trans-Pacific Life Lines*. Chichester, West Sussex: Wiley-Blackwell.
Soennecken, Dagmar. 2010. "Commentary: Merkel's Integration Rhetoric." *European Union Centres of Excellence Newsletter* 5(1): 5. EUCE Canada: www.euce-network.carleton.ca.

Contributors

Pauline Gardiner Barber is Professor and Chair of the Department of Sociology and Social Anthropology at Dalhousie University, Canada. She has published ethnographic works on two regions considered through a similar theoretical lens. Her work on industrial Cape Breton, Canada tackled questions of social reproduction, class, culture, and history. More recently, her Philippine research examines issues of political economy, class, and gender associated with Philippine migration, citizenship, and development. Recent articles on Filipinos as global migrants appear in volumes published by Berghahn, Blackwell, and Routledge, as well as in journals such as the *Third World Quarterly*, *Focaal*, and *Anthropologica*. She is co-editor of the Ashgate Press series Gender in a Global/Local World. Recent co-edited volumes (with Winnie Lem) include *Class, Contention, and a World in Motion* (Berghahn, 2010).

Lindsay Bell is a PhD candidate in the Department of Sociology and Equity Studies in Education at the University of Toronto. Her research interrogates the social relations engendered by large-scale natural resource extraction. Her current work focuses on labor migration and class inequalities in Canada's diamond basin.

Catherine Bryan is a PhD candidate in the Department of Social Anthropology at Dalhousie University. She holds a Masters degree from McGill University. Over the last two years she has been involved in research on Canada's Provincial Nominee Programs. A Social Science and Humanities Research Council Joseph-Armand Bombardier Canada Graduate Scholarship recipient, her own research explores Philippine-Canada migration, the gendered consequences of transnationality, and the intersection of political economy, migration, and social reproductive labor.

Bela Feldman-Bianco, PhD Columbia University with post-doctoral studies in history at Yale, teaches at the Graduate Program of Social Anthropology at the State University of Campinas (UNICAMP) in Brazil and is currently the president of ABA, the Brazilian Association of Anthropology.

She has extensive research experience both in small towns of Brazil and the United States as well as major cities of Brazil and Portugal. In addition to editing several books, she directed the 1991 documentary film *Saudade* (Nostalgia) about the experience of seven Portuguese-Americans in New Bedford, Massachusetts (Watertown: D.E.R). Among her books and special issues of journals are *La construcción social del sujeto migrante en América Latina: Prácticas, Representaciones y Categorías* (The social construction of migrants: Practices, representations and categories) (with L. Rivera-Sanchez, C. Stefoni, and M. Villa Martinez, Quito: Flacso, 2011); *Nações e Diásporas: Estudos comparativos entre Brasil e Portugal* (Nations and diasporas: Comparative studies in between Brazil and Portugal) (Campinas: Editora da Unicamp, 2010).

Nina Glick Schiller is Professor of Social Anthropology and the Director of the Research Institute for Cosmopolitan Cultures, University of Manchester. Glick Schiller's research and writings explore a comparative and historical perspective on migration, cities, transnational processes, social relations, long distance nationalism, methodological nationalism, and diasporic cosmopolitanisms. Founding editor of the journal *Identities: Global Studies in Culture and Power*, her publications include *Nations Unbound: Transnational Projects, Postcolonial Predicaments, and Deterritorialized Nation-States* (co-authored with L. Basch and C. Szanton Blanc, 1994); *Georges Woke Up Laughing: Long Distance Nationalism and the Search for Home* (co-written with G. Fouron, 2001); *Migration, Development, and Transnationalization: A Critical Stance* (co-edited with T. Faist, 2010); *Cosmopolitan Sociability: Locating Transnational Religious and Diasporic Networks* (co-edited with T. Darieva and S. Gruner-Domic, 2012); and *Locating Migration: Rescaling Cities and Migrants* (co-edited with Ayse Çaglar, 2011).

Yan Hairong is an anthropologist at Hong Kong Polytechnic University. She is the author of *New Masters, New Servants: Migration, Development, and Women Workers in China* (Duke University Press, 2008); co-author of *East Mountain Tiger, West Mountain Tiger: China, Africa, the West and "Colonialism"* (Maryland Monograph Series in Contemporary Asian Studies, no. 186); and co-editor of *What's Left of Asia?* (a special issue of *Positions* 15, no. 2 [2007]).

Josiah McC. Heyman (PhD, CUNY 1988) is Professor of Anthropology and Chair of the Department of Anthropology and Sociology at University of Texas El Paso. He is currently doing research on access and barriers to health care for immigrants, and Latinos more generally, in El Paso, Texas. Previous work has examined US border enforcement, US border officers, and border communities and cultures. He is the editor of *States and Illegal Practices* (Oxford: Berg, 1999), and the author of *Finding a*

Moral Heart for U.S. Immigration Policy: An Anthropological Perspective (Washington, DC: American Anthropological Association); *Life and Labor on the Border: Working People of Northeastern Sonora, Mexico, 1886–1986* (Tucson: University of Arizona Press); and more than fifty scholarly articles and book chapters. He was Chair of the Society for Applied Anthropology Public Policy committee from 2001–2007, and has participated extensively in the US-Mexico Border and Immigration Task Force. He can be contacted at jmheyman@utep.edu.

Belinda Leach is Professor in the Department of Sociology and Anthropology at the University of Guelph, and Associate Dean (Research) for the College of Social and Applied Human Sciences. Her research is concerned with livelihoods, gender, migration, class, and rurality and she has published in *Critique of Anthropology*; *Labour-Le Travail*; *Signs*; and *Identities*. She isthe author of *Contingent Work, Disrupted Lives: Labour and Community in the New Rural Economy* (with Tony Winson, University of Toronto Press, 2002); co-editor with Winnie Lem of *Culture, Economy, Power: Anthropology as Critique, Anthropology as Praxis* (SUNY Press, 2002); and co-editor of *Reshaping Class and Gender in Rural Spaces* (with Barbara Pini, Ashgate, 2011). She has been co-editor of the journal *Identities: Global Studies in Culture and Power*.

Winnie Lem is an Anthropologist and is Professor of International Development Studies and Women's Studies at Trent University in Canada. She is currently conducting research on migration between China and France, focusing on the political economy of migrant entrepreneurship and questions of citizenship in urban France. Her research focuses on questions of transnationalism, citizenship; regionalism, nationalism, gender relations in marginal economies, migrant livelihoods, women and small enterprises, diasporas, ethnicity, work, women and nationalism, gender and household economies; agrarian change; women and rural politics; racism; culture and class. Among her publications are *Cultivating Dissent: Work, Identity and Praxis in Rural Languedoc*, 1997 (Albany: State University of New York Press); *Culture, Economy, Power: Anthropology as Critique; Anthropology as Praxis*, 2002 (co-edited with Belinda Leach) (Albany: State University of New York Press); *Class and Contention in a World in Motion*, 2009 (co-edited with Pauline Gardiner Barber) (London: Berghahn); *Confronting Capital*, forthcoming (co-edited with Belinda Leach and Pauline Gardiner Barber). She has also been Editor-in-Chief and Editor of manuscripts in English of *Anthropologica*.

Janet McLaughlin is Assistant Professor of Health Studies and a Research Associate with the International Migration Research Centre (IMRC) at Wilfrid Laurier University. A socio-cultural and medical anthropologist, her research explores issues of health, human rights, development, food systems, labor, citizenship, and transnational migration in the Americas, with a specific focus on migrant farmworkers in Canada.

Donald M. Nonini is Professor of Anthropology at the University of North Carolina, Chapel Hill. He is the author and editor of numerous reviewed books, chapters, and journal articles on the political economy and cultural politics of ethnicity and race among Chinese populations of Southeast Asia, and on the political economy of local politics in the United States. He is the co-editor (with Aihwa Ong) of *Ungrounded Empires: The Cultural Politics of Modern Chinese Transnationalism* (Routledge, 1997); and the second author, with six others, of *Local Politics under Siege: Activism, Public Interests, and Private Politics* (New York University Press, 2007). This book won the Delmos Jones and Jagna Sharf Award for the Best Book in the Critical Study of North America, 2008–2009. He is currently (2010–2012) serving as president of the Society of Urban National and Transnational Anthropology.

Index

A

Aboriginal, 9, 132–135, 137–147, 149, 150; land claims, 138, 140, 141, 149–150
agency: ; of migrants, 5, 7, 48, 90, 92–93, 95, 102–103, 105, 112, 217, 221, 233, 239, 240; political, 105, 205, 206, 209
airplane jumpers, 80–81, 84
anti-immigrationism, 165–166
Asia Pacific, 11, 65, 70–71, 77, 83,
assimilation, 3, 9, 39–40, 43, 52, 140, 168, 179, 181
asylum seekers, 51
Australia, 7, 67, 71, 74, 76–79, 94, 98, 139, 149
Azorean, 9, 177, 181, 182, 189, 191
Azores, 11, 175, 177, 186, 187, 189, 190

B

belonging, 64, 66, 67, 69, 95, 98, 106, 169, 192, 202
Big Dan Rape, 179, 192–193
Binford, Leigh, 115, 128, 162, 221,
border, 1, 3, 4, 9, 17, 40, 53, 57, 99, 112, 118, 122, 124, 128, 153–170, 171, 238,
Bourdieu, Pierre, 75; symbolic violence, 223

C

Canada, 7, 8, 11, 52, 67, 71, 74, 76–78, 90–92, 95–97, 100, 103–104, 106, 107, 109–120, 122, 123–126, 127, 128, 129, 132–133, 135–137, 141, 143, 145, 149, 225, 228, 234
capital: accumulation, 6, 9, 25, 27, 44, 50, 65–67, 71, 73, 78–79, 178, 215, 217–219, 230, 238;
British, 137; finance, 64, 71, 77, 90, 95, 136; flows, 4, 17, 44, 45, 56, 71, 77, 95, 167, 204
capitalism, 1–5, 7, 10–11, 18–23, 30–31, 32, 44, 56, 64–65, 69–70, 83, 93, 109, 114, 148, 153, 165, 170, 176, 178, 182, 186, 193, 196–197, 204, 215–218, 220, 224, 230–231, 233, 236–240; contemporary, 1, 5, 30, 56, 69, 171; neoliberal, 215, 216, 218, 220, 230, 231; petty, 76; petty accumulation trap, 74–75, 78
care chain, 230–232
care labor, 10, 215–220, 224–225, 228–233; as commodity, 217–219
care migration, 10, 215–216, 221–222, 227–228, 233
Caribbean, 8, 11, 90, 92–101, 103–105, 106, 110–113, 115–117, 162, 168, 171, 186
Castles, Stephen, 11, 31, 33, 51, 112, 236
China, 11, 23–29, 32, 33, 57, 67, 72–74, 77–78, 95, 100–102, 196–197, 204, 206, 209, 210, 211, 212; Chinese, 5, 6, 7, 10, 18, 23–25, 28–29, 57, 65, 67, 70–75, 77–78, 80–84, 89, 90, 91, 100–102, 104, 105, 196, 199, 200, 206–207, 210, 211; Chinese labor, 80, 82–84, 91, 101–102, 104, 105, 196
citizenship, 7, 9, 29, 33, 52, 66–67, 70, 79, 97, 98, 103, 106, 111, 114, 133–135, 138, 140, 147–148, 153–154, 163, 168–169, 180, 181, 187, 190, 191, 229, 238–239, 240, 243; differentiated, 9,

114, 133–135, 148, 149, 154; dual, 98, 187, 190
class: analysis, 4, 21, 31, 240; and power, 4, 9, 31, 154, 233; differentiation, 5, 23, 30, 79; formation, 4–9, 21, 29, 70; inequalities, 90, 237; middle, 38, 91, 96, 224, 225, 226; mobility, 82, 111, 228–229; reproduction, 72, 74, 78; working, 26, 29, 64, 65, 66, 68, 69, 70, 80, 81, 83, 89, 90, 92, 105, 142, 144, 145, 175, 186, 217, 226, 236
colonialism, 1, 20, 21, 135
coloniality of power, 50–51, 54
communication technologies, cellular, 227, 231
container theory, 41
construction work, 80–81, 83, 91–96, 98, 99, 101–102, 106, 124, 142, 143, 157, 159, 164, 165, 176, 186, 196
cultural codes, 175, 181–183; cultural misunderstandings, 179, 183
cultural industries, 45
cultural pluralism, 176, 179, 180

D

depersonalization, 53
deskilling, 216, 217, 221, 222
development, 1, 2, 6, 8, 10, 11, 18, 21–25, 28, 31, 33, 38, 39, 40, 41, 42, 46–52, 55–56, 78, 89, 93–95, 101, 103, 106, 132, 133, 134, 136–143, 147, 148, 149, 150, 178, 189, 190, 197, 203–207, 209, 210, 212, 220, 240
DeWind, Josh, 2, 17, 18, 31, 35
diamonds, 8, 140, 141, 143, 150
diaspora, 43, 89, 139, 182, 187, 229
dispossession, 5, 6, 23, 25, 27, 32, 138
domestic helpers, 224
domestic labor, 69, 70, 97, 116, 199, 201, 218, 219, 228
domestication, 207, 209
double burden, 198–201

E

Eagleton, Terry, 236
economic: downturn, 1, 145, 146, 237; recession, 1, 76, 91, 148, 169, 226, 237; rescaling, 44–47, 53, 176, 177, 184

employment, 25–28, 49, 53, 80, 82, 84, 101, 105, 111–113, 115–119, 123, 124, 127, 134, 135, 142, 144, 145, 149, 158, 159, 162, 171, 185–186, 196–197, 201, 215, 219, 221, 225–228, 231, 233, 234
entrepreneurs, 29, 78, 164, 223, 240
ethnic group, 9, 43, 57, 74, 83, 90, 134, 138, 183, 188, 191–192, 233
ethnicity, 4, 23, 46, 135, 175, 180–181, 183, 184, 220, 232–233, 245

F

feminism, 10, 68, 175, 179, 180, 182, 183, 185, 191, 193, 215
finance capital, 64, 71, 77, 90, 95, 136
financial institutions, 1, 38, 40, 45, 50, 52, 56, 100, 104, 136, 190, 239
floating population, 26–28, 33
flows, 4, 8, 9, 11, 17, 26, 29, 47, 48, 50, 89–106, 126, 154, 156, 157, 159, 160, 161, 166, 167, 170, 211, 216, 220, 221, 222, 239; global, 4, 7, 48
France, 27–29, 42, 240
frontier, 3, 109, 133, 135, 140, 147

G

gender, 4, 8–10, 21, 23, 31, 50, 54, 80–81, 83, 85, 90, 92, 97–98, 104, 106, 107, 110, 111, 115, 116, 117, 121, 128, 129, 140, 149, 175, 180–184, 191, 198–200, 209, 211, 215–218, 220–224, 226–233; differences, 50, 66; identity, 66, 70; relations, 182; roles, 181–183, 209
global care chain, critique of, 230–232
global talent, 39
globalization, 17, 23, 31, 33, 40, 42, 54, 56, 90–91, 93–94, 105–106, 165–166, 191–192
guestworker programs, 109, 112, 128, 166

H

Harvey, David, 32, 44, 45, 54, 71, 138, 204, 218
hegemonic processes, 6, 41, 43, 50, 54, 66, 106, 125, 126, 212, 220, 238
housewifization, 10, 215, 217, 220, 222, 224, 226–230, 233

Hukou, 26, 28, 33
human rights, 118, 127, 128, 166, 170

I
ideal migrants, 8, 110, 112, 115, 118, 126, 127, 128
identities, 4, 8, 9, 10, 39, 40, 43, 54, 66, 83, 105, 106, 112, 127, 128, 135, 138, 140, 154, 175–179, 181–183, 188–189, 191–192, 198, 202, 207, 209–210, 215, 221, 225, 229, 232, 233; politics of, 135, 181, 192
ideologies, 10, 40, 41, 43, 66, 69, 153, 160, 163, 164, 165, 167, 176, 177, 178, 180, 182, 187, 188, 191, 192, 204, 206, 207, 209, 215, 218, 230
immigration, 3, 39, 77, 79, 81, 94, 95, 97, 98, 99, 104, 106, 114, 127, 128, 129, 153, 158, 159, 160, 162–169, 178, 179, 181–183, 185–187, 189–192, 237–238; policies, 97, 98, 104, 153, 186, 190, 238
indigeneity, 8, 82, 92, 132, 134–141, 147, 149, 150
International Organization of Migration, 100
interregional, 26, 30, 33
intra-regional, 72, 90, 98–99

J
Jamaica, 92, 95, 98, 110–112, 116–117, 119–123, 128
Japan, 7, 67, 71, 78, 80–81, 83, 143, 198, 206

L
labor: contract, 51, 52, 55, 159, 196; feminized, 18, 180, 232; markets, 10, 31, 52, 53, 64–66, 76, 80, 83, 91, 100, 104, 112, 114, 166, 167, 182, 202, 216, 218, 221, 227, 229, 232; power, 24, 66–69, 72, 80, 197, 207, 219; segmented, 6, 31, 80; sexual division of, 215, 217, 230; shortage, 9, 101, 133, 145, 226; skilled, 25, 39, 45, 84, 91, 95, 96, 97, 99–101, 104–105, 123–126, 128, 129, 144, 146, 178, 186, 187, 216, 225, 227, 228, 238; surplus, 8, 26, 132, 199, 202, 207, 219
laborer, 7, 11, 25, 26, 65–70, 72, 80, 82–84, 91, 101–102, 104, 105, 106, 109, 114, 116, 118, 119, 121, 126, 168, 186, 192, 196, 198, 207, 218–219, 222, 230–232, 240
law enforcement, 153, 157–159, 161, 166
locality, 9, 43, 44, 46–50, 57, 91, 92, 132–135, 138, 147, 176, 178, 179, 181, 184, 186, 187, 192; analysis, 6, 46, 91, 92, 106; migrant incorporation, 33, 41, 43, 46, 47, 56

M
Malaysia, 7, 67, 71–76, 78–81, 83–84
Manila, 10, 226, 227, 234
Marx, Karl, 1, 4, 6, 18, 20–24, 26–27, 32, 67–70, 109, 196–197, 203, 210, 219, 236–267, 240
Marxism, 4, 5, 19, 20–23, 30–31, 44, 215, 236, 240; analysis, 5, 21, 22, 31, 32, 36; classical Marxists, 240; framework, 44; Marxian, 1, 70
Massey, Doreen, 92
Massey, Douglas, 2, 11, 12, 17, 18, 19, 29, 30, 31, 33, 48, 109, 128
methodological nationalism, 3, 6, 7, 40–44, 55, 56, 170
Metropolis, 3
Mexico, 8, 9, 11, 69, 94, 110, 111, 112, 116–125, 128, 153–159, 161–162, 165–166, 169, 170, 178, 186, 191, 220
Mies, Maria, 10, 215, 217, 218, 233
migrants: as gentrifiers, 47; farmworkers, 8, 25, 65, 70, 110, 111, 113, 114, 116, 125, 126, 128; undocumented, 51, 156, 159, 178, 186, 190
migration: and development, 10, 11, 38, 39, 41, 47, 48, 49, 55, 57; and Caricom policy, 92, 99, 103, 104; and crime, 93, 99, 101, 105, 120, 175, 179, 180; circular, 2, 51, 52, 65, 110, 229; migration development nexus, 11, 47, 100, 178, 236; global perspective on, 39, 42, 48, 54, 55, 56, 89, 176, 193; temporary,

52, 65, 80, 97, 99, 104, 109–114, 125, 126, 127, 128, 129, 135, 142, 164, 169; return, 42, 52, 74, 76, 78, 81, 91, 98, 103, 105, 106, 112, 114, 115, 118, 120, 122, 125, 156, 164, 177, 186, 196, 202, 209, 228, 229
Miller, Mark, 11, 31, 33, 236
missions, 136–139; missionaries, 136, 148
mobile proletariat, 23, 25, 28, 29, 83
modernity, 10, 203–210
multiculturalism, 176–180, 187, 191, 192, 238, 240

N

nationality, 8, 46, 57, 70, 115, 137, 178, 187, 220, 230, 232
nation-state, 6, 39–44, 47, 50, 54–56, 57, 34, 33, 70, 78, 95, 109, 134, 136, 147, 192
negotiation, 102, 135, 145, 146, 148, 149, 175, 181, 182, 233
neoliberal, 1, 3, 6, 10, 11, 29, 44, 45, 48, 49, 51, 55, 77, 79, 109, 110, 114, 126, 128, 176–179, 190–192, 215–216, 218, 220, 230–231, 238, 240; neoliberalism, 4, 11, 23, 24, 33, 44, 45, 93, 114, 128, 220, 230, 233, 239; projects, 6, 40, 44, 45; restructuring, 41, 44, 45, 48, 51, 53–55
New Bedford, 9, 10, 175–192

O

Ong, Aihwa, 22, 78, 79

P

place, 7, 27, 33, 39, 44–50, 64, 65, 91–94, 105, 106, 132, 169, 176, 177, 178, 189, 202, 209, 210
passport, 42, 170, 240
patriarchal, 10, 68, 85, 119, 199–201
patriarchy, 198–202
performances of subordination, 110, 111, 120, 123, 133
Philippines, 11, 69, 97, 101, 104, 113, 216, 217, 220–222, 224, 227, 229, 231, 234
policy, 3, 7, 8, 26, 45, 52, 53, 74, 84, 91, 92, 95, 96, 99, 106, 136, 138, 143, 150, 153, 154, 157, 158, 160, 161, 164, 166, 167, 189, 204, 238; migration, 3, 6, 8, 11, 53, 97, 98, 104, 153, 157, 160, 167
political economy, 1, 4–11, 18–23, 30–31, 32, 42, 50, 72, 84, 91, 104, 109, 132, 136, 147, 148, 153, 155, 164, 170, 176, 197, 219, 231, 236–240; global, 9, 11, 50, 72, 219
politics: identity, 135, 179, 181, 192; of culture, 45, 167, 177, 188, 190; of unequal incorporation, 9, 175, 187; of exclusion, 3, 51, 53, 57, 125, 139, 162, 176, 177, 191, 239
postfordism, 9
post-socialist, 10, 196, 197
Portugal, 176, 177, 181, 183, 186–190, 192
Portes, Alejandro, 2, 17, 18, 31, 40, 52, 109
power, 4, 5, 6, 7, 9, 10, 11, 24, 31, 40–51, 54–56, 66–69, 72, 77, 80, 89, 90, 92, 94, 97, 102, 104, 109, 119, 124, 146, 154, 155, 158, 161, 162, 163, 164, 166, 167, 169, 170, 176–179, 182, 187, 188, 196, 197, 201, 202, 204, 205, 206, 207, 215, 219, 224, 225, 228, 232–234, 237–240
production, 2, 4, 21, 23, 24, 27, 28, 29, 44, 45, 51–54, 64–69, 72–73, 77, 84, 85, 94, 114, 116, 124, 126, 132, 133, 134, 136, 140, 141, 142, 145, 149, 155, 177, 185, 197–201, 203–207, 209, 217, 220, 222
primitive accumulation, 6, 24, 25, 32, 196, 203
pro-immigrationism, 39, 166
proletarianization, 23, 27
protest, 91, 101–103, 105, 125, 139, 179, 180, 184, 239

R

race, 8, 9, 43, 50, 72, 77, 90, 104, 110, 111, 114, 129, 135, 136, 149, 153, 156, 163, 168, 175, 180, 188; racism, 42, 49, 94, 98, 104, 154, 168, 180, 185; racialization, 23, 90, 100, 104, 137
Ratzel, Friedrich, 42
refugees, 39, 51, 103, 109, 239

remittances, 2, 6, 25, 29, 30, 38, 39, 40, 41, 46–53, 56, 69, 39, 105, 113, 122, 125, 126, 144, 210, 220, 221, 226, 228–230
reproduction, 6, 22, 23, 39, 44, 46, 64, 65, 67, 68, 72, 74, 75, 78, 83, 109, 138, 140, 199
rescaling, 44–47, 53, 176, 177, 184
resistance, 40, 55, 91, 125, 137, 138, 140, 182
resource extraction, 8, 132–134, 138, 143, 149; mining 8, 133, 142, 143, 144, 147, 150
Roseberry, William, 19, 20, 21, 32

S

Sassen, Saskia, 11, 31, 33, 148
scalar positioning, 41, 45, 46
Seasonal Agricultural Workers Program, 8, 110, 112–116, 118, 122, 125, 126, 127, 128, 129
securitization, 3, 4, 9, 163, 165, 166, 238
Sider, Gerald, 32, 114, 142, 148, 149
Smith, Gavin, 21, 22, 32, 127
social location, 183, 230, 232, 233
social reproduction, 2, 4, 5, 6, 7, 10, 25, 64–67, 69–70, 74, 77–79, 81, 83, 84, 85, 132, 133, 135, 142, 147, 215–218, 222–224, 229–232, 238; fictions of, 217
spatial scales, 231, 232, 233
speculation, 25, 32, 71, 77, 78; speculative practice, 71, 72, 77–79
state, 3, 9, 19, 22, 23, 24, 26, 31, 41, 42, 43, 44, 45, 48, 50, 53, 54, 64, 66, 68, 69, 72, 75, 77, 79, 83, 84, 90, 93, 94, 101, 105, 110, 111, 112, 114, 122, 127, 132, 134–142, 145, 147–148, 149, 157, 161, 163, 165–168, 171, 178, 179, 185, 186, 187, 188, 189, 190, 191, 192, 197–201, 203–207, 209, 211, 216, 217, 219–222, 231, 233; agendas, 3, 4; formation, 20, 21, 79; policies, 12, 10, 26, 48, 75; of exception/system of exception, 110, 111, 127
subjectivity, 10, 110, 183, 197, 198, 207, 209, 210, 233

surplus population, 5, 6, 8, 9, 26–29, 133, 238, 239
surplus value, 67, 71, 72, 77, 79, 218–220; indirect, 220

T

temporary foreign workers, 80, 97, 99, 104, 109–114, 125, 127, 128, 169
The World Trade Organization, 24, 26, 45, 53
transnational: community, 31, 105, 176; labor, 7, 64, 65, 66, 67, 80, 83; middling transnationalists, 67; migration, 5, 18, 27, 30, 40, 43, 47, 52, 53, 57, 94, 110, 153, 176, 191; movement, 65–67, 70, 72, 74, 75, 77, 78, 167; social fields, 47; transnationalism, 3, 31, 93, 94; transnationality, 38, 231
transregional, 5, 7, 10, 18, 27, 30
Trinidad and Tobago, 7, 8, 89–105, 106, 107, 234

U

unemployment, 26, 27, 81, 93, 105, 179, 185, 186
unfree labor, 53, 111, 114, 129, 210, 233
units of analysis, 40, 42, 43, 44, 55, 56

V

"value plus plus," 216

W

wall, 153–157, 159, 161, 163–169, 170
Wenzhou, 27–29, 33
women, 33, 68, 69, 80, 81, 83, 84, 85 93, 96–99, 115, 117, 118, 119, 150, 168, 180–183, 185–186, 191, 197–204, 207–210, 211, 215–233, 234
Wolf, Eric, 11, 20, 21, 23, 32, 41, 89, 90, 218, 219, 220
World Bank, 38, 54, 93, 206
world systems theory/analysis, 19, 20, 21, 31, 69

Y

youth, 10, 69, 150, 197, 200, 203, 204, 206–210

CPSIA information can be obtained
at www.ICGtesting.com
Printed in the USA
FFOW02n0312290717
38201FF